Six-Guns & Saddle Leather

SIX-GUNS & SADDLE LEATHER

A Bibliography of Books and Pamphlets on Western Outlaws and Gunmen

Compiled by RAMON F. ADAMS

UNIVERSITY OF OKLAHOMA PRESS
NORMAN

By Ramon F. Adams

Six-Guns & Saddle Leather: A Bibliography of Books and Pamphlets on Western Outlaws and Gunmen (NORMAN, 1954)

Come an' Get It: The Story of the Old Cowboy Cook (NORMAN, 1952)

Charles M. Russell, the Cowboy Artist (with Homer E. Britzman) (PASADENA, 1948).

Western Words: A Dictionary of the Range, Cow Camp, and Trail (NORMAN, 1944)

Cowboy Lingo (BOSTON, 1936)

Library of Congress Catalog Card Number 54-5939

Copyright 1954 by the University of Oklahoma Press, Publishing Division of the University. Composed and printed at Norman, Oklahoma, U.S.A., by the University of Oklahoma Press. First edition.

Dedicated

with sincere friendship to LORING CAMPBELL, *a real book scout and collector, but above all a big-hearted friend whose generous impulses make one love him. His friendship has been an inspiration to me.*

Acknowledgments

ALTHOUGH a large percentage of the books listed herein are in my own private library, I needed to search far and wide to see and examine certain rare items which I do not possess. To do this, I needed help, and I am happy to say that this world is still filled with co-operative souls if one but looks for them. I wish to thank the Texas State Historical Association for a Rockefeller Foundation grant which made it possible for me to visit libraries of various states and institutions, as well as several important private libraries. In these travels I met many old friends and, I hope, made a few new ones. I found librarians and book collectors everywhere most co-operative and willing helpers, and if by chance I overlook any who took the trouble and time to search their shelves for me, it is not intentional.

I would like to express my appreciation to the Henry E. Huntington Library, of San Marino, California, and its Grant-in-Aid Committee for extending me a second grant for extended research in that institution. My thanks to Dr. Robert Glass Cleland and Dr. Godfrey Davies of the Committee; Dr. John E. Pomfret, director of the Library; Mr. Leslie E. Bliss, librarian, Mr. Carey Bliss, assistant curator of rare books, Miss Mary Isabel Fry, reference librarian and registrar, Mrs. Margaret L. Packer, supervisor of the rare reading room, and Dr. French Fogle for the many favors extended me.

Aside from the members of the staff of the Huntington Library, my greatest benefactor in California was my friend and an outstanding collector of books on western outlaws, Loring Campbell. He not only went to a great deal of trouble to dig out books for my examination, but cheerfully transported me over wide areas of Los Angeles County to inspect other private libraries. Among these was that of my good friend Mr. Robert J. Woods, of Hollywood, in which I spent one whole day and where I found some unusual and rare books in what is perhaps the greatest private collection it has been my pleasure to examine.

My friend Mr. Paul W. Galleher, of the Arthur H. Clark Company, Glendale, was most kind in helping me locate certain books and in allowing me to take his valuable time discussing points of reference in first editions, and I shall ever be in his debt for acting as my cordial host at two dinners given by the Westerners of Los Angeles.

I wish to thank my old friend Mr. Glen Dawson, of the Dawson Book Shop, Los Angeles, for the many favors extended me and for transportation to places not easily accessible.

Mrs. Ella L. Robinson, librarian of the Southwest Museum Library, Los Angeles, was most kind to let me spend a day searching the shelves of this institution. Her welcome and help make this day a very pleasant memory.

My gratitude is extended to Dr. E. E. Dale, curator of the Phillips Collection, University of Oklahoma; to Miss Ina T. Aulls, Western History Room, Denver Public Library; to Mrs. Agnes Wright Spring, a friend of long standing, of the same department, but now of the Colorado Historical Society, for digging out many books for me; to Miss Frances Shea, librarian, Colorado State Historical Society, for her help and interest; to Mrs. Eulalia Chapman of the Bibliographical Center for Research, Denver Public Library, for her valuable aid in locating certain rare titles; to Miss Mae Cody, of the Wyoming State Library, Cheyenne; to Miss Mary E. Marks, librarian, University of Wyoming, Laramie; and to Miss Lola Homsher, archivist of the Western Room, University of Wyoming, and her able assistant, Miss Henryetta Berry. Not only did the last two accord me every courtesy among the bookshelves, but they also took the time to show me some of the beautiful scenery of that section of the country.

My thanks also to Mr. Frederick Cromwell, librarian of the University of Arizona, Tucson, and his assistants for allowing me to search through the bookshelves of that institution; to Mr. Mulford Winsor, director of the State Library and Archives of Arizona, Phoenix, and Mrs. Alice B. Good, librarian, for giving me free access to their shelves; to Miss Harriett Smither, archivist, Texas State Library, for research and photostats; to Mr. E. W. Winkler, University of Texas Library, Austin; and to Miss Llerna Friend, University of Texas, Texas Collection, for her untiring effort to locate new acquisitions not yet catalogued by that institution. My thanks are also extended to Mrs. Margaret D. Ulridge, University of California Library, Berkeley; Mrs. Eleanor A. Bancroft, assistant to the director of the Bancroft Library of the same institution, and Mr. Walter Muir Whitehill, director and librarian of the Boston Athenaeum Library.

Many personal friends are due my thanks for assistance in varied directions: Mr. J. C. Dykes, of College Park, Maryland, for calling my attention to certain books and giving me pointers on them; Mr. and Mrs. John J. Lipsey, of Colorado Springs, in whose home and library I spent several days; and Mr. Don Bloch, of Denver, for his constant words of encouragement.

I wish especially to acknowledge my indebtedness to my good friends Mr. J. Frank Dobie, Mr. Frank Caldwell, and Captain R. W. Aldrich, all of Austin, Texas, for allowing me the freedom of their private libraries. They possess a number of unusual books and a great willingness to help others. My gratitude to that experienced bookman and good friend Mr. Fred A. Rosenstock, of Denver, for inviting me to his home to search through his private library and examine his most precious collection. My thanks also to Mr. Thomas M. Bogie, Interlibrary Loan Department of the Dallas Public Library, for his most friendly co-operation.

I wish to thank the Reverend Robert W. Shields, of Alcester, South Dakota, for his help with some books and stories on the Reno brothers, on whom he has perhaps done more genuine research than any other man. My thanks also to Mrs. Elsie D. Hand, librarian of the Oklahoma Historical Society, Oklahoma City, for her aid in securing a photostat of one of the very rare books in that collection. Mr. Don Russell, associate editor, *American Peoples' Encyclopedia*, Chicago, has given me helpful information and suggestions.

My friend and fellow collector of Dallas, Texas, Mr. Dan Ferguson, was most kind to bring me books from his office to read and examine, and to allow me to visit his home library with every freedom to examine its contents. My friend Mr. Wayne Gard, of the *Dallas Morning News*, has extended me every help and encouragement. My thanks to Mr. Walter S. Campbell, University of Oklahoma, to Mr. F. B. Streeter, librarian, Fort Hays Kansas State College, and to Miss Joyce McLeod, assistant reference librarian, University of Kansas, Lawrence, for their cordial co-operation.

Among the book dealers who have helped me in locating rare volumes for my own library, and to whom I am grateful, are Mr. Charles Eberstadt and Mr. Peter Decker, both of New York; Mr. H. M. Sender, Kansas City, Missouri, and Mr. H. C. Revercomb, Kansas City, Kansas; Mr. M. J. Walsh, of Goodspeed's, Boston, and Glen Dawson, Paul Galleher, Fred A. Rosenstock, John J. Lipsey, and that good bookman Mr. William F. Kelleher, of Cliffside Park, New Jersey.

I would indeed be ungrateful if I did not express appreciation to my good wife for her encouragement, the giving of her time that I might work on this project which has taken unlimited hours, and her willingness for me to buy expensive books with money which could well have been used for her own comfort.

A compilation of this kind demands much time, labor, travel, and expense, with the expectation of only a limited financial return, but when the compiler takes into consideration the many friends made during his excursions, he feels that his reward is richly abundant.

RAMON F. ADAMS

Dallas, Texas
January 19, 1954

Contents

Illustrations

Six-Guns & Saddle Leather

Introduction

ONE OF THE PHENOMENA of our times is the vitality of the western tradition and the strength and continuity of its claim upon the interest of Americans. The late Eduard Lindeman, writing in the *Saturday Review* shortly before his death, called attention to the fact that "the frontier is a cherished element in our experience as a people. Every American is a potential pioneer. In every American there lies dormant the feeling that he too might play the part of a hero. Every American is a latent out-of-doors person. . . . In short, the West is 'in our blood.' "

Of all the figures of the American frontier, the bad man with a single-action Colt's revolver in his hand has surest claim upon the attention of American readers. A latecomer to the western scene, and a social product of settlement rather than of self-sufficient isolation, he treads in the footsteps of four great predecessors: the mountain man, the explorer, the military man, and the Indian. Arrayed against the virtuous settler or small townsman, he is the stuff of which action is made. Without him, the more or less orderly processes of settlement could have been as dull as neighborhood gossip in a country store. With him, the West was in ferment from the moment of its social emergence.

The outlaw antedates the Civil War, but he becomes the most notable mark upon the western landscape after 1865. He was a natural product of his time. Men from more settled sections of the country flocked west when they got into trouble at home, often dropping their real names when they reached the frontier, for this was a new land where every man was a law unto himself and where there was a "longer distance between sheriffs." Many of the early

3

Texas outlaws got a start because of their quick-tempered resistance to carpetbagger rule after the Civil War and their rebellion against the Negro police. At a time when six-guns were necessary accouterment, thorough familiarity with them bred contempt for bloodshed, and hasty use led to a career of "ridin' the high line."

When a working cowhand found his boss mavericking calves under the guise of legitimate branding, he saw no crime in trying to build a herd of his own with rope and running iron. But the big cattleman viewed things in a different light, and the ambitious cowboy soon found himself considered a cow thief and outlaw—unless he was clever enough to "steal himself rich" and become another influential cattleman, free of the threat of a long rope. The horse thief, on the other hand, was not tolerated by any westerner except one of his own kind. If captured, he seldom was accorded a trial by law, but was taken to the nearest tree, where his body was left to sway in the breeze as an example to others.

No matter what form of outlawry he might follow—stage or train robbing, cattle rustling, horse stealing, or killing—the bad man led an exciting and colorful life. Often his name became celebrated in both deed and legend around campfires, and his exploits epitomized the daring and excitement of chase and battle. His survival depended upon quick thinking, good judgment, and abundant practice of the fast draw. Generally speaking, he trusted no man. When he sat, he did so with his back to the wall, facing the door, cat-eyed to every movement around him. If his reputation had become widespread, he knew that there were other gunmen of lesser caliber seeking to down him for the fame it would bring them. It is natural for men to become fascinated by such adventurous characters and easily mistake cold nerve for bravery, for killers are rarely brave. The brave man never shoots until he has to. As Struthers Burt once wrote, "The real heroes of the West saved their cartridges."

It is true that some of the western outlaws followed a code which might be considered honorable, such as never shooting an unarmed man, or shooting a man in the back, or molesting a decent woman. But this code resulted from fear of an enraged citizenry rather than any conception of honor. Most outlaws were bloodthirsty killers thinking of self-preservation first and last. Biographers of bad men often seek to justify their subjects' outlawry on the grounds of persecution of themselves or their families, but such was rarely the

4

case. Usually they got their start from their own foolhardiness, hot tempers, or desire for a reputation of being feared by other men. Once they took the fatal step, there was no turning back. As one of them once said, "You couldn't stop no more'n a loser in a poker game."

Although most outlaws departed from physical life with their boots on, some of the more famous ones—such as Billy the Kid, Joaquín Murieta, Jesse James, Sam Bass, and John Wesley Hardin— live on forever in both song and legend. Many books have been written about them and their kind. Numbers of books on the cattle industry and cowboy life have included outlaws because many men outside the law were associated with the range. It was easy for the reckless cowboy to drift into outlawry. Not a few reminiscences of westerners include accounts of outlaws because it seemed inevitable that most men in the West would sooner or later run into some of them.

Because of the widespread interest in, and extensive writing about, outlaws, I have compiled this bibliography of books which have come under my personal observation, many of them diligently sought by the great number of collectors of outlaw material. Please bear in mind that this compilation has been made by a book collector, not a professional bibliographer. No doubt the latter would have followed certain rules which have been grossly neglected in this work. I have merely tried, in a manner dictated by common sense and, I hope, unconfusing simplicity, to slant this whole collection toward the antiquarian bookman, the book collector, and the li- brarian, with the added hope that the future historian may take notice, particularly of the margin I have tried to establish between fact and fancy, between contemporary truth and subsequent legend.

The perfect bibliography has not yet been compiled, and perhaps never will be, even by the professional bibliographer. This one, like others preceding it, will be criticized, I am sure. Many critics will accuse me of leaving out this or that, or of including items of no importance. No one man can know every elusive book or pamph- let, even in a narrowly delimited field or for a brief historical period. Too many are memoirs of old-timers, printed without copyright by country presses in small editions and not distributed beyond the bounds of their place of origin. By the time the outside world has discovered them, they have been lost or thrown away, or the pulp paper upon which they were printed has disintegrated.

I freely confess that I have omitted a number of possible items in this bibliography, some on purpose and some through my ignorance of their existence. While the ink is still fresh on its pages, I will undoubtedly discover other outlaw books and wish that they had been included. I think this happens to every compiler.

Perhaps it would be in order here to discuss some of the volumes excluded purposely from this compilation. The first large category consists of county and state histories. To include all such books which deal with or touch upon the western outlaw, I would have to list practically every state and county history for all states west of the Mississippi. This would pose a problem of space, and therefore of practicality. Hence, if you find some favorite work of this nature omitted, the reason may not be my ignorance, but rather the necessity of using the space for books of larger importance, or for those needing severe criticism. I have attempted, however, to list enough of these volumes to give them representation.

There are many books of poetry and cowboy songs which refer to western outlaws, but these, too, have been excluded because they do not serve the purpose of this work.

Almost every state and territory of the early West had vigilance committees, and the California committees were perhaps the most publicized. Books concerned with these California committees I have also purposely excluded, because they do not deal with the true western outlaw. The work of California vigilance committees was mostly against petty thieves, arsonists, "Sydney Ducks," and political enemies. The vigilantes of territories such as Montana, Idaho, New Mexico, and the like dealt with road agents such as the Plummer gang and killers such as Vicente Silva and Joel Fowler of New Mexico—genuine western outlaws and gunmen—and are therefore included.

It would be impractical to attempt to include all the "butcher boy" books, "penny dreadfuls," and dime novels written about the western outlaws in a work of the proportions I have chosen. All are wild fiction of no historical value, written to enrich the publishers and to thrill and stir young imaginations. I have tried, however, to include enough of those which appeal to collectors to provide more than a sampling of the class. Some of the old *New York Police Ga-*

zette publications, especially, are expensive collectors' items, and some, like *Bella Starr*, unfortunately have provided the foundation for "histories" by careless writers who have sought the sensational rather than the true. It has seemed necessary to list a number of the latter in order to point out the pitfalls they contain for the researcher. To include all would be but a waste of space, of no value to the historian, and of little value to the collector.

There were a few female outlaws in the West, notably Belle Starr, Rose of Cimmaron, and Pearl Hart, and I have tried to list books containing information about them. In addition, although Calamity Jane, Poker Alice, and Madam Moustache cannot be classed as outlaws, it seems to me that these unique characters deserve a place here as part of the gunman's West.

In including many less worthy books than some I have omitted, I have had a definite purpose. Very little that is trustworthy has been printed about the old outlaws, aside from the court records and the accounts in the honest but scattered newspapers of their day. In all truth, one would not have to use an adding machine to count the really reliable books on the subject; they are greatly outnumbered by the unreliable ones.

For many years I have collected books pertaining to our western outlaws, but only when I approached the task of compiling this bibliography did I attempt to relate, analyze, and refine the information they contain. Now, after reading hundreds, I am like many another researcher before me: never would I have believed, before my investigations began, that so much false, inaccurate, and garbled history could have found its way into print.

Unfortunately, no matter how historically worthless many books are, they remain collectors' items. The book collector often fails to make, or disregards, the distinction between trustworthy and inaccurate accounts. It is not entirely his own fault, because the search for books is an end in itself, whereas the evaluation of them is a science which has history for its name. There are few among us, however, who would pass up a book like John Rollin Ridge's *Life and Adventures of Joaquín Murieta*, even though it does not contain the materials of historical accuracy. To know when to honor a legend is a fine act of judgment which will always be in dispute. Collecting the book that contains it is a quite different thing from arriving at the past event which is sought by other, historical, means.

But the historian or biographer should be concerned with the veracity of what he reads, and I think it extremely important to point out inaccurate sources so that the student of history can better appreciate factually reliable accounts. Many historians and would-be historians and biographers in the past have perpetuated false statements because they did not take the trouble to question what they had read or make investigations of their own.

A characteristic of the western American, as I have pointed out, has ever been to create legends about outlaws. Billy the Kid's living out his natural life in Mexico, Tom Horn's being seen walking the streets of Denver after his hanging in Cheyenne, a dummy's having been hanged in Giddings, Texas, instead of Bill Longley, and the half-dozen men during the last generation claiming to be Jesse James at various times—all of these tales and improvisations are by-products of western hero worship. Cumulatively, they offer a distortion of character and career which makes the search for the real man an almost impossible task. And I might add that not even the most heedless collector can escape, in time, the attraction of recognizable facts. Nor is it necessary to embellish a fourteen-carat hero in order to make him worthy of worship.

I know of no more striking example of handing down false history from author to author, and from generation to generation, than the account of Wild Bill Hickok's fight with the McCanles faction. This spurious report was started by Colonel George Ward Nichols in an article published in *Harper's Magazine*, in February, 1867. Purported to be an interview with Wild Bill himself, it has now been proved highly imaginary and exaggerated sensationalism, pure fabrication throughout. Nevertheless, most of the subsequent books on Wild Bill rehashed this legend, and Wild Bill himself made the story credible by not denying it.

In order to contrast the fabrications of these early unreliable historians with what actually happened, it may be desirable to give a brief account of the truth of this fight as it took place.

David McCanles had sold the Rock Creek Station property to the Overland Stage Company, which had fallen behind in its payments to him. He went to the station to talk with Wellman, its keeper, about the delinquency, taking with him his twelve-year-old son, Monroe, and two friends, Gordon and Woods. These four comprised the notorious "McCanles gang" of "cutthroats" which,

8

through the efforts of certain yellow journalists, became so identified in the minds of the public. If McCanles had expected trouble, he certainly would not have taken his young son along. In addition, he was a powerful man physically and did most of his fighting with his fists. There is no evidence that any of his party were armed.

Wellman refused to come out and talk with McCanles, but Wild Bill stepped to the door. Surprised at seeing Hickok, McCanles asked for a drink of water to gain time to collect his thoughts. After handing the dipper back to Hickok, he walked to another door to try again to talk with Wellman. It was then that Wild Bill shot him through the heart from a concealed position behind a curtain, using a rifle which McCanles had left at the station.

Woods and Gordon, meantime, had gone to the barn. Hearing the shots, they came running to see what was going on. Wild Bill stepped to the door and shot Woods, severely wounding him; then he shot Gordon as he was running away from the trouble. The brave Wellman now came out and finished the wounded Woods by beating his brains out with a heavy hoe, and would have done the same to the McCanles boy had the youngster not fled.

Simply told, these are the facts of the so-called "fight" with the "McCanles gang."

J. W. Buel, in nearly all his books, repeated the false Nichols story; then Emerson Hough seized it and enlarged upon it, and with his popularity and reputation convinced the public of its truth even more. Today it is still being repeated by writers who, for lack of better evidence, assume it to be reliable.

Many books and pamphlets have been written about Billy the Kid, concerning whose career most writers are in agreement on one point: he killed a man for every year of his life. However, writers disagree as to his age when he was killed by Pat Garrett, despite the commonly accepted statement that he died at the age of twenty-one years after having killed twenty-one men. His age and the number of men killed vary up to twenty-seven. From my own investigations, I think it is doubtful that he killed a total of ten men.

Even to the initiated, it is astonishing to discover how many accounts of his life have been written. Many have appeared in autobiographies of men who claimed acquaintance with the young outlaw. Others deal only with Billy. Most of them contain preposterous statements which will be discussed in the comments I make on individual works in this volume.

Joaquín Murieta of California is hardly second to Billy the Kid in demonstrating the power of legend to overcome fact. And it may be worthy of note at this point that the development of this kind of legend is of the order of conscious artifice, not of accident in an oral or unwritten tradition. If the study of human institutions and conventions teaches us anything, it is that an oral tradition has a singular purity, even among the most primitive. Nor do I think that Joaquín is necessarily the product of a bookless frontier, admitting, however, that it is upon the frontier that the tall tale and its characters—Paul Bunyan and Pecos Bill, for example—are developed. The tall tale is of another order: it exhibits a knowing wink and a conscious sense of tongue in cheek.

Today's historians have proved that Joaquín Murieta was nothing more than a low, brutal, and vicious cutthroat, but in the early 1850's he was seized upon by Californians as a subject to fill men's folk-memories. In 1854, John Rollin Ridge wrote a story of Murieta which was issued as an unpretentious little paper-bound book. Ridge was anything but a historian and biographer, but he could write with a certain rhetorical flourish. His account, though pure fiction, was greedily received by the waiting public, and it was believed. Ridge's creation was pirated, copied, made into plays and poems, and translated into foreign languages until it was, and is, accepted as truth.

An unsuccessful newspaperman with a vivid imagination, Ridge was merely trying to make enough money to pay some debts. But in common with many of his contemporaries, he possessed in abundance those techniques of the dime novelist which were to make the last half of the nineteenth century notable in the history of mass-reading phenomena. Indeed, he acknowledged that he wrote his book for the profit he expected to make from it. He could not guess how strongly it would appeal to an adventure-hungry people, or how little money he would realize from it because of difficulties with his own publishers and widespread pirating by others.

His story was seized and, with a few changes, published by the *California Police Gazette*, running serially for ten issues. It was illustrated by Charles Christian Nahl, a well-known artist of his day, and issued in book form in 1859, five years after the publication of Ridge's original story. By this time the legend was well on its way. Soon afterward it began to appear, with slight changes and under different author's names, in Mexico, Spain, France, and Chile. Later this same legend was used by Walter Noble Burns and such careful historians as Bancroft and Hittell until now it is hard to convince the reader that it is fiction. Thus the history of Ridge's fabrication demonstrates the peculiar credibility and vitality of a fabrication, once it gets under way.

It may also demonstrate an even larger principle, namely the search for a series of writing conventions which would make a vast and little-inhabited land beyond the Missouri understandable to American society in the nineteenth century. It is only unfortunate that the search was not always conducted by well-informed writers, with a regard for the line of distinction between legitimate factual narrative and gross distortion of events. But to inveigh against the fabrications in this field is to miss the essential point that, in a developing urban and industrial society east of the Mississippi, the "penny dreadful" was the order of the day, and the pattern it set could hardly miss application to an exciting land and adventurous personalities needing no embellishment.

After studying hundreds of books on our western outlaws, I have classified the writers into four groups. The earliest writers were those of the penny dreadfuls and dime novels. They were hired by the publishers to turn out sensational stories in modern production-line style. By no stretch of the imagination could they be classed as lovers of the truth. They merely wrote what was expected of them—and here the word "expect" is of the essence, for it represents not so much a concession to popular taste as it does a hard-pressed hack's view of what the public should have. It must never be forgotten that this was still the age of marvels.

My chief complaint against such writers is not their fictitious histories, but their attempt at deception by leaning so heavily upon the disarming words "true" and "authentic" in their titles and sub-titles. This was their stock in trade. But for the careful reader these misleading words serve as a warning, and rarely do they fail to prove the book so identified to be historically questionable.

The second type of author in the western outlaw field who has posed problems for us is the old-timer who attempts a book of memoirs. To begin with, he has rarely had previous writing experience, a handicap which often causes him to choose a worse instead of a better writing model, usually something dimly appreciated from his younger years. Memory, even in youth, is never entirely reliable, but in old age it offers pitfalls of an alarming kind. By a special variety of osmosis, the story heard around a campfire becomes an established fact of personal experience. Dates become transposed haphazardly, family connections take bizarre turns, and action which was fast enough at the time acquires extra tempo.

If the old-timer places his work in the hands of an editor, the latter is often enough quite ignorant of the West, its language and history, and like the average reader is too ready to accept the author's statements as gospel truth, mainly because none can dispute remembered events not of his own knowing. Old-timers' books are usually entertaining when they have not been spoiled by academic editing, but the serious student of western life and history is urged to accept them only with several grains of salt.

The third group of writers I call "rocking chair historians." They do not have the energy or the acumen to dig out for themselves the records requisite to authentic narrative, or the critical powers needed to analyze the secondary sources upon which they mainly rely. Rewriting earlier spurious accounts in their own words —oftentimes not even taking the trouble to change the original phrasing—they sometimes succeed in passing along unreliable information from generation to generation. The complicating factor here is that highly respected writers occasionally accept, quite unwittingly, the substance of transmitted error, thus hardening into accepted doctrine the false and untrustworthy. From this point on, the public is unwilling to discount the word of a favored and competent author, even if subsequent research casts doubt upon his findings. As Mr. E. DeGolyer, the well-known collector of Western Americana, has said, any attempt to make of Billy the Kid a character less admirable than Robin Hood is practically foredoomed to failure, in spite of the facts.

My fourth class of writers on the western outlaw consists of those thoroughly able and scrupulous men who, by their tireless efforts, their imagination, and their grasp of the methods of history, can in fact be called true historians. These are the men who go back to the newspaper files and court records, who check and compare, and who reconstruct personalities and events with a careful regard for manner and action and conflicting claims. The work of many of them will appear in this bibliography.

It is my earnest hope that the facts, as I have found them, will be valuable to librarians, to book collectors, and to followers of the western tradition in history, letters, and the arts. To say that my informal bibliographical effort has been a labor of love is tempting but untrue. In the words of a cowhand grown old, having just roped a Brahma bull, "it sweated the hell out of me."

Table of Abbreviations

adv.	advertisement, advertisements
col.	colored
dec.	decorated
diagr., diagrs.	diagram, diagrams
dif.	differs, different
ed.	edition, editor
facsm., facsms.	facsimile, facsimiles
fold.	folding, folded
front.	frontis
illus.	illustrated, illustration, illustrations
imt.	imitation
l.	leaf, leaves
ltd.	limited
n.d.	no date
No., Nos.	number, numbers
n.p.	no place
OP.	out of print
p.	page, pages
pict.	pictorial
p.l.	preliminary leaf, preliminary leaves
port., ports.	portrait, portraits
prelim.	preliminary
pseud.	pseudonym
pub.	published, publisher
pub. device	publisher's device
t.p.	title page
Vol., Vols.	volume, volumes

Six-Guns and Saddle Leather

A Bibliography of Books and Pamphlets
on Western Outlaws and Gunmen

1   Abbott, Newton Carl

Montana in the making, by Newton Carl Abbott.   Billings, Mont., Gazette printing co., 1931.   Cloth.   OP.

> 4 p.l., ₃₁–520 p. front. (relief map), illus., plates, ports., maps, facsm. 20 cm.
> Appendix: p. 504–514; index: p. 515–520.
> Map on end papers (dif.).

Although this book went through several editions, the eighth with complete revision issued on March 15, 1943, it is difficult to find a copy. It contains chapters on the outlaws and vigilantes of Montana.

2   Abbott, E. C. (Teddy Blue)

We pointed them north; recollections of a cowpuncher, by E. C. Abbott ("Teddy Blue") and Helena Huntington Smith. Illustrated with drawings by Ross Santee, and photographs.   New York, Toronto, Farrar & Rinehart, inc. ₁₁₉₃₉₁.   Pict. cloth.   OP.

> xv p., 1 l., 3–281 p. front. (map), illus., ports., facsm. map, music. 22cm.
> Index: p. 271–281.
> Half title; vignette; t.p. magenta; first edition "F R" in device on copyright p.

This is one of the best books in recent years depicting cowboy life, and although it was recorded by a woman, she was nice enough to leave in all the flavor and saltiness of the cowboy lingo. Too often an erudite editor spoils a work of this kind by making it conform to academic standards. The book contains many references to the outlaws of the period covered, but the author's knowledge of outlaws, like that of

17

most old-timers, was from hearsay and thus unreliable. He says that Sam Bass was his father's wagon boss before he went to Texas. This statement I doubt very seriously, because Bass went directly to Texas from Mississippi when he was in his teens and was inexperienced in cow work. He stayed around Denton, Texas, until he went north with Joel Collins to help drive a herd of cattle. Abbott says that Sam was a nice boy and never would have turned outlaw if it had not been for his loyalty to Collins. When Collins sold the herd he had driven to South Dakota and blew in the money, Sam helped him rob the Union Pacific train.

Abbott also declares that American cowboys, as a class, had no use for Billy the Kid—"it was the Mexicans that made a hero of him." He repeats the legend about Chisum's owing the Kid a large sum of money and says that the Kid sent word to Chisum that he would kill one of his men for every fifty dollars owed him, "and he had already killed three and sent Chisum the receipt." He further states that the first time he saw Calamity Jane she was dressed in purple velvet and wearing diamonds, and that she was a madam running a big gambling hall in Deadwood. He tells how Granville Stuart, his father-in-law, and his vigilantes hanged horse thieves, and of the killing of Rattlesnake Jake Fallon and Long-Haired Owens.

3   Adler, Alfred

"Billy the Kid; a case study in epic origins."   Berkeley, Calif., University of California press, 1951. Pamphlet. OP.

[10] p. staples. 25.4 cm.

A reprint from *Western Folklore*, Vol. X, No. 2 (April, 1951), published for the California Folklore Society by the University of California Press.

4   Agee, George W.

Rube Burrows, king of outlaws, and his band of train robbers. An accurate and faithful history of their exploits and adventures, by G. W. Agee . . . .   Chicago, the Henneberry co., publishers [1890]. Cloth. Rare.

x, 194 p. front., ports. 19 cm.

Published same year by the C. J. Krehbiel co., Cincinnati.

The author was superintendent of the Western Division of the Southern Express Company and gives a fairly accurate account of Burrows' life and activities.

18

5   Aiken, Albert W.

Rocky Mountain Rob, the California outlaw; or, the vigilantes of Humbug Bar, by Albert W. Aiken.   New York, Beadle & Adams, 1871.   Pict. wrappers.   Rare.

206 p.   17 cm.

A wildly imaginary account of western outlawry, like many of Beadle and Adams' novels of the period. Robert Ernest Cowan, in his *A Bibliography of the History of California and the Pacific West, 1510–1906* (San Francisco, Book Club of California, 1914), gives the 1871 date for the publication of this book; but Albert Johannsen, in *The House of Beadle and Adams and Its Dime and Nickel Novels* (Norman, University of Oklahoma Press, 1950), does not show publication until 1873 as a serial in the *Saturday Journal*, with subsequent reprints in book form in 1875, 1878, and 1897.

6   Aikman, Duncan

Calamity Jane, and the lady wildcats, by Duncan Aikman. New York, Henry Holt and co. [1927].   Cloth.   OP.

xii p., 1 l., 3–347 p.   front., illus., plates, ports.   21 cm.
Illus. end papers (col.); vignette; untrimmed.

Republished, New York, Blue Ribbon, inc., 1937.

vii p., 2 l., 347 p.   front., ports.   19.5 cm.

This book deals with Calamity Jane, Belle Starr, Cattle Kate, Pearl Hart, Poker Alice, and other female characters of the early West, and is much better written than its predecessors, but still fails to separate some of the legend from fact. In the Belle Starr chapter the author admits drawing liberally from Harman's *Hell on the Border*, and also follows some of the legends created by the Police Gazette's *Bella Starr*. See Item 951.

7   Alldredge, Eugene Perry

Cowboys and coyotes, by Eugene Perry Alldredge.   [Nashville, Marshall & Bruce co., 1945.]   Cloth.   OP.

v, 7–184 p.   illus., plates.   23.5 cm.
Illus. chapter headings.

The author makes some mention of Billy the Kid and Pat Garrett, but makes the erroneous statement that Pete Maxwell's daughter lured Billy the Kid upon the front porch where he was shot from ambush. In a footnote he refers to Mrs. Sophie Poe's book, *Buckboard Days*, pages 111–16, but she tells no such tale as that of the Kid's being lured by Maxwell's daughter and ambushed.

8   Altrocchi, Julia Cooley

Traces in folklore and furrow. The old California trail, by Julia Cooley Altrocchi. Illustrated from photographs by the author. Caldwell, Idaho, the Caxton printers, ltd., 1945.   Cloth.   In print.

> 12 p.l., [25]–327 p.   front., plates, ports.   23.5 cm.
> Bibliography: p. [317]–320; index: p. [321]–327.
> At head of title: "Traces of Folklore and Furrow"; cover and half title: "The Old California Trail"; map on end papers; pub. device.

Has some information on the killing of Jesse James by Bob Ford, and on some other western outlaws, but the author misnames Clell Miller as "Clem."

9   Alvarez, N.

The James Boys in Missouri. A western drama in four acts, by N. Alvarez. To which is added a description of the costumes—cast of characters—entrances and exits—relative positions of the performers on the stage, and the whole of the stage business . . . . [N.p.], Ames' publishing co., 1906.   Wrappers.   (Cover title.) Scarce.

> [3]–31 p.   19.3 cm.

This little four-act play is wildly imaginary as to fact and has no historical value, but is a scarce collector's item.

10   American Guide Series

Arizona, a state guide. Compiled by workers of the Writers' Program of the Work Projects Administration in the state of Arizona. . . . Illustrated . . . . New York, Hastings House, publishers, MCMXL.   Cloth.   First ed. scarce.

> xxv p., 1 l. 3–530 p.   illus., plates, ports., maps.   21 cm.
> American guide series.
> Appendix: p. 499–[520]; index: p. 521–530.
> Half title; map on end papers.

Contains some information on many of the outlaws of Arizona, including the robbery of the Southern Pacific by Alvord and Stiles, the O K Corral fight in Tombstone between the Earp-Clanton factions, and the Tonto Basin War.

11 ———

California. A guide to the golden state. Compiled and written by the Federal Writers' Project of the Works Progress Administration for the state of California.... New York, Hastings House, publishers, MCMXXXIX. Cloth. First ed. scarce.

> xxxl p., 1 l. 3–713 p. plates, ports., maps. 20.2 cm.
> American guide series.
> Chronology: p. 687–693; selected reading list: p. 694–698; index: p. 699–713.
> Half title.

Gives some high lights on the California outlaws and stage robbers such as Murieta, Vásquez, Black Bart, and others.

12 ———

Colorado. A guide to the highest state. Compiled by workers of the Writers' Program of the Work Projects Administration in the state of Colorado.... Illustrated.... New York, Hastings House, publishers, MCMXLI. Cloth. First ed. scarce.

> xxxiii p., 1 l., 3–511 p. illus., plates, ports., maps. 21 cm.
> American guide series.
> Appendices: p. 467–[496]; index: p. 497–511.
> Half title; map on end papers.

Contains reliable material on such outlaws as Butch Cassidy, the Espinosa brothers, Joseph Slade, and Soapy Smith, and gives an account of Alfred Packer, the "man eater." The book tells of the killing of Bob Ford, but misnames his killer Kelly as "O'Kelly." This has been done frequently, probably because Kelly's full name was Ed O. Kelly.

13 ———

Kansas. A guide to the sunflower state. Compiled and written by the Federal Writers' Project of the Work Projects Administration for the state of Kansas.... Illustrated. New York, the Viking press, MCMXXXIX. Cloth. First ed. scarce.

> xviii [2] p., 538 p. front., plates, ports., map. 20.8 cm.
> American guide series.
> Chronology: p. 511–522; bibliography: p. 523–529; index: p. 431–538.
> Half title.

Contains material on Wild Bill Hickok and other Kansas cowtown gunmen.

14 ———

Missouri. A guide to the "show me" state. Compiled by workers of the Writers' Program of the Work Projects Administration in the state of Missouri. . . . New York, Duell, Sloan and Pearce [1941]. Cloth. First ed. scarce.

> 15 p.l., 3–652 p. plates, ports., maps. 20 cm.
> American guide series.
> Chronology: p. 577–595; selected bibliography: p. 596–611; map section: p. 614–[627]; index: p. 629–652.
> Half title.

Gives some information on Sam Hilderbrand, the James and Younger gangs, and the killing of Jesse James.

15 ———

Montana, a state guide book. Compiled and written by the Federal Writers' Project of the Work Projects Administration for the state of Montana. . . . Illustrated . . . . New York, the Viking press, MCMXXXIX. Cloth. First ed. scarce.

> xxiii [3] p., 3–430 [12] p. illus., plates, ports., maps, fold. map in pocket at end. 21 cm.
> American guide series.
> Appendices: p. 413–423; bibliography: p. 425–429; index: p. 430–[442].
> Half title; map on end papers; device.

Has some reliable material on Calamity Jane, Kid Curry, the vigilantes of Montana, and many of the state's outlaws. The writers here misname James Butler Hickok as "Charles" Butler Hickok.

16 ———

Nebraska, a guide to the cornhusker state. Compiled and written by the Federal Writers' Project of the Works Progress Administration for the state of Nebraska. . . . Illustrated . . . . New York, the Viking press, MCMXXXIX. Cloth. First ed. scarce.

> xxiii [3] p., 3–424 p. front., plates, ports., maps, plans, fold. map in pocket at end. 21 cm.
> American guide series.
> Chronology: p. 401–406; bibliography: 407–412; index: p. 413–424.
> Half title; map on end papers.

Gives an account of the Hickok-McCanles fight.

17 ⸻

New Mexico, a guide to the colorful state. Compiled by workers of the Writers' Program of the Work Projects Administration in the state of New Mexico. . . . Illustrated . . . . New York, Hastings House, publishers, MCMXL. Cloth. First ed. scarce.

> xxxvii p., 1 l., 3–458 p. illus., plates, ports., maps. 21 cm.
> American guide series.
> Appendices: p. 423–439; index: p. 441–458.
> Half title; map on end papers; vignette.
>
> Republished by University of New Mexico press, 1945, with a road map in pocket at end.

Has material on the Lincoln County War, Billy the Kid, Elfego Baca, Clay Allison, Black Jack Ketchum, and other outlaws. In the account about Billy the Kid, Jesse Evans is called "Joe," and the writers make the statement that the Kid was twenty-two years old when he was killed.

18 ⸻

Oklahoma. A guide to the sooner state. Compiled by workers of the Writers' Program of the Work Projects Administration in the state of Oklahoma. . . . Illustrated. . . . Norman, University of Oklahoma press, MCMXLI. First ed. scarce.

> xxvi p., 1 l., 3–442 p. plates, ports., maps (6 on one fold. map in pocket at end). 20 cm.
> American guide series.
> Chronology: p. 415–421; selected reading list: p. 422–426; index: p. 427–442.

Contains material on the outlaws and law officers of Oklahoma. Also gives information on some of the lesser-known outlaws, such as Ray Terrell, Mat Kimes, and Wilbur Underhill.

19 ⸻

The Oregon trail, the Missouri river to the Pacific ocean. Compiled and written by the Federal Writers' Project of the Works Progress Administration. Sponsored by the Oregon Trail Memorial Association, inc., New York, Hastings House, publishers [1939]. Pict. cloth. OP.

> xii, 244 p. front., plates, fold. map at end. 19.8 cm.
> [American guide series.]
> Appendices: p. 215–227; bibliography: p. 228–230; index: p. 233–244.
> Half title.

Contains some material on Butch Cassidy, Tom Horn, and J. A. Slade.

20 _____

Provo, pioneer Mormon city. Compiled by the workers of the Writers' Program of the Work Projects Administration for the state of Utah. . . . Illustrated . . . .   Portland, Ore., Binfords & Mort, publishers [1942].   Cloth.   OP.

> 8 p.l., [17]–223 p.   plates.   20.3 cm.
> American guide series.
> Notes: p. [190]–201; bibliography: p. [202]–208; index: p. [209]–223.
> Half title; map on front end papers; plan on rear end papers; vignette.

Contains some material on Butch Cassidy and his gang.

21 _____

A South Dakota guide. Compiled by the Federal Writers' Project of the Works Progress Administration for the state of South Dakota. Sponsored by the state of South Dakota.   [Pierre, State publishing co.], 1938.   Cloth.   First ed. scarce.

> xxii p., 1 l., 441 p.   illus., plates, ports., maps, facsm.   21 cm.
> [American guide series.]
> Bibliography: p. 429–435; index: p. [436]–441.

Tells of the killing of Wild Bill Hickok by Jack McCall. The authors give Calamity Jane's birthplace as LaSalle, Illinois, and the date of her birth as May 1, 1852.

22 _____

Texas. A guide to the lone star state. Compiled by the workers of the Federal Writers' Program of the Work Projects Administration in the state of Texas. . . . Illustrated.   New York, Hastings House, publishers, 1940.   Cloth.   First ed. scarce.

> xxxiii [3] p., 3–718 p.   plates, ports., maps.   20.2 cm.
> American guide series.
> Glossary: p. 669–670; chronology: p. 671–676; selected reading list:
> p. 677–682; index: p. 701–718.
> Half title; illus. end papers.

Goes to some extent into the activities of such outlaws as Sam Bass, King Fisher, Ben Thompson, and John Wesley Hardin.

23 _____

Tulsa, a guide to the oil capital. Compiled by the workers of the Federal Writers' Project of the Works Progress Administration in the State of Oklahoma. Sponsored by the Tulsa Federation of Women's Clubs. Tulsa, Okla., published by the Mid-West printing co., 1938. Stiff pict. wrappers. OP.

> 3 p.l., 9–79 p. front., plates, plans, map. 21.3 cm.
> ₍American guide series.₎
> Bibliography: p. 75; index: p. 76–79.

This little book has a section on the Oklahoma outlaws who hung around Tulsa, such as the Glass gang, the Dalton boys, the Buck gang, Bill Doolin's gang, Cherokee Bill, and Henry Starr. None of these outlaws ever bothered the people of Tulsa; for the most part they rode to town to drink and gamble.

24 ———

Utah, a guide to the state. Compiled by workers of the Writers' Program of the Work Projects Administration for the state of Utah. . . . Illustrated . . . . New York, Hastings House, publishers, MCMXLI. Cloth. First ed. scarce.

> xxvi p., 1 l., 3–595 p. illus., plates, ports., maps. 21 cm.
> American guide series.
> Appendices: p. 531–566; index: p. 567–595.
> Half title; map on end papers.

Has some information on Butch Cassidy, Joseph Slade, and other bad men.

25 ———

Wyoming. A guide to its history, highways, and people. Compiled by workers of the Writers' Program of the Work Projects Administration in the state of Wyoming. . . . Illustrated . . . . New York, Oxford University press ₍1941₎. Cloth. First ed. scarce.

> xxvii p., 1 l., 3–490 p. illus., plates, ports., maps, fold. map in pocket at end. 21 cm.
> American guide series.
> Appendices: p. 441–468; index: p. 469–490.
> Half title; map on end papers.

Has some information on Butch Cassidy, the Johnson County War, Calamity Jane, Bill Carlisle, Cattle Kate, Nate Champion, and others.

26   Anderson, Abraham C.

The pioneer life of George W. Goodhart, and his association with the Hudson's bay and American fur company's traders and trappers. Trails of early Idaho, as told to Abraham C. Anderson. Illustrations: photos by Abraham C. Anderson, drawings by Jo G. Martin.   Caldwell, Idaho, the Caxton printers, ltd., 1940. Cloth.   OP.

> 9 p.l., [15]–368 p.   front. (col.), plates, ports.   23.5 cm.
> Half title; map on end papers; pub. device.

Contains some firsthand material on some of Plummer's road agents.

27   Anderson, George B. (ed.)

History of New Mexico, its resources and people. Illustrated.   Los Angeles, Chicago, New York, Pacific States publishing co., 1907.   Pub. in two volumes.   Three-quarter leather.   Scarce.

> Vol. I, xxvii, 522 p.   front. (port.), plates, ports. (part with tissues).
> 26 cm.
> Both volumes paged continuously.

Volume I contains a long chapter entitled "Local Wars and Crimes," and deals with the Lincoln County War and Billy the Kid, the Harrold War, the train robbery by Taggart, Joy, and Lee, and the capture and trial of Black Jack Ketchum and other criminals. As in many accounts of this period, quite a few proper names are misspelled. This history quotes much material from the unreliable writings of Emerson Hough.
Volume II is biographical.

28   Angel, Myron (ed.)

History of Nevada with illustrations and biographical sketches of its prominent men and pioneers.   Oakland, Cal., Thompson & West, 1881.   Cloth.   Scarce.

> xiv p., 2 l., [17]–680 p.   illus., plates, ports. (part with tissues), facsm.,
> tables.   20.5 cm.
> Double column.

One chapter, which includes a short sketch of Sam Brown and Langford Peel, gives a long list of the killings by years.

29   ———

History of Placer county, California, with illustrations and biographical sketches of its prominent men and pioneers.   Oakland, Cal., Thompson & West, 1882. Three-quarter leather. Rare.

> viii, [9]–416 p. front. (with tissue), plates (1 fold.), ports. 31 cm.
> Double column.

In a long chapter on crime, the author deals at length with Richard Barter, alias "Rattlesnake Dick," one of the most notorious outlaws of California.

30 ———

History of San Luis Obispo county, California, with illustrations and biographical sketches of its prominent men and pioneers. Oakland, Cal., Thompson & West, 1883. Three-quarter leather. Rare.

> viii, [11]–391 p. plates, ports. 31 cm.

This rare book has three long chapters on crime and criminals, giving accounts of such California outlaws as Jack Powers, Joaquín Murieta, and Joaquín Valenzuela.

31 Appler, Augustus C.

The guerrillas of the west; or, the life, character and daring exploits of the Younger brothers. With a sketch of the life of Henry W. Younger, father of the Younger brothers, who was assassinated and robbed by a band of Jayhawkers. . . . Also a sketch of the life of the James boys whose names are familiar to every household in the country, and whose reputed deeds of blood, robbery & crime of almost every kind, equal the most desperate brigand of the nineteenth century, etc., etc., by Augustus C. Appler . . . . St. Louis, John T. Appler, publisher and proprietor, 1875. Cloth. Exceedingly rare.

> iv, 208 p. front., plates. 19 cm.
> Cover title: "Younger Brothers."

Reprinted in 1876, St. Louis, Eureka publishing co.

> iv, 5–224 p. front., plates. 21.2 cm.

An edition was published in 1878 with 215 pages, eight pages of the Northfield Bank robbery being omitted at the end. Another edition was printed in Chicago by Bedford, Clark and Company, with 287 pages. The original illustrations are used, but have a different placement. Although the text is the same, there are more pages because larger type was used. "The Guerrillas of the West" is omitted at head of title page. On page 32 the word "Ohio" is substituted for "Iowa" on page 23 of the original. This edition has no date of publication. Reprinted again in a cloth edition in the Pinkerton Detective Series, No. 48, Chicago, Laird and Lee, 1893.

viii, [9]–287 p. front., plates, ports. 19 cm.

The author, being a friend of the Youngers, painted them with a kindly brush, and did much to prove that these outlaws did not commit all the crimes of which they were accused. However, such accusations were a part of the lives of all outlaws. As long as they were free and active, they received credit for many crimes committed by others. Being editor of the Osceola, Missouri, *Democrat*, the author had the honesty of the old-time newspaperman, and most of his statements are fairly accurate. This book served as the fountainhead for many later and less accurate volumes.

32   Armor, Samuel (ed.)

History of Orange county, California, with biographical sketches of the leading men and women of the county, who have been identified with the growth and development from the early days to the present time. Illustrated . . . .   Los Angeles, Calif., Historic Record co., 1911.   Leather.   Scarce.

x, [5]–705 p.   plates, ports. (part with tissues), fold. map.   28.2 cm.

Chapter XXI deals with the killing of Sheriff Barton and the capture and lynching of Juan Flores and his gang.

Rewritten ten years later (1921) and published by the same company.

11 p.l., [33]–1669 p.   plates, ports.   27.6 cm.

Chapter XXIV again tells of Barton's murder, and gives the story of the capture and lynching of Juan Flores written by an eyewitness to the hanging.

33   Arizona

History of Arizona territory showing its resources and advantages; with illustrations descriptive of its scenery, residences,

farms, mines, mills . . . .   San Francisco, Cal., Wallace W. Elliott
& co., publishers, 1884.   Cloth.   Scarce.

> 4 p.l., [25]-332 [1] p.   front. (with tissue), plates (1 col.), ports.   34.7 cm.
> Double column.

In a chapter entitled "Crime and Criminals," there is material on the
Heath gang.

34   Arnold, Oren

Thunder in the southwest. Echoes from the wild frontier,
by Oren Arnold, with drawings by Nick Eggenhofer.   Norman,
University of Oklahoma press [1952].   Cloth.   In print.

> ix p., 1 l. 3-237 p.   illus.   21.9 cm.
> Half title; "First edition" on copyright page.

The author here tells of much lawlessness in the Southwest, some of
which has become legendary. In one chapter he repeats the Murieta
legend and uses the Carmen version of the California *Police Gazette*.
Like several others he misspells Murieta's name. He has Carmen raped
and killed before the very eyes of the wounded Murieta. He repeats that
old legend about the reward notice and Murieta's writing beneath the
poster. This incident never happened. The author admits that three
movies have been made of this outlaw's life, "none of them historically
accurate," yet his chapter on Murieta is inaccurate in every detail.

In his chapter on the Earp-Clanton feud, he is favorable to the Earp
faction. There is one typographical error which may later identify the
first state of this work. On page 39, line 11, the word "beheld" is
spelled "behld."

35   Arrington, Alfred W.

The desperadoes of the southwest; containing an account of
the Cane-Hill murders. Together with the lives of several of the
most notorious regulators and moderators of that region, by Charles
Summerfield [pseud.].   New York, William H. Graham, 1847.
Pict. wrappers.   Rare.

> iv, [5]-48 p.   front., illus.   24.5 cm.
> Illus. t.p.

This rare book was published to sell for fifteen cents, but now brings a
high price.

29

36 ———

Duelists and dueling in the south-west. With sketches of southern life. Being the second and concluding part of "The Desperadoes of the South-West," by Charles Summerfield [pseud.] of Texas. New York, William H. Graham; H. Long and brother; Philadelphia, Zeiber and co.; St. Louis, E. K. Woodward, 1847. Wrappers. Rare.

> iv, [5]–54 p. front. 22.4 cm.
> 2 p. adv. at end.

37 ———

Illustrated lives and adventures of the desperadoes of the new world; containing an account of the different modes of lynching; the Cane-Hill murders . . . together with the lives of the notorious regulators and moderators in the known world, by Charles Summerfield [pseud.] . . . . Philadelphia, T. B. Peterson [1849]. Wrappers. Rare.

> 2 p.l., 11–117 p. wood-block engravings. 24 cm.

38 ———

The lives and adventures of the desperadoes of the south-west; containing an account of the duelists and dueling; together with the lives of several of the most notorious regulators and moderators of that region, by Charles Summerfield [pseud.]. New York, W. H. Graham, 1849. Wrappers. Rare.

> iv, [5]–98 p. wood-block engravings. 24 cm.

39 ———

The rangers and regulators of the Tanaha; or, life among the lawless. A tale of the republic of Texas, by Charles Summerfield [pseud.] . . . . New York, Robert M. DeWitt, publisher . . . [1856]. Cloth. Scarce.

> xi, [13]–397 p. front., plates. 19.2 cm.
> 5 l. adv. at end.
> Tissues.

Later published under the title "A Faithful Lover" by G. W. Carleton and co., 1884.

> 1 p.l., [13]–396 p. front. 19.5 cm.

All of Judge Arrington's books are fictionized accounts of life in Texas during the Shelby County War between the Moderators and Regulators and are written in the flowery style of the period. Most of his writings are a repetition of the same theme.

40   Arthur, George Clinton

Bushwhacker, by George Clinton Arthur. A true history of Bill Wilson, Missouri's greatest desperado; a story in blood. Rolla, Mo., Rolla printing co., 1938.   Thin cloth.   OP.

x, [11]–108 [1] p.   front., illus., ports.   17.8 cm.
Half title.

The only book I know devoted to this famous Missouri outlaw. It tells of Wilson's hardships and daring exploits.

41   Artrip, Louise and Fullen

Memoirs of Daniel Fore (Jim) Chisholm and the Chisholm trail, by Louise and Fullen Artrip.   [Boonville, Ark., published by Artrip publications, 1949.]   Stiff wrappers.   In print.

4 p.l., 11–89 p.   front., plates, ports.   19.6 cm.

The authors here erroneously claim that Daniel Chisholm bossed the first herd of cattle to leave Texas and that the Chisholm Train was named after him. They also state that this trail led through Vernon, Texas, and crossed Red River at Doan's Crossing. This was not the original Chisholm Trail, but the Western Trail, which was established several years after Jesse Chisholm had blazed the original Chisholm Trail. Their account of the Sutton-Taylor feud and John Wesley Hardin's participation in it is more reliable.

42   [Ash, George]

Captain George Ash. His adventures and life story as cowboy, ranger and soldier . . . .   Eastleigh [England], Eastleigh printing works . . . [n.d.].   Pict. boards.   Scarce.

6 p.l., 17–180 p.   plates, ports.   18.8 cm.

This scarce little book deals with cattle rustling and some outlawry along the Mexican border country.

43 Ashton-Wolfe, H.

Outlaws of modern days, by H. Ashton-Wolfe . . . with eight plates. London, Toronto, Melbourne & Sydney, Cassell & co., ltd. [1927]. Cloth. OP.

xiii, 277 [1] p. front., plates, ports., facsm. 22.2 cm.

Has a long chapter on Red López, the outlaw of Utah.

44 Aten, Ira

Six and one-half years in the ranger service. The memoirs of Ira Aten, sergeant, Company D, Texas rangers. Bandera, Texas, published by Frontier Times, 1945. Wrappers. (Cover title.) OP.

64 p. front., plates. 26.8 cm.
Double column.

This is a separate reprint of a series which ran in the *Frontier Times* and deals with Aten's efforts to suppress wire cutting and other outlawry in Texas.

45 Axtell, Gov. Samuel B.

Message of Gov. Samuel B. Axtell to the legislative assembly of New Mexico, twenty-third session. Santa Fé, Manderfield & Tucker, public printers [1878]. Wrappers. (Cover title.) Exceedingly scarce.

16 p. 20.3 cm.

A rare issue of Governor Axtell's speech. Also contains some material on outlaws and conditions in that territory.

46 Ayers, I. Winslow

Life in the wilds of America, and wonders of the west in and beyond the bounds of civilization. Illustrated . . . . By I. Winslow Ayers . . . . Grand Rapids, Mich., published by the Central publishing co., 1880. Cloth. Scarce.

5 p.l., [13]–528 p. front., illus., plates. 22 cm.
Vignette.

Here is some minor material on road agents and the vigilantes of Montana.

47   Ayers, Col. James J.

Gold and sunshine; reminiscences of early California, [by] Colonel James J. Ayers. Illustrations from the collection of Charles B. Turrill.   Boston, Richard G. Badger . . . [1922].   Cloth.   Scarce.

> xiv p., 1 l., 11–359 p.   front. (port.), plates, ports.   21 cm.
> Index: p. 347–359.
> Illus. end papers; pub. device; untrimmed.

48   Ayers, Nathaniel M.

Building a new empire, by Nathaniel M. Ayers. A historical story of the settlement of the wild west. Taking up the wild scenes incident to the settlement of a country inhabited by buffalo and hostile Indians . . . .   New York, Broadway publishing co. . . . [1910].   Cloth.   Scarce.

> 3 p.l., 7–221 p.   front. (port.), illus., plates.   20 cm.
> Pub. device; untrimmed.

Several chapters on horse thieves and outlaws.

49   Baber, Daisy F.

Injun summer. An old cowhand rides the ghost trails, by Daisy F. Baber as told by Bill Walker. Illustrated with photographs. Caldwell, Idaho, the Caxton printers, ltd., 1952.   Cloth.   In print.

> 9 p.l., [19]–223 p.   front., plates, ports.   23.5 cm.
> Half title; headpieces; vignette; pub. device.

The teller of this tale, Bill Walker, claims to have talked with Billy the Kid in Colorado, but, like many old-timers, has much of his information incorrect. He claims that the Kid was a bank and stagecoach robber, and that when the law got after him in Colorado and was closing in "and he knew his gun was going empty, Billy the Kid took a high dive into the *Missouri River*, but he saved one last shot for Black Bess" (his horse, which the posse wanted to get).

He claims that the Kid was a great favorite in Lincoln County and had many good points and many friends. He severely condemns Pat Garrett for hiding in the dark "and *behind a curtain*" to shoot the Kid. He says Pat Garrett "was small-time and small-town before he shot Billy the Kid." He further states that neither grass, flowers, nor trees will grow above the Kid's grave; yet on the next page is shown a photograph of the Kid's grave covered with grass and a bush in bloom.

33

50 ──────

The longest rope; the truth about the Johnson county cattle war, by D. F. Baber as told by Bill Walker. Illustrated by R. H. Hall. Caldwell, Idaho, the Caxton printers, ltd., 1940. Pict. cloth. OP.

> 9 p.l., [19]–320 p. front., illus., plates. 23.5 cm.
> Appendix: p. [297]–320 (George Dunning's confession).
> Half title; map on end papers; headpieces; double t.p. in red.

This is much the better book of the two and gives some inside information never told before on the Johnson County War and the battle between the invaders and Nate Champion.

51 Baca, Carlos C. de

Vicente Silva, New Mexico's vice king of the nineties. [N. p., n. d.] Wrappers. Rare.

> 1 p.l., [5]–39 p. 15.3 cm.

The author admits he used Manuel C. de Baca's book as his foundation and it is very similar, but he does add a little new material.

52 Baca, Manuel Cabeza de

Historia de Vicente Silva sus cuarenta bandidos sus crímenes y retribuciones. Escrita por Manuel C. de Baca. Corregida y aumentada por Francisco L. López. Las Vegas, Spanish-American publishing co. [n. d.]. Wrappers. Exceedingly rare.

> 4 p.l., 97 p. 21.3 cm.

An exceedingly rare and crudely printed little volume dealing with the reign of Vicente Silva and his band of criminals. I have in my private library another edition with 112 pages, plates, and ports., 17.7 cm., the most crudely printed and bound book it has even been my privilege to examine. The author was a police reporter for a Spanish-language newspaper in Las Vegas, New Mexico, and wrote the first account of this group of killers.

53 ──────

Historia de Vicente Silva sus cuarenta bandidos sus crímenes y retribuciones. Escrita por Manuel C. de Baca. Las Vegas, N. M., Imprenta la voz del Pueblo, 1896. Wrappers. Rare.

> 5 p.l., 128 p. front., plates, ports. 18.4 cm.

34

54 ————

Vicente Silva & his 40 bandits, [by] Manuel C. de Baca. Translation [by] Lane Kauffmann. Illustrations [by] Fanita Lanier. Washington, Edward McLean, Libros escogidos, 1947. Boards and cloth. OP.

> vi p., 3 l., 7–77 [1] p. 32.5 cm.
> Illus. chapter headings; lettering in red and black.
> Colophon: "500 copies of this book have been printed by E. L. Hildreth and Co., of Battleboro, Vermont, for Libros Escogidos under the supervision of Edward McLean. The text is set in Intertype Garamond Bold; the paper is Strathmore's all rag Old Stratford. Miss Lanier's drawings are adapted from the illustrations of the edition in Spanish.
> "25 numbered copies hand bound in full Niger Goatskin signed by the translator, the illustrator, and the binders, Hazel Dries and Edward McLean. 300 copies case bound and signed by the translator and illustrator. 25 copies in French wrappers."

A translation of the original.

55 Badger, Joseph E., Jr.

Joaquín, the saddle king. A romance of Murieta's first fight, by Joseph E. Badger, Jr. New York, Beadle & Adams, 1881. Pict. wrappers. Rare.

> 29 p. 31.5 cm.
> Beadle's Dime Library, Vol. XIII, No. 154.
> Triple column.

56 ————

Joaquín, the terrible. The true history of the three bitter blows that changed an honest man into a merciless demon, by Joseph E. Badger, Jr. New York, Beadle & Adams, 1881. Pict. wrappers. Rare.

> 29 p. 31.5 cm.
> Beadle's Dime Library, Vol. XIII, No. 165.
> Triple column.

57 ————

Pacific Pete. The prince of the revolver, by Joseph E. Badger, Jr. New York, Beadle & Adams, 1875. Pict. wrappers. Rare.

> 172 p. 17 cm.

Ernest Cowan's *A Bibliography of the History of California and the Pacific West, 1510–1906* gives the above information. According to Albert Johannsen (*The House of Beadle and Adams and Its Dime and Nickel Novels*), *Pacific Pete* appeared serially in the *Saturday Journal* in 1875–76 and was published as a twenty-cent novel in 1876.

58 ———

The pirate of the placers; or, Joaquín's death-hunt, by Joseph E. Badger, Jr. New York, Beadle & Adams, 1882. Pict. wrappers. Rare.

> 29 [3] p. 31.5 cm.
> Beadle's Dime Library, Vol. XVI, No. 201.
> Triple column.

All these Badger items are exceedingly rare and are placed in this work as examples of the early writings on outlaws. None of them are of any value historically, being mostly wild fiction, but they have become valuable as collector's items.

59   Bailey, Harry H.

When New Mexico was young, by Harry H. Bailey. His autobiography. Edited by Homer E. Gruver. [Las Cruces, N. M., published by the Las Cruces Citizen, 1948.] (Copyright 1946.) Wrappers. In print.

> 202 [1] p. illus., ports. 22.8 cm.
> Double column; port. of author on cover; foreword on verso of t.p.; copyright notice on verso of flyleaf preceding t.p.

This book tells of life in early New Mexico and contains some material on Jim Miller and the Oliver-Lee feud, but the author makes a statement I have never seen before when he says that Billy the Kid was married to Pete Maxwell's daughter and that they had two children. The book is a separate reprint from a series which ran in the *Las Cruces Citizen* from 1946 to 1948, which accounts for the fact that copyright antedates the book by two years. The author pictures Billy the Kid as one who shot his victims in the back.

60   Bakarich, Sarah Grace

Gun-smoke, by Sarah Grace Bakarich . . . . [N. p.], 1947. Pict. wrappers. In print.

> 3–152 [1] p. 15.3 cm.
> Device.

This little book deals with the gunmen and outlaws of Tombstone, Arizona. It is full of typographical errors and crudely printed. The author misspells the names of some of her characters, using for example "Chisholm" for Chisum and "Seringo" for Siringo. When I see a supposedly factual book filled with conversation, I feel that it has become more or less fictionized. Who recorded the conversation from actual life?

61   Baker, Joseph E. (ed.)

Past and present of Alameda county, California. Joseph E. Baker, editor. Illustrated.   Chicago, the S. J. Clarke co., 1914. Pub. in two volumes.   Three-quarter leather.   OP.

> Vol. I., 4 p.l., 7–463 p.   front. (port.), plates, ports., map.   26.8 cm.
> Vol. II, biographical.

Chapter X deals with the outlaws of that county, such as Juan Soto, José Piazarro, and Tomaso Rondedo, alias Procopio.

62   Ballou, Robert

Early Klititat valley days, by Robert Ballou . . . .   ₁Goldendale, Wash., printed by the Goldendale Sentinel, 1938.₁   Cloth. Scarce.

> 3 p.l., 7–496 p.   front., illus., ports.   23.5 cm.
> double column; errata on last page.

This little-known book contains material on bank and stagecoach robbers, the vigilantes of Idaho, and, most surprisingly, a correct version of the Hickok-McCanles "fight" as reported by a pony-express rider who arrived at Rock Creek Station immediately after the shooting.

63   Bancroft, Hubert Howe

Works of Hubert Howe Bancroft. Vol. XVII. History of Arizona and New Mexico, 1530–1888.   San Francisco, the Historical co., publishers, 1889.   Calf.   Scarce.

> xxxvii, 829 p.   maps (1 fold.).   23.6 cm.
> Index: p. 802–829.

Contains some material on Billy the Kid and Pat Garrett.

64   ———

Works of Hubert Howe Bancroft. Vol. XXV. History of

Nevada, Colorado and Wyoming, 1540–1888. San Francisco, the Historical co., publishers, 1890. Calf. Scarce.

> xxxii, 828 p. illus. maps. 23.6 cm.
> Index: p. 802–828.
> Half title.

65 ———

Works of Hubert Howe Bancroft. Vol. XXXI. History of Washington, Idaho, and Montana. San Francisco, the Historical co., publishers, 1890. Calf. Scarce.

> xxvi, 836 p. maps. 23.6 cm.
> Index: p. 809–836.

Some material on George Ives, Henry Plummer, and the Montana vigilantes.

66 ———

Works of Hubert Howe Bancroft. Vol. XXXIV. California pastoral, 1769–1848. San Francisco, the Historical co., publishers, 1888. Calf. Scarce.

> vi, 808 p. 23.6 cm.
> Glossary: p. 793–800; index: p. 801–808.

Information on train and stagecoach robberies, Murieta, Juan Soto, and Vásquez.

67 ———

Works of Hubert Howe Bancroft. Vol. XXXVI. Popular tribunals. San Francisco, the Historical co., publishers, 1887. Calf. Scarce.

> Vol. I, xiii, 749 p. fold. map. 23.6 cm.
> Half title.
> Vol. II, viii, 772 p. 23.6 cm.
> Index: p. 749–772.
> Half title.

All these works give some history of the outlaws of the various states handled in the volumes.

68 Banditti of the Rocky Mountains

and vigilance committee in Idaho. An authentic record of

startling adventures in the gold mines of Idaho. Chicago, Post-office box 3179, 1865. Pict. wrappers. Exceedingly rare.

vi, 25–143 [1] p. illus. 23.5 cm.

This exceedingly rare item has crude illustrations and careless pagination throughout. It is a history of the Plummer gang of outlaws published a year before the well-known one by Dimsdale. An article in the *Montana Post*, dated Saturday, August 26, 1865, announces the publication of the first installment of Dimsdale's book in that paper and condemns the above work, but I believe the condemnation arises from jealousy on Dimsdale's part because this unknown author "beat him to the draw." No one seems to know who the author was, and I know of only one copy of this work. It is written in the exaggerated style of that period.

69 [Bank of Douglas]

Arizona, 1887–1950. [Phoenix, Arizona, 1949, published by the Bank of Douglas, 1949.] Wrappers. OP.

2 p.l., 7–30 p. plates, ports. 30.6 cm.
Illus. t.p.; double column.

This booklet of pictures and short sketches was issued by the Phoenix Bank of Douglas. It contains material on many of the outlaws and gunmen of Arizona, and on the hanging of the Heath gang.

70 Banning, Capt. William and George Hugh

Six horses, by Captain William Banning and George Hugh Banning, with a foreword by Major Frederick Russell Burnham. New York, and London, the Century co. [1930]. Cloth. OP.

xx p., 1 l., 410 p. front. (port.), illus., plates, ports, map. 21 cm.
Bibliography: p. 377–387; acknowledgments signed: G.H.B.
Map on end papers.

A well-written history of the western stage lines containing some information about the early stage robbers.

71 [Bannorris, Amanda]

The female land pirate; or, awful, mysterious, and horrible disclosures of Amanda Bannorris, wife and accomplice of Richard Bannorris, a leader of that terrible band of robbers and murderers, known far and wide as the Murrell men . . . . Cincinnati, printed for, and published by E. E. Barclay, 1848. Pict. wrappers. Exceedingly rare.

3 p.l., [7]-32 p. front. (2 full p. plates), illus. 22 cm.
Vignette.

A very rare and curious work. "The following manuscripts were found in the cell of Amanda Bannorris, who, as all will recollect who have noticed the lists of crime in the New Orleans papers, within the past year, was found dead in her cell, from having taken poison. As she has narrated the case, it is senseless to say more; save that these manuscripts procured of the jailer, who claimed them as his property, at a heavy expense, and are now, for the first time, put before the world."—Publisher's note on verso of title page.

72   Barler, Miles

"Early days in Llano," by Miles Barler.   [N. p., n. d.]   Stiff wrappers.   (Cover title.)   Scarce.

76 p.   14.6 cm.
Later reprinted in a small edition.

A scarce little book which tells about cattle thieves and the author's battles with them.

73   Barnard, Evan G.

A rider of the Cherokee strip, [by] Evan G. Barnard. With illustrations.   Boston, New York, Houghton Mifflin co., 1936. Cloth.   OP.

xviii p., 1 l., 233 p.   front., plates, ports.   21.3 cm.
Appendix: p. [225]-227; index: p. [229]-233.
Half title; map on end papers; pub. device; untrimmed; first edition, 1936 under imprint.

Contains information on some of Oklahoma's outlaws, such as Tulsa Jack, Dick Yeager, the Daltons, and others, and has an account of the battle between Charlie Bryant and Ed Short.

74   Barnes, William Croft

Apaches & longhorns; the reminiscences of Will C. Barnes, edited and with an introduction by Frank C. Lockwood . . . with

40

THE

FEMALE LAND PIRATE;

OR

AWFUL, MYSTERIOUS, AND HORRIBLE DISCLOSURES

OF

AMANDA BANNORRIS,

WIFE AND ACCOMPLICE OF RICHARD BANNORRIS, A LEADER IN THAT TERRIBLE BAND OF ROBBERS AND MURDERERS, KNOWN FAR AND WIDE AS THE

MURRELL MEN.

At length the door opened, and two large fellows, with masks on their faces, carrying a dark lantern, entered, and in a gruff voice said I must go with them. Their first operatioa was to blindfold me—which done, one of them seized me in his brawny arms, bore me out, mounted me on a horse, and rode swiftly away--the other following. (*See page* 17.)

CINCINNATI.

PRINTED FOR, AND PUBLISHED BY E. E. BARCLAY.

1848.

NUMBER 71

a decoration by Cas Duchow. Los Angeles, the Ward Ritchie press, MCMXLI. Pict. cloth. OP.

> xxiii p., 1 l., 3–210 p. front., plates, ports., plan. 21.5 cm.
> Half title; vignette.

An interesting book containing accounts of the Tonto Basin feud and the killing of Andy Cooper by Commodore Owens.

75 Bartholomew, Ed

Wild Bill Longley, a Texas hard-case, by Ed Bartholomew .... Illustrated from the famous Rose collection. Houston, Texas, the Frontier press of Texas, 1953. Cloth. In print.

> 1 p.l., 5–117 [3] p. front., (port.), plates. 22.3 cm.
> 3 p. plates at end.

Published in both cloth and wrappers. This book gives some previously undisclosed facts about Bill Longley, but it needs proofreading for misspelled words. Crudely printed, but a genuine contribution to Western Americana. The first plate shows Longley standing between his two captors, both of whom wear long, heavy beards. It is said that he requested this photograph be made to prove to the world that he was not captured by two "boys."

76 Barton, O. S.

Three years with Quantrell [*sic*]. A true story told by his scout John McCorkle, written by O. S. Barton. Armstrong, Mo., Armstrong Herald print. [n. d.]. Wrappers. OP.

> 2 p.l., 1 p., [6]–157 p. front., ports. 23 cm.

An account of Quantrill and his activities, repeating legends about this famous guerrilla since disproved. Also tells of some of the escapades of Cole Younger and Frank James while they were members of the guerrillas.

77 [Bass, Sam]

Life and adventures of Sam Bass, the notorious Union Pacific and Texas train robber, together with a graphic account of his capture and death—sketch of the members of his band, with thrilling pen pictures of their many bold and desperate deeds, and the capture and death of Collins, Berry, Barnes, and Arkansas Johnson.

With illustrations.   Dallas, Texas, Dallas Commercial Steam print.,
1878.   Wrappers.   Exceedingly rare.

> 110 [2] p.   illus.   23 cm.

This exceedingly rare little book was reprinted with eighty-nine pages
by John A. Norris, of Austin, Texas, in blue wrappers, and later reprinted by N. H. Gammel, of Austin, in tan wrappers. Neither reprint
edition is illustrated. The most common one seen is the Norris reprint
in blue wrappers. Very few copies of the original edition seem to exist.
This book is quite similar to the one written by Thomas E. Hogg and
published in Denton, Texas, the same year. See Item 484. In 1952 another
reprint, with photographs, was made by the Frontier Press, Houston,
Texas.

> [3]–89 [4] p.   front. (port.), plates, ports.   20.7 cm.   Stiff wrappers.
> Last four pages plates and ports.

78 ———

From ox-teams to eagles. A history of the Texas and Pacific railway. [Dallas, Texas, 1948.]   Stiff wrappers.   OP.

> 2 p.l., 5–50 [2] p.   front., illus.   26.7 cm.

A little book issued by the Texas and Pacific Railroad, now scarce. It
contains some material on Sam Bass and his robberies of the Texas and
Pacific trains.

79 ———

True story of Sam Bass, the outlaw.   Round Rock, Texas,
written and published for the Sam Bass Café [1929].   Pamphlet.
(Cover title.)   In print.

> 11 [1] p.   front.   16 cm.

A pamphlet published by the Sam Bass Café of Round Rock, Texas,
where Sam Bass was killed. First issues of the pamphlet are scarce, but
its publisher keeps it in print for advertising purposes. This condensed
history of Bass was especially written from the files of the Adjutant
General of Texas by a son of a Texas Ranger. He merely hits the high
spots of Bass' career, and is in error in stating that the robbers got $65,000
in the Union Pacific robbery and also in stating that the Eagle Ford
robbery was the first in Texas by the Bass gang. The robbery of the
Texas Central at Allen, Texas, was the gang's first Texas train robbery; the Eagle Ford robbery of the Texas Pacific was the third.

80   Bates, Mrs. D. B.

Incidents on land and water; or, four years on the Pacific coast. Being a narrative of the burning of the ships Nonantum, Humayoon and Fanchon, together with many startling and interesting adventures on sea and land, by Mrs. D. B. Bates. Boston, James French and co., 1857. Pict. cloth. Rare.

5 p.l., [11]–336 p. front., 4 plates (incl. front.). 20.2 cm.

Contains a chapter on Murieta. This chapter is numbered XVII, but should be XIV, as it follows XIII and is followed by XV. The proper Chapter XVII is in order.

81   Bates, Edmund Franklin

History and reminiscences of Denton county, by Ed F. Bates . . . . Denton, Texas, McNitzky printing co. [1918]. Cloth. Scarce.

xi p., 2 l., 412 p. front., plates, ports., 2 fold. photographic scenes.
23.5 cm.
Index: p. 408–412.
Half title.

This book contains a chapter on Sam Bass, telling of his life in Denton, Texas, his start in crime, and his career to his death. The author's account of the capture of Joel Collins after the Union Pacific robbery is all wrong. Murphy did not break jail at Tyler, Texas, but skipped bond in a frame up arranged with the officers so that he might betray his friend Sam Bass. Nor did the killing of Grimes at Round Rock occur in a saloon, but in Copperel's store, where Bass had gone to purchase tobacco.

82   Beal, M. D.

A history of southeastern Idaho. An intimate narrative of peaceful conquest by empire builders. The fruits of their labors along tortuous rivers and valleys now sparkle like pearls in the diadem that is Idaho, the gem of the mountains, by M. D. Beal . . . . Illustrated with photographs. Caldwell, Idaho, the Caxton printers, ltd., 1942. Cloth. OP.

10 p.l., [23]–443 p. front., plates, ports. 19.7 cm.
Bibliography: p. [385]–392; notes: p. [395]–432; index: p. [433]–443.

Chapter 9 deals with road agents, outlaws, and rustlers of Idaho.

83   Beattie, George William and Helen Pruitt

Heritage of the valley; San Bernardino's first century, by George William Beattie and Helen Pruitt Beattie. With a foreword by Henry R. Wagner. Pasadena, Calif., San Pasqual press, 1939. Cloth. OP.

> xxv, 459 p. plates, ports., maps (1 fold.), facsm. 25.4 cm.
> "List of references": p. 427–439; index: p. 449–459.

84   ———

Heritage of the valley, San Bernardino's first century, by George William Beattie and Helen Pruitt Beattie. Oakland, Calif., Biobooks, 1951. Cloth. In print.

> xxix, 459 [1] p. plates, maps (all col.). 25.6 cm.
> "List of references": p. 427–439; index: p. 441–459.
> Half title, "California Southeast"; illus. front end papers; map on rear end papers; vignette.
> Colophon: "1000 copies printed by Lederer, Street and Zeus co., inc. Typography by Arthur G. Henry, art work by Wm. F. M. Kay."

Both the de luxe and the original edition have some minor material on Joaquín Murieta.

85   Bechdolt, Frederick Ritchie

Tales of the old-timers, by Frederick Bechdolt . . . . New York, and London, the Century co. [1924]. Pict. cloth. OP.

> 6 p.l., 3–367 p. front. 19.4 cm.
> Half title; device.

Has a chapter on the Lincoln County War and Billy the Kid. The author makes the error of spelling Alex McSween's name as "McSwain" and Tom O'Folliard's name as "O'Phalliard." The book also contains several chapters on the outlaws of the Northwest.

86   ———

When the west was young, by Frederick Bechdolt . . . . New York, the Century co., 1922. Cloth. OP.

> 7 p.l., 3–309 p. front. 19.3 cm.
> Half title.

45

Here the author still perpetuates the Wild Bill Hickok fable of the ten men in the McCanles fight, and calls Dave McCanles, "Jim." He also continues to spell O'Folliard's name as "O'Phalliard."

87   Beebe, Lucius, and Charles Clegg

Hear the train blow. A pictorial epic of America in the railroad age, [by] Lucius Beebe and Charles Clegg. With ten original drawings by E. S. Hammack and 860 illustrations.   New York, E. P. Dutton & co., inc., publisher, 1952.   Pict. cloth.   In print.

> 4 p.l., 1 p., 10–[415] p.   illus., plates, ports., facsms.   28.7 cm.
> Half title; illus. double t.p. (col.); illus. end papers; "First edition" on copyright p.

A chapter entitled "Car Robbers and Bindle Stiffs" deals largely with train robbers, such as the James boys and the Daltons.

88   ———

U. S. west, the saga of Wells Fargo, by Lucius Beebe and Charles Clegg.   New York, E. P. Dutton & co., inc., publishers, 1949.   Pict. cloth.   In print.

> 8 p.l., 17–320 p.   illus., plates, ports., map., facsms.   26.3 cm.
> Chronology: p. 304–310; bibliography: p. 311–313; index: p. 315–320 (triple column).
> Illus. half title; illus. double t.p. (col.); "First edition" on copyright p.

The authors write that Wild Bill Hickok was quite surprised when he read Nichols' account of his Rock Creek Station fight with the McCanles' in *Harper's Magazine*, although Nichols said that it was taken from a personal interview with Wild Bill.

"There is one item of photographic evidence in the McCanles shooting," says the authors, "a daguerreotype in the California State Library showing Dave McCanles on horseback with a bottle in his hand in front of the Rock Creek Pony Express Station. No less authority than Arthur Chapman says that the bottle contained whiskey. The inference is tenable that, when the time arrived for McCanles to draw and defend himself, his hand and aim were palsied from a low way of life. No other available moral seems to attach to the affair at Rock Creek." It is not possible that this picture was made anywhere near the day of the fight, and it has never been proved that McCanles ever drew a gun.

This excellent book also has a long chapter on the various robberies of Wells Fargo throughout sections of the West.

89   Beers, George A.

Vásquez; or, the hunted bandits of the San Joaquin. Containing thrilling scenes and incidents among the outlaws and desperadoes of southern California. With a full and accurate account of the capture, trial and execution of the noted bandit, by George A. Beers, esq.   New York, Robert M. DeWitt, publisher ₁1875₁.   Pict. wrappers.   Very rare.

> 2 p.l., ₁7₁–141 p.   diagrs.   23.5 cm.
> Double column; 2 p. adv. at end; port. of Vásquez with facsm. of his signature on cover.

Before he wrote this book for the New York publisher, Beers, a young newspaperman from the *San Francisco Chronicle*, was with the posse which chased Vásquez. Although the book sold well, the author realized only a pittance from it. It is now extremely scarce and sells at a premium.

90   Belden, John J.

Life of David Belden ₁by John J. Belden₁.   New York, and Toronto, Belden brothers, 1891.   Cloth.   Scarce.

> vi p., 1 l., 9–472 p.   front., ports.   25 cm.

Belden became one of the leading judges of early California, and among his collection of speeches is his sentence of Tiburcio Vásquez, the notorious outlaw.

91   Bell, Horace

On the old west coast; being further reminiscences of a ranger, ₁by₁ Major Horace Bell. Edited by Lanier Bartlett.   New York, William Morrow & co., 1930.   Cloth (label pasted on).   OP.

> xiv p., 1 l., 336 p.   front., plates, ports, facsms.   24.3 cm.
> Notes: p. 308–329; index: p. 330–336.
> Illus. end papers; cattle brand at end of each chapter; pub. device.

Published from the wealth of unpublished material that Major Bell left at his death, containing many things he did not wish to make public while his subjects were still alive. There is much material on Murieta and other California outlaws.

92   ———

Reminiscences of a ranger; or, early times in Southern California, by Major Horace Bell. Los Angeles, Yarnell, Caystile & Mathes, printers, 1881. Pict. cloth. Scarce.

> 7 p.l., [17]–457 p. 23.5 cm.

Reprinted at Santa Barbara by William Hebberd in 1927 and again in 1933. Foreword written by Arthur M. Ellis, with illustrations by James S. Bodrero.

> 8 p.l., 499 p. front., illus. 20 cm.

This later edition contains an index identifying many of the characters mentioned in the original edition. The first edition is said to be the first clothbound book to be printed, bound, and published in Los Angeles. Much information on the lawlessness of early California.

93 Bell, John C.

The pilgrim and the pioneer. The social and material developments in the Rocky mountains, by John C. Bell ... Lincoln, Nebr., printed by the International publishing ass'n [1906]. Cloth. OP.

> xii, 13–531 p. front., illus., plates. 20.8 cm.
> Leaf of errata, 7th preliminary page.

Contains some information on Alfred Packer, his crime and trial.

94 Bell, Katherine M.

Swinging the censer. Reminiscences of old Santa Barbara, by Katherine M. Bell. Compiled by Katherine Bell Cheney . . . . Santa Barbara, Calif., MCMXXXI. Dec. cloth. Scarce.

> xx p., 3 l., 3–287 p. front. (port.), illus., plates, ports. 20 cm.
> Half title; illus. end papers.

Some heretofore unrevealed information about Jack Powers and his gang of outlaws.

95 Belle, Frances P.

Life and adventures of the celebrated bandit Joaquín Murrieta [*sic*], his exploits in the state of California. Translated from the Spanish of Ireneo Paz by Frances P. Belle. Chicago, Reagan publishing corp., 1925. Cloth. OP.

> x, 174 p. 21.2 cm.
> Untrimmed.

Colophon (on copyright p.): "This first edition printed on London Feather weight paper consists of 975 copies."

Republished in 1937 by the Charles T. Powner co., Chicago.

This is a translation from the Spanish of the fifth edition published in Los Angeles.

96　[Benders, The]

The five fiends; or, the Bender hotel horror in Kansas. This family of fiends have for a number of years been systematically murdering travellers who stopped at their hotel or store, by a most singular method, which has never been discovered until the killing of Dr. York, the brother of Senator York, of Kansas. This book contains full and startling details of their lives and awful crimes . . . . Philadelphia, Old Franklin publishing house, 1874. Pict. wrappers. Exceedingly rare.

> 1 p.l., 3–60 [1] p. illus., plates, plan. 23.2 cm.
> Captions under plates in both English and German.

This rare book is crudely printed and illustrated. The first part gives some history of the Benders, but soon switches to wild fiction told through another character, who claims that there were three identical Bender girls (operating at that time under the name of Liefens), who, with their husband (same man married to all three sisters), were committing wholesale murders near Nagadotches [*sic*], Texas.

97　Benedict, John D.

Muskogee and northeastern Oklahoma, including the counties of Muskogee, McIntosh, Wagoner, Cherokee, Sequoyah, Adair, Delaware, Mayes, Rogers, Washington, Nowata, Craig and Ottawa, by John D. Benedict. Chicago, the S. J. Clarke publishing co., 1922. Pub. in three volumes. Cloth. OP.

> Vol. I, 9 p.l., 19–693 p. front. (port. with tissue), plates, ports. 27.7 cm.
> Index: p. 687–693.

Volume I is the only one with material on outlaws, containing a condensed history of Henry Starr.

98　Bennett, Estelline

Old Deadwood days, by Estelline Bennett. New York, J. H. Sears & co., inc., publishers [1928]. Pict. cloth. OP.

THE FIVE FIENDS:

OR,

The Bender Hotel Horror in Kansas.

THIS FAMILY OF FIENDS HAVE FOR A NUMBER OF YEARS
BEEN SYSTEMATICALLY MURDERING TRAVELLERS
WHO STOPPED AT THEIR HOTEL OR STORE,

BY A MOST SINGULAR METHOD,

WHICH HAS NEVER BEEN DISCOVERED UNTIL THE KILLING
OF DR. YORK, THE BROTHER OF SENATOR YORK,
OF KANSAS.

THIS BOOK CONTAINS FULL AND STARTLING DETAILS OF
THEIR LIVES AND AWFUL CRIMES.

*IT IS CERTAIN THAT THEY HAVE MURDERED OVER
ONE HUNDRED PEOPLE!*

PUBLISHED BY

OLD FRANKLIN PUBLISHING HOUSE IN PHILADELPHIA, PA.

Entered According to Act of Congress, in the year 1874, by C. W. Alexander,
in the office of the Librarian of Congress, at Washington, D. C.

NUMBER 96

xi p., 1 l., 3–300 p. front. (port.), plates. 21 cm.
Half title; illus. t.p.; untrimmed.

Reprinted in 1929; republished by Charles Scribner's sons in 1935.

A long chapter on Calamity Jane discusses the various dates and places of her birth as recorded by other writers. There is also some new information on Calamity Jane that I have not seen in other books.

99   Bennett, William P.

The first baby in camp. A full account of the scenes and adventures during the pioneer days of '49 . . . , by Wm. P. Bennett . . . . Salt Lake City, Utah, the Rancher publishing co., 1893. Wrappers. Scarce.

3 p.l., [9]–68 p. fold. plates. 17 cm.

Pictures 22x28 cm. are supposed to accompany this book, but are seldom seen. The book contains material on road agents and holdups.

100   Benton, Jesse James

Cow by the tail, by Jesse James Benton, with an introduction by Richard Summers. Boston, Houghton Mifflin co., 1943. Cloth. OP.

xii p., 1 l., 225 p. 20.4 cm.
Half title; illus. double t.p.; signature in facsm. at end; headpieces; first edition, 1943 over imprint.

Here is another old-timer who claims he knew Billy the Kid well and that the Kid had come up the trail from Uvalde, Texas, when Benton met him. Benton also claims the Kid went by the name of Billy LeRoy, and makes the statement that Pat Garrett stepped into Pete Maxwell's bedroom from an adjoining room when Garrett killed Billy the Kid. Could it be that this author had read the popular *Police Gazette* novel *Billy LeRoy* and become confused in his memory fifty years later?

101   Biggers, Don H.

Shackleford county sketches, [by] Don H. Biggers. Done into a book in the Albany News office, October, 1908. Boards. Rare.

[71] p. (no pagination). front. 26.5 cm.
Appendix (articles first published in the Dallas *News*): last 35 p.

This exceedingly rare little book contains material on the Millet Ranch outlaws and John Laren, of Fort Griffin, Texas.

102 [Billy the Kid]

Cowboy's career; or, the daredevil deeds of Billy the Kid, the most noted New Mexico desperado, by "One of the Kids." Chicago, St. Louis, Belford, Clarke & co., 1881. Pict. wrappers. Exceedingly rare.

There is no complete copy of this work known to exist so far as I can learn, and even the remnants have been lost. This no doubt is one of the books referred to in Pat Garrett's introduction to his *Billy the Kid* as preceding his own work. It is mentioned here with the hope that someone may resurrect a copy and let it be known.

103 Birney, Herman Hoffman

Vigilantes, by Hoffman Birney. A chronicle of the rise and fall of the Plummer gang of outlaws in and about Virginia City, Montana, in the early '60s; drawings by Charles Hargens. Philadelphia, the Penn publishing co. [1929]. Cloth. OP.

9 p.l., [17]–346 p. front., illus., plates, ports., facsm. map. 21 cm. Half title; illus. end papers; vignette.

Also published in a de luxe edition of 250 copies.
Colophon: "Two hundred and fifty copies of this edition have been specially bound and signed by the author, This is number ____."

About a third of this book appeared in the *Saturday Evening Post* in short articles before the publication of the book. It contains little new information on the vigilantes.

104 Bivins, Mrs. J. K.

Memoirs. [By Mrs. J. K. Bivins. N. p., n. d.] Cloth. Scarce.

2 p.l., 138 p. front., plates. ports. 23 cm.

A privately printed book with a chapter on Cullen Baker, an early Texas outlaw.

105 Black, A. P. (Ott)

The end of the long horn trail, by A. P. (Ott) Black. Selfridge, N. D., published by Selfridge Journal [n.d.]. Stiff wrappers. (Cover title.) OP.

4–59 p. front., illus., plates. 22.5 cm.
Blank leaf following each of the first three chapters.

The author tells of knowing Bill Powers when he was wagon boss of the Hashknife outfit and before he went to Oklahoma to join the Dalton gang. Writing of the Cherokee Strip, he calls it the "Chesakee Strip," but of course this might be an error on the part of the printer; however, he misspells other names, such as "Quantrell" for Quantrill, and he misnames Bat Masterson, "Bob" Masterson.

He tells of Bob Ford's running a honkytonk in Cripple Creek, Colorado, and is entirely wrong in saying that George Scarborough (which he spells "Scarbar") killed John Wesley Hardin. He makes the statement that "Hardin had killed thirty-one men and Scarbar [*sic*] had killed thirty when they met. Scarbar killed his thirty-second when he put Hardin away." He also declares that Calamity Jane was Wild Bill Hickok's wife.

106   Blake, Herbert Cody

Blake's western stories. The truth about Buffalo Bill (William F. Cody,) Wild Bill (J. B. Hickok,) Dr. Carver, California Joe, Yellow Hand, Tall Bull, the pony express, the old .44 Colt, derailing of the Union Pacific, reprisal on the Cheyennes under Turkey Leg. History and busted romances of the old frontier. Brooklyn, N. Y., published by Herbert Cody Blake, 1929.   Wrappers.   (Cover title.)   Scarce.

32 [1] p.   plates, ports.   23 cm.

Most of this book is devoted to debunking Buffalo Bill and the claims of the marvelous shooting of Wild Bill Hickok. The author makes the strong statement that Buffalo Bill never killed an Indian in his life.

107   Blanchard, Leola Howard

Conquest of southwest Kansas, by Leola Howard Blanchard. A history and thrilling stories of frontier life in the state of Kansas. [Wichita, printed and bound by the Wichita Eagle press, 1931.] Pict. cloth.   OP.

3 p.l., 7–355 p.   illus., plates, ports.   20.3 cm.
Vignette; copyright notice on verso of flyleaf.

Material on Dodge City and on Hendry Brown and Ben Wheeler, the bank robbers.

108   Bliss, Frank E.

The life of Hon. William F. Cody known as Buffalo Bill, the

53

famous hunter, scout and guide. An autobiography [by Frank E. Bliss]. Hartford, Conn., Frank E. Bliss [1879]. Cloth. Rare.

> xvi, 17–365 p. front. (port, signed in facsm.), illus., plates, letter in facsm. 22 cm.
> Frontis tissue.

This rare book is the earliest authentic biography of William F. Cody. It contains material on Wild Bill Hickok, but gives another false account of the McCanles fight. At least it is different from the usual accounts. The author has Wild Bill a pony express rider, and has him arriving at Rock Creek Station just in time to save the stock tender's wife, who was being assaulted by five of the McCanles "desperadoes." Wild Bill succeeded in killing four of them, the fifth escaping. The author at least holds his odds within the bounds of reason and does not have Wild Bill wounded. "Wild Bill remained at the station," Bliss writes, "with the terrified woman until the stage came along, and then he consigned her to the care of the driver. Mounting his horse he at once galloped off, and soon disappeared in the distance, making up for lost time."

109   Boethel, Paul C.

The history of Lavaca county, by Paul C. Boethel. San Antonio, Texas, the Naylor co., 1936. Pict. cloth. OP.

> 5 p.l., 151 p. 23.5 cm.
> Half title.

110   Boggs, Mae Hélène Bacon

My playhouse was a Concord coach. An anthology of newspaper clippings and documents relating to those who made California history during the years 1822–1888. Compiled by Mae Hélène Bacon Boggs. [Oakland, Calif., printed at the Howell-North press, 1942.] Cloth. OP.

> xvi, 763 p. illus., plates, ports., maps (incl. 7 fold.), facsms. 31.5 cm.
> Index: p. 749–763.
> Illus. end papers; illus. t.p.; double column.
> Colophon: "My Playhouse Was a Concord Coach is not for sale, but is presented to ____."

This is practically a history of western stagecoaching as taken from contemporary newspapers, and contains much information on road agents such as Black Bart and Tom Bell and on their robberies.

111 Boller, Henry A.

Among the Indians. Eight years in the far west: 1858–1866, embracing sketches of Montana and Salt lake, by Henry A. Boller. Philadelphia, T. Ellwood Zell, 1868. Cloth. Rare.

xvi, 17–428 p. front. (fold. map). 19 cm.
Half title.

Has a short chapter on the vigilantes and outlaws of Montana and the hanging of Henry Plummer, but most of the book is devoted to the author's life with the Indians. Most of the existing copies of this rare book lack the map.

112 Bonney, Edward

Banditti of the prairies; or, the murderer's doom! A tale of the Mississippi valley, by Edward Bonney. Chicago, E. Bonney, 1850. Cloth. Exceedingly rare.

2 p.l., [9]–196 p. plates, ports. 22 cm.
Imprint on cover: "Chicago, W. W. Davenport, 1850."

Republished by D. B. Cooke and co., 1856; and by the Homewood publishing co., 1890. An undated edition was later published in Chicago on cheap paper and with poor printing.

This exceedingly rare book is something of a history of the Mormons during the Navoo period and contains much material on the outlaws of the early Middle West.

113 Bonsal, Stephen

Edward Fitzgerald Beale, a pioneer in the path of empire, 1822–1903, by Stephen Bonsal, with 17 illustrations. New York and London, G. P. Putnam's sons, 1912. Cloth. OP.

xii p., 1 l., 312 p. front., plates, ports. 22.5 cm.
Index: p. 307–312.
T.p. in red and black; untrimmed.

Contains some material on Joaquín Murieta and Three-Fingered Jack García. Beale said that the head of Murieta and the hand of Three-Fingered Jack were brought to his camp "but a few hours after these scoundrels were shot."

114 Booker, Anton S.

Wildcats in petticoats. A garland of female desperadoes—

Lizzie Merton, Zoe Wilkins, Flora Quick Mundis, Bonnie Parker, Katie Bender and Belle Starr, by Anton S. Booker. Girard, Kan., Haldeman-Julius publications [1945]. Wrappers. In print.

> 3–24 p. 21.5 cm.

Another of those cheap and unreliable little pamphlets issued by these publishers.

115 Botkin, B. A. (ed.)

Folk-say, a regional miscellany, 1930, edited by B. A. Botkin. Norman, University of Oklahoma press, 1930. Pict. cloth. OP.

> 10 p.l., 21–473 [1] p. front., illus., music. 23.6 cm.
> Notes: p. 429–439; contributors: p. 443–454; index: p. 457–473.
> Half title; vignette.

The section entitled "Aprocrypha of Billy the Kid," by Maurice G. Fulton, presents a story of Billy the Kid's life as published in the *Las Vegas Optic* as a serial in the latter part of 1882. Fulton confesses that the first chapters are missing and begins the narrative with Chapter VII. Chapter VIII is also missing, but beginning with Chapter IX, the account continues to the end.

This newspaper serial has the Kid doing the talking as he tells the story of his life. He says that the first man he killed was a Chinaman whose throat he cut "from ear to ear," and the next man he killed was an abusive blacksmith with whom he found work.

116 ———

Folk-say. A regional miscellany, 1931, edited by B. A. Botkin. Norman, University of Oklahoma press, 1931. Dec. cloth. OP.

> 5 p.l., [11]–354 p. 23.5 cm.
> Contributors: p. [347]–354.
> Half title.

This collection has a chapter on the Apache Kid.

117 ———

A treasury of American folklore. Stories, ballads, and traditions of the people. edited by B. A. Botkin . . . with a foreword by Carl Sandburg.   New York, Crown publishers [1944].   Pict. cloth.   In print.

> xxvii [2] p., 2–932 p.   music.   22 cm.
> Index: p. 919–932.
> Half title; vignette.

Many pages are devoted to western outlaws and gunmen. The editor's section on Wild Bill is quotations from George Ward Nichols' article in *Harper's Magazine*, and Frank J. Wilstach's *Wild Bill Hickok*. His material on Billy the Kid is largely from Burns' *Saga of Billy the Kid*, chapters V–VII from *The Cowboy's Career*, and Charlie Siringo's *History of Billy the Kid*. Most of the Jesse James material is from Love's *Rise and Fall of Jesse James*, and his Sam Bass material from Gard's *Sam Bass*.

118 ———

A treasury of western folklore, edited by B. A. Botkin. Foreword by Bernard DeVoto . . . .   New York, Crown publishers, inc. [1951].   Pict. cloth.   In print.

> xxvi p., 3 l., 7–806 p.   music.   21.6 cm.
> Index (triple column): p. 793–806.
> Illus. t.p.

Published also in special Southwest, Rocky Mountain, and West Coast editions. The Southwest edition has a special foreword by J. Frank Dobie. (2 l. before t.p.).

In a long chapter entitled "Law and Order, Ltd.," the compiler quotes from various books on many of the western gunmen such as Clay Allison, Joaquín Murieta, Black Bart, Jesse James, Bill Doolin, Billy the Kid, Al Jennings, Tom Horn, Apache Kid, Cherokee Bill, Belle Starr, Calamity Jane, Sam Bass, Harry Tracy, Elfego Baca, Wild Bill Hickok, and others. Nothing new has been added.

119   Bracke, William B.

Wheat country, by William B. Bracke.   New York, Duell, Sloan and Pearce [1950].   Cloth.   In print.

> viii p., 1 l., 3–309 p.   22 cm.
> American folkways series.
> Index: p. 299–309.
> Half title; map on end papers.

One of the American Folkways Series edited by Erskine Caldwell, this book contains some information on Wild Bill Hickok and his death, and a brief account of the Daltons robbing the banks at Coffeyville.

120   Bradley, Glenn Danforth

The story of the Santa Fe, by Glenn Danforth Bradley . . . . Boston, Richard G. Badger . . . [1920]. Cloth.   Scarce.

> 7 p.l., 17–288 p.   front., plates, ports.   20.5 cm.
> Source material: p. 272–279; index: p. 281–288.
> Map on end papers (dif.); thesis (Ph.D.), University of Michigan, 1915.

This book has a chapter on Dodge City, Kansas, in its wild days and gives some information on its gunmen.

121   Bradley, R. T.

The outlaws of the border; or, the lives of Frank and Jesse James, their exploits, adventures and escapes, down to the present time. Together with the achievements, robberies and final capture of the Younger brothers, by R. T. Bradley . . . .   St. Louis, J. W. Marsh, publishers, 1880.   Cloth.   Rare.

> ix, [3]–302 p.   front., illus., ports.   20 cm.

The last half of this book is taken from Edwards' *Noted Guerrillas*. Like most of the books of this period about the James boys, it is not too reliable.

122   Brady, Jasper Ewing

Tales of the telegraph. The story of a telegrapher's life and adventures in railroad, commercial and military work, by Jasper Ewing Brady . . . .   New York, Doubleday & McClure co., 1899. Dec. cloth.   OP.

> viii p., 1 l., 272 p.   front., plates, facsm.   19.3 cm.
> Half title; device.

Contains some minor material on train robbery.

123   Branch, E. Douglas

The cowboy and his interpreters, [by] Douglas Branch; illustrations by Will James, Joe DeYong, Charles M. Russell.   New York, London, D. Appleton and co., 1926.   Dec.   Cloth.   OP.

ix [1] p., 1 l., 277 [1] p. front., illus. 21.3 cm.
Bibliography: p. 271–[278].
Half title; illus. end papers; pub. device; untrimmed; first edition: figure
(1) at end of bibliography.

In a chapter on Sam Bass, the author says that the Union Pacific robbery netted the outlaws $5,000 from the passengers, and that they made a haul of $15,000 in twenty-dollar gold pieces from the express car. He is mixed up in his amounts. They did not get near that amount from the passengers and got $60,000 from the express car.

124 ———

Westward. The romance of the American frontier, by E. Douglas Branch. Woodcuts by Lucina Smith Wakefield. New York, and London, D. Appleton and co., 1930. Cloth. OP.

ix [1] p., 2 l., 3–626 [1] p. illus. incl. maps (1 double p.) 22.2 cm.
Notes on material: p. 598–[609]; index: p. 611–[627].
Half title; map on end papers; illus. chapter headings; vignette; untrimmed;
first edition: figure (1) at end of index.

Contains some material on the Lincoln County and Johnson County wars, with a slight mention of Billy the Kid and other outlaws.

125 Breakenridge, William M.

Helldorado. Bringing the law to the mesquite, by William M. Breakenridge. With illustrations. Boston and New York, Houghton Mifflin co., 1928. Cloth. OP.

xix, 256 p. front., plates, ports. 23.2 cm.
Half title; pub. device; first edition: 1928 under imprint.

A most interesting book about Tombstone, Arizona, in its wild days, told by one of the law officers of that period.

126 Bridwell, J. W.

The life and adventures of Robert McKimie, alias "Little Reddie," from Texas. The dare-devil desperado of the Black Hills region, chief of the murderous gang of treasure coach robbers. Also, a full account of the robberies committed by him and his gang in Highland, Pike and Ross counties; with full particulars of Detective Norris' adventures while effecting the capture of members of the gang. Compiled from authentic sources by J. W. Bridwell. Hills-

———THE———

LIFE AND ADVENTURES

OF

ROBERT McKIMIE,

ALIAS "LITTLE REDDY," FROM TEXAS.

The Dare-Devil Desperado of the Black Hills Region,
Chief of the Murderous Gang of Treasure
Coach Robbers.   Also, a full

ACCOUNT OF THE ROBBERIES COMMITTED

By him and his Gang in Highland, Pike and Ross
Counties; with full particulars of Detective
Norris' Adventures while effecting the
Capture of Members of the Gang.

Compiled from Authentic Sources by J. W. BRIDWELL.

HILLSBORO, O., DECEMBER, 1878.

PRINTED AND PUBLISHED AT THE
HILLSBORO GAZETTE OFFICE.

NUMBER 126

boro, O., printed and published at the Hillsboro Gazette office, December, 1878.   Pict. wrappers.   Rare.

[3]–56 p.   ports.   22.6 cm.

An exceedingly rare item about an outlaw of the Black Hills who made a specialty of robbing the treasure coaches of the Deadwood and Cheyenne run. McKimie is credited with the daring holdup at Cheyenne Crossing and South Pass City and with the murder of Johnny Slaughter, the well-known stage driver. He was a member of the Joel Collins–Sam Bass gang at the start of their criminal career. I know of but three copies of this book.

127   Briggs, Harold E.

Frontiers of the northwest. A history of the upper Missouri valley, by Harold E. Briggs . . . . Illustrated.   New York, London, D. Appleton-Century co., inc., 1940.   Cloth.   OP.

xiv p., 1 l., 3–629 p.   front., plates (4 ports. on 1 plate), maps.   22.8 cm.
Bibliography: p. 595–612; index: p. 613–629.
Half title; map on end papers; pub. device; first edition: figure (1) at end of index.

In one section, entitled "The Calamity Jane Myth," some space is devoted to the debunking of this well-known character. In another, labeled "Justice in the Mining Camps," the author deals with the Vigilance Committee of Montana and with Henry Plummer's road-agent gang.

128   Brininstool, Earl Alonzo

Fighting Red Cloud's warriors. True tales of Indian days when the west was young, by E. A. Brininstool . . . . Columbus, Ohio, the Hunter-Trader-Trapper co., 1926.   Pict. cloth.   OP.

7 p.l., 17–241 p.   front., plates, ports.   18.7 cm.
7 p. adv. at end.
"The Frontier Series," Vol. 2.

There is a long chapter on Calamity Jane, in which the author quotes from her book and that of Brown and Willard. In the footnotes he tries to correct some of the legends about her.

129   Bronaugh, Warren Carter

The Youngers' fight for freedom. A southern soldier's twenty years' campaign to open northern prison doors—with anecdotes of war days, by W. C. Bronaugh ... who spent the period from 1882 to 1902 to secure the release of Cole, Jim and Bob Younger from the Minnesota state penitentiary .... Columbia, Mo., printed for the author by E. W. Stephens publishing co., 1906. Cloth. OP.

> 6 p.l., 15–398 p. front. (port.), plates, ports. 21 cm.

A book different from all the others dealing with the James and Younger brothers, and reliable. The author spent twenty years of his life working to get the Youngers pardoned from the Minnesota penitentiary. From 1882 to 1902 he wrote letters, spent his money, raised funds from friends, traveled thousands of miles, and camped on the trail of governors, pardon boards, and wardens. He did not give up until the Youngers were released.

130   Bronson, Edgar Beecher

Red blooded, by Edgar Beecher Bronson .... Chicago, A. C. McClurg & co., 1910. Pict. cloth. OP.

> viii, 3–341 [1] p. front., plates. 21 cm.

Partly reprinted from various publications. Republished by George H. Doran Co., New York, with some changes in the title page.

An excellent piece of Western Americana with a chapter on Clay Allison; one entitled "Triggerfingeritis" is on stagecoach robberies by Dunc Blackburn, shotgun messengers, such as Boone May, and horse thieves, such as Doc Middleton. A long chapter on "The Evolution of a Train Robber" relates the story of the robbing of the Southern Pacific by Kit Joy, Mitch Lee, Taggart, and George Cleveland.

131   ———

The vanguard, by Edgar Beecher Bronson. New York, George H. Doran co. [1914]. Pict. cloth. OP.

> 5 p.l., 9–316 p. 19.6 cm.
> Half title; illus. end papers (col.).

The author spells John Chisum's name "Chisholm." He tells of the hanging of Lame Johnny and gives some material on Apache Kid.

132   Brosnan, C. J.

History of the state of Idaho, by C. J. Brosnan .... New York, Chicago, Boston, Charles Scribner's sons [1918]. Cloth. OP.

xiii p., 2 l., 237 p.   front., (double p. col. map), illus., plates, ports., maps.
20 cm.
Supplements: p. 213–231; index: p. 233–237.

Contains some material on the vigilantes of Idaho.

133   Brothers, Mary Hudson

Billy the Kid. The most hated, the most loved outlaw New Mexico ever produced. Story by Bell Hudson. Written by Mary Hudson Brothers. ₁Farmington, New Mexico, Hustler press, 1949.₁ Pict. stiff wrappers with 2 hole tie.   In print.

5 p.l., 13–52 p.   2 ports. (incl. front.).   24.7 cm.
Half title.

This is largely taken from the author's previous book, *A Pecos Pioneer*. She repeats the legend of the Kid's shooting off the heads of snowbirds, but most of her account is fairly accurate.

134   ———

A Pecos pioneer, by Mary Hudson Brothers. Albuquerque, published by the University of New Mexico press, 1943.   Cloth.   OP.

vii p., 1 l., 169 p.   front. (group port.).   23.5 cm.
Half title; device.

This book is based upon notes taken from the author's father, Bell Hudson, but she makes the mistake of crediting the Chisholm Trail to John Chisum, and the book contains other errors of locale and events.

135   Brown, Dee, and Martin F. Schmitt

Trail driving days. Text by Dee Brown, picture research by Martin F. Schmitt.   New York, Charles Scribner's sons; London, Charles Scribner's sons, ltd., 1952.   Pict. cloth.   In print.

xxii p., 1 l., 264 p.   plates, ports., cattle brands, facsms.   30.5 cm.
Bibliography: p. 255–264.
Half title; errata leaf tipped in; vignette; first edition: letter "A" on copyright p.

This is mostly a picture book containing many familiar photographs of various outlaws, but does contain a new picture said to be that of Billy the Kid. In the chapter on the Kid, the authors repeat the old legend about the judge's sentencing of the Kid and his impudent answer, and also the one about his being in a card game with Bell when he killed Bell. Most of the chapter on the Kid follows Walter Noble Burns' account.

136   Brown, James Cabell

Calabaza; or, amusing recollections of an Arizona "city," by J. Cabell Brown. Illustrated with original drawings. San Francisco, published by Valleau and Peterson, printers and publishers [1892]. Wrappers. Scarce.

> 5 p.l., [13]–251 p.   front., illus.   18.4 cm.

Calabaza was a rugged camp in the Santa Cruz Valley, Arizona, just north of the Mexican border. It was the refuge of tough *hombres* from all parts of the West. The town was broken up by riots. What was left of it was moved to Nogales, where it is said its citizens "could keep one foot on the bar-rail and the other on the boundary line."

137   Brown, Jesse, and A. M. Willard

The Black Hills trails. A history of the struggles of the pioneers in the winning of the Black Hills, by Jesse Brown and A. M. Willard, edited by John T. Milek.   Rapid City, S. D., Rapid City Journal co., 1924.   Cloth.   Scarce.

> 6 p.l., [17]–572 p.   front., illus., plates, ports.   23.6 cm.

One of the standard histories of the Black Hills, this book contains much information on the outlaws of that section. The authors' version of the birthplace of Calamity Jane is Burlington, Iowa. They also write of Billy the Kid McCarthy as a member of the Axelbee gang in the Black Hills. This Billy is not Billy the Kid Bonney, although some of the early dime novels did get the two names confused. The authors also state that Calamity Jane's father was a Baptist preacher, but most accounts of her parentage say that he was a simple farmer who married her mother out of a bawdy house.

138   Brown, John

Twenty-five years a parson in the wild west; being the experience of Parson Ralph Riley, by Rev. John Brown . . . .   Fall River, Mass., printed for the author, 1896.   Cloth.   OP.

> 4 p.l., 9–215 p.   front. (port.).   18.7 cm.

Experiences with stagecoach robbers in Nevada and with train robbers in Texas.

64

139 Bruffey, George A.

Eighty-one years in the west, by George A. Bruffey. Butte, Mont., the Butte Miner co., printers, 1925. Cloth. Scarce.

4 p.l., [11]–152 p. front. (port.). 20 cm.
Half title; device.

Material on the Montana vigilantes and outlaws, the hanging of Slade and the rest of the Plummer gang.

140 Buckbee, Edna Bryan

Pioneer days of Angel's Camp, by Edna Bryan Buckbee. Angel's Camp, Calif., published by Calaveras Californian [1932]. Stiff pict. wrappers. OP.

3 p.l., 80 p. front., plates, ports. 19.4 cm.

Has some stories about Black Bart.

141 ———

The saga of old Tuolumne, by Edna Bryan Buckbee. Sixteen full page illustrations from photographs. New York, the Press of the Pioneers, inc., 1935. Cloth. Scarce.

x p., 3 l., 526 p. front., plates. 23.5 cm.
Bibliography: p. [492]–500; pioneers of Tuolumne County: p. 501–521; towns and camps of Tuolumne region: p. 523–526.
Half title.

Contains some material on Murieta and other California outlaws.

142 Buel, James William

The border outlaws. An authentic and thrilling history of the most notorious bandits of ancient and modern times, the Younger brothers, Jesse and Frank James, and their comrades in crime. Compiled from reliable sources only and containing the latest facts in regard to these celebrated outlaws, by J. W. Buel . . . . Illustrated with portraits and colored plates. St. Louis, Historical publishing co., 1881. Cloth. Rare.

4 p.l., [11]–252 p. front. (port. of 3 Youngers), illus., ports., plates (8 col.).

[Published with]

The border bandits. An authentic and thrilling history of the noted outlaws, Jesse and Frank James, and their bands of highway-men. Compiled from reliable sources only and containing the latest facts in regard to these desperate freebooters, by J. W. Buel . . . . Illustrated with late portraits and colored plates. St. Louis, Historical publishing co., 1881. Scarce.

> 4 p.l., [7]–148 [4] p. front. (port. of 2 James brothers), plates (4 col.), ports. 19.2 cm.

> Republished by same publishers in 1882, and in later years, and published several times in cheap editions, both together and separately, by I. & M. Ottenheimer, of Baltimore.

Buel is unreliable in all his books, and his writings seem to border upon the sensational rather than to rely upon historical fact.

143 ———

Heroes of the plains; or, lives and wonderful adventures of Wild Bill, Buffalo Bill . . . and other celebrated Indian fighters . . . including a true and thrilling history of Custer's "last fight" . . . also a sketch of the life of Sitting Bull and his account of the Custer massacre as related to the author in person, J. W. Buell . . . . St. Louis and Philadelphia, Historical publishing co., 1883. Scarce.

> 2 p.l., [9]–612 p. front., illus., plates (col.), ports. 21 cm.

This is no dime novel, though it reads like one. It is a thick book re-printed many times, and its large circulation caused readers to believe it to be fact. Thus the legends about Wild Bill and Buffalo Bill were created and are still being quoted by careless writers.

This book retains the false story started by Nichols in *Harper's Magazine*, the author also claiming to have come into possession of Wild Bill's diary, given him by his widow, Mrs. Agnes Lake. Her son-in-law denies Wild Bill kept a diary. Buel, too, puts Rock Creek Station in Kansas instead of Nebraska. He calls McCanles "Bill" instead of David, his real name. He also incorrectly claims the McCanles' were horse thieves, which they were not. Like Nichols, he claims corroboration for his story. He has Wild Bill's skull fractured, three gashes in his breast, fore-arm cut, one deep wound in the hip and two in the right leg, and his right cheek cut open, besides all the bullet wounds. Research has proved that Wild Bill was not even wounded in this so-called battle with the McCanles'.

"This combat," says Buel, "of one man fairly whipping ten ac-knowledged desperadoes, has no parallel, I make bold to say, in any authentic history. The particulars as has been here recorded are unquestionably correct, for they are obtained from Captain Kingsbury, who heard Bill's first recital of the facts right on the battle front."

Nichols and Buel both quote a Captain Kingsbury; and Colonel Prentiss Ingraham, in his dime novel on Wild Bill, also states that the *Harper's* story was undoubtedly correct because "the particulars were obtained from Captain Kingsbury." Connelley thinks him fictional.

144 ———

Jesse and Frank James and their comrades in crime, the Younger brothers, the notorious border outlaws. An authentic account of the most daring bandits of modern times, the Younger brothers, also Jesse and Frank James and their comrades in crime. Compiled from the most reliable sources, and containing the latest facts, by J. W. Buel. Fully illustrated. Baltimore, I. & M. Ottenheimer [n. d.]. Pict. wrappers. OP.

> 2 p.l., 7–188 p.   front., illus.   19 cm.

A cheap reprint of the author's *Border Outlaws*, with omissions.

145 ———

Life and marvelous adventures of Wild Bill, the scout. Being a true and exact history of all the sanguinary combats and hairbreadth escapes of the most famous scout and spy America ever produced, by J. W. Buel .... Illustrated. Chicago, Belford, Clarke & co., 1880. Pict. wrappers. Rare.

> 4 p.l., 7–92 [1] p.   front. (port.), illus.   18 cm.
> Republished in 1888, and published again in Chicago, by G. E. Wilson, in 1891 with same format.

This is the first and perhaps the rarest book written about Wild Bill Hickok, and is a continuation of the legend about the Hickok-McCanles fight. In later years the Hickok-McCanles fight proved to be just an example of highly imaginary and exaggerated sensationalism. In February, 1867, *Harper's Magazine* published a story about Hickok written by Colonel George Ward Nichols purportedly told by Wild Bill himself to the author. This tale has proved to be pure fabrication throughout, but most of the books on Wild Bill which followed Buel rehashed this wild but untrue tale. Emerson Hough probably used this book for his chapter on Hickok in his *Story of the Outlaw*.

146   [Buffalo Bill]

Buffalo Bill (Hon. Wm. F. Cody,) and his wild west com-

LIFE AND MARVELOUS ADVENTURES

OF

WILD BILL,

THE SCOUT.

BEING A TRUE AND EXACT HISTORY OF ALL THE
SANGUINARY COMBATS AND HAIR-BREADTH
ESCAPES OF THE MOST FAMOUS SCOUT
AND SPY AMERICA EVER PRODUCED.

BY
J. W. BUEL,
OF THE ST. LOUIS PRESS.

ILLUSTRATED.

CHICAGO:
BELFORD, CLARKE & CO.
1880.

NUMBER 145

panions, including Wild Bill, Texas Jack, California Joe, Captain Jack Crawford, and other famous scouts of the western plains. Chicago, George M. Hill co., [1893]. Pict. wrappers. Scarce.

> 2 p.l., 7–234 p. illus. 19 cm.
> Device.

A laudatory, but undependable, "life" of Buffalo Bill by an anonymous writer. In his chapter on Wild Hill Hickok he quotes from the dime novelist Prentiss Ingraham, who was always unreliable.

147 Buffum, George Tower

On two frontiers, by George T. Buffum . . . . Frontispiece by Maynard Dixon, pen-and-ink illustrations by Frank T. Merrill. Boston, Lothrop, Lee & Shepard co. [1918]. Dec. cloth. OP.

> vii p., 1 l., 3–375 p. front. 19.7 cm.
> Half title; illus. chapter headings; device; untrimmed.

This book has a chapter on Curly Bill Brocius and some of his actions in Charleston, Arizona, one on the vigilantes of Bonanza Gulch, and one on Wild Bill Hickok. In the chapter on Wild Bill the author has the McCanles fight taking place at "Widow Waltman's cottage." He repeats the early false account of the fight and states that "when he [Hickok] had only six shots left, with nine opponents left [he had already killed Dave McCanles], he learned that he was thoroughly efficient with the bowie knife."

148 ———

Smith of Bear City, and other frontier sketches, by George T. Buffum. Illustrated with six photogravures from original drawings by F. T. Wood. New York, the Grafton press, 1906. Dec. cloth. OP.

> xii [1] p., 1 l., 248 [1] p. front., plates. 21.4 cm.
> Half title; device; untrimmed.

Several chapters are included on outlaws, such as Soapy Smith, Curly Bill, and Clay Allison, most of them highly fictitious. In the chapter on Clay Allison the author calls Chunk Colbert, "Chutt," and has Allison kill him with a *derringer* when they sat down together. Of Billy the Kid he says, ". . . at the age of twenty-six he had killed twenty-seven men," which is, as we know, incorrect. Further, he makes the statement that "when he was pursued after having killed his jailer he displayed the white flag, and when the posse came near to receive his surrender he shot the entire band." He also has the account of the mob holding up the departure of the train at Las Vegas, on which the Kid was prisoner, all wrong. Pat Garrett, not Stewart as the author states, had Billy the Kid under arrest, and Dave Rudabaugh was the man the mob was after.

149 Buntline, Ned (pseud. of Edward Zane Carrol Judson)

Buffalo Bill, by Ned Buntline. New York, American publishers corp. ₁n. d.₁. Pict. wrappers. Scarce. Also published in cloth.

₁3₁–314 p. front., illus. 19 cm.

One of the lurid early accounts of Buffalo Bill. Said to be the book that introduced Cody to the circus world.

150 ———

Buffalo Bill and his adventures in the west, by Ned Buntline. New York, J. S. Ogilvie publishing co., 1886. Pict. wrappers. Scarce.

₁3₁–314 p. front., illus. 19.4 cm.
2 p. adv. at end.

This is the same book as Item 149, with a different title. Both contain the most brazen of all the falsehoods written about the Hickok-McCanles fight. The author calls David McCanles "Jake" and wrongly spells the last name as "McKandlas." He has McCanles kill Buffalo Bill's father before the eyes of his entire family, and the whole account is written in a sickening, cheap theatrical style.

Buntline thought he knew what the East expected of the West, so taking up his pen, he dashed off his first Buffalo Bill story. It was read by Cody with the utmost amazement. It "told of deeds he had never done and could never hope to match, of talents he did not possess, and noble sentiments which he did not boast."

Buffalo Bill himself signed fabulous ghost-written tales and let them be published under his own name. He once wrote his publishers: "I am sorry to have to lie so outrageously in this yarn. My hero has killed more Indians on one war trail than I have killed all my life. But I understand this is what is expected of border tales. If you think the revolver and bowie knife are used too freely, you may cut out a fatal shot or stab wherever you deem it wise."

151 Burch John P.

Charles W. Quantrell [sic], a true history of his guerrilla warfare on the Missouri and Kansas border during the civil war of 1861 to 1865, by John P. Burch. Illustrated. As told by Captain Harrison Trow, one who followed Quantrell [sic] through his whole course. ₁Vega, Texas, 1923.₁ Dec. cloth. OP.

> 7 p.l., 15–266 p. front. (port.), illus., plates. 20.2 cm.

Somehow one loses confidence in a biographer who does not even know how to spell his subject's name correctly. "Quantrell" spelled his name "Quantrill," and his Christian names were William Clarke, not "Charles W." The text of the book is just as unreliable.

152 Burdick, Usher Lloyd

Jim Johnson, pioneer. A brief history of the Mouse river loop country, by Usher L. Burdick. ₁Williston, N. D., privately printed, 1941₁. Wrappers. OP.

> 2 p.l., 7–32 ₁1₁ p. front. (port.). 22.8 cm.
> "Edition limited to 300 copies."

Contains a good account of the vigilantes and some bad men of North Dakota.

153 ——

Life and exploits of John Goodall, by Usher L. Burdick . . . . Watford City, N. D., published by the McKenzie County Farmer, 1931. Wrappers. OP.

> 3 p.l., ₁7₁–29 p. front., port. 22.7 cm.
> Copyright notice and "First edition" on t.p.

Contains information on the Montana vigilantes organized by Granville Stuart to rid the country of horse thieves.

154 ——

Tales from buffalo land. The story of George "W." Newton . . . , by Usher L. Burdick. Baltimore, Wirth brothers, 1939. Wrappers. OP.

> 3 p.l., 9–27 p. front. (port.), plates. 22.8 cm.
> Vignette.
> Reprinted same year.

More material on horse thieves and Montana vigilantes.

155 _____

Tales from buffalo land. The story of Fort Buford, by Usher L. Burdick. Baltimore, Wirth brothers, 1940. Cloth. OP.

> 3 p.l., [7]-215 p. front. (port.), plates, ports., fold. letter in facsm. 20.6 cm.

Although this book has practically the same title as the preceding one, it is an entirely different item. However, it does contain information on the horse thieves and vigilantes of Montana.

156 Burk, Mrs. Clinton (Calamity Jane)

Life and adventures of Calamity Jane, by herself. [N. p., *ca.* 1896.] Pict. wrappers. Rare.

> 7 p. 16.5 cm.

Reprinted later in Livingston, Montana, by Post Print [n. d.].

> 8 p. 16.5 cm.

> Modern reprints have been made available within the last few years.

Calamity Jane wandered about the country selling these pamphlets for an income during her declining years. Since she had a propensity for romancing and seeking notoriety, much of her book should be "taken with a grain of salt." She claims that the killing of Wild Bill took place in the Bella Union Saloon when it really happened in Saloon No. 10, and she claims also that she pursued Jack McCall and captured him, but records show that she was not at the scene when the killing took place. Written, or rather dictated, many years after her active days, her account is based upon a bad memory and exaggeration. Her statement that she chased Jack McCall and captured him with a meat cleaver in Shurdy's butchershop has been repeated by many writers, but reliable eyewitnesses say she was nowhere near the scene.

157 Burke, John M.

"Buffalo Bill" from prairie to palace. An authentic history of the wild west, with sketches, stories of adventure, and anecdotes of "Buffalo Bill," the hero of the plains. Compiled by John M. Burke ("Arizona John") with the authority of General W. F. Cody ("Buffalo Bill"). Chicago and New York, Rand McNally & co., 1893. Pict. cloth. Scarce.

> 6 p.l., 13-275 p. front. (port. with signature in facsm.), illus., plates, ports., facsm. 20 cm.
> Half title.

The author does not repeat here the often told tale of the McCanles fight, but does dwell at length on Wild Bill's bravery. He spells Jack McCall's name as "McCaul," and also misspells Jules Reni's name as Jules "Bevi" in telling of Slade's killing of this Frenchman.

158   Burlingame, Merrill G.

The Montana frontier, by Merrill G. Burlingame . . . . End plates and maps by George A. Balzhiser.   Helena, Mont., State publishing co. [1942].   Cloth.   OP.

> xiii p., 1 l., 418 p.   front. (relief map), illus., plates, ports., maps, diagr., tables.   22.2 cm.
> Footnotes: p. 357–381; appendix (chronological outline): p. 385–390; bibliography: p. 391–397; index: p. 399–418.
> Map of Montana, 1863 (front end papers); map of Montana, 1890, back end papers; vignette.

Contains a chapter on the vigilantes and Henry Plummer's gang of road agents.

159   Burnham, Frederick Russell

Scouting on two continents, by Major Frederick Russell Burnham . . . , elicited [sic] and arranged by Mary Nixon Everett. Garden City, N. Y., Doubleday, Page & co., 1926.   Cloth.   OP.

> xxii p., 1 l., 370 p.   front., illus., plates, ports., maps, facsms.   23.5 cm.
> Half title; t.p. in red and black; device.
>
> Reprinted in 1927.

Contains some material on the Tonto Basin War.

160   Burns, Walter Noble

The Robin Hood of El Dorado; the saga of Joaquin Murrieta [sic], famous outlaw of California's age of gold, by Walter Noble Burns.   New York, Coward-McCann, inc. [1932].   Cloth.   OP.

> 5 p.l., 304 p.   front. (facsm.).   21 cm.
> Half title; untrimmed; first edition: "C M" in device at bottom of copyright page.

This has become perhaps the most widely read book on Murieta because it is modern and written in a charming style. Being made into a motion picture also made it popular. It is, more or less, a gathering together and rewriting by an able writer of material in other, earlier books on Murieta. The author combines the Ridge and *Police Gazette* versions, the former

73

using the name Rosita for Joaquín's sweetheart and the latter Carmela. Burns combines the two and calls her Rosita Carmen, but he still follows the fictitious account created by Ridge. This book is said to be a "biography," but should be classed as fiction just as his *Saga of Billy the Kid* should be.

161 ———

The saga of Billy the Kid, by Walter Noble Burns . . . . Garden City, N. Y., Doubleday, Page & co., 1926. Cloth. OP.

> 5 p.l., 322 p.   21.3 cm.
> Half title; illus. end papers (col.); vignette; "First edition" on copyright p.
>
> Reprinted many times, and reprints are available.

A well-written book, but, in my opinion, done in a too romantic style, the whole sounding like a tale of folklore. The author cites no sources and gives few dates. He makes the statement that Mrs. McSween played the piano while her home was burning. Mrs. McSween later emphatically denied this statement as being preposterous. Although conversation makes a book more readable, I always wonder about this feature in a historical work. This book is filled with it, all the invention of the author. Yet this romantic piece of folklore has been taken for fact and become so popular that it has been kept in print in both this country and England. Many librarians, however, keep it in the fiction section of their shelves, where it should be.

162 ———

Tombstone, an Iliad of the southwest, by Walter Noble Burns.   Garden City, N. Y., Doubleday, Page & co., 1927.   Cloth. OP.

> ix p., 1 l., 388 p.   21.4 cm.
> "Sources": p. vii–ix.
> Half title; t.p. in red and black; vignette; untrimmed; "First edition" on copyright p.
>
> Reprinted in 1929 with added material, and reprinted many times since.

The author writes entertainingly, and this is perhaps the first complete book dealing with Tombstone, Arizona. He makes this turbulent old town live vividly, but again I wonder who recorded all the conversation.

163   [Burrows, Rube]

Complete official history of Rube Burrows and his celebrated gang. A story of his life and exploits, without a parallel in

crime and adventure. Birmingham, Ala., Lyman and Stone publishers and stationers [n. d.]. Wrappers. (Cover title.) Exceedingly rare.

> 2 p.l., [5]–141 p.   front., illus., ports.   16.8 cm.
> 3 p. adv. at end.

This is perhaps the rarest of the books on Rube Burrows and gives a
fairly accurate account of his operations.

164 ——————

Rube Burrows' raids. Historic highwayman. Night riders
of the Ozarks; or, the Bald Knobbers of Missouri .... New York,
R. K. Fox, 1891.   Pict. wrappers.   Rare.

> 17 [4] p., 20–45 [2] p., 6–42 p.   illus.   24 cm.
> Double column.

Two books bound in one, both just another of the *Police Gazette's* pieces
of sensational fiction, but a collector's item.

165   Burt, Maxwell Struthers

The diary of a dude-wrangler, by Struthers Burt.   New
York, London, Charles Scribner's sons, 1924.   Pict. cloth.   OP.

> viii p., 2 l., 3–331 p.   front.   21 cm.
> Half title; vignette; frontis tissue; untrimmed.
>
> Reprinted in 1938 with "List of Ranches" p. 333–343.

The author here touches upon the Johnson County War, but he makes
the mistake of stating that two freighters had escaped from the besieged
house of Nate Champion and spread the alarm. The "two freighters"
were Bill Walker and Ben Jones, two trappers, and they did not escape.
When they went to the river for water, they were captured and held
prisoner by the attacking party. Jack Flagg, a neighboring ranchman,
was the man who spread the alarm.

166   ——————

Powder river; let 'er buck, by Struthers Burt. Illustrated by
Ross Santee.   New York, Toronto, Farrar & Rinehart, inc. [1938].
Cloth.   First ed. scarce.

> xi p., 1 l., 3–389 [13] p.   front. (map), illus.   20.8 cm.
> [Rivers of America series.]
> Bibliography: p. 377–380; index: p. 381–389.

Half title: t.p. in red and black; vignette; first edition: "F R" in device on
copyright p.
Last 11 pages "Rivers and American Folk" by Constance Lindsay Skinner.
Reprinted several times.

Quite a bit of space is devoted to the Johnson County War, and the
author corrects the error he made in his *Diary of a Dude-Wrangler* about
Walker and Jones. He tells of the Hole-in-the-Wall gang and Tom
Horn. This excellent writer has written one of the best books of the
Rivers of America series.

167   Burton, Richard Francis

The city of the saints, and across the Rocky mountains to
California, by Richard F. Burton. With illustrations.   New York,
Harper and brothers, publishers, 1862.   Cloth.   Scarce.

xii p., 2 l., 547 p.   front., illus., fold. map, fold. plan.   23.5 cm.

The original edition is now quite scarce, but the book was reprinted by
the Long Book Company in 1951. It contains some material on road
agents and Joseph Slade.

168   Bush, I. J.

Gringo doctor, by Dr. I. J. Bush. Foreword by Eugene Cunningham. Illustrated by James Wallis.   Caldwell, Idaho, the Caxton
printers, ltd., 1939.   Pict. cloth.   OP.

9 p.l., [17]–261 p.   front., illus.   23.6 cm.
Half title; illus. end papers; pub. device.

Some minor material on John Wesley Hardin, John Selman, and Jim
Miller.

169   Bushwick, Frank H.

Glamorous days, by Frank H. Bushwick.   San Antonio,
Texas, the Naylor co., 1934.   Cloth.   OP.

vi, 308 p.   front. (port.), plates, ports.   23.8 cm.
Appendix: p. 305–308.
Half-title; device; "first edition" on t.p.

Touches upon many western outlaws, with chapters on King Fisher,
Ben Thompson, and John Wesley Hardin. The author claims that his
account of the killing of Ben Thompson is related for the first time.
"The actual facts were not made public at the time," he writes, "nor
for many years afterward, for reasons that can be readily understood."
He then proceeds to name McLaughlin, a bartender, Canada Bill, a

gambler, and Harry Tremaine, an English Jew variety actor, as the men who shot Thompson from a near-by box in the theater. They immediately left town.

170   Butcher, Solomon D.

Pioneer history of Custer county and short sketches of early days in Nebraska, [by S. D. Butcher].   Broken Bow, Nebr., [privately printed at Denver, by the Merchants publishing co.], 1901. Cloth.   OP.

> 3 p.l., [7]–403 p.   front. (port. signature in facsm.), plates, ports.   24 cm.
> 5 p. adv. at end; leaf of errata; frontis tissue.

A long chapter on the lynching of Kid Wade, the horse thief, and on the exploits of Dick Milton.

171   [Cahuengas Valley]

In the valley of the Cahuengas. The story of Hollywood. Written by the publicity department, Hollywood Branch, Security Trust & Savings Bank. Hollywood, published by Hollywood Branch of the Security Trust & Savings Bank [n. d.].   Pict. wrappers.   OP.

> 48 p.   plates (1 double p.), ports., map at end.   19.8 cm.

Has a section on Tiburcio Vásquez.

172   California's Age of Terror.
Murieta and Vásquez (general cover title)

Crimes and career of Tiburcio Vásquez. The bandit of San Benito county and notorious early California outlaw. Compiled from newspaper accounts of the period and first hand information from some of those who played a part in this story.   Published by the Evening Free Lance, Hollister, Calif., copyright 1927 by M. F. Hoyle.

> 5–26 p.   front. (port.)

[Published with]
The history of Joaquín Murieta, the king of California outlaws, whose band ravaged the state in the early fifties, by John R. Ridge. Revised edition . . . .   Pict. wrappers.   OP.

> 3–84 p.   22.5 cm.

This is a later reprint of the 1874 edition published by Fred'k MacCrellish and co. See Item 835.

173 [California Assembly]

Journal of the assembly, California. 1853. Vol. II. ₁N. p., 1853.₁ Cloth and calf. Rare.

722 p. 23.4 cm.

At the Assembly meeting of March 26, 1853, a joint resolution was introduced to offer a reward for the capture of Murieta. In the appendix, Document No. 49 contains argument against offering this reward. The chairman of the committee says in part: "To set a price upon the head of any individual who has not been examined and convicted by due process of law, is to proceed upon an assumption of his guilt. . . . Unless the said Joaquín be endowed with supernatural qualities, he could not have been seen at the same time in several places, widely separated from each other. The offer of such a reward would be likely to stimulate cupidity, to magnify fanciful resemblance, and dozens of heads similar in some respect to that of Joaquín might be presented for identification." Murieta's sister denied that the head later brought in was that of her brother, and many old-timers still think it was that of "just another Mexican."

174 Callison, John J.

Bill Jones of Paradise valley, Oklahoma. His life and adventures for over forty years in the great southwest. He was a pioneer in the days of the buffalo, the wild Indian, the Oklahoma boomer, the cowboy and the outlaw. Copiously illustrated from photographs and drawings from real life, by John J. Callison . . . . ₁Chicago, printed by M. A. Donohue & co., 1914.₁ Cloth. Scarce.

6 p.l., 13–328 p. front., illus. 19.5 cm.

This privately printed book is written in humorous vein, and contains some material on the Dodge City gunmen and Billy the Kid. Like one or two others, the author says the Kid had killed twenty-three men when he was killed at the age of twenty-three. Jones also says that he worked on a ranch owned by Jesse and Frank James, Cole Younger, and three more of their gang, and that when Billy the Kid stole some cattle from them, they chased his gang of rustlers and killed all of them except Billy the Kid and one other. I corresponded with this old-timer before his death and bought all the remaining copies of his book. It was a very scarce item until I began turning this remainder loose.

175 Calvin, Ross

Sky determines. An interpretation of the southwest, by Ross Calvin. New York, the Macmillan co., 1934. Dec. cloth. OP.

xii p., 1 l., 354 p. front., plates. 20.2 cm.
Bibliography: p. 343–346; index: p. 347–354.
Half title; untrimmed.

Republished in a revised and enlarged edition in 1948 by the University of New Mexico press, Albuquerque.

Has a chapter containing information on the robbery of the Southern Pacific by Mitch Lee, Kit Joy, and Frank Taggart, their capture and death. He also debunks Billy the Kid as the Robin Hood he is pictured to be by some writers.

176 Canton, Frank M.

Frontier trails. The autobiography of Frank M. Canton, edited by Edward Everett Dale. With illustrations. Boston and New York, Houghton Mifflin co., 1930. Cloth. OP.

xvii p., 1 l., [3]–236 [1] p. front., ports. 21.3 cm.
Half title; pub. device; first edition: 1930 under imprint.

This autobiography of Frank Canton, written shortly before his death and edited from the manuscripts he left, tells of his experiences during the Johnson County War. Canton was hired by the large cattle interests to fight the smaller owners and so-called rustlers in the Johnson County War, and naturally he tells their side of the story. The group picture following page 110 is erroneously labeled "the Dalton brothers and their sister." It is a picture of the Youngers and their sister. Much of the book is devoted to the better-known outlaws of Oklahoma and the "Wild Bunch" of Butch Cassidy.

177 Cantonwine, Alexander

Star forty-six, Oklahoma. [Oklahoma City, printed by Pythian Times publishing co.], 1911. Cloth. Very scarce.

334 p. front. (port.), illus. 24 cm.

Contains some material on the Daltons and other Oklahoma outlaws.

178 Carey, Henry L. (ed.)

The thrilling story of famous Boot Hill and modern Dodge City . . . , edited by Henry L. Carey, publisher. Dodge City, Herbert Etrick printers, 1937. Pict. wrappers. OP. Caption title.

[25] p. (no pagination). illus., plates, ports. 19.5 cm.
8 p. adv. at end.

Tells of the founding of Dodge City, its gun marshals, and Boot Hill.

179   Carlisle, William L.

Bill Carlisle, lone bandit. An autobiography; illustrations by
Charles M. Russell; introduction by J. R. Williams; end papers by
Clarence Ellsworth. Pasadena, Trail's End publishing co., inc.
[1946]. Cloth. In print.

4 p.l., [9]–220 p. front., plates, ports., facsm. 21 cm.
Map and legend on end papers; pub. device.

Also published in a de luxe limited and signed edition, bound in morocco.

This is the honest autobiography of the last of the lone train robbers,
a man who allowed himself to be captured rather than take a human life.

180   Carr, Harry

Los Angeles, city of dreams, by Harry Carr; illustrations by
E. H. Suydam. New York, London, D. Appleton-Century co.,
inc., 1935. Cloth. OP.

ix [1], 3–403 p. front. (col., with tissue), illus., plates. 23.5 cm.
Index: p. 353–403.
Illus. end papers; headpieces; vignette; first edition: figure (1) at end of
index.

This book devotes some space to the outlaws of southern California,
such as Murieta, Vásquez, Jack Powers, and others.

181   Carter, Capt. Robert Goldthwaite

The old sergeant's story. Winning the west from the In-
dians and bad men in 1870 to 1876, by Captain Robert G. Carter . . . .
New York, Frederick H. Hitchcock, publisher, MCMXXVI.
Cloth. Scarce.

9 p.l., 17–220 p. front., plates, ports. 23.5 cm.
Half title; pub. device.

The author devotes a chapter to the outlaw Red McLaughton, and
calls the Earps "the most desperate criminals Arizona ever knew." Much
of his information on Wild Bill Hickok is incorrect. He states that he

was in Deadwood when Wild Bill was killed and that Wild Bill was killed in Al Swiner's [*sic*] Dance Hall. There seems to be much confusion among writers as to the place where Wild Bill was killed. Colonel Wheeler, in his *Frontier Trail*, places it at Nuttall and Mann's Saloon, and Wilstach says the Bella Union, while Harry Young says the Sixty-Six; but most authorities concede it to be the saloon known as Number 10. The author here also states that Jack McCall was rearrested in Omaha, but he was, in fact, rearrested at Laramie, Wyoming.

182 Carter, W. N.

Harry Tracy, the desperate outlaw. A fascinating account of the famous bandit's stupendous adventures and daring deeds. The most thrilling man-hunt on record . . . , by W. N. Carter.   Chicago, Laird and Lee, publishers [1902].   Wrappers.   Scarce.

> 7 p.l., [9]–296 p.   front., illus., plates, ports., maps, plan.   18.8 cm.
> 4 p. adv. at end.

183 ———

Harry Tracy, the desperate western outlaw . . . . The most thrilling man-hunt on record . . . . Melodramatic scenes and tragic death, by W. N. Carter. Over 90 half-tones and text-etchings.   Chicago, Laird and Lee, publishers [1902].   Pict. wrappers.   Scarce.

> 8 p.l., [9]–296 p.   front., plates, ports., maps.   18.5 cm.
> 4 p. adv. at end.

184 Casey, Robert J.

The Black hills and their incredible characters. A chronicle and a guide, by Robert J. Casey. Indianapolis, New York, the Bobbs-Merrill co., inc., publishers [1949].   Cloth.   In print.

> 6 p.l., 11–383 p.   front., plates, ports., 31 p. guide in pocket at end.   22 cm.
> Appendix: p. 345–371; index: p. 372–383.
> Half title; map on end papers; "First edition" on copyright p.

In his chapter on Hickok, the author relates the corrected version of the McCanles fight, but writes as if he does not believe it. He says, "It is an established fact that Hickok was seriously wounded. He was thought to be dying when the stage line finally got him to a St. Louis hospital, and he was in bed for several weeks." He does not cite any references for the truth of this statement. Buel, Hough, and other writers stated that Hickok was gravely wounded, but all their accounts have been proved false. The book also contains chapters on Calamity Jane, Jack McCall, Fly-Specked Billy, and others.

185 ⸺

The Texas border and some borderliners. A chronicle and a guide, by Robert J. Casey. Indianapolis, New York, the Bobbs-Merrill co., inc., publishers [1950]. Cloth. In print.

> 6 p.l., 13–440 p. front., plates, ports., guide in pocket at end. 22 cm.
> Appendix: p. 397–417; bibliography: p. 418–425; index: p. 427–440.
> Half title; map on end papers; untrimmed; "First edition" on copyright p.
>
> Published also in a special "Lone Star Edition" signed and tipped in.

The author takes in some large territory and covers practically all the outlaws of the Southwest, including those involved in the Lincoln County War. In his account of the Kid's killing of Bell, he uses the Burns' version. In his chapter on Sam Bass, he has the Union Pacific "jackpot" at $75,000 instead of $60,000.

186 Castleman, Harvey N.

Sam Bass, the train robber. The life of Texas' most popular bandit [by] Harvey N. Castleman. Girard, Kan., Haldeman-Julius publications, 1944. Wrappers. In print.

> [2]–24 p. 21.5 cm.

A fairly accurate account, but the author does say that the butcher-boy on the train being robbed at Mesquite, Texas, was seen with a revolver, but went back into the coach without firing a shot when Sam Bass said to him, "We don't need any peanuts." All other accounts I have seen report that he did shoot a couple of the robbers with his little "peashooter," though he did no more damage than break the skin. The author is also wrong in stating that Jim Murphy "died of poison administered by his own hand."

187 ⸺

The Texas rangers. The story of an organization that is unique, like nothing else in America, [by] Harvey N. Castleman. Girard, Kan., Haldeman-Julius publications, 1944. Wrappers. OP.

> 24 p. 21.5 cm.

A brief history of the Texas Rangers, including the story of the killing of Sam Bass and the treachery of Jim Murphy.

188   [Catalogue]

Catalogue of Wells, Fargo and company historical exhibit at the World's Columbian Exposition, Chicago, 1893.   [San Francisco, printed by H. S. Crocker co., 1893.]   Wrappers.   (Cover title.)   Scarce.

> 32 p.   19.5 cm.

A listing of 175 exhibits, including material concerning the California stage and train robbers.

189   Caughey, John Walton

History of the Pacific coast, by John Walton Caughey . . . . Los Angeles, privately published by the author, 1933.   Cloth. (Label pasted on.)   OP.

> xiii, 429 p.   illus., ports., maps.   25 cm.
> Index: p. 407–429.
> Half title; map on end papers.

Has some material on Joaquín Murieta and Juan Flores.

190   Chaffin, Lorah B.

Sons of the west; biographical account of early-day Wyoming, [by] Lorah B. Chaffin. Illustrated with photographs.   Caldwell, Idaho, the Caxton printers, ltd., 1941.   Pict. cloth.   OP.

> 10 p.l., [21]–284 p.   plates, ports.   23.5 cm.
> Bibliography: p. [277]–279; appendix: [280]–284.
> Half title; pub. device.

Touches lightly on the Johnson County War and the killing of Nate Champion and Nick Ray.

191   Chalfant, Willie Arthur

Outposts of civilization, by W. A. Chalfant.   Boston, the Christopher publishing house [1928].   Cloth.   OP.

> 3 p.l., 9–193 p.   20.5 cm.
> Pub. device.

A chapter on the gunmen and vigilantes of Nevada, and one on the bandits of California. His account of Murieta follows the Ridge version, repeating the legend about the reward notice.

192 ———

The story of Inyo, by W. A. Chalfant. [Chicago, W. B. Conkey co.], published by the author, 1922. Cloth. OP.

xviii, 358 p. front. (fold. map). 19.6 cm.
Leaf of errata pasted inside back cover.

Republished [Los Angeles, Citizen's print shop, inc., 1933].

6 p.l., 13–430, vii p. front. (map). 23.4 cm.

Contains a chapter on lawlessness and quite a bit of material on Tiburcio Vásquez.

193 Chamberlain, Newell D.

The call of gold. True tales on the gold road to Yosemite, by Newell D. Chamberlain. Illustrated. [Mariposa, Calif., Gazette press, 1936.] Cloth. OP.

xii p., 1 l., 183 p. front., plates, ports., maps, facsm. 20 cm.

Tells of the killing of Murieta and uses the Ridge version of his wife's being "mistreated and killed before his eyes."

194 Chapman, Arthur

The pony express. The record of a romantic adventure in business, by Arthur Chapman. Illustrated with contemporary prints and photographs. New York and London, G. P. Putnam's sons, 1932. Cloth. OP.

7 p.l., 13–319 p. front., plates, ports., facsm. 23 cm.
Bibliography: p. 311–314; index: p. 317–319.
Half title; map on end papers.

Here is another author who tried to correct the wild legend of the Hickok-McCanles fight at Rock Creek Station. He also devotes a chapter to Joseph Slade.

195 Chapman, Berlin Basil

The founding of Stillwater. A case study in Oklahoma history, by Berlin Basil Chapman . . . . [Oklahoma City, Okla., published by the Times Journal publishing co., 1948.] Cloth. OP.

xii, 245 p. front., plates, ports., maps, facsms., plans. 23.8 cm.
Appendices: p. 160–230; bibliography: p. 231–233; index: p. 234–245.

Has some material on the Doolin gang and Henry Starr.

196 Chisholm, Joe

Brewery Gulch. Frontier days of Old Arizona—last outpost of the great southwest, by Joe Chisholm. San Antonio, Texas, the Naylor co. [1949]. Cloth. In print.

> xi, 180 p. front. 21.7 cm.
> Index: p. 177–180.
> Half title.

This most interesting book, assembled from Chisholm's earlier writings, was published twelve years after his death. It deals with a majority of the better-known outlaws of Arizona, and the writer's opinion of the Earps is not favorable. He seems to think that it was the Earp clique which robbed the stages, and that it was Doc Holliday who killed Bud Philpot.

197 City Directory

of Abilene, Kansas, 1904–05. [N. p.], American Directory co. [1905]. Stiff wrappers. Scarce.

> 2 p.l., [5]–156 p. illus. 20.6 cm.
> 24 l. telephone directory at end.
> Advertisements interspersed throughout.

Contains some information on Wild Bill Hickok while he was marshal of Abilene.

198 Clampitt, John Wesley

Echoes from the Rocky mountains; reminiscences and thrilling incidents of the romantic and golden age of the west; with graphic accounts of its discovery, settlement and grand development, by John W. Clampitt .... Chicago, New York, ... Bedford, Clark and co., 1889. Pict. cloth. OP.

> xvi, 19–671 p. front., illus., plates, ports., facsm. 25 cm.

Has a chapter on outlaws and vigilantes.

199 Clapp, Mrs. Louise Amelia Knapp Smith

The Shirley letters from California mines in 1851–52. Being a series of twenty-three letters from Dame Shirley ... to her sister in Massachusetts and now reprinted from the *Pioneer Magazine* of 1854–55, with synopses of the letters, a foreword, and many typographical and other corrections and emendations by Thomas C. Russell, together with "an appreciation" by Mrs. M. V. T. Lawrence. Illustrated. San Francisco, printed by Thomas C. Russell at his private press . . . , 1922. Boards and cloth. Scarce.

> L p., 2 l., 3–350 p. front., 8 plates (all col., incl. front., with tissues). 24 cm.

Although she calls no names, the author gives an account of the start of Murieta's difficulties which led him to outlawry. Many think that her letters perhaps gave Ridge the idea for his story about this outlaw.

Republished in 1949 with an introduction by Carl I. Wheat. New York, Alfred A. Knopf. Dec. cloth. OP.

> xix p., 1 l., 3–216 p. plates (col.). 21.7 cm. Half title; map on end papers; pub. device.

200 Clark, Barzilla W.

Bonneville county in the making, by Barzilla W. Clark. Idaho Falls, Idaho, published by the author, 1941. Cloth. OP.

> 6 p.l., 140 p. front., ports., maps (incl. front.). 23.5 cm. Addenda: p. 136–140.

Has a chapter on the vigilantes and another on stage robbery.

201 Clark, Henry W.

History of Alaska, by Henry W. Clark. New York, the Macmillan co., 1930. Cloth. OP.

> x p., 3 l., 208 p. plates, maps. 22.6 cm. Index: p. 193–208. Half title.

Contains some material on Soapy Smith.

202 Clark, O. S.

Clay Allison of the Washita, first a cow man then an extinguisher of bad men. Recollections of Colorado, New Mexico and the Texas Panhandle. Reminiscences of a '79er. [By O. S. Clark.] [Attica, Ind., G. M. Williams], 1920. Stiff wrappers. Exceedingly rare.

> 1 p.l., 38 p. 24.5 x 13.2 cm. Three loose-leaf inserts.

This little book, privately printed for friends, is exceedingly rare, espe-

CLAY ALLISON

OF

THE WASHITA

FIRST A COW MAN AND THEN AN EXTINGUISHER
OF BAD MEN

—

RECOLLECTIONS

OF

COLORADO, NEW MEXICO AND THE
TEXAS PANHANDLE

REMINISCENCES OF A '79ER

—

TO MY FRIENDS IN THE ENCHANTING EAST
TO *Mis Compadres* IN THE FASCINATING WEST

COMPLIMENTS OF
O. S. CLARK,
ATTICA, INDIANA.

NUMBER 202

cially with the inserts. Part of the final insert reads: "And finally when the curiosity and novelty has worn off and the little thing [the book] is scuffed about, trampled on, battered around, and shoved behind the clock, and from there to the old garret, where all the old literary gems are often stored, then eventually it will reach the woodhouse ready for the junk pile." Perhaps the prophecy of the author came true, as it is almost impossible to find a copy today. The author tells of his experiences in meeting Clay Allison on the trail and of some of his subsequent killings. He also quotes a long story of Clay Allison from Alfred Henry Lewis' *Sunset Trail*.

203 ———

Clay Allison of the Washita. First a cowman and then an extinguisher of bad men. Recollections of Colorado, New Mexico and the Texas Panhandle. Reminiscences of a '79er. [Attica, Ind., 1922.] Stiff wrappers. Rare.

4 p.l., 9-135 p. front., plates, ports., map. 24 cm.

Although this volume has the same title as the 1920 edition, it is quite different and contains much added material by other writers. This edition has also become rather scarce and is the only edition known to many bibliophiles. It contains an introduction not in the first edition, and the author also names his two trail companions, which he failed to do in the first. His own writing is very much like that in the 1920 edition; for several pages before new material is found, paragraphing and wording are the same. The bulk of this book was written by others, and it contains illustrations and a map not in the first edition.

204 Clarke, Donald Henderson

The autobiography of Frank Tarbeaux, as told to Donald Henderson Clarke . . . . New York, the Vanguard press, MCMXXX. Boards and cloth. Scarce.

ix [1] p., 3 l., 3-386 [1] p. 21.3 cm.
Half title; illus. end papers; pub. device; untrimmed.

The subject of this autobiography claims that he and his father opened the Chisholm Trail in 1863. He says the herds were divided into "*bands*" of five thousand each and with each "band" were a mess wagon and ten or fifteen cowboys. According to the cowman's standard this would be a rather unwieldy herd for fifteen cowboys. He speaks disparagingly of Buffalo Bill and says that "all his history is pure fiction." He makes the strong statement that "Buffalo Bill never killed an Indian in his life, and those people who say they saw him do it are suffering from hallucinations." He further states that he had just left the poker game when Wild Bill was killed and that he was killed by "one of the *McCoys*, and was sent to do the job by Johnny Varnes who had it in for Bill." Like many of his other unreliable statements is the one that Calamity Jane was first heard of in Deadwood, where she was just an ordinary dance hall girl. He also claims to have been a close friend of Wild Bill, the James boys, and many other western outlaws.

205   Clay, John

My life on the range, by John Clay.   Chicago, privately printed [1924].   Cloth.   Rare.

> 4 p.l., 365 [1] p.   front. (port., signature in facsm.), plates, ports.   23.5 cm.
> Half title; device; gilt top; untrimmed.

This well-written book about the author's ranch experiences has become scarce and is one of the most-sought-after cattle books. It is said that the author kept copies on his desk and friends helped themselves until the supply became exhausted. He was one of the better-known ranch owners of the Northwest and a well-educated Scotchman. His picture of ranch life is well written and authentic. He relates some incidents in the Johnson County War.

206   ———

The tragedy of Squaw mountain, by John Clay.   [Chicago, designed and printed by Maders printing co., n. d.]   Stiff wrappers. Scarce.

> 19 [1] p.   ports.   22 cm.
> Top of each page decorated with colored drawings.

A very scarce little item containing a story about Tom Horn.

207   Cleaveland, Agnes Morley

No life for a lady, by Agnes Morley Cleaveland. Illustrations by Edward Borein.   Boston, Houghton Mifflin co., 1941.   Cloth. OP.

> ix p., 1 l., [3]–356 p.   illus.   23.5 cm.
> Life in America series.
> Half title; map on end papers; illus. chapter headings; device; first edition: 1941 under imprint.
>
> Reprinted several times.

One of the really good western books, it contains some information on Clay Allison and a few other New Mexico outlaws.

89

208 ———

Satan's paradise, from Lucien Maxwell to Fred Lambert, by Agnes Morley Cleaveland. With decorations by Fred Lambert. Boston, Houghton Mifflin co., 1952. Cloth. In print.

> viii p., 1 l., 274 p. 21.4 cm.
> Half title; tailpieces; vignette; first edition: 1952 over imprint.

A well-written book, it is largely about a peace officer named Fred Lambert, and contains chapters on the Black Jack gang, Clay Allison, and other outlaws in New Mexico. But compared to the author's first book, it is a little disappointing.

209 Cleland, Robert Glass

California pageant, the story of four centuries, by Robert Glass Cleland. Illustrated by Raymond Lufkin. New York, Alfred A. Knopf, 1946. Dec. cloth. OP.

> x p., 1 l., 257 p. front. (col.), illus. (col.). 21.7 cm.
> Index: p. 247–257.
> Illus. chapter headings (some in col.).

Gives a brief account of Murieta.

210 ———

The cattle on a thousand hills; southern California, 1850–1870, by Robert Glass Cleland. San Marino, Calif., the Huntington Library, 1941. Cloth. OP.

> xiv p., 1 l., [3]–327 p. facsm., map, cattle brands. 23.3 cm.
> Appendix: p. [277]–315; index: p. [319]–327.
> Half title: Huntington Library Publications; vignette.

Republished with additions in 1951.

> xvi p., 1 l., 3–365 p. plates, ports., map, facsms. 23.3 cm.
> Appendices: p. 235–279; notes: p. 281–338; bibliography: p. 339–349; index: p. 351–365.
> Vignette.

Much on Murieta and Vásquez. Although this edition has the same chapters as the first, there are some changes in the text, paragraphing, maps, and illustrations; and the 1951 edition has added a long section of notes as well as a bibliography. An added Section V in the appendix is devoted to Tirbucio Vásquez—an interview by the Los Angeles *Star* in 1874.

211 ———

History of California: the American period, by Robert Glass Cleland. New York, the Macmillan co., 1922. Cloth. OP.

xiii p., 1 l., 512 p. front. (fold. map), plates, map. facsm. 22.6 cm.
Appendices: p. 469–502; index, p. 503–512.
Half title.

Some material on Murieta and other California outlaws.

212 ———

The Irvine ranch of Orange county, 1810–1950, by Robert Glass Cleland. San Marino, Calif., the Huntington Library, 1952. Cloth. In print.

vii p., 1 l., 3–163 p. plates, ports., map. 23.5 cm.
Index: p. 155–163.
Half title.

Chapter VI deals with the outlaws of Orange County, the killing of Sheriff Barton, and the hanging of Juan Flores.

213 Clemens, Samuel Langhorne
(Mark Twain, pseud.)

Roughing it, by Mark Twain (Samuel L. Clemens) . . . . Hartford, Conn., American publishing co.; Chicago, F. G. Gilmer and co. [etc., etc.], 1872. Cloth. Scarce.

xviii, [19]–591 p. front., illus., plates. 22 cm.
Republished in 1886, 1888, 1891, 1895, 1899, 1903, 1913, 1924, and many other years.

Contains some material on road agents, Joseph Slade, and other bad men.

214 Clover, Samuel Travers

On special assignment; being the further adventures of Paul Travers; showing how he succeeded as a newspaper reporter, by Samuel Travers Clover . . . . Illustrated by H. G. Laskey. Boston, Lothrop publishing co. [1903]. Pict. cloth. Scarce.

5 p.l., 11–307 p. front., illus. 18.3 cm.
2 l., adv. at end; device.

The author was a reporter sent out by a Chicago paper to cover the Johnson County War. Although written in the form of fiction, this book calls actual names and relates factual incidents as the author witnessed them.

215   Clum, Woodworth

Apache agent. The story of John P. Clum. With illustrations. By Woodworth Clum. Boston and New York, Houghton Mifflin co., 1936. Cloth. OP.

> xv [1] p., 3–297 [1] p. front. (col.), illus., plates, ports. 21.5 cm.
> Half title; first edition: 1936 under imprint.

Contains information on some of the Arizona gunmen.

216   Coan, Charles Florus

A history of New Mexico, by Charles F. Coan . . . assisted by a board of advisory editors . . . . Chicago and New York, the American Historical Society, inc., 1925 . Pub. in three volumes. Leather. Scarce.

> Vol. I, xlviii, 586 p. front., illus., plates, ports., maps, tables. 26.7 cm.
> Vols. II and III, biographical; bibliography at end of some chapters of Vol. I.

Volume I contains a chapter on the livestock industry with an account of the Lincoln County War. The author is careless with the spelling of proper names, such as "Chisom" for Chisum, "McSwain" for McSween, and "Tunstel" for Tunstall.

217   Coates, Robert M.

The outlaw years. The history of the land pirates of the Natchez Trace, by Robert M. Coates. New York, the Literary Guild of America, 1930. Pict. cloth. OP.

> 7 p.l., 3–308 p. front., plates, facsm. 21.2 cm.
> Bibliography: p. 303–308.
> Half title; map on end papers; vignette; untrimmed.

Here we have short histories of the Harpes, the Murrells, Joseph Hare, and Samuel Mason, the land pirates of the Mississippi.

218   Coblentz, Stanton Arthur

Villains and vigilantes. The story of James King of William, and pioneer justice in California, by Stanton A. Coblentz. Illustrated from contemporary prints and portraits.   New York, Wilson-Erickson, inc., 1936.   Cloth.   OP.

> vii p., 1 l., 261 p.   front., plates, ports.   23.5 cm.
> Principal authorities consulted: p. 255–256; index: p. 257–261.
> Half title.

The author's account of Murieta follows the Ridge version.

219   Cody, Louisa Frederici

Memories of Buffalo Bill, by his wife Louisa Frederici Cody, in collaboration with Courtney Ryley Cooper.   New York, London, D. Appleton and co., MCMXIX.   Cloth.   Scarce.

> 3 p.l., 325 [1] p.   front. (port.)   21 cm.
> Half title; pub. device; first edition: figure (1) at end of text.

220 Cody, William Frederick

An autobiography of Buffalo Bill (Colonel W. F. Cody). Illustrated by N. C. Wyeth.   New York, Cosmopolitan book corp., 1920.

> 4 p.l., 328 p.   front. (port.), plates.   20.4 cm.
> Lettered on cover: "Buffalo Bill's Life Story."

221   ———

Life and adventures of "Buffalo Bill," Colonel William F. Cody. This thrilling autobiography tells in Col. Cody's own graphic language the wonderful story of his long eventful and heroic career, and is supplemented with a chapter by a loving, life-long friend covering his last days, death and burial . . . . The whole work comprising an authentic history of many events inseparably interwoven with the exploration, settlement and development of our great western plains. Illustrated with many rare engravings.   New York, Wiley book co. [1927].   Cloth.   Scarce.

> 352 p. illus., plates.   20 cm.
> "The End of the Trail," by Col. William Lightfoot Visscher: p. 338–352;
> port. of W. F. Cody on cover; initials.

Republished, Lookout Mountain, Golden, Colo., Mrs. "Johnny" Baker [1939].   Cloth.   Scarce.

> xiii [1], 15–352 p.   front. (port.), illus., plates.   20.5 cm.

222 ———

Story of wild west and camp-fire chats, by Buffalo Bill (Hon. W. F. Cody). A full and complete history of the renowned pioneer quartet, Boone, Crockett, Carson and Buffalo Bill's conquest of England with his wild west exhibition . . . . Richmond, Va., B. F. Johnson and co. [1888]. Cloth. Scarce.

> xvi, 17–766 p. illus., plate (col.), ports. 20 cm.

223 ———

True tales of the plains, by Buffalo Bill (William F. Cody), frontiersman and late chief of scouts, U. S. Army. New York, Cupples & Leon co., 1908. Cloth. (Port. pasted on.) Scarce.

> 2 p.l., 259 p. front. (port., signature in facsm.), illus., plates, ports. 19.2 cm.
> 6 p. adv. at end; headpieces; device.

Most of the Cody books were ghost written and contain chapters on Wild Bill Hickok which follow the pattern set by Buel. This author also places the Rock Creek Station in Kansas instead of Nebraska, has ten men in the McCanles gang, and calls McCanles "Jacob." All of this goes to show how closely one writer used material from another without checking the truth of his statements. Cody numbers Wild Bill's wounds as three bullet, eleven buckshot, and thirteen knife wounds.

224 Coe, Charles H.

Juggling a rope; lariat roping and spinning, knots and splices; also the truth about Tom Horn, "King of the Cowboys," by Charles H. Coe . . . . Pendleton, Ore., Hamley & co., 1927. Cloth. OP.

> 4 p.l., 9–114 p. front., plates, ports. 19.7 cm.
> Index: third prelim. leaf.

Part V is devoted entirely to the defense of Tom Horn.

225 Coe, George Washington

Frontier fighter, the autobiography of George W. Coe, who fought and rode with Billy the Kid. As related to Nan Hillary Harrison. Boston and New York, Houghton Mifflin co., 1934. Pict. cloth.

94

xiv p., 1 l., 220 p.   front. (port.), plates, ports., facsm.   21.2 cm.
Half title; pub. device; first edition: 1934 under imprint.

Republished in 1951 by the University of New Mexico press, Albuquerque. Cloth.   In print.

Though an active friend of Billy the Kid, the author was never considered an outlaw. As a participant in the Lincoln County War, he gives, I believe, a reliable account of the affair and the activities of Billy the Kid. He waited a long time to give his story to the world, but it is accurate so far as I have been able to check, and it makes most interesting reading.

226   Colburn, J. G. W.

The life of Sile Doty, the most noted thief and daring burglar of his time. The leader of a gang of counterfeiters, horse thieves and burglars of the New England, middle and western states. The terror of Mexico during 1849. Illustrated. Compiled by J. G. W. Colburn.   Toledo, O., Blade printing & paper co., 1880.   Cloth. Rare.

2 p.l., 5–269 p.   front., illus.   22.8 cm.

I hesitated for some time to include this book in a bibliography of western outlaws, but Doty did operate to a certain extent in the Middle and Southwestern states. Although he cannot be considered a western outlaw in the sense we think of one, he was a notorious lawbreaker in his day.

227   ———

The life of Sile Doty, 1800–1876. A forgotten autobiography. The most noted thief and daring burglar of his time. A foreword by Randolph G. Adams.   Detroit, Alved of Detroit, inc., 1948.   Cloth.   In print.

x p., 2 l., 288 p.   front., illus.   21.7 cm.

A modern reprint of the rare first edition.

228   Cole, Cornelius

Memoirs of Cornelius Cole, ex-senator of the United States from California. [By Cornelius Cole.]   New York, McLoughlin brothers, 1908.   Cloth.   Scarce.

x, 354 p.   front. (port.).   24.5 cm.
Device; untrimmed.

Contains some material on the arrest of Vásquez, the California outlaw.

229   Coleman, Max M.

From mustanger to lawyer, by Max M. Coleman . . . . ₁San Antonio, Texas, printed in the United States of America by the Carleton printing co., 1952.₁ Cloth. In print.

> 13 p.l., ₁29₁–156 p. illus., plates, ports. 23.6 cm.
> Colophon (verso of third prelim. leaf): "This limited first edition of Part A From Mustanger to Lawyer consists of 500 copies signed by the author of which this is number _____."

In one chapter the author tells of the arrest of Bill Cook and Skeeter Baldwin, the Oklahoma outlaws. A typographical error on page 130 names Pat Garrett as "Barrett." The table of contents is labeled "index" and is the first page of the book.

230   Collier, William Ross, and Edwin Victor Westrate

Dave Cook of the Rockies, frontier general, fighting sheriff and leader of men, by William Ross Collier & Edwin Victor Westrate . . . . Illustrated from contemporary photographs by Joseph Collier. New York, Rufus Rockwell Wilson, inc., 1936. Cloth. OP.

> xv, 224 p. front. (port.), plates, ports. 23.5 cm.
> Half title.

A history of this famous Colorado detective, with an extended account of the capture of Musgrove and his gang, as well as of other outlaws.

231   ———

The reign of Soapy Smith, monarch of misrule in the last days of the old west and the Klondike gold rush, by William Ross Collier and Edwin Victor Westrate. Illustrated from photographs. Garden City, N. Y., Doubleday, Doran and co., inc., 1935. Pict. cloth. OP.

> vi p., 2 l., 299 p. front. (port.), plates. 20.6 cm.
> Half title; illus. end papers; untrimmed; "First edition" on copyright p.

About the only life story of this unusual character and swindler. In a chapter on Bob Ford the authors tell of his life and death, but make the mistake of naming his killer "Ed O'Kelly" (his name was Ed O. Kelly), but this mistake is made by many others.

232 Collins, Dennis

The Indians' last fight; or, the Dull Knife raid, by Dennis Collins. ₁Girard, Kan., Press of Appeal to Reason, 1915.₁ Cloth. Scarce.

3 p.l., ₁9₁–326 p. front., plates, ports. 23.7 cm.

In telling of western outlaws, the author claims that one of the principal causes of their development was the publication of Wild West fiction and dime novels which created false impressions of the West and inflamed the imaginations and corrupted the minds of the younger generation.

233 Collins, Hubert Edwin

Warpath & cattle trail, by Hubert E. Collins; with a foreword by Hamlin Garland. Illustrated by Paul Brown. New York, William Morrow & co., 1928. Cloth. OP.

xix p., 1 l., 296 p. front., illus., plates. 24 cm.
Notes: p. 289–296.
Illus. front end papers; map on rear end papers; vignette; untrimmed.

This volume contains a chapter on Cherokee Bill, telling about this outlaw's life before he started upon his career of crime.

234 Compendious History

of Ellsworth county, Kansas, from its early settlement to the present time. Embracing the executive and educational departments, population, sketches of prominent men, general character of the land, and condition of the people . . . . Ellsworth, Kan., printed at the Recorder office, 1879. Wrappers. Rare.

2 p.l., 5–59 p. 17.7 cm.
3 p. business cards at end; "First edition" on t.p.

This exceedingly rare little book contains some material on Wild Bill Hickok.

235 Conn, William

Cow-boys and colonels. Narrative of a journey across the prairie and over the Black Hills of Dakota. From *"Dans les montagnes rocheuses"* of Baron E. de Mandat-Grancey, with additional notes not contained in the original edition, by William Conn.

London, Griffith, Farran, Okeden & Welsh . . . , 1887. Cloth. Scarce.

> xi, 352 p. front., plates. 22 cm.
> Pub. device.

> Another edition of 364 pages was published in New York the same year.

A translation of the French of Mandat-Grancey, with the addition of a few unimportant notes. As in the original, there is a most ridiculous account of the killing of Wild Bill Hickok. See Item 665.

236 Connell, Robert, Sr.

Arkansas, by Robert Connell, Sr. New York, the Paebar co., publishers, 1947. Cloth. OP.

> ix, 9–128 [2] p. front., plates, ports. 21 cm.

This book has nothing to do with the state of Arkansas, but of a character who goes by that name. The author writes of some of his western experiences and has some information on Bucky O'Neill.

237 Connelley, William Elsey

Quantrill and the border wars, by William Elsey Connelley . . . . Cedar Rapids, Iowa, the Torch press, publishers, 1909. Cloth. OP.

> 9 p.l., [17]–542 p. front. (port.), illus., fold. map, diagrs. 24 cm.
> Index: p. [485]–539; errata: p. [541]–542.
> Half title; device; untrimmed.

A thoroughly reliable book relating many of the actions of the James and Younger brothers while fighting as guerrillas.

238 ——

Wild Bill and his era. The life & adventures of James Butler Hickok, by William Elsey Connelley . . . with introduction by Charles Morceau Harger. New York, the Press of the Pioneers, 1933. Pict. cloth. Scarce.

> xii p., 1 l., 229 p. front. (port.), plates, port. 24.2 cm.
> Notes: p. 215–221; index: p. 223–229.
> Half title; untrimmed.

Perhaps the most reliable and complete book done on Wild Bill Hickok, it is a work showing wide research. The author makes an honest effort to correct some of the false accounts in other books. Yet he repeats the legend that Calamity Jane captured Jack McCall with a meat cleaver in a butchershop. He also says that a Mrs. Josephine Blake wrote the little pamphlet on Calamity's life which Jane sold. Connelley's book was published three years after his death, being edited by his daughter, Edith Connelley Clift. She admits that she was forced to leave out much material and condense what she retained. Her father made a thorough study of Wild Bill, and it is unfortunate that all the material he collected could not be used.

239 Connolly, Christopher P.

The devil learns to vote. The story of Montana, [by] Christopher P. Connolly. New York, Covici Friede, publishers [1938]. Cloth. OP.

89219

5 p.l., 13–310 p. front. (port.), plate, ports. 21 cm.

The first few chapters deal with the outlaws, road agents, and vigilantes of Montana, giving a good account of Henry Plummer and his gang.

240 Convict Life

at the Minnesota state prison, Stillwater, Minnesota. Profusely illustrated. St. Paul, Minn., published by W. C. Heilbron [1909]. Wrappers. Scarce.

3 p.l., [7]–155 [3] p. front., plates, ports., facsm. 19.5 cm. Device.

One chapter, entitled "Real Facts About the Northfield, Minnesota, Bank Robbery," is related by Cole Younger.

241 Cook, David J.

Hands up; or, twenty years of detective life in the mountains and on the plains. Reminiscences of Gen. D. J. Cook, superintendent of the Rocky Mountain Detective Association. A condensed criminal record of the far west. Denver, Republican print, 1882. Wrappers. Exceedingly rare.

285 p. front. (port.), plates. 23 cm. Illus. half title.

This rare book was originally published to be sold on trains by butcher boys. Reprinted the same year and bound in cloth. When the cloth edition was first brought out, there was a picture of two upraised hands with a scalping knife on the cover. The knife is said to have belonged formerly to Wild Bill Hickok and to have been given to Cook. The design was made from a photograph of Wild Bill's hands and his scalping knife. It is said that the book was largely written by Thomas Fulton Dawson, a prolific writer and editor.

The book was reprinted in 1897, Denver, W. F. Robinson printing co., in cloth binding.   Now scarce also.

7 p.l., [13]-442 p. front. (port. signature in facsm.), illus., plates, ports. 23.5 cm.

242   Cook, James Henry

Fifty years on the old frontier, as cowboy, hunter, guide, scout and ranchman, by James H. Cook; with an introduction by Brigadier-General Charles King, U. S. V. . . . .   New Haven, Yale University press . . . , MDCCCCXXIII.   Cloth.   OP.

xix p., 1 l., 3-291 p. front., plates (1 col., 2 fold.), ports. 24 cm.
Index: p. 283-291.
Half title; pub. device.

Reprinted in several editions, including one by the Lakeside press of Chicago.

An outstanding western book with much on outlawry and a good first-hand account of the battle between cowboys and Elfego Baca, a fight in which the author participated. The author states that Billy the Kid was a New York City tough and "doubtless he read some yellow novels about the bandits of the West before he started on his career of crime in New Mexico." Evidently he did not know that the Kid left New York while still a baby.

243   ———

Longhorn cowboy, by James H. Cook, edited and with an introduction by Howard R. Driggs, and with drawings by Herbert Stoops.   New York, G. P. Putnam's sons [1942].   Pict. cloth.   OP.

xi p., 1 l., 241 p. front., illus. (double p.). 20.5 cm.
Half title; illus. end papers; headpieces.

This book is founded upon the original edition and arranged for younger readers.

244   Cook, Jim (Lane)

Lane of the Llano, being the story of Jim (Lane) Cook as

told to T. M. Pearce; illustrated by Walter J. Heffron. Boston, Little, Brown and co., 1936. Pict. cloth. OP.

> xiv p., 1 l., [3]–269 p. front. (port.), illus. 21.3 cm.
> Half title; pict. map on end papers; vignette.

The author at one time assumed the name Jim Lane (cf. p. 144, 188). This book is supposedly an autobiography, but it is unreliable, for the author put too much trust in a faulty memory. He claims to have been in the burning house of McSween with Billy the Kid during the Lincoln County War, but his name is not mentioned in any other account. Unlike some other writers, he says that Mrs. McSween was not in the house while it was burning, but that the boys played the piano and sang while the bullets were coming into the house.

245 Cook, John R.

The border and the buffalo. An untold story of the southwest plains. The bloody border of Missouri and Kansas. The story of the slaughter of the buffalo. Westward among the big game and wild tribes. A story of mountain and plain, by John R. Cook. Topeka, Kan., monotyped and printed by Crane & co., 1907. Pict. cloth. Scarce.

> xii, 351 [1] p. front. (port.), plates, ports. 23.5 cm.

Republished as a Lakeside Classic in Chicago by R. R. Donnelley and Sons Co., 1938. Edited with a historical introduction by M. M. Quaife.

Contains some information on the Benders of Kansas, and the reprint has an added footnote on Billy the Kid. The author's information on the Benders I have not seen elsewhere. A friend told him that fifteen men followed the Benders when they tried to escape in a wagon, and that they killed the entire family where they were camped on the Verdigris River, dividing their money and swearing themselves to secrecy.

246 Coolidge, Dane

Arizona cowboys, by Dane Coolidge, with photographs by the author. New York, E. P. Dutton and co., inc., 1938. Pict. cloth. OP.

> 5 p.l., 13–160 p. front., plates. 20.8 cm.
> Half title; "First edition" on copyright p.

Contains a chapter on the Pleasant Valley War between the Grahams and the Tewksburys.

247 ———

Fighting men of the west, by Dane Coolidge; with an introduction by the author; illustrated with halftones. New York, E. P. Dutton & co., inc., publishers [1932]. Cloth. OP.

> 7 p.l., 13–343 p. front., plates, ports. 22.2 cm.
> Index: p. 339–343.
> Half title; vignette; "First edition" on copyright p.

This author makes the statement that after the Kid had killed his guards, Bell and Ollinger, Pat Garrett lost his nerve, and John Poe was put in Garrett's place. We know this is not true, for Garrett stayed on the job until the Kid was killed. Coolidge also makes the preposterous statement that Billy the Kid "was not satisfied to have a woman in every *placita*, but cast his ruthless eyes on one of a different class, who met his advances with scorn. *It was to save her that Billy the Kid was killed.* And, to protect her good name, John Poe himself built up a fictitious account of the event." His account of the Kid's death is different, too. He says that the Kid went to Pete Maxwell's to cut off a slab of bacon to take with him to the sheep camp where he had been hiding out.

He has Poe and McKinney sitting near the gate instead of on the porch. In fact, he says that McKinney was sitting on the edge of the board sidewalk because one of his spurs was hung under a plank and he couldn't move.

248 ———

Gringo gold; a story of Joaquín Murieta the bandit, by Dane Coolidge. New York, E. P. Dutton & co., inc., 1939. Cloth. OP.

> 5 p.l., 13–249 p. 19.6 cm.
> Half title; untrimmed.

This is the life of Murieta told in fictional form, and, as history, is unreliable.

249 Cooper, Courtney Ryley

High country, the Rockies yesterday and today, by Courtney Ryley Cooper. Illustrated. Boston, Little, Brown and co., 1926. Cloth. OP.

> 6 p.l., [3]–294 p. front., plates. 21.2 cm.
> Half title; device.

The last chapter deals with the psychology of the gunman and contains material on Wild Bill Hickok and the killing of Bob Ford.

250 Cooper, Frank C.

Stirring lives of Buffalo Bill, Colonel Wm. F. Cody, last of the great scouts, and Pawnee Bill, Major Gordon W. Lillie, white chief of the Pawnees..., by Frank C. Cooper. ₁New York, Parsons and co., inc., 1912.₁ Dec. cloth. (Col. label pasted on.) OP.

> 5 p.l., 11–223 ₁1₁ p. double front. (ports.), plates, ports. 18.8 cm.
> Frontis tissue.

Although this book was published in 1912, four years later than Cody's *True Tales of the Plains,* the author uses Cody's account practically verbatim and continues to hand down the same false history started by Nichols. He states that Wild Bill was "wounded by three bullets, eleven buckshot, and cut in thirteen places," although he never received a single injury. He adds that it took Wild Bill six months to recover. Emerson Hough claimed it took a year. Cooper also misnames David McCanles, calling him "Jacob." He, too, has ten men in the McCanles party, five of them being killed at the outset.

251 Corle, Edwin

Desert country, by Edwin Corle. Edited by Erskine Caldwell. New York, Duell, Sloan & Pearce ₁1941₁. Cloth. OP.

> viii p., 1 l., 3–357 p. 22.2 cm.
> American folkways series.
> Index: p. 349–357.
> Half title; map on end papers; "First edition" on copyright p.

This book tells of the O K Corral fight between the Clantons and the Earps and also has some minor material on Billy the Kid.

252 ———

The Gila river of the southwest, by Edwin Corle. Illustrated by Ross Santee. New York, Toronto, Rinehart & co., inc. ₁1951₁. Cloth. In print.

> 9 p.l., 5–402 p. front. (double p. map), illus. 21 cm.
> Bibliography: p. 377–386; index: p. 387–402.
> Half title; illus. t.p.; first edition: "R" in device on copyright p.

The author is confused in his facts concerning Pearl Hart, who he says robbed a *train* in 1899. Her only robbery was of a stagecoach in 1898.

253 ———

Mojave; a book of stories, by Edwin Corle. New York, Liveright publishing corp. [1934]. Pict. cloth. OP.

> 5 p.l., 11–272 p. 19.5 cm.
> Half title; device; untrimmed.

A chapter entitled "The Ghost of Billy the Kid" is a piece of well-written fiction which has been reprinted in many anthologies since its first appearance.

254 ———

The royal highway (El Camino Real), by Edwin Corle. Indianapolis, New York, the Bobbs-Merrill co., inc. [1949]. Pict. cloth. OP.

> 6 p.l., 13–351 p. plates, ports., maps. 22.2 cm.
> Appendix: p. 331–334; bibliography: p. 335–339; index: p. 341–351.
> Half title; map on end papers. "First edition" on copyright p.

In his chapter entitled "Your Money or Your Life," the author gives an account of Murieta and makes some mention of Vásquez.

255 Cossley-Batt, Jill Lillie Emma

The last of the California rangers, by Jill L. Cossley-Batt. New York, and London, Funk & Wagnalls co., 1928. Cloth. OP.

> xix, 299 p. front., illus., plates, ports., facsm. 21.4 cm.
> Index: p. 295–299.
> Half title; illus. end papers; untrimmed.

This English author devotes several chapters to Murieta and other California outlaws. She continues to rehash Ridge's account of Murieta. She claims that Murieta divided his gang into five different squads, each one having as its leader one of the numerous Joaquíns, thus allowing Joaquín Murieta seemingly to commit crimes in widely separated sections.

256 Coursey, O. W.

Beautiful Black Hills; a comprehensive treatise on the Black Hills of South Dakota . . . for popular readings, by O. W. Coursey . . . . Mitchell, S. D., published by the Educator Supply co. [1926]. Cloth. OP.

> 4 p.l., [11]–265 p. plates, ports. 19.4 cm.
> 3 p. adv. at end; "References"; fourth prelim. leaf.

Contains chapters on Wild Bill Hickok and Calamity Jane. The author says that *Harper's Magazine* sent a reporter "out to the field" to get the facts and that this story turned out to be a preposterous tale written by George Ward Nichols.

257 ———

Wild Bill (James Butler Hickok), by O. W. Coursey . . . . Mitchell, S. D., published by the Educator supply co., [1924]. Cloth. OP.

> 4 p.l., [9]–80 p. illus. 18.8 cm.
> "Reprinted from the Sioux Falls Daily Argus-Leader."

Only a few of these little books were printed. The author tames down the McCanles-Hickok fight somewhat. While some writers have claimed that the fight was the result of McCanles' horse stealing, others stated that he was trying to collect a debt. This writer makes the statement that the trouble started over the woman Kate Shell.

258 Court of Appeals

at Tyler [Texas], October term, 1882. Ex parte Ben Thompson for bail. [N. p. and no t.p.] Pamphlet. Rare.

> 17 p. 21 cm.

259 Cowan, Robert Ellsworth (Bud)

Range rider, by Bud Cowan; an introduction by B. M. Bower; illustrations by Ross Santee. Garden City, N. Y., Doubleday, Doran & co., 1930. Pict. cloth. OP.

> x p., 1 l., 289 p. front., plates. 21.2 cm.
> Half title; device; untrimmed.
>
> Reprinted in Garden City, Sun Dial Press, same year.

This book has a chapter on Big Nose George Parrott and gives some new information on his capture and lynching. The author was the third husband of B. M. Bower (Mrs. Bertha M. Sinclair-Bower), who wrote the introduction, and she is the better writer of the two.

260 Cowling, Mary Jo

Geography of Denton county, by Mary Jo Cowling . . . . Dallas, Banks Upshaw and co., 1936. Cloth. OP.

xii., 132 p. front. (cattle brands), plates, ports., map, tables. 22.3 cm.
Bibliography: p. 126–130; index: p. [131]–132.
Map on end papers; vignette.

A condensed account of the high lights in the life of Sam Bass.

261 Craig, Newton N. ("Nute")

Thrills 1861 to 1887, by Nute Craig. [Oakland, Calif., published by N. N. Craig, 1931.] Morocco. OP.

5 p.l., [7]–62 [1] p. front. (port.), plates, facsm. of letter from Thomas A. Edison. 20 cm.

262 Crawford, Lewis Ferandus

Rekindling camp fires. The exploits of Ben Arnold (Conner) (Wa-si-cu-Tam-a-he-ca). An authentic narrative of sixty years in the old west as Indian fighter, gold miner, cowboy, hunter and army scout. Map, illustrations, bibliography, index and notes by Lewis F. Crawford . . . . Bismark, N. Dakota, Capital book co. [1926]. Cloth. OP.

8 p.l., 15–324 p. front. (port.), plates, map. 22.4 cm.
Bibliography: p. 311–313; index: p. 315–324.
Illus. half title; untrimmed.

Also published in a de luxe edition of one hundred signed and numbered copies, three-quarter leather, boxed.
Colophon: "This edition is limited to one hundred copies of which this is No. _____."

The author claims that Calamity Jane's real name was Jane Somers and that she was born in Princeton, Missouri, in 1851. He says that the stories of her being a scout and guide are the inventions of people who never knew her. This book also contains a chapter on Joseph Slade and some stories about "Doc" Middleton.

263 Crichton, Kyle S.

Law and order, ltd. The rousing life of Elfego Baca of New Mexico, by Kyle S. Crichton. Santa Fé, New Mexican publishing corp., 1928. Cloth. OP.

viii p., 1 l., [3]–219 p. plates, ports. 22.2 cm.
Pub. device.

Also published in a limited, numbered, and signed de luxe edition of 375 copies.
Colophon: "Three hundred and seventy-five copies of this first edition of

two thousand copies have been inscribed by Mr. Baca and the author. Of
the three hundred and fifty autographed copies which are for sale, this is
Copy No. _____."

The only book written about this notorious gunman, it includes much
information about his now famous fight at Frisco, his association with
Billy the Kid, and two chapters on Joel Fowler. Some of the stories about
Billy the Kid have been heretofore untold, but the author errs in placing
the Kid's trial at Lincoln instead of Mesilla.

264 Crittenden, Henry Huston

The Crittenden memoirs, compiled by H. H. Crittenden.
Fully illustrated.   New York, G. P. Putnam's sons, 1936.   Cloth
OP.

> xv, 17–542 p.   front., plates, ports., facsm., fold. geneal. table, coat of arms.
> 24.2 cm.
> Addenda: p. [513]–529; index: p. 531–542.
> Half title; pub. device.

A large portion of this book is devoted to the life of the James brothers
and the trial of Frank James. Governor Crittenden offered the reward
which ultimately led to Jesse's death.

265 Crockett, George Louis

Two centuries in east Texas. A history of San Augustine
county and surrounding territory, from 1685 to the present time,
by George Louis Crockett . . . .   Dallas, Texas, the Southwest press
[1932].   Cloth.   OP.

> xi, 372 p.   23.8 cm.
> Bibliography: p. 355–357; corrigenda *et* addenda: p. 359–364; index: p.
> 365–372.

This book contains a history of the Moderator and Regulator feud
and the lawlessness running rampant at that time.

266 Crouch, Carrie J.

Young county, history and biography, by Carrie J. Crouch.
Dallas, Dealey and Lowe, 1937.   Imt. leather.   OP.

> 7 p.l., 339 [3] p.   front., plates, ports., cattle brands, diagr.   22.3 cm.
> Bibliography and index on unnumbered pages at end.
> Map on end papers; pub. device; "First Edition" on copyright p.

In a chapter entitled "Young County Trials," the author gives a brief
history of the Marlow brothers.

267 Crowe, Pat

Spreading evil. Pat Crowe's autobiography.   New York, the Branwell co. [1927].   Cloth.   OP.

xvi, 3–331 [1] p.   19.4 cm.
Half title.

A good account of this outlaw and his crimes.

268 Croy, Homer

Corn country, by Homer Croy. Edited by Erskine Caldwell.   New York, Duell, Sloan & Pearce [1947].   Cloth.   In print.

vi p., 2 l., 3–325 p.   21.8 cm.
Index: p. 319–325.
Half title; map on end papers; "First edition" on copyright p.

This book gives a brief account of Lame Johnny.

269 ———

He hanged them high. An authentic account of the fanatical judge who hanged eighty-eight men, by Homer Croy.   New York, Duell, Sloan and Pearce; Boston, Little, Brown and co. [1952].   Cloth.   In print.

viii p., 2 l., [3]–278 p.   front. (port.), plates, ports.   21 cm.
Sources: p. [239]–271; index: p. [273]–278.
Half title; "First edition" on copyright p.

A well-written book, not without humor, which gives some information on Judge Parker's background and boyhood that Mr. Harrison did not include in his *Hanging Judge*. On page 83 the proofreader missed the spelling of Fort Smith as "Fourth Smith"; this error will identify the book in its first state. The author makes one statement about Belle Starr which I do not think he intended to make: ". . . one item of her attire was a holster which she wore becomingly at her waist. It contained *two revolvers*." No one wore two guns in one holster.

270 ———

Jesse James was my neighbor, by Homer Croy.   New York, Duell, Sloan and Pearce [1949].   Cloth.   In print.

xii p., 2 l., 3–313 p.   21 cm.
Sources, including a necrology of the bandits and a note on the James family today: p. 265–307; index: p. 309–313.
Half title.

To me this is the most refreshing book on Jesse James in some time. The author's notes and sources throw much new light on the subject.

271   Crumbine, Samuel J.

Frontier doctor, by Samuel Crumbine, M. D. The autobiography of a pioneer on the frontier of public health.   Philadelphia, Dorrance & co. [1948].   Cloth.   OP.

> ix, 11–284 p.   20.5 cm.
> Pub. device.

The author not only did much for the good health of later Dodge City, but also doctored some of her early marshals, and he tells of Boot Hill.

272   Culley, John Henry (Jack)

Cattle, horses & men of the western range, by John H. (Jack) Culley. Illustrations by Katherine Field.   Los Angeles, Calif., the Ward Ritchie press [1940].   Cloth.   OP.

> xvi p., 1 l., [3]–337 p.   front. (port.), illus., plates.   23.5 cm.
> Index: p. [333]–337.
> Half title; illus. t.p.

This excellent book, written by a well-educated Englishman who came to America and became manager of the large Bell Ranch of New Mexico, devotes some space to the various gunmen of that state. Among them are Clay Allison, Black Jack Ketchum, and Joel Fowler. The author does, however, make the mistake of calling Chunk Colbert by the name of Chunk "Cooper."

273   Cummins, Jim

Jim Cummins' book, written by himself. The life story of the James and Younger gang and their comrades, including the operations of Quantrell's [sic] guerrillas, by one who rode with them. A true but terrible tale of outlawry. Illustrated.   Denver, Colo., the Reed publishing co., 1903.   Pict. cloth.   Rare.

> xv [1] p., [17]–191 p.   front. (port.), plates, ports., facsm.   20 cm.

An exceedingly rare book giving heretofore untold information concerning the Missouri outlaws. In his old age Jim Cummins' memory went bad. I used to correspond with him while he lived in the Old Soldiers Home at Higginsville, Missouri, and he wrote me on Septem-

JIM CUMMINS' BOOK

WRITTEN BY HIMSELF

The Life Story

OF THE

JAMES AND YOUNGER GANG

AND THEIR COMRADES, INCLUDING
THE OPERATIONS OF

QUANTRELL'S GUERRILLAS

BY

ONE WHO RODE WITH THEM

A TRUE BUT TERRIBLE
TALE OF OUTLAWRY

ILLUSTRATED

DENVER, COLORADO
THE REED PUBLISHING COMPANY
NINETEEN HUNDRED THREE

NUMBER 273

ber 29, 1926, that he did not remember ever having written such a book. Yet in the next sentence he wrote: "The book I sent you [Burch's *Quantrill*] was copied off my original book with about one-third of this present book added."

He had been written about so much in Wild West fiction, and in real life was such a meek-looking man, that when he tried several times to give himself up after the breakup of the James gang, no one would believe him. He was never brought to trial.

274   Cunningham, Eugene

Famous in the west, by Eugene Cunningham . . . . Cover design and decorations by Forrest Wood.   El Paso, Texas, Hicks-Haywood co., 1926.   Pict. col. wrappers.   Exceedingly rare.

> 3 p.l., 25 p.   front., illus.   20.5 cm.

This rare little pamphlet was originally published as an advertisement for free distribution by a firm dealing in cowboy clothes. It is said to have been published in an edition of sixty thousand copies, but after the dealer found out how much postage it would take to distribute the books, he gave up the idea and destroyed the edition; hence its scarcity. It deals with rangers and the outlaws of the Southwest.

275   ———

Triggernometry, a gallery of gunfighters. With technical notes on leather slapping as a fine art, gathered from many a loose holstered expert over the years, by Eugene Cunningham. Foreword by Engene Manlove Rhodes. Illustrations from the Rose Collection, San Antonio.   New York, the Press of the Pioneers, inc., 1934.   Pict. cloth.   Scarce.

> xvii p., 1 l., 441 p.   illus., plates, ports.   23.5 cm.
> Bibliography: p. 440–441.
>
> Republished, Caldwell, Idaho, the Caxton Printers, ltd., 1941. These publishers have kept it in print to date, but the first edition is hard to come by.

This book has become a standard work and is reliable on most points. The author also corrects the fable about Wild Bill's fight with McCanles. I think he errs, however, in spelling Tom O'Folliard's name "O'Phalliard," and he is certainly mistaken in saying that Calamity Jane captured Jack McCall with a meat cleaver in a butchershop after he murdered Wild Bill. It has been proved that Calamity was nowhere near at the time. This is merely one of her own claims.

276   Cunningham, James Charles

The truth about Murietta [*sic*]; anecdotes and facts related by those who knew him and disbelieve his capture, by J. C. Cunningham. Los Angeles, Calif., Wetzel publishing co., inc. [1938]. Cloth. OP.

9 p.l., 13–286 p.   4 l. plates and ports. at front.   19.2 cm.

Gives a quite controversial side of the death of Murieta, and the author records the testimony of old-timers to prove his point.

277   Dacus, Joseph A.

Life and adventures of Frank and Jesse James, the noted western outlaws, by Hon. J. A. Dacus, Ph. D. Illustrated. St. Louis, N. D. Thompson & co., publishers . . . ; Chicago, J. S. Goodman . . . , 1880.   Cloth.   Scarce.

5 p.l., [11]–383 [1] p.   front., illus., ports.   19 cm.

278   ———

Illustrated lives and adventures of Frank and Jesse James, and the Younger brothers, the noted western outlaws, by Hon. Joseph A. Dacus . . . . New edition. Enlarged and improved with history complete to 1881.   St. Louis, N. D. Thompson and co., 1881.   Cloth.   Scarce.

8 p.l., [13]–458 [1] p.   front., illus., ports., facsm.   19 cm.

279   ———

Illustrated lives and adventures of Frank and Jesse James, and the Younger brothers, the noted western outlaws, by Hon. Joseph A. Dacus . . . . Illustrated with portraits from life and numerous engravings made expressly for this book. New edition enlarged and improved with history complete to 1882, including the death and funeral of Jesse James.   St. Louis, N. D. Thompson and co., 1882.   Cloth.   Scarce.

2 p.l., 498 p.   front., illus., ports., facsm.   19 cm.

This edition has forty-two pages on the Youngers not in the 1880 edition and has different portraits and illustrations. All of these books are more sensational than reliable.

280 [Daggett, Thomas F.]

Billy LeRoy, the Colorado bandit; or, the king of American highwaymen. A complete and authentic history of this famous desperado. His crimes and adventures. New York, published by Richard K. Fox, Police Gazette [1881]. Pict. wrappers (col.). Rare.

> 2 p.l., 7–66 p. front., illus. 23.8 cm.
> 10 p. adv. at end.

Another of the *Police Gazette* series on criminals printed upon the familiar pink paper. Purporting to be the life of Billy the Kid, it is nothing but the vivid imagination of a hack writer, with just enough half-truths to make it confusing. Its author makes his hero an actor impersonating a female character even though he is a killer. He lays the scene in Colorado instead of in New Mexico; and though a rare collector's item, the whole thing is a piece of worthless trash. The author has invented a brother Sam who joined the Kid. (In one place he calls him "Arthur.") Although the author calls no names, he has the killing of Bell and Ollinger all wrong, and repeats the fable about the Kid's shooting cowboys who worked for Chisum. Fox's writers were running out of subjects, hence created imaginary characters to keep the presses rolling. The book ends with a preposterous account of Billy and his brother being *hanged* at Del Norte, Colorado.

281 Dale, Edward Everett

Cow country, by Edward Everett Dale. Norman, University of Oklahoma press, 1942. Cloth. OP.

> ix p., 2 l., [3]–265 p. illus. 21 cm.
> Index: p. [259]–265.
> Half title; headpieces; vignette; "First edition" on copyright p.

Contains minor mention of certain outlaws and of the Johnson County and Lincoln County wars.

282 Dale, Henry

Adventures and exploits of the Younger brothers, Missouri's most daring outlaws, and companions of the James boys, by Henry Dale .... New York, Street & Smith, 1890. Wrappers. Scarce.

> [5]–191 p. front. 19 cm.
> [Secret service series, No. 32.]
> 16 p. adv. at end.

For the most part unreliable. The author says that Belle Starr's maiden name was Starr, and that she married Cole Younger. The whole account is written in the sensational dime-novel style.

283 [Dalton Brothers]

The Dalton brothers and their astounding career of crime, by an eye witness. With numerous illustrations reproduced from photographs taken on the spot . . . . Chicago, Laird & Lee, publishers, 1892. Pict. wrappers. Rare.

> 3 p.l., 9–220 p. front., illus., facsm., plan. 19.3 cm.
> [Pinkerton detectives series, No. 6, 1892.]
> 4 p. adv. at end.

This scarce book is correct in most details, but contains some inaccuracies. United States Marshal Ransom Payne is made a hero in this account, but later he lost his job for allowing his name to be used.

284 Dalton, Emmett

Beyond the law, by Emmett Dalton, only survivor of the famous Dalton gang. New York, J. S. Ogilvie publishing co., 1918. Wrappers. Scarce.

> vi, iii, 5–190 p. front., illus. 18.3 cm.
> Copyright notice on t.p.

285 ———

When the Daltons rode, by Emmett Dalton, in collaboration with Jack Jungmeyer. Garden City, N. Y., Doubleday, Doran & co., inc., 1931. Pict. cloth. OP.

> viii, 313 p. front. (port.), plates, ports. 21.5 cm.
> Half title; illus. end papers; vignette; untrimmed; "First edition" on copyright p.

> Republished in 1937 by Sun Dial Press.

Although Emmett Dalton's name is used as author, it is doubtful that he wrote any part of this book. It seems to be founded upon the earlier book, *The Dalton Boys*, by "an eye witness" (Item 283). Although this earlier book was a cheap paper-bound two-bit thriller, it is the more accurate of the two.

286 Dalton, Kit

Under the black flag, by Capt. Kit Dalton, a Confederate

soldier. A guerrilla captain under the fearless leader Quantrell [*sic*] and a border outlaw for seventeen years following the surrender of the Confederacy. Associated with the most noted band of free booters the world has ever known. ₁Memphis, Tenn., Lockhart publishing co., 1914.₁ Stiff pict. wrappers. OP.

2–252 p. front., illus., plates, ports. 19.6 cm.
Text starts on verso of t.p.

One cannot understand why a writer, like this one, supposedly telling about his own life could possibly make the statements he does, unless in his dotage his memory had turned to fantastic hallucinations. Not only does he say that Belle Starr was a half-blood Cherokee and was educated in Carlisle Indian School, but he claims to have served as marshal under Wild Bill Hickok at Deadwood, *Colorado* (!) and later at Cheyenne. "I know nothing," he writes, "of William Hickock's [*sic*] career after we parted in Cheyenne except that he was assassinated several years later in *Tombstone, Arizona*."

287 David, Robert Beebe

Malcolm Campbell, sheriff, by Robert B. David. The reminiscences of the greatest frontier sheriff in the history of the Platte valley, and the famous Johnson county invasion of 1892. Casper, Wyo., Wyomingana, inc. ₁1932₁. Cloth. OP.

4 p.l., ₁7₁–361 ₁5₁ p. front., plates, ports., maps, facsms. plan. 20.2 cm.
Chronological table of contents at end; half title.

A good account of the Johnson County War, this book contains some material on Alfred Packer.

288 Davis, Clyde Brion

The Arkansas, by Clyde Brion Davis; illustrated by Donald McKay. New York, Toronto, Farrar & Rinehart, inc. ₁1940₁. Cloth. OP.

x p., 1 l., 3–340 p. front. (map), illus. 20.9 cm.
₁Rivers of America series.₁
Acknowledgments: p. 328–330; index: p. 331–340.
Half title; illus. end papers; illus. t.p.; first edition: "F R" in publisher's device on copyright p.

The author here gives an accurate sketch of Judge Parker's court and tells of the bad men and peace officers of Dodge City.

289 Davis, George Wesley

Sketches of Butte (from vigilante days to prohibition), by

George Wesley Davis. Boston, the Cornhill co. [1921]. Cloth. Scarce.

> vi p., 3 l., 3–179 p. plates, ports. 19.3 cm.
> ·Half title; pub. device.

Contains a chapter on the Montana vigilantes and outlaws.

290 Dawley, T. R.

Mercedes; or, the outlaw's child. An original tale of California, the scenes of which are laid at the time mobs, riots and lawless men were as plenty in San Francisco as golden slugs. New York, 1866. Pict. wrappers. Rare.

> 67 p. 17.5 cm.

An early example of the dime novel on western outlaws.

291 Dawson, Charles

Pioneer tales of the Oregon Trail and of Jefferson county, by Charles Dawson. Topeka, Kan., Crane & co., 1912. Pict. cloth. Scarce.

> xv, 488 p. front., ports., maps (1 fold.), tables. 23.4 cm.

This book is the first one in which an author tried to publish a correct account of the Hickok-McCanles fight and to show "the wide variance between the truth and fiction as told by Emerson Hough." He was also the first to claim that Wild Bill shot McCanles from behind a curtain and ambushed Woods and Gordon from an unseen shelter.

292 Day, Donald

Big country: Texas, by Donald Day. Edited by Erskine Caldwell. New York, Duell, Sloan & Pearce [1947]. Cloth. OP.

> x p., 1 l., 3–6 p., 1 l., 9–326 p. 21.7 cm.
> [American folkways series.]
> Index: p. 316–326.
> Half title.

The author makes the statement that the "Alamo" Saloon in Abilene, Kansas, was presided over by Wild Bill Hickok, which is not true. Wild Bill drank and gambled in many different saloons, but he never worked in, or owned, one of them. There are also accounts of several Texas feuds in this book.

293   Day, Jack Hays

The Sutton-Taylor feud, by Jack Hays Day. Authentic. [San Antonio, produced by the presses of Sid Murray & son, printers, n.d.] Stiff wrappers.   Scarce.

6 p.l., 9–40 p.   front., plates, ports.   21.5 cm.

This scarce little book tells some of the inside facts of the feud from the Taylor side by one of the participants and a kinsman of the Taylors.

294   DeBarth, Joe

The life and adventures of Frank Grouard, chief of scouts, U. S. A., by Joe DeBarth. Illustrated.   St. Joseph, Mo., Combe printing co. [1894].   Pict. cloth.   Scarce.

xii p., 5 l., [21]–545 p.   plates, ports.   23 cm.

There is some material on lawlessness and the James boys.

295   Debo, Angie

Prairie city, the story of an American community, by Angie Debo.   New York, Alfred A. Knopf, 1944.   Cloth.   OP.

xiv p., 1 l., [3]–245 p.   plates.   21.8 cm.
Index: p. i–viii.
Half title; vignette; untrimmed.

Tells of the killing of Dick Yeager and Isaac Black, well-known Oklahoma outlaws.

296   ———

The cowman's southwest, being the reminiscences of Oliver Nelson, freighter, camp cook, cowboy, frontiersman in Kansas, Indian Territory, Texas, and Oklahoma 1878–1893. Edited by Angie Debo . . . .   Glendale, Calif., the Arthur H. Clark co., 1953.   Cloth. In print.

9 p.l., [19]–343 p.   front. (map), plates, cattle brands, map.   24 cm.
Index: p. [333]–343.
Half title: "Western Frontiersman Series No. IV"; pub. device; untrimmed.

A most interesting book of reminiscences, with some material on many of the outlaws of Oklahoma and Texas.

297   Delay, Peter J.

History of Yuba and Sutter counties, California, with biographical sketches of the leading men and women of the counties who have been identified with their growth and development from the early days to the present. History by Peter J. Delay. Illustrated . . . . Los Angeles, Calif., Historic Record co., 1924.   Three-quarter leather.   OP.

11 p.l., [39]–1328 p.   plates, ports.   27.5 cm.

Contains much material on Tom Bell and some minor information on Joaquín Murieta.

298   Delony, Lewis S.

Forty years a peace officer. A true story of lawlessness and adventure in the early days in southwest Texas, by Lewis S. Delony. [N.p., n. d.]   Stiff wrappers.   (Cover title.)   Scarce.

2 p.l., 61 p.   21.8 cm.
First 8 p. unnumbered.
Double column; stapled.

This interesting and little-known book contains material on the Taylor-Sutton feud, the hanging of Bill Longley, the capture and killing of John Wesley Hardin, as well as on many other crimes in Texas. The author, however, errs in saying that John Selman killed Sam Bass.

299   Denison, Merrill

Klondike Mike. An Alaskan odyssey, by Merrill Denison. Seattle, Wash., Leslie O. Johnson, publisher, 1948.   Cloth.   In print.

xi p., 10 l., 3–393 p.   plates, ports., map, facsms.   21 cm.
Half title; device; 8 p. of plates and ports. before text.

This well-written story of the far North gives some new and interesting material on Soapy Smith during his stay in Skagway, where he met his death.

300   Denton, B. E. "Cyclone"

A two-gun cyclone. A true story, by B. E. (Cyclone) Denton. Illustrated by Jack Patton.   Dallas, Texas, B. E. Denton . . . [1927].   Pict. cloth.   OP.

viii p., 2 l., 145 p.   front. (port.), plates (1 col.).   19.4 cm.
Half title.

A little book of reminiscences written by an old-timer after he had reached his seventies. He was a typical old-time Texas cowboy, uneducated and big hearted. I knew him well, and he could have written a much better story if he had tried.

301 Devil Anse:

or, the Hatfield-McCoy outlaws. A full and complete history of the deadly feud existing between the Hatfield and McCoy clans. Thrillingly narrated and graphically illustrated.

[Published with]

Trujillo; or, Bob Montclair, the terror of Eldorado. A truthful portrayal of the life and adventures of this noted bandit and desperado. Profusely illustrated.   New York, Richard K. Fox, publisher, 1889.   Pict. wrappers.   Rare.

> Part I, [Devil Anse] 2 p.l., [5]-32 p. front., illus.
> Part II, [Trujillo] 2 p.l., [5]-28 p. front., illus.   21.8 cm.
> Double column.

Another of the familiar pink-paper *Police Gazette* publications of no historical truth, but now a collector's item. Though it is claimed that the latter section is a "truthful" account of a "noted" bandit, the character has been created out of whole cloth.

302 Dewey, Frederick H.

Spanish Jack, the mountain bandit; or, the pledge of life. New York, Beadle and Adams, 1873.   Pict. wrappers.   Rare.

> 100 p.   16.5 cm.

A story of an outlaw who operated between San Francisco and San Diego. Another example of the early Beadle novels, this one from Starr's American Novels series.

303 DeWolf, J. H.

Pawnee Bill (Major Gordon W. Lillie), his experience and adventures on the western plains; or, from the saddle of a "cowboy and ranger" to the chair of a "bank president," by J. H. DeWolf. [N.p.], published by Pawnee Bill's historic Wild West co., 1902. Col. pict. boards.   Rare.

119

> 4 p.l., 13–108 p.   front., illus., plates, ports.   23.7 cm.
> Vignette.

Contains some information on the James brothers.

304   Dibble, Roy Floyd

Strenuous Americans, [by] R. F. Dibble . . . .   New York, Boni and Liveright, publishers [1923].   Cloth.   Scarce.

> 9 p.l., 15–370 p.   front., ports.   22.4 cm.
> Short bibliography after each chapter.
> Half title; pub. device.

Chapter I is about Jesse James.

305   Dick, Everett

The sod-house frontier, 1854–1890. A social history of the northern plains from the creation of Kansas & Nebraska to the admission of the Dakotas, by Everett Dick . . . . Illustrated.   New York, London, D. Appleton-Century co., inc., 1938.   Pict. cloth. OP.

> xviii p., 1 l., 550 p.   illus., plates.   22.8 cm.
> Bibliography: p. 519–528; index: p. 529–550.
> Half title; pub. device; untrimmed; first edition: figure (1) at the end of index.

A scholarly book which covers life on the frontier thoroughly, it contains a chapter on lawlessness and the vigilantes, and another on the homesteader-cattleman war of the early frontier.

306   ———

Vanguards of the frontier. A social history of the northern plains and Rocky mountains from the earliest white contacts to the coming of the homemaker, by Everett Dick . . . . Illustrated.   New York, London, D. Appleton-Century co., inc., 1941.   Pict. cloth. OP.

> xvi p., 1 l., 574 p.   front. (port.), plates.   23 cm.
> Bibliography: p. 519–545; index: p. 547–574.
> Half title; map on end papers; pub. device; untrimmed; first edition: figure (1) at end of index.

Another extensive work by this author touching upon, among many other subjects, road agents, vigilantes, and the Johnson County War.

307 Dickson, Arthur Jerome

Covered wagon days. A journey across the plains in the sixties, and pioneer days in the northwest. From the private journals of Albert Jerome Dickson, edited by Arthur Jerome Dickson. Cleveland, the Arthur H. Clark co., 1929. Cloth. OP.

> 8 p.l., [19]–287 p. front., plates, ports., fold. map at end. 24.6 cm.
> Index: p. [281]–287.
> Half title; pub. device; untrimmed; tissues.

Excellent history from the journal of a man who went west in the early days. He gives some firsthand information about the outlaws and vigilantes of Virginia City.

308 Dimsdale, Thomas Josiah

The vigilantes of Montana; or, popular justice in the Rocky mountains. Being a correct and impartial narrative of the chase, trial, capture and execution of Henry Plummer's road agent band, together with accounts of the lives and crimes of many of the robbers and desperadoes, the whole being interspersed with sketches of life in the mining camps of the "Far West"; forming the only reliable work on the subject ever offered the public, by Prof. Thos. J. Dimsdale. Virginia City, M. T., Montana Post press, D. W. Tilton & co., book and job printers, 1866. Pict. wrappers. Exceedingly rare.

> iv, [5]–228 p. 16 cm.
> 4 p. adv. at end.

Republished in 1882, 1915, and later, all editions issued by different publishers except the second. The third edition in 1915 was issued by Al Noyes, with footnotes and illustrations and with an appended history of southern Montana.

> 4 p.l., [9]–290 p. front., plates, ports. facsms. 24 cm.
> The table of contents is labeled "index" and placed at end.

The original edition is said to be the first book produced by a printing press in Montana. Perhaps no other book excels Dimsdale's in presenting the picture of the lawless conditions that characterized the mining camps of the Rocky Mountain country. The author was editor of the Virginia City *Montana Post* and a participant in this extraordinary campaign against lawlessness. The book ran serially in the *Post* before being published in book form.

309   Dixey, Harry (pseud.)

The Collis express robbers [or hunting down two desperate criminals by Harry Dixey]. New York, Street and Smith co., Oct. 20, 1897. Pict. wrappers. Rare.

> 31 p.   21.5 cm.
> Double column.
> No. 449 of the Old Log Cabin series.

A dime-novel version of the activities of the Evans-Sontag gang, including its California train robberies.

310   Dobie, J. Frank

Apache gold & Yaqui silver, by J. Frank Dobie. Illustrated by Tom Lea. Boston, Little, Brown and co., 1939. Cloth. OP.

> xvii p., 1 l., 3–366 p.   front. (col.), illus., plates (col.), plan.   22.5 cm.
> Appendix: p. 357–366.
> Half title; vignette.
> Colophon: "Two hundred and sixty-five numbered copies of this Sierra Madre edition have been printed . . . and autographed by the author and . . . artist. This is No. _____."
> Extra set of colored plates in envelope laid in.
>
> Also published in a trade edition which has gone through many subsequent reprintings.

This fascinating book on lost mines contains some interesting material on Apache Kid.

311   ———

Coronado's children. Tales of the lost mines and buried treasure of the southwest, by J. Frank Dobie. Illustrated by Ben Carlton Mead. Dallas, Texas, the Southwest press [1930]. Pict. cloth. OP.

> xv, 367 p.   front., illus., plates, map, charts.   24 cm.
> Notes: p. 343–359; glossary, p. 361–367.
> Map on end papers; tailpieces; device; untrimmed.

Republished many times, but the first state can be identified by the dedication. The original manuscript read in part: ". . . to the memory of my father R. J. Dobie, a *clean* cowman of the Texas soil." The publishers deleted the work "clean," an act which displeased the author, and the word was restored in subsequent editions. This is another book on lost mines. In the chapter entitled *"Los Muertos No Hablan,"* there is some information on Zwing Hunt and Russian Bill.

312 ———

Flavor of Texas, by J. Frank Dobie, with illustrations by Alexandre Hogue. Dallas, Dealey and Lowe, 1936. Cloth. OP.

> 6 p.l., 287 p. front., illus. 22.5 cm.
> Index: p. [285]–287.

Some information on Clay Allison and other gunmen.

313 ———

Guide to life and literature of the southwest, with a few observations, by J. Frank Dobie. Illustrated. Austin, University of Texas press, 1943. Wrappers. OP.

> 2 p.l., [7]–111 p. front., illus., plates, music. 22.8 cm.

Originally mimeographed for distribution to Mr. Dobie's students, this book was later printed in wrappers, only a few being bound in cloth. It was not for sale, but for free distribution, although a few copies did get upon the shelves of booksellers. With the same plates lent to the Southern Methodist University Press, a run was made under that imprint. This book is not a true biblography, but an excellent check list with comments on many western books, some of which deal with outlaws.

314 ———

Guide to life and literature of the southwest. Revised and enlarged in both knowledge and wisdom, [by] J. Frank Dobie. Dallas, Southern Methodist University press, 1952. Cloth. In print.

> viii, 222 p. illus., music. 23.5 cm.
> Index: p. 197–222.
> Half title; double t.p.; facsimile of signature on cover.

A greatly enlarged edition of the original. In writing of Pat Garrett's book on Billy the Kid, the author misspells Ash Upson's name as "Upton." At first I thought this might be a typographical error, but the same mistake is found in the index.

315 ———

A vaquero of the brush country, by J. Frank Dobie, partly from the reminiscences of John Young. Illustrated by Justin C. Gruelle. Dallas, Texas, the Southwest press, 1929. Cloth and boards. (Imt. rattlesnake skin.) OP.

> xv, 314 p. front. (col.), illus., plates, facsm. 24 cm.
> Appendix: p. 299–303; index: p. 305–314.
> Map on end papers; pub. device; untrimmed.

The first edition may be identified by the word "river" after "Rio Grande" on map of end papers. The author told me: "I have always had a particular dislike for the redundance of 'river' in conjunction with 'Rio.' When I found this idiotic redundancy in my own book I was not happy. I had not seen the proof of these end papers. I immediately had 'river' taken out and also made other corrections."

The book contains some side lights on such gunmen as King Fisher, Ben Thompson, and Billy the Kid. A chapter entitled "Billy the Kid Interpreted" contains interesting information on this young outlaw, some of which is new.

316 Dobie, J. Frank (ed.)

Southwestern lore, edited by J. Frank Dobie. Publications of the Texas Folk-lore Society, Number IX, 1931 . . . . Dallas, the Southwest press [1931]. Cloth. OP.

v, 198 [1] p. illus., music. 23.4 cm.
Index: p. 193–198.

In a chapter on folklore shooting, there is much debunking of the marvelous shooting of such gunmen and outlaws as Wild Bill Hickok and Billy the Kid.

317 Donaghey, George Washington

Autobiographical sketch of George W. Donaghey. The first three stages in the drama of a life . . . . [By George W. Donaghey. N. p., 1924.] Pict. wrappers. (Cover title.) Scarce.

[5]–31 [1] p. front. (port.). 26 cm.
Double column.

This former governor of Arkansas tells of his early experiences as a cowboy in Texas; he makes some mention of Bill Longley and Sam Bass.

318 Donald, Jay

Outlaws of the border. A complete and authentic history of the lives of Frank and Jesse James, the Younger brothers, and their robber companions, including Quantrell [sic] and his noted guerrillas, the greatest bandits the world has ever known. A wonderful record of crime and its consequences, drawn with great care from reliable sources. A thrilling narrative, vividly written by Jay Donald. Fully illustrated. Chicago, Coburn & Newman publishing co. . . . , 1882. Pict. cloth. Scarce.

ix, 11–520 p. front., plates, ports. 19.7 cm.

Republished same year in Philadelphia.

One of the better early histories of the Jameses and Youngers. This author, like so many other writers on the James boys, seems determined to bring these outlaws into the Big Springs holdup of the Union Pacific engineered by Joel Collins and Sam Bass. Like many others, too, he is wrong concerning the amount of money obtained in this robbery, stating that there was $62,000 from the express car and enough from the passengers to bring the total to near $100,000. He has Sam Bass and Bill Longley in the James gang, and calls Bill Chadwell a Minnesota horse thief and outlaw who joined the James gang when they went north to rob the bank at Northfield, Minnesota.

319   Donaldson, Thomas Corwin

Idaho of yesterday, by Thomas Donaldson. Introduction by Thomas B. Donaldson. Illustrated by photographs. Caldwell, Idaho, the Caxton printers, ltd., 1941. Cloth. OP.

9 p.l., [19]–406 p. front. (port.), plates, ports., facsms. 23.5 cm.
Index: p. [403]–406.
Half title; pub. device.

Contains a chapter on lawlessness and the vigilantes of early Idaho.

320   Donoho, Milford Hill

Circle dot, a true story of cowboy life forty years ago, by M. H. Donoho. Topeka, monotyped and printed by Crane & co., 1907. Cloth. Scarce.

3 p.l., 7–256 p. front. 20 cm.

Includes material on some of the outlaws of the Indian Territory and the gunmen of Dodge City.

321   Doughitt, Katherine Christian (Mrs. J. W.)

Romance and dim trails. A history of Clay county [Texas], [by] Katherine Christian Doughitt (Mrs. J. W.), editor-in-chief. Dallas, Texas, William T. Tardy, publisher, 1938. Imt. leather. OP.

7 p.l., 280 p. front., plates, ports. 23.2 cm.
Cattle brands: p. 269–280.
Map on end papers; leaf of errata tipped in; device.

In one chapter the author writes that the James and Younger brothers visited Clay County, where a sister lived for a time. She also tells of a man who came there in 1936 claiming to be the real Jesse James, and says he was quite convincing. This story has been going around for years.

322   Douglas, Claud Leroy

Cattle kings of Texas, by C. L. Douglas. Dallas, Texas, published by Cecil Baugh [1939]. Cloth. OP.

> xiv p., 1 l., 376 p. front., illus., plates, ports., map. 22.5 cm.
> Half title; illus. end papers; device.

First appeared serially in *The Cattleman* magazine. Some copies bound in cowhide with the hair left on. The author says that Billy the Kid often "likkered" up at the bars of Tascosa; but Dr. Hoyt of Tascosa, who knew the Kid well, says that he never took a drink while there.

323   ———

Famous Texas feuds, [by] C. L. Douglas . . . . Dallas, Texas, the Turner co. . . . [1936]. Pict. cloth and leather. OP.

> v p., 1 l., 173 p. front., ports. 20.4 cm.

Treats many of the feuds of Texas.

324   ———

The gentlemen in the white hats; dramatic episodes in the history of the Texas rangers, by C. L. Douglas. Dallas, Texas, South-west press . . . [1934]. Cloth. OP.

> vii, 205 p. front., illus., plates, ports. 22.5 cm.
> Pub. device.

Most of this book contains nothing new. In his chapter on John Wesley Hardin, the author repeats what has gone before.

325   Drannan, Capt. William F.

Thirty-one years on the plains and in the mountains; or, the last voice from the plains. An authentic record of a life time of hunting, trapping, scouting and Indian fighting in the far west, by Capt. William F. Drannan . . . . Copiously illustrated by H. S. DeLay, and many reproductions from photographs. Chicago, Rhodes & McClure publishing co., 1899. Dec. cloth. Scarce.

6 p.l., 17–586 p.   front. (port. signed in facsm.), plates, ports.   20.2 cm.
8 p. adv. at end.

Republished by Thos. W. Jackson publishing co., Chicago, 1900.

This quite scarce book deals largely with the Montana vigilantes.

326   Draper, William R.

A cub reporter in the old Indian territory, by Wm. R. Draper. Girard, Kan., Haldeman-Julius publications ₁1946₁. Wrappers. OP.

3–32 p.   21.5 cm.
Notes and comments: p. 25–32 (double column).

Tells of the capture of Cherokee Bill and other Oklahoma outlaws.

327   ———

Exciting adventures along the Indian frontier. A reporter's experiences in the red man's territory and in the old Cherokee Strip during the '90s, by Wm. R. Draper.   Girard, Kan., Haldeman-Julius publications ₁1946₁.   Wrappers.   OP.

2 p.l., 5–32 p.   21.5 cm.
Notes and comments: p. 30–32 (double column).

328   Driggs, Benjamin Woodbury

History of Teton valley, Idaho, by B. W. Driggs. Caldwell, Idaho, the Caxton printers, ltd., MCMXXVI.   Boards.   Scarce.

6 p.l., ₁13₁–227 p.   front., plates.   23.5 cm.

Has a chapter on outlawry.

329   Driggs, Howard Roscoe

Westward America, by Howard R. Driggs. With reproductions of forty water color paintings by William H. Jackson. Trails edition.   New York, G. P. Putnam's sons ₁1942₁.   Cloth. OP.

x p., 1 l., 312 p.   40 col. plates (incl. front.).   29.3 cm.
Bibliography: p. 301–302; index: p. 305–312.
Half title.

Also published in trade edition.

A chapter entitled "Rock Creek" contains a true account of the Hickok-McCanles fight.

127

330 Driscoll, R. E.

Seventy years of banking in the Black Hills, by R. E. Driscoll. First National Bank of the Black Hills, 1876–1946. ₍Rapid City, S. D., the Gate City Guide, publishers, 1948.₎ Stiff pict. wrappers. In print.

> 4 p.l., 11–87 p. front. (port.). 23 cm.

In writing of the various banks of the Black Hills, the author gives some information on a bank robbery in which Tom O'Day was involved.

331 Drumheller, Daniel

"Uncle Dan" Drumheller tells thrills of the western trails in 1854, by "Uncle Dan" Drumheller. Spokane, Wash., Inland-American printing co., 1925. Raised leather. Scarce.

> xi, 131 p. 2 ports. (incl. front.). 19.5 cm.
> Half title; frontis tissue; chapter and divisions printed in red.

The author writes of his long experience in the West as a miner, rider of the pony express, cattleman, and rancher. He tells of some of the outlaws, including Boone Helm and Brocky Jack.

332 Drury, Aubrey

California, an intimate guide, by Aubrey Drury. New York., London, Harper & brothers, publishers, 1935. Cloth. Pict. label pasted on. OP.

> xvi p., 1 l., 592 p. plates, maps. 22.2 cm.
> Acknowledgments: p. 559–561; index: p. 563–592.
> Half title; pub. device; t.p. in red and black.

A little information on Vásquez and Black Bart.

333 ———

John A. Hooper and California's robust youth, by Aubrey Drury. Together with a foreword by Arthur W. Hooper. San Francisco, Calif. ₍Lawton Kennedy, printer₎, 1952. Cloth. In print.

> 3 p.l., 85 p. front. (port.), plates, ports. 27 cm.
> Vignette; t.p. in red and black.

Contains slight, but new, material on Murieta.

128

334 Drury, Wells

An editor on the Comstock Lode, by Wells Drury. Fore-word by Ella Bishop Drury. Illustrated with photographs. New York, Toronto, Farrar & Rinehart, inc. [1936]. Cloth. Scarce.

xx, 343 p. front., illus., plates, ports., map, diagr. 23.5 cm.
Half title; first edition: "F R" in device on copyright p.

Republished by Pacific Books, Palo Alto, Calif., in 1948.

xx p., 1 l., 3–307 p. plates, ports., map. 23.5 cm.
Index: p. 295–307.

These books have material on road agents, such as Henry Plummer and Boone Helm.

335 Dudley, J. H.

The climax in crime of the 19th century, being an authentic history of the trial, conviction and execution of Stephen Morris Ballew for the murder of James P. Golden, in Collin County, Texas, on the 21st day of October, 1870, with a short sketch of the early life of the murderer, by J. H. Dudley. Quincy, Feb. 28, 1872. Wrappers. Exceedingly rare.

208 p. front. (port.). 20.8 cm.

336 Du Fran, Dora (D. Dee, pseud.)

Low down on Calamity Jane, by D. Dee. Rapid City, S. D. [1932]. Pict. wrappers. (Cover title.) Scarce.

12 p. 22 cm.
Foreword on verso of cover; port. on cover.

This little pamphlet was written by a woman who claimed to have known Calamity Jane, and it is said that she was in a position to know the "seamy side of her character," since she was quite a character her-self. But in dealing with facts, she is unreliable. Established historical facts make many of the statements in her book highly improbable.

Although other writers are as unreliable regarding Jane's birth-place and the date of her birth, this author is the only one to claim that Jane was born at Fort Laramie, Wyoming, giving the date as 1860. Jane herself states she was born in Princeton, Missouri, May 1, 1852. The author of this book says that Calamity Jane was "often called Mary

Jane Canary [*sic*], but this was nothing but a nickname. She liked to sing, but her voice was anything but musical, so they called her Canary after the mules, which were also called Rocky Mountain canaries."

337 Duke, Thomas S.

Celebrated criminal cases of America, by Thomas S. Duke, captain of police, San Francisco. Published with approval of the Honorable Board of Police Commissioners of San Francisco. San Francisco, Calif., the James H. Barry co., 1910. Cloth. Scarce.

xii p., 3 l., [3]–657 p. front., plates, ports. 23.5 cm.
Tipped-in slip on p. 14; tissues between double p. ports.

This work deals with outlaws and murderers, crime and criminals over the whole nation. The chapters on the Pacific Coast outlaws treat Murieta, Vásquez, Black Bart, the Evans-Sontag gang, and Harry Tracy. Chapters on the Middle West discuss Alfred G. Packer, the Daltons, the Benders, and the James-Younger gang. The chapter on Murieta is taken from the Ridge book, and the one on Vásquez is from the Sawyer account of this outlaw.

338 Dykes, Jefferson C.

Billy the Kid, the bibliography of a legend, [by] J. C. Dykes. Albuquerque, the University of New Mexico press, 1952. Wrappers. In print.

5 p.l., 11–186 p. front. 22.8 cm.
Index: p. 179–186.
Device.
Head of title: "University of New Mexico publications in language and literature, No. 7."
Five hundred copies also bound in cloth, thirty of which were numbered and signed. Very shortly after publication a second printing was made, mostly bound in cloth.

This is more a check list than a true bibliography, but each entry contains much information on the contents of the book listed, and the author points out many false and inaccurate statements made by various writers. It is the first complete list of materials on this young outlaw and includes songs, plays, motion pictures, phonograph records, and magazine articles.

339 Earle, J. P.

History of Clay county and northwest Texas, by J. P. Earle. [Henrietta, Texas, 1900.] Wrappers. Scarce.

64 p. front., ports. 22.4 cm.

Some material on the Jameses and Youngers and on the Jesse Brown gang.

340   Eaton, Frank

Pistol Pete, veteran of the old west, by Frank Eaton. With illustrations. Boston, Little, Brown and co., 1952. Cloth. In print.

x p., 1 l., [3]–278 p. plates, ports. 21 cm.
Half title; pub. device; "First edition" on copyright p.

A wild tale of a man who trained himself, as he grew up, to be able to kill all the men who took part in the murder of his father. The writer tells of having a horse race with Belle Starr and losing his Winchester to her. He says that when Belle refused to let Edgar Watson take her home from a dance, he hid out on her trail home and shot her. Since Watson was a happily married man, this tale does not hold water. Watson was never convicted. Yet Eaton declares that he and his friends heard the shot and chased Watson for a hundred miles and killed his horse in a gun battle which followed, and that Belle's friends hanged Watson with Belle's lariat. He tells of his killing of the last man on his "want list" in Albuquerque, New Mexico, with Pat Garrett looking on and with his sanction. The book reads like Wild West fiction and is filled with doubtful statements. The author turns out to be a regular one-man army, and though just a boy when he started on his chase, he matched his skill against a number of hardened killers.

341   Eaton, Jeannette

Bucky O'Neill of Arizona, by Jeannette Eaton. Illustrated by Edward Shenton. New York., William Morrow and co., 1949. Pict. cloth. In print.

6 p.l., 14–219 p. illus. 20.8 cm.
Half title; illus. t.p.; illus. chapter headings.

A story of this Arizona Ranger for young readers.

342   Edwards, J. B.

Early days in Abilene, by J. B. Edwards. Edited and published by C. W. Wheeler, printed in the *Abilene Chronicle*, 1896; reprinted in *Abilene Daily Chronicle*, 1938, with added material from the papers of J. B. Edwards. [N. p., n. d.] Pict. wrappers. (Caption title.) Scarce.

> 16 p. illus., plates, ports. 20.5 x 23.5 cm.
> Triple column; tissues inside front and back wrappers.

The author relates some events in early Abilene. He lived there from its founding and knew its history firsthand. The last letter I received from him was written when he was 102 years old, but he has since died. He writes of Wild Bill Hickok, Calamity Jane, and Jack McCall.

343   Edwards, Jennie (Mrs. John N. Edwards)

John N. Edwards, biography, memoirs, reminiscences and recollections. His brilliant career as soldier, author and journalist. Choice collection of his most notable and interesting newspaper articles, together with some unpublished poems and many private letters. Also a reprint of Shelby's expedition to Mexico, an unwritten leaf of the war. Compiled by his wife, Jennie Edwards.   Kansas City, Mo., Jennie Edwards, publisher, 1889.   Cloth.   Scarce.

> 3 p.l., 9–428 p.   front. (port.).   19.2 cm.

Contains a chapter on the killing of Jesse James reprinted from the *Sedalia Democrat*, April, 1881, which has become a classic.

344   Edwards, John N.

Noted guerrillas; or, the warfare of the border. Being a history of the lives and adventures of Quantrell [sic], Bill Anderson, George Todd, Dave Poole, Fletcher Taylor, Peyton Long, Oll Shepherd, Arch Clements, John Maupin, Tuck and Woot Hill, Wm. Gregg, Thomas Maupin, the James brothers, the Younger brothers, Arthur McCoy and numerous other well known guerrillas of the west, by John N. Edwards .... Illustrated.   St. Louis, Bryan, Brand & co.; Chicago, Thompson & Wakefield; San Francisco, Cal., A. L. Brancroft & co., 1877.   Cloth.   Scarce.

> xi, [13]–488 p.   front., plates, ports.   21.8 cm.
> 2 p. adv. at end.
>
> Reprinted in 1879.

This book is not considered reliable. The author was an honest man and believed what he wrote, but he got most of his information, which proved to be false, from Frank and Jesse James while they were hiding out. The book went through several editions, but has since been repudiated. The author seemed to strive to glorify outlaws and outlawry.

345 Eisele, Wilbert E.

The real Wild Bill Hickok, famous scout and knight chivalric of the plains—a true story of pioneer life in the far west, by Wilbert E. Eisele (Ross Lyndon) .... Denver, Colo., William H. Andre, publisher, 1931. Pict. cloth. OP.

> 9 p.l., 15–364 p. front. (port.), illus. 20 cm.
> Half title; vignette; port. of author on verso of dedication page; first edition: "Collector's edition" on copyright p.

This author also claims that the McCanles' were desperate horse thieves who were overrunning the country. He closely follows preceding false accounts, names the McCanles' "Jim" and "Jack," and states that "Jim was the biggest cutthroat of them all." He follows Hough in placing the fight in a dugout, and has the usual ten men in the McCanles party. Using the Buel and Nichols accounts as a pattern, he makes even stronger statements than they, as "the bowie in Bill's hands now did desperate work, plunging from one heart to another, and drawing great fountains of blood which spurted about until the floor was fairly flooded; but his own life current assisted largely to swell the bright red streams, for his body was punctured by bullet holes and knife thrusts, yet the inner recesses of his life had not been touched and his strong arm continued to do its deadly work." He brings in Captain Kingsbury, as Buel did, and uses Buel's own words without quotation marks in saying, "This combat, of one man fairly whipping ten acknowledged desperadoes, has no parallel, I make bold to say, in any authentic history." See Item 143.

Eisele is the only author to write an account of this fight who acknowledges that he has read later accounts than the first preposterous ones, yet he claims that the statement that Wild Bill killed only three men is "incorrect and a distortion of the real facts," and indignantly says that such stories were started by Southern sympathizers trying to take the glory from his hero.

He claims that the accounts by Nichols, Buel, and Hough have been accepted as authentic for many years, and therefore must be true. This claim only shows how the lazy historian works. He also misspells Phil Coe's name, calling him Phil "Cole," as his predecessors had done. Most of his quotations are from unreliable sources, among them Sutton's *Hands Up*, a most unreliable book.

133

346 El Comancho (pseud. of Walter Shelley Phillips)

The old timer's tale, by El Comancho. Chicago, the Canterbury press, 1929. Pict. boards. Scarce.

> 5 p.l., 114 p. front. (port.), plates. 20.3 cm.
> Half title; pub. device.
> Two errata slips inserted, the first reading: "Page 15, line 7 should be line 6;" the second reading: "Page 47, line 5 should follow line 24."

The author writes of Wild Bill Hickok, Joseph Slade, Bat Masterson, and others.

347 Elliott, David Stewart

Last raid of the Daltons. A reliable recital of the battle with the bandits at Coffeyville, Kansas, October 5, 1892, by David Stewart Elliott .... First edition. Illustrated by E. A. Filleau. Coffeyville, Kan., Coffeyville Journal print, 1892. Pict. wrappers. Rare.

> 5 p.l., [13]-71 [1] p. front. (port.), illus., ports., plan at end. 19.2 cm.
> "First edition" on t.p.
>
> Later reprinted in a 60 p. edition.

This exceedingly rare little book is an accurate account of this battle written by the editor of the *Coffeyville Journal* immediately after the raid when details were fresh.

348 Emmett, Chris

Shanghai Pierce, a fair likeness, by Chris Emmett, with drawings by Nick Eggenhofer. Norman, University of Oklahoma press [1953]. Cloth. In print.

> xiii p., 1 l., 3–326 p. illus., plates, ports., maps. 24 cm.
> Bibliography: p. 313–319; index: p. 321–326.
> Half title; illus. double t.p.; illus. chapter headings; "First edition" on copyright p.

An interesting book on one of Texas' most colorful cattlemen. There is some material on the Taylor-Sutton feud and on John Wesley Hardin, Jack Helms, Ben Thompson, Wild Bill Hickok, and other gunmen. I cannot, however, agree with the author when he says that two pistols were a "necessary part of his [the cowboy's] accoutrement ... he would have felt too light on his feet if not wearing two six-shooters, or out of balance at the hips were he wearing only one." (Page 62.)

LAST RAID

OF THE

DALTONS

A RELIABLE RECITAL OF THE BATTLE
WITH THE BANDITS

...AT...

COFFEYVILLE, KANSAS
OCTOBER 5, 1892

By DAVID STEWART ELLIOTT
Editor Coffeyville Journal

FIRST EDITION
ILLUSTRATED BY E. A. FILLEAU

1892:
COFFEYVILLE JOURNAL PRINT,
COFFEYVILLE, KANSAS.

NUMBER 347

349   Emrich, Duncan

It's an old wild west custom, [by] Duncan Emrich.   New York, the Vanguard press, inc. [1949].   Pict. cloth.   In print.

> xiv p., 1 l., 3–313 p.   illus., cattle brands.   21.3 cm.
> Half title; illus. t.p.; illus. chapter headings.

Has a chapter on bad men, but tells nothing new.

350   Enfield, Dr. J. E.

The man from Packsaddle, by Dr. J. E. Enfield.   Holly-wood, House-Warven, publishers, 1951.   Cloth.   In print.

> 3 p.l., 5–186 p.   23.5 cm.
> Device.

Although this is an autobiography and the author rode the outlaw trail, he does not give the reason for his start as a hunted man. He uses fictitious names for his characters instead of their real names and thus spoils the historical value of the book, although he does save some embarrassment (and perhaps avoids charges of libel).

351   Erskine, Mrs. Gladys (Shaw)

Broncho Charlie; a saga of the saddle, by Gladys Shaw Erskine. The life story of Broncho Charlie Miller, the last of the pony express riders.   New York, Thomas Y. Crowell co., publishers [1934].   Cloth.   OP.

> xiv p., 1 l., 316 p.   plates, ports., maps (1 fold.), facsm.   22.5 cm.
> Half title; map on end papers; vignette.

Contains information on several of the Dodge City gunmen whom Broncho Charlie knew while there.

352   Evans, Clyde (ed.)

Adventures of the great crime-busters, edited by Clyde Evans. New York, New Power publications [1943].   Cloth.   OP.

> 5 p.l., 11–256 p.   21 cm.
> Half title.

A chapter on Jesse James gives an account of the Northfield Bank raid, and one on Billy the Kid is a reprint of part of Chapter XII of Pat Garrett's book. Nothing of value is added to the books on outlaws except to make the list longer.

353 Evans, James W., and A. Wendell Keith

Autobiography of Samuel S. Hildebrand, the renowned Missouri "bushwhacker" and unconquerable Rob Roy of America; being his complete confession recently made to the writers, and carefully compiled by James W. Evans and A. Wendell Keith, M. D., of St. Francois county, Mo., together with all the facts connected with his early history. Jefferson City, Mo., State Times book and job printing house, 1870. Wrappers. Rare.

12 p.l., [25]–312 p. front., illus., plates. 19 cm.

A scarce and reliable account of this notorious outlaw's activities.

354 Fable, Edmund, Jr.

Billy the Kid, the New Mexican outlaw; or, the bold bandit of the west! A true and impartial history of the greatest of American outlaws. His adventures and crimes committed in the west. The history of an outlaw who killed a man for every year of his life . . . . Denver, Colo., published by the Denver publishing co. [1881]. Col. pict. wrappers. Exceedingly rare.

3 p.l., [9]–83 p. plates, ports. 23 cm.
Western border series, No. 1.

A most amazing distortion of facts. Although the author states in the title that it is a "true and impartial" history, there is scarcely a sentence from beginning to end which contains a grain of truth. The foreword is dated July 15, 1881, the day after Billy the Kid was killed. The author must have been a fast writer or had the book written except for the last chapter when the Kid was killed. Most of the proper names are misspelled, and all the facts are wrong. He makes John Chisom [sic] the head of a band of cattle thieves, and his account of the killing of Bell and Ollinger is just the reverse of the truth. He records the innermost thoughts of the Kid and has him coming to the West after he was grown.

His descriptions of the Kid's clothes will bring a smile to anyone who knows the West. "His dress," he writes, "was arranged with a view to attract attention. He wore a blue dragoon jacket of the finest broadcloth, heavily loaded down with gold embroidery, buckskin pants, dyed a jet black, with small tinkling bells sewed down the sides. . . . Underneath this garment were his drawers of fine scarlet broadcloth, extending clear down to the ankle and over his feet, encasing them like stockings. But his hat was the most gorgeous and the crowning feature of his getup. . . . And this whole structure of a hat was covered with gold and jewels until it sparkled and shone in a dazzling and blinding manner when one looked upon it. There was a gold cord around the crown as large as a man's thumb, and a great bright rosette at the left side set it off in all its glory. The *shoes* worn by this young prince of the plains were *low quartered*, with patent silver spurs fixed *in the heels*, which took the place of the common clumsy arrangements that ordinary equestrians use."

The italics are mine, and I would love to have seen anyone atempt to dress in this theatrical fashion in the old West and live to enjoy his glory. This description of Billy the Kid's clothing gives one an idea of the absurdity of the whole book. No wonder Pat Garrett complained bitterly that the several books (of which this is one) preceding his own account were inaccurate.

J. C. Dykes, in his recent bibliography of Billy the Kid, asks doubt-fully, "Was this item ever printed?" I succeeded in locating only one copy, and so far as I know this is the only one extant.

355 Fairfield, Asa Merrill

Fairfield's pioneer history of Lassen county, California; con-taining everything that can be learned about it from the beginning of the world to the year of our Lord, 1870. The chronicles of a border county settled without law, harassed by savages, and in-fested by outlaws . . . , by Asa Merrill Fairfield. San Francisco, published for the author by H. S. Crocker co. ₁1916₁. Pict. cloth. Scarce.

xxii p., 1 l., 3–506 ₁1₁ p. front. (port.), plates, fold. map at end. 22.3 cm.
Half title.

A scarce, privately printed history of early California and some of its lawlessness.

356 Fairfield, Ula King

Pioneer lawyer. A story of the western slope of Colorado, by Ula King Fairfield. ₁Denver, W. H. Kistler stationery co.₁, 1946. Cloth. Scarce.

x p., 1 l., 156 p. front., plates, ports., facsm. 22.2 cm.
Half title; device.
"Only 300 copies printed in private edition."

Some material on bank robbery and feuds.

357 Fanning, Peter

Great crimes of the west. Pete Fanning, author, for thirty-seven years a San Francisco police officer. ₁San Francisco, printed by Ed Barry co., 1929.₁ Cloth. OP.

> 4 p.l., 9–292 p. 19.5 cm.
> Author's port. on t.p.; copyright notice on verso of flyleaf.

The author of this work, for many years a San Francisco peace officer, brought together in this book a number of stories on crime and outlaws. The only chapters which fit our purpose are the one on Black Bart and the one on the Daltons. Neither is accurate; Fanning names the participants in the Coffeyville bank robbery as Bob, Gratt, and Emmett Dalton, Tom Evans, "Texas Jack" Moore, and Ollie Ogee. The last three I had never heard of before.

358 Farber, James

Texans with guns, by James Farber. Illustrations by R. L. McCollister. San Antonio, Texas, the Naylor co. ₁1950₁. Cloth. In print.

> xi p., 1 l., 3–196 p. illus. 21.6 cm.
> Index: p. 191–196.
> Half title; vignette.

Covers most of the Texas gunmen. The author, in his introduction, makes this modest statement: ". . . 'Texans With Guns' makes claim to great accuracy. You may possibly nail me on a date or so, but you'll probably find these stories the most accurate versions ever written." However, before reading many pages, I found that he makes the statement that the John Selman of Fort Griffin was not to be connected with the John Selman who killed John Wesley Hardin in El Paso. As a matter of fact, they were one and the same person. This is just an example of the many other mistakes he makes.

359 ———

Those Texans, by James Farber. Illustrations by John H. McClelland. San Antonio, Texas, the Naylor co. ₁1945₁. Cloth. In print.

> xi p., 1 l., 3–171 p. front., illus., plates. 21 cm.
> Index: p. 167–171.
> Half title.

Has a chapter on gunplay, in which the author gives short sketches of many of the outlaws of the Southwest. He says the Younger brothers were "as dastardly a collection of murdering cutthroats as the American scene has ever beheld," and he claims that Belle Starr got her name by marrying *Jim* Starr.

360   Fast, Howard Melvin

The last frontier, [by] Howard Fast .... New York, Duell, Sloan and Pearce [1942]. Cloth. OP.

> xii p., 1 l., 3–307 p. 22 cm.
> Half title; map and illus. on end papers; "First edition" on copyright p.

Contains a chapter on Dodge City and some of its gunmen.

361   Fenley, Florence

Grandad and I. A story of a grand old man and other pioneers in Texas and the Dakotas, as told by John Leakey to Florence Fenley. Leakey, Texas, John Leakey, publisher, 1951. Cloth. In print.

> 4 p.l., 9–179 p. front., plates, ports. 21.2 cm.
> Last 18 p. plates and ports.

There is a chapter on King Fisher, relating some of his escapades not found in other books.

362   Fergusson, Erna

Murder & mystery in New Mexico, [by] Erna Fergusson. Frontispiece by Peter Hurd. Albuquerque, N. M., Merle Armitage editions [1948]. Cloth. In print.

> 6 p.l., 15–[193] p., 5 l. plates, ports. at end. 23.5 cm.
> Half title; double t.p. in red and black; map on front end papers; headpieces in silhouette; pub. device; "First edition" on copyright p.

A well-written book with chapters on several of the New Mexico outlaws, such as Vicente Silva, Billy the Kid, and Tom Ketchum.

363   ———

Our southwest, by Erna Fergusson; photographs by Ruth Frank and others. New York & London, Alfred A. Knopf, 1940. Cloth. OP.

> 7 p.l., 3–376, vi p., 1 l. front., plates, 2 fold. maps, 1 col. double p. map. 22.5 cm.

Index: p. i–vi.
Half title; map on end papers; pub. device; untrimmed; "First edition" on copyright p.

The author says Billy the Kid was killed by Pat Garrett when he went to Pete Maxwell's to visit his sweetheart. This account is untrue, but the legend has been repeated by many writers.

364 Fergusson, Harvey

Rio Grande, by Harvey Fergusson.   New York, Alfred A. Knopf, 1933.   Cloth.   OP.

x p., 1 l., 3–296, i–viii p. (index), 1 l.   15 p. plates at end.   22.4 cm.
Bibliography: p. 293–296; index: p. i–viii (at end).
Half title; vignette; untrimmed; "First edition" on copyright p.

Quite a lot of material on Elfego Baca, as well as some on Billy the Kid, Joel Fowler, and others. Harvey Fergusson admits that Billy the Kid briefly ruled a region "as large as France because he was faster on the draw than any other man in it," but he has his towns mixed when he says that Ben Thompson likewise dominated *Houston*. He speaks of Wild Bill Hayward as a famous gunman. I wonder if he means Wild Bill Hickok?

365 Finger, Charles Joseph

Adventure under sapphire skies, by Charles J. Finger, with sketches made en route by Helen Finger.   New York, William Morrow & co., 1931.   Cloth.   OP.

viii p., 2 l., 3–293 p.   illus., maps.   18.8 cm.
Index: p. 289–293.
Half title.

Telling of the Lincoln County War and Billy the Kid, the author ends his account by having the Kid killed at Pete Maxwell's house, but he places the house in Fort Stanton instead of Fort Sumner.

366 ———

The distant prize. A book about rovers, rangers and rascals, by Charles J. Finger. Decorations by Henry Pitz.   New York, London, D. Appleton-Century co., inc., 1935.   Cloth.   OP.

ix, 330 p.   21 cm.
Index; p. 325–330.
Half title; illus. end papers; illus. chapter headings; untrimmed; first edition: figure (1) at end of index.

Some mention of many outlaws, such as Billy the Kid, Jesse James, Bob Ford, and Sam Bass. The author repeats that old legend about Murieta's reading the sign offering a reward for him and scribbling under it, adding to the reward.

367 Fisher, Anne B.

The Salinas, upside-down river, by Anne B. Fisher. Illustrated by Walter K. Fisher. New York, Toronto, Farrar & Rinehart, inc. [1945]. Cloth. OP.

> xviii p., 2 l., 5–316 p. illus., map (double p.). 21 cm.
> Bibliography: p. 305–308; note by illustrator: p. 309–310; index: p. 311–316.
> Half title; illus. end papers; pict. t.p.; first edition: "F R" in device on copyright p.

This book contains much information on Murieta and Vásquez.

368 Fisher, O. C.

It occurred in Kimble, by O. C. Fisher; illustrations by Lonnie Rees, cover design by Hal Jones. Houston, Texas, the Anson Jones press, MCMXXXVII. Pict. cloth. OP.

> 13 p.l., [29]–237 [3] p. front., illus., ports. 23.6 cm.
> "Printed sources consulted": p. [239].
> Half title; on cover: "The Story of a Texas County."
> Colophon: "Of this first edition . . . 500 copies have been printed of which this is ____."

Two chapters, "The Big Outlaw Roundup of '77" and "Outlaws and Trigger-pulling," are devoted to the outlaws of this Texas county.

369 Fisher, Walter M.

The Californians, by Walter M. Fisher . . . . London, the Macmillan co., 1876. Cloth. Rare.

> x, 236 p. 19.2 cm.
> Half title; 31 p. adv. at end, numbered [1] to 28 [3].

Contains a chapter on lawlessness, including the activities of Vásquez and Chávez.

370 Fitzpatrick, George (ed.)

This is New Mexico, edited by George Fitzpatrick. Sketches by Wilfred Stedman. Santa Fé, the Rydal press [1948]. Cloth. In print.

x p., 2 l., 3–328 p.   23.5 cm.
Half title; map on end papers; vignette.

A collection of stories from the *New Mexico Magazine*. It contains a story about Billy the Kid, by Eugene Cunningham, and one on Clay Allison, by J. Frank Dobie.

371   Ford, Tirey L.

Dawn and the dons. The romance of Monterey, by Tirey L. Ford. With vignettes and sketches by Jo Mora.   San Francisco, A. M. Robertson, MCMXXVI.   Pict. boards.   OP.

xiii p., 1 l., 236 p.   illus., facsms.   23.5 cm.
Index: p. 233–236.
Map on end papers; headpieces; tailpieces; vignette.

In Chapter XVIII, devoted entirely to Murieta, the author repeats the legend about Murieta's scrawling beneath the reward notice.

372   Forest, Col. Cris

Hildebrand, the outlaw; or, the terror of Missouri, by Col. Cris Forest . . . .   New York, Robert M. DeWitt, publishers . . . , 1869.   Pict wrappers.   Rare.

[9]–100 p.   front.   16 cm.
One p. adv. on verso of t.p.

A ten-cent thriller which has now become scarce.

373   Forrest, Earle Robert

Arizona's dark and bloody ground, by Earle R. Forrest; with introduction by William MacLeod Raine.   Caldwell, Idaho, the Caxton printers, ltd., 1936.   Cloth.   OP.

10 p.l., [21]–370 p.   illus., plates, ports.   19.5 cm.
Notes: p. [310]–339; acknowledgments: p. [340]–341; bibliography: p. [342]–343; principal characters: p. [344]–352; index: p. [353]–370.
Half title; map on end papers; pub. device.

Reprinted in 1948 with additions and changes.

Perhaps the best and most complete history of the Graham-Tewksbury feud, this book reveals intelligent research.

374   ——, and Edwin B. Hill

Lone war trail of Apache Kid, by Earle R. Forrest and Edwin B. Hill. Illustrations by Charles M. Russell. Pasadena, Trail's End publishing co., inc. [1947]. Cloth. In print.

> 12 p.l., 27–143 [1] p. plates (1 col.), ports. 23.6 cm.
> Notes: p. 115–132; bibliography: p. 133–136; index: p. 137–143.
> Half title; legend and map on end papers; pub. device.
> Also published in a de luxe edition of 250 copies, signed and bound in morocco.

A well-written history, and perhaps the most complete work done on this notorious Arizona Indian outlaw.

375 Forsee, Peter A.

Five years of crime in California; or, the life and confession of G. W. Strong, alias G. W. Clark, who was tried, convicted, and hung, August 31st, 1866 at Ukiah City, Mendocino county, California, for the murder of Frances Holmes. A truthful record of this most extraordinary man . . . together with evidence . . . legal proceedings . . . rulings of the courts before whom he was tried . . . . Compiled and arranged by deputy sheriff and one of his prison guards, George Washinton [sic] Thompson. Ukiah City, Mendocino county, California, published by Peter A. Forsee, January 25th, 1867. Wrappers. Rare.

> 46 p. 23.3 cm.

376 Fouts, Burnett W. "Bob"

The gunfight of the age in verse form, by Burnett W. "Bob" Fouts. The story of the famous Earp-Clanton feud which culminated in the historical gunfight at the "O. K." Corral in Tombstone, Arizona, October 26, 1881. [Tombstone], 1946. Stiff pict. wrappers. OP.

> 8 p. 19.7 x 8.2 cm.

377 Fowler, Gene

Timber line; a story of the Bonfils and Tammen, by Gene Fowler. New York, Covici, Friede, publishers, MCMXXXIII. Cloth. OP.

> 8 p.l., 13–480 p. front. (2 ports.). 21.8 cm.
> Half title; t.p. in black and green; facsm. of signature on cover; untrimmed.

This book has been republished several times, but the first printing has become quite scarce. It contains a long chapter on the life of Tom Horn and his execution.

378 Foy, Eddie

Clowning through life, by Eddie Foy and Alvin F. Harlow. Illustrated.   New York, E. P. Dutton & co. [1928].   Cloth.   OP.

4 p.l., 3–331 p.   front., plates, ports.   23 cm.
Half title; device; untrimmed.

The author tells of his experiences in Dodge City, Kansas, and Tombstone, Arizona, as an early-day actor among the gunmen of those wild towns.

379 Frackelton, Will

Sagebrush dentist, as told by Dr. Will Frackelton to Herman Gastrell Seely.   Chicago, A. C. McClurg & co. [1941].   Cloth. OP.

3 p.l., 9–246 p.   22.3 cm.
Half title.

Reprinted with added material (publisher's preface, introduction, and a chapter on Buffalo Bill's divorce suit) in 1947 by Trail's End publishing co., Pasadena.

6 p.l., 13–258 p.   front. (port.).   22 cm.
Half title; pub. device.

The author spins an interesting yarn, and among other things tells of his experiences with Butch Cassidy, Harry Longabough, Tom O'Day, and the rest of the Wild Bunch in their own lair.

380 Franke, Paul

They plowed up hell in old Cochise, by Paul Franke. Douglas, Arizona, Douglas Climate Club, 1950.   Stiff wrappers. In print.

2 p.l., 5–58 [2] p.   front., illus., plates, ports., map.   19.7 cm.
Half title; map on inside of each cover; t.p. on verso table of contents; headpieces.

Much material on the outlaws of Arizona.

381 Franks, J. M.

Seventy years in Texas; memories of the pioneer days, Indian depredations and the northwest cattle trail, by J. M. Franks. Gatesville, Texas, 1924. Wrappers. Scarce.

2 p.l., [5]–133 [1] p. front. (port.). 23.5 cm.

The author says Wild Bill was killed in 1880 instead of 1876. He also tells of the killing of Phil Coe by Wild Bill, and calls him Phil "Cole," a mistake often made by others.

382   Frederick, James Vincent

Ben Holladay, the stagecoach king. A chapter in the development of transcontinental transportation, by J. V. Frederick. . . . Glendale, Calif., the Arthur H. Clark co., 1940. Cloth. OP.

8 p.l., [19]–334 p. front., plates, fold. map, facsm. 24.3 cm.
Appendix: p. 281–303; bibliography: p. [307]–313; index: p. [319]–334.
Half title; pub. device; tissues.

Tells of some of the early stagecoach robberies.

383   Freeman, George D.

Midnight and noonday; or, dark deeds unraveled, giving twenty years experience on the frontier. Also the murder of Pat Hennesey [sic], and the hanging of Tom Smith, at Ryland's Ford, and facts concerning the Talbert raid on Caldwell. Also the death dealing career of McCarty and incidents happening in and around Caldwell, Kansas, from 1871 until 1890, by G. D. Freeman. Caldwell, Kan. [the author], 1890. Boards. Exceedingly rare.

4 p.l., 9–405 p. front. (port.). 20 cm.

Reprinted in 1892 in cloth and with the same text, but in the second printing there is appended on page 406 a certificate signed by seven old-time pioneers attesting to the truth of the narrative. They, in turn, are vouched for by the editor of the *Caldwell News*. The second printing is bound in red cloth, and the first edition is so scarce that some collectors think that the 1892 edition was the only one published. The book contains much material on the gunmen and their gun battles in Caldwell.

384   Freeman, James W. (ed.)

Prose and poetry of the live stock industry of the United States, with outlines of the origin and ancient history of our live stock animals . . . . Illustrated. Prepared by authority of the National Live Stock Association, Denver and Kansas City. [Franklin Hudson publishing co., 1905.] Dec. leather. Vol. I (all that was published). Exceedingly rare.

11 p.l., 25–757 p. illus., plates, ports. 27.8 cm.
Double column; tissues; gilt top.

One of the most important and most sought-after books on the cattle industry. In all my years of book collecting, I have never seen this book listed in a dealer's catalog. When a dealer finds a copy, he always has a waiting list. All copies of this exceedingly rare book, bound in leather, were issued to members of the National Livestock Association, each with the name of the individual member stamped in gold on the cover and a certificate with seal bound in. It is said that the publication of this one volume broke one printing company and almost broke the association. Originally three volumes were planned; but, after the expense of the first volume, the project was abandoned.

The book is said to have been written by Charles F. Martin. The chapter entitled "The Range Rustler" contains material on the Johnson County and Lincoln County wars. The writer calls Billy the Kid an "infamous cutthroat" and says he "died a violent death at the ripe age of twenty-three and at that time had killed twenty-three men—one for each year of his horrible life—having committed his first murder when he was but fourteen years old."

385 Freeman, Lewis Ransome

Down the Yellowstone, by Lewis R. Freeman . . . With illustrations. New York, Dodd, Mead and co., 1922. Cloth. OP.

12 p.l., 282 p. front., plates, ports. 22.6 cm.
Half title; t.p. in red and black; device.

Republished in London by William Heineman, ltd., in 1923.

Contains much new information on Calamity Jane.

386 French, George (ed.)

Indianola scrap book. Fiftieth anniversary of the storm of August 20, 1886. History of a city that once was the gateway of commerce for this entire section. Victoria, Texas, compiled and published by the Victoria Advocate, 1936. Cloth. Scarce.

3–198 p. plates, ports., map, facsm. 23.5 cm.

Contains some material on the Taylor-Sutton feud and the killing of Bill Sutton by Jim Taylor.

387 French, Joseph Lewis (ed.)

A gallery of old rogues, edited by Joseph L. French. New York, Alfred H. King, inc. [1931]. Cloth. OP.

vi p., 2 l., 11–285 p.   23 cm.
Half title.

An anthology concerning outlaws, some from the American West, such as Billy the Kid, Al Jennings, and Joseph Slade. The chapter on Billy the Kid is from Burns' *Saga of Billy the Kid,* and there are two chapters by Al Jennings, both from his *Beating Back.*

388 ———

The pioneer west. Narratives of the westward march of empire. Selected and edited by Joseph Lewis French, with a foreword by Hamlin Garland. Illustrations in color by Remington Schuyler.   Boston, Little, Brown and co., 1923.   Pict. cloth.   OP.

xiv p., 1 l., 386 p.   front. (col.), plates (col.).   21 cm.
Republished in 1924.

An anthology of the West containing, among other subjects, a chapter on Alder Gulch from Nathaniel Langford's *Vigilante Days and Ways,* and one on Joseph Slade from Mark Twain's *Roughing It.*

389 French, William

Some recollections of a western ranchman, New Mexico, 1883–1899, by the Hon. William French.   New York, Frederick A. Stokes co., publishers [1928].   Cloth.   OP.

vi p., 1 l., 283 p.   22.4 cm.
Half title.

One of the really good, but little-known, books on the West, it contains information heretofore unknown about many of the western outlaws, such as the Wild Bunch, Joel Fowler, Black Jack Ketchum.

390 [Fridge, Ike]

History of the Chisum war; or, life of Ike Fridge. Stirring events of cowboy life on the frontier [as told to Jodie D. Smith. Electra, Texas, J. D. Smith, 1927.] Stiff pict. wrappers.   Scarce.

70 [1] p.   front. (port.), illus.   22 cm.

For some years this little book was so scarce that J. Frank Dobie, in the introduction of his *Life and Literature of the Southwest* (1943 edition), said that it was unprocurable. As a book collector, I found my interest aroused by this statement, and after much diligent search, I finally located and bought the small number of remaining copies which had been stored in a country print shop. Since then I have scattered a few copies among other collectors and dealers; and the book has become better known, although it is still considered comparatively rare and the edition is now practically exhausted.

Like most of the old-timers who have written books, Fridge seems to have had a bad memory and little knowledge of his characters before his association with them. He says that Billy the Kid's father died when Billy was sixteen, and that when his mother married again he began to drift. According to his account, the Kid killed his first man when he entered a deserted sheep camp and prepared himself a meal. The Mexican sheepherder came back and began abusing him; then he ran at him with a knife, and Billy shot him.

Fridge relates that once when the outlaw returned home, he found the house surrounded. During his escape Billy was wounded, and, the author says, "the faithful mother made trips to his mountain rendezvous daily and nursed her outlaw son back to health." I have never seen this statement elsewhere.

Fridge states that the Kid fell for a girl who did not return his love but, instead, helped Pat Garrett (whom he calls a United States marshal) to trap him. As he tells the story, Garrett went to Maxwell's house, holed up out of sight, and finally received a signal from the girl that Billy was in her parlor, the room next to Maxwell's. Maxwell left the house, purposely making a lot of noise so that the Kid would think the guest was leaving. Billy had heard them talking, but the girl had convinced him that the voices were those of Maxwell and a friend. The Kid, thinking Maxwell had remained in the room, went in to talk with him.

"As he came through the door," reports Fridge, "Garrett had him covered. Just as soon as the Kid discovered the marshal he went for his guns. But Garrett had only to pull the trigger and the most dangerous outlaw ever on the western Texas and New Mexico ranges was no more." Fridge also says that Garrett asked the government for troops to run down the rest of the gang.

391 Fritz, Percy Stanley

Colorado, the centennial state, by Percy Stanley Fritz . . . . New York, Prentice-Hall, inc., 1941. Cloth. OP.

xii p., 2 l., 3–518 p.   front. (double p. col. map), illus., plates, maps, facsms.,
music.   23.5 cm.
Bibliography after each chapter.
Appendix: p. 493–495; index: p. 497–518.
Half title.

Gives a short history of Alfred Packer.

392   Fuller, George W.

A history of the Pacific northwest, by George W. Fuller ....   New York, Alfred A. Knopf, 1931.   Dec. cloth.   OP.

xvi p., 1 l., [3]–383 [15] p.   front., plates, ports., maps (1 fold.).   24.2 cm.
Notes: p. [341]–383; index: p. [385]–[399].
Half title; pub. device.

Contains the same material on Henry Plummer that is found in the
author's *The Inland Empire of the Pacific Northwest*, published three
years earlier. See Item 393.

393   ———

The inland empire of the Pacific northwest. A history, by
George W. Fuller ....   Spokane, Denver, H. G. Linderman, 1928.
Pub. in three volumes.   Cloth.   OP.

Vol. I, xiii p., 1 l., 240 p.   plates, ports., maps (1 fold.).
Half title.
Vol. II, vii, 258 p.   plates, ports., maps (1 fold.).
Half title.
Vol. III, vii, 259 p.   plates, ports., maps.   23.5 cm.
Index: p. 241–259 (Vol. III).

Volume III contains some new material on the life of Henry Plummer
before he went to Montana Territory.

394   Fuller, Henry Clay

Adventures of Bill Longley. Captured by Sheriff Milton
Mast and Deputy Bill Burrows, near Keatchie, Louisiana, in 1877,
and was executed at Giddings, Texas, 1878, by Henry C. Fuller.
Nacogdoches, Texas [Baker printing co., n.d.].   Stiff pict. wrappers.   OP.

4 p.l., [68] p. (no pagination).   front. (port.).   21.8 cm.
Double column; illus. t.p. on verso of flyleaf; business cards scattered
throughout.

A complete story of the life of one of Texas' most notorious outlaws.

395 ——————

"A Texas sheriff"; a vivid and accurate account of some of the most notorious murder cases and feuds in the history of east Texas, and the officers who relentlessly pursued the criminals till they were brought to justice and paid the full penalty of the law. Also many illustrations of the most prominent characters. by Henry C. Fuller . . . . Nacogdoches, Texas, Baker printing co., 1931. Pict. wrappers. OP.

> 6 p.l., 11–80 p. front., illus., ports. 22 cm.
> Double column.
> "Short biography of A. J. Spradley" (before title page), p. 3–8.

Tells of many Texas murders and has a chapter on the Border-Wall-Broocks feud, one of the well-known feuds of Texas.

396 Fulton, Maurice Garland, and Paul Horgan

New Mexico's own chronicle. Three races in the writings of four hundred years. Adapted and edited by Maurice Garland Fulton and Paul Horgan. Dallas, Banks Upshaw and co. [1937]. Cloth. OP.

> xxviii p., 1 l., 3–155 p., i–xxiv [2], 159–372 p. illus., ports., maps (1 double p.), facsms. 23. cm.
> Notes: p. 351–364; index: p. 367–372.
> Half title; t.p. in brown and black.

Consisting of excerpts from books on New Mexico history, this volume contains some information about outlaws of New Mexico. There are two articles on Billy the Kid, one from R. B. Townshend's *The Tenderfoot in New Mexico,* and an article by J. N. Marchand from *Century Magazine,* entitled "The Old Regime in the Southwest: the Reign of the Revolver in New Mexico." There is also an article on Joel Fowler from William French's *Some Recollections of a Western Ranchman.*

397 Furlong, Thomas

Fifty years a detective, by Thomas Furlong . . . . 35 real detective stories. Hitherto unpublished facts connected with some of Mr. Furlong's greatest cases . . . . Illustrated . . . . St. Louis, C. E. Barnett . . . [1912]. Pict. cloth. OP.

> 2 p.l., 5–352 [2] p. illus., plates, ports. 19.5 cm.
> Copyright notice on flyleaf preceding t.p.; table of contents at end.

Much of this book is about crimes which are not concerned with western outlaws, but there are several chapters on various train robberies in the West.

398 [Gamel, Thomas W.]

Life of Thomas W. Gamel. ₁N. p., n.d. (*ca.*1932).₁ Wrappers. Rare.

> 32 p. 22.5 cm.
> Caption title.

A little-known book containing some material on the Mason County War and on Scott Cooley.

399 Gann, Walter

Tread of the longhorns, by Walter Gann. Illustrations by R. L. McCollister. San Antonio, Texas, the Naylor co. ₁1949₁. Cloth. In print.

> ix, 188 p. 21.5 cm.
> Index: p. 187–188.
> Half title; illus. chapter headings.

Contains a chapter on cattle thieves and range wars, including the Lincoln County and Johnson County wars.

400 Gantt, Paul H.

The case of Alfred Packer, the man-eater, ₁by₁ Paul H. Gantt. ₁Denver₁, University of Denver press ₁1952₁. Cloth. In print.

> 6 p.l., 13–157 p. plates, ports., facsms. 22.2 cm..
> Appendix: p. 115–127; bibliography: p. 128–129; notes and references: p. 130–153; index: p. 154–157.
> Half title; illus. map on end papers; vignette.

The only book that I know of devoted exclusively to this unusual character, this volume is well annotated and reliable.

401 Ganzhorn, Jack

I've killed men, by Jack Ganzhorn. Illustrated. London, Robert Hale, ltd. ₁1940₁. Cloth. OP.

> ix, 11–288 p. front., plates, ports. 22 cm.
> Half title.

An excellent and little-known book which, in my opinion, gives the true account of the Earp-Clanton feud and the O K Corral fight.

402   Gard, Wayne

The fence cutters, ₁by₁ Wayne Gard. Reprinted from the *Southwestern Historical Quarterly*, Vol. LI, No. 1 (July, 1947). Wrappers.   (Cover title.)   OP.

15 p.   24 cm.

A chapter from the author's *Frontier Justice*, read as a paper before the Texas Historical Association, this reprint deals with the lawlessness of wire cutting in the range country.

403   ———

Frontier justice, by Wayne Gard.   Norman, University of Oklahoma press, 1949.   Cloth.   In print.

xi p., 1 l., 3–324 p.   illus., plates, ports., map, facsms.   22 cm.
Bibliography: p. 291–308; index: p. 309–324.
Half title; vignette; "First edition" on copyright p.

This book, apparently the result of scholarly research, deals with western feuds, the vigilantes, and the many outlaws of all sections of the West.

404   ———

Sam Bass, by Wayne Gard. With illustrations.   Boston and New York, Houghton Mifflin co., 1936.   Cloth.   Scarce.

vi p., 2 l., 262 p.   front., plates, ports., facsms.   21.2 cm.
Bibliography: p. ₁249₁–251; index: p. ₁253₁–262.
Map on end papers; pub. device; first edition: 1936 under imprint.

The most complete and reliable work on Sam Bass to date. The author is the only biographer to trace the ancestry of Bass.

405   Gardner, Roy

Hellcatraz, by Roy Gardner . . . . ₁N. p., n. d.₁   Stiff pict. wrappers.   OP.

4 p.l., 9–109 p.   plates, ports.   19.5 cm.

These little books on life at Alcatraz were sold by the author while he was serving as a guide at the Golden Gate Exposition.

406   Gardner, Raymond Hatfield (Arizona Bill)

The old wild west. Adventures of Arizona Bill, by Raymond Hatfield Gardner (Arizona Bill) in collaboration with B. H. Monroe; illustrated by Grady Sowell.   San Antonio, Texas, the Naylor co., 1944.   Cloth.   In print.

> 4 p.l., 315 p.   front. (port.).   21 cm.
> Index: p. 309–315.
> Half title; illus. end papers; illus. chapter headings.

Occasionally an author claims a personal acquaintance with all of the old outlaws, as does Gardner in this book. He says that he often met Wild Bill Hickok in *Tombstone, Arizona!* Although his account was published as late as 1944, he persists in having ten horse thieves in the McCanles party, retains the names "Jack" and "Jim," and places the fight in a dugout. By claiming that Wild Bill *told him all this himself,* he tries to convince the reader that his statements must be true.

According to Gardner, in this fight Wild Bill suffered a fractured skull that caused his scalp to hang over his eyes, a jagged wound which laid open his cheek, three knife wounds in his chest, a knife wound in his left forearm, a bullet in his left hip, and two bullets through his right leg. Yet he did most of his fighting after his skull was fractured. The author even has the much-wounded hero run down a hill to kill the men trying to escape. Every paragraph shows that this account was patterned from earlier ones such as those of Buel and Hough.

In telling of Billy the Kid, Gardner makes just as many errors. He says that when Billy the Kid was a child, he played on the streets of New York with wooden guns, yet it is a known fact that his parents left New York when he was three years old. He attributes some miraculous shooting to the Kid, such as aiming backward over his shoulder while looking in a mirror back of a bar, and hitting his man. Another such feat, which even the author admits is an "almost impossible trick" but accomplished by the Kid, was to shoot with a gun in each hand at two different targets at the same time and hit both of them. And, of course, the Kid could fan a six-shooter so fast that it sounded like a submachine gun.

When Governor Lew Wallace invited the Kid to come to see him, the author, Johnny-on-the-spot for everything, was called in to take part in the conferences. He makes the statement that the cattlemen of Lincoln County hired the Kid to kill sheepmen. Pat Garrett told him personally how he killed the Kid, saying that when the Kid passed the two deputies outside and they didn't answer his challenge, "he darted into the house and *upstairs* in his stocking feet." He has Garrett saying

154

further: "My face was in the shadow when he appeared in the doorway, and he darted over to me with his knife in one hand and his gun in the other. He had his gun within a foot of me when he *laid his hand on my knee* and demanded 'Who are you?'

"He sprang back instantly and fired. But I had fired first and the ball went through his heart."

The author continues with the old fable that Calamity Jane captured Jack McCall with a meat cleaver. He has almost everything wrong, even to the story of Clay Allison's pulling the dentist's teeth. He says that Calamity Jane had a little son who used to accompany his mother on her freighting trips. Further proof of Gardner's inaccuracy is his statement that Calamity Jane helped Wild Bill make his raids against robbers while he was in *Dodge City*, although Wild Bill was never an officer in Dodge.

In the rest of his book he deals with practically every western outlaw, and, of course, he knew them all personally. One could almost point out enough errors in his account to make another book.

407 Garrett, Patrick Floyd

The authentic life of Billy, the Kid, the noted desperado of the southwest, whose deeds of daring and blood made his name a terror in New Mexico, Arizona and northern Mexico, by Pat F. Garrett . . . by whom he was finally hunted down and captured by killing him . . . . Santa Fé, New Mexican printing and publishing co., 1882. Pict. wrappers. Exceedingly rare.

> 3 p.l., [7]-137 p. front. (port.), plates, port. 21 cm.
> Leaf of errata tipped in.
> Page 121 should read 113, and from that page to the end of the book the pagination is wrong.

Because of widespread criticism of his method of killing the Kid, Garrett wanted the world to have his version of the killing, which appears in this book. Although Garrett gave his name to the book, it is said to have been written by his friend Ash Upson, with whom he lived. Upson, a newspaperman who could write with a flourish, gave Garrett the best of the controversy and painted the young outlaw in dark hues; the more he built him up as a super bad man, so much more to the credit of his friend Garrett. Whoever the author, he made the mistake of calling Tom O'Folliard "Tom O. Folliard."

W. A. Keleher, in an article published in Volume IV of the *New Mexico Folklore Record*, gives this interesting information about the book: "It sold in Santa Fé after publication for $1.00, then for 75¢, and

THE

AUTHENTIC LIFE

—OF—

BILLY, THE KID,

THE NOTED DESPERADO OF THE SOUTHWEST, WHOSE DEEDS OF DARING AND
BLOOD MADE HIS NAME A TERROR IN NEW MEXICO,
ARIZONA AND NORTHERN MEXICO.

By PAT. F. GARRETT,

SHERIFF OF LINCOLN CO., N. M.,

BY WHOM HE WAS FINALLY HUNTED DOWN AND CAPTURED BY
KILLING HIM.

A FAITHFUL AND INTERESTING NARRATIVE.

———•◦•———

SANTA FE, NEW MEXICO:
NEW MEXICAN PRINTING AND PUBLISHING CO
1882.

NUMBER 407

finally the New Mexican printing office which printed it, sold the rem-
nant of several dozen volumes to an early day Billy the Kid enthusiast in
Santa Fé for 25¢ the copy. The purchaser trundled the books away in
a wheel-barrow, and they are lost to posterity." The book has now
become one of the rarities of Western Americana.

408 ────

Pat F. Garrett's authentic life of Billy the Kid, edited by
Maurice Garland Fulton. New York, the Macmillan co., 1927.
Cloth. Paper label pasted on; also paper title on back strip. OP.

xxviii p., 2 l., 233 p. front. (col.), plates, ports., map. facsm., plan. 22.2cm.
Half title.

The facsimile of the original title page depicted in this volume is not the
same as that of any of the originals I have ever examined, either in position or in size of type. The illustrations, too, are different. The original
is illustrated by a few drawings; the reprint, by many photographs. This
edition has been well edited, much of the paragraphing being changed;
it has been well annotated by a man who has made a thorough study of
Billy the Kid, and therefore is much more valuable historically than the
original edition. It is strange, however, that no one attempted to reprint
the original text until forty-five years after the book was first issued.

409 ────

Authentic story of Billy the Kid, by Pat F. Garrett, greatest
sheriff of the old southwest. Foreword by John M. Scanland, and
eye witness reports. Edited by J. Brussel. New York, Atomic
books, inc., 1946. Pict. wrappers. OP.

5 p.l., 11–128 p. 18.5 cm.

This is a cheap reprint with a new foreword and occasional editing.
Some new material has been added, including an analysis of Billy the
Kid's handwriting.

410 Garst, Doris Shannon

The story of Wyoming and its constitution and government,
by Doris Shannon Garst. ₁Douglas, Wyo.₁, printed by Douglas
Enterprise ₁1938₁. Cloth. OP.

3 p.l., 179 p. front. (col. flag), ports., map. 19 cm.
Index: p. 173–179.
Questions and references after each chapter.

Like other histories of the state, this book treats the Johnson County War.

411 ⸻

When the west was young, by Shannon Garst. Drawings by F. C. Reed. Douglas, Wyo., Enterprise publishing co., 1942. Cloth. OP.

> 6 p.l., [13]–248 [1] p. front., illus. 23.4 cm.
> Illus. half title; illus. end papers.

Contains a chapter on the Johnson County War.

412 ⸻, with Warren Garst

Wild Bill Hickok, [by] Shannon Garst with Warren Garst. New York, Julian Messner, inc. [1952]. Cloth. In print.

> viii, 183 p. front. 21.8 cm.
> Chronology: p. 178; bibliography: p. 179–180; index: 181–183.
> Half title; headpieces.

The authors have written this book for young readers. They do not follow the old fable of the McCanles fight, but they do make the statement that "Woods was found dead at the rear of the house, and later Gordon's body was found near the creek. For several minutes Bill stared at the corpses in silence. The sight made him ill."

All this I doubt. It would have been some stunt to have gazed at both dead men at once, since Gordon died some distance from the house. The authors also repeat the story about Calamity Jane's rushing into the butchershop where McCall was hiding and dragging him out.

413 Garwood, Darrell

Crossroads of America. The story of Kansas City, [by] Darrell Garwood. New York, W. W. Norton & co., inc. [1948]. Cloth. In print.

> 6 p.l., 13–331 p., 1 l. plates, ports. 21.7 cm.
> Sources and acknowledgments: p. 323–326; index: p. 327–331.
> Half title; map on end papers; pub. device; "First edition" on copyright p.

Contains a chapter on Jesse James and information on the Youngers and the Northfield Bank robbery. The author of this book is another who has Quantrill's given name as "Charley."

414   Gay, Beatrice Grady

"Into the setting sun." A history of Coleman county, by Beatrice Grady Gay. Drawings by Mollie Grady Kelley . . . . ₁N. p., n. d.₁   Pict. cloth.   Scarce.

> x, 193 p.   front., illus., plates, ports., maps.   20.4 cm.

In one chapter an old-timer tells of his experiences as a Ranger and sheriff, his capture of John Wesley Hardin, his part in capturing Sam Bass near Round Rock after Bass had been shot, and his part in capturing lesser-known outlaws.

415   George, Andrew L.

A Texas prisoner, by Andrew L. George. Sketches of the penitentiary, convict farms and railroads, together with poems and illustrations.   ₁Charlotte, N. C.₁, 1895.   Pamphlet.   Scarce.

> 32 p.   illus., plates.   17 cm.

The author was in prison with John Wesley Hardin but only mentions him.

416   Gibbons, Rev. James Joseph

In the San Juan Colorado. Sketches, by Rev. J. J. Gibbons. ₁Chicago, Calumet book & engraving co., 1898.₁   Cloth.   Scarce.

> 3 p.l., 7–194 p.   plates.   18.2 cm.

Tells of the bank robbery at Telluride.

417   Gillett, James B.

Six years with the Texas rangers, 1875 to 1881, by James B. Gillett . . . .   Austin, Texas, von Boeckmann-Jones co., publishers ₁1921₁.   Cloth.   Scarce.

> 5 p.l., 11–332 ₁1₁ p.   front., ports.   19.2 cm.
> Device; frontis tissue.

One of the better Texas Ranger books, this book deals with many of the Texas outlaws and early feuds. Published in a small edition by the author and sold personally by him; republished by Yale University Press in 1925, edited by Milo M. Quaife. This edition, in turn, was republished by the Lakeside Press, Chicago, in 1943. Also published under the title *The Texas Ranger*, in collaboration with Howard Driggs, by the World Book company, Yonkers-on-Hudson, N. Y., 1927.

418   Gish, Anthony

American bandits. A biographical history of the nation's outlaws—from the days of the James boys, the Youngers, the Jennings, the Dalton gang and Billy the Kid, down to modern bandits of our own day, including Dillinger, "Pretty Boy" Floyd, and others, by Anthony Gish.   Girard, Kan., Haldeman-Julius publications [1938].   Stiff wrappers.   OP.

> 2 p.l., [5]–101 [11] p.   21.5 cm.
> 11 p. adv. at end.

A cheap rehash of many stories about western outlaws, as well as some about modern city gangsters.

419   Glasscock, Carl Burgess

Bandits and the Southern Pacific, by C. B. Glasscock. New York, Frederick A. Stokes co., MCMXXIX.   Cloth.   OP.

> 5 p.l., 294 p.   front., ports.   19.8 cm.
> Pub. device; untrimmed; illus. end papers.

This book is mostly about the train robbers of California. In a chapter on the Daltons, the author discusses their raid on the banks at Coffeyville, Kansas. Although he devotes only a few pages to this final exploit of the Dalton gang, he gets many details wrong. He has two members of the ill-fated gang named "Tom Heddy" and "Allie Agers." The real names of the two members of the gang he has in mind were Dick Broadwell and Bill Powers. His information on Chris Evans and the Sontags is more accurate.

420   ———

Gold in them hills. The story of the west's last wild mining days, by C. B. Glasscock . . . . Illustrated.   Indianapolis, the Bobbs-Merrill co., publishers [1932].   Cloth.   OP.

> xiii p., 1 l., 17–330 p.   front. (port.), plates, ports.   22.5 cm.
> Index: p. 325–330.
> Half title; map on end papers; untrimmed; "First edition" on copyright p.

Contains some new information on Wyatt Earp. It is said that the mention of Earp's name in Tonopah made claim jumpers move on to other claims.

421 ———

A golden highway. Scenes of history's greatest gold rush yesterday and today, by C. B. Glasscock . . . . Illustrated. Indianapolis, the Bobbs-Merrill co., publishers [1934]. Cloth. OP.

8 p.l., 13–333 p. front., plates, ports. 22.5 cm.
Bibliography: p. 317–321; index: p. 325–333.
Half title; map on end papers; untrimmed; "First edition" on copyright p.

Contains some material on Black Bart and Murieta. The author tells a story about Murieta which he says he has never read in any other book. "It seems," he writes, "that when the bullets began to fly too frequently in Joaquín's direction a Frenchman sought out the bandit and offered to have a shirt of chain mail made for him, for one thousand dollars in gold. When the armor arrived from France, Murrietta [sic] ordered the Frenchman to put it on. Then he stood at a distance and emptied his revolver into the armor, while the salesman fainted with fright. When the victim was revived and found unwounded, however, Joaquín promptly paid over the one thousand dollars in gold."

422 ———

Then came oil. The story of the last frontier, by C. B. Glasscock. Indianapolis, New York, the Bobbs-Merrill co., publishers [1938]. Cloth. OP.

6 p.l., 11–349 p. front., plates, ports. 22.3 cm.
Bibliography: p. 327–329; index: p. 333–349.
Half title; map on end papers; "First edition" on copyright p.

This book has several chapters on Oklahoma outlaws, but it tells nothing new. There is a rehash of Belle Starr's life and well-known facts about Cherokee Bill and the Daltons are repeated.

423 ———

The war of the copper kings; builders of Butte and wolves of Wall Street, by C. B. Glasscock . . . . Indianapolis, and New York, the Bobbs-Merrill co., publishers [1935]. Cloth. OP.

ix p., 3 l., 17–314 p. front., plates, ports. 22.3 cm.
Half title; untrimmed; "First edition" on copyright p.

The second chapter deals with the Montana vigilantes and the Plummer gang of road agents.

424 Gollomb, Joseph

Master highwaymen, [by] Joseph Gollomb. New York, the Macaulay co. [1927]. Cloth. OP.

5 p.l., 11–312 [1] p. 22.5 cm.
Half title; untrimmed.

Contains a long chapter on the life of Joaquín Murieta. Founded upon the *Police Gazette* version, it adds many preposterous situations, such as Murieta's being bodyguard of Santa Anna, though Murieta could have been but a boy in his teens at the time. The author also portrays Murieta with a passion for reading the classics.

425 Good, Milton

Twelve years in a Texas prison, by Milt Good, as told to W. E. Lockhart. (Illustrations drawn by Isabel Robinson.) Amarillo, Texas, printed by Russell stationery co., 1935. Stiff pict. wrappers. Scarce.

4 p.l., 7–88 p. front. (port.), illus., ports. 24 cm.

The story of a somewhat well-known cattle rustler of recent years.

426 Gordon, S.

Recollections of old Milestown, by S. Gordon. Miles City, Mont. [Independent printing co.], 1918. Thin cloth. Scarce.

2 p.l., 3–42 [3] p. front., plates, ports. 23.2 cm.

A scarce book containing material on vigilante action in Miles City.

427 Gordon, Welche

Jesse James and his band of notorious outlaws, by Welche Gordon. Chicago, Laird & Lee, publishers, 1890. Col. pict. wrappers. Rare.

2 p.l., [7]–238 p. front., illus., plates, ports. 18.8 cm.
2 l. adv. at end.

A scarce book on these outlaws, but, like many others, not too reliable. The author misspells Quantrill's name and calls Dick Liddill, Dick "Little."

162

428 Graves, Richard S.

Oklahoma outlaws. A graphic history of the early days in Oklahoma; the bandits who terrorized the first settlers and the marshals who fought them to extinction; covering a period of twenty-five years, by Richard S. Graves .... ₁Oklahoma City, State printing and publishing co., 1915.₁ Pict. wrappers. Scarce.

3 p.l., ₁3₁–131 p. front., ports. 17.5 cm.

Touches upon most of the better-known Oklahoma outlaws and marshals. The serious student or researcher may wish to make a detailed comparison of this book with Zoe A. Tilghman's *Outlaw Days* (1926), Item 995. Further comparison of the two with J. A. Newsom's *The Life and Practice of the Wild and Modern Indian* (1923), Item 725, may prove rewarding.

429 Gray, Arthur Amos

Men who built the west, by Arthur Amos Gray. Illustrated by photographs. Caldwell, Idaho, the Caxton printers, ltd., 1945. Pict. cloth. OP.

7 p.l., ₁15₁–220 p. front., plates, ports., maps, facsms. 23.5 cm.
Index: p. ₁217₁–220.
Half title; pub. device.

This book devotes a chapter to stagecoach robbery and such road agents as Black Bart and Henry Plummer and his gang, and tells of the criminal activities of Joseph Slade.

430 Gray, Farmer

The bandit judge, by Farmer Gray. Lansing, Mich., Readers Union publishing co., 1892. Wrappers. Scarce.

₁5₁–122 p. 18.5 cm.

431 Great American Parade

Garden City, N. Y., Doubleday, Doran & co., inc., 1935. Cloth. OP.

xiv p., 1 l., 611 p. 21 cm.
Half title.

An anthology containing a chapter on Billy the Kid taken from Walter Noble Burns' *The Saga of Billy the Kid.*

432 Greer, James Kimmins

Bois d'arc to barb'd wire; Ken Carey: Southwestern frontier born, by James K. Greer.   Dallas, Texas, Dealey and Lowe, 1936. Pict. cloth.   OP.

7 p.l., 428 p.   plates, maps.   22.5 cm.
Bibliographical notes: p. [411]–423; index: p. [425]–428.
Illus. double t.p.; map on end papers (dif.).

433 ———

Grand prairie, by James K. Greer.   Dallas, Texas, Tardy publishing co. [1935].   Cloth.   Scarce.

4 p.l., 284 p.   plates, maps.   19.7 cm.
Notes: p. 235–264; index: p. 265–284.

For some reason this book has become exceedingly scarce, although it was published comparatively recently. It contains a great deal of information on various outlaws of Texas. On page 169, however, the author erroneously states that John Selman killed John Wesley Hardin in 1865. This incident actually occurred in 1895, thirty years later.

434 Grey, F. W.

Seeking a fortune in America, by F. W. Grey. With a frontispiece.   London, Smith, Elder & co. . . . ,1912.   Cloth.   Scarce.

xiv, 307 p.   front. (port.).   20.8 cm.
Half title; frontis tissue; 2 l. adv. at end.

This English author erroneously states that Billy the Kid was a half-breed Indian. He also says that when Pat Garrett discovered the house of the Kid's Mexican sweetheart, "after tying and gagging her," he lay in wait there for the Kid. When the outlaw appeared, Garrett shot him from behind a sofa. He claims that he got his story from Kip McKinney, with whom he worked on a mining venture; but if McKinney told him this story, he was only "jobbing" him. He also gives some minor information about Luke Short and an untrue account of the killing of Ben Thompson.

435 Griggs, George

History of Mesilla valley, or the Gadsden purchase, known in Mexico as the Treaty of Mesilla . . . , by George Griggs . . . .
[Las Cruces, N. M., Bronson printing co.], 1930.   Stiff wrappers. Scarce.

7 p.l., [3]-128 p.   illus., maps.   22.6 cm.
Index: p. 125-128.
Map on t.p.; double column.

This book is a local history containing some information on Billy the Kid and Pat Garrett. The author credits Billy the Kid with killing twenty-seven men. His account differs from most others in stating that the Kid's first victim was a miner who had run off with the Kid's fifteen-year-old sister. Like the authors of several other accounts, he states that the Kid killed Chisum's riders to get even with Chisum. He also says that Garrett killed the Kid with a rifle and that the Kid was twenty-six years old when he died. He tells that Billy's father, Frank Bonney, was killed by the Apaches in Arizona. He is mistaken also about the circumstances of the killing of Bell and in stating that Billy killed Ollinger with a Winchester instead of a shotgun.

436   Guernsey, Charles Arthur

Wyoming cowboy days. An account of the experience of Charles Arthur Guernsey, in which he tells in his own way of the early territorial cattle days and political strifes, and deals with many of the state's and nation's famous characters . . . . True to life, but not autobiographical. Romantic, but not fiction. Facts, but not history. Profusely illustrated. New York, G. P. Putnam's sons, 1936. Cloth.   OP.

x p.l., 1 l., 13-288 p.   front., plates, ports., facsms.   24.3 cm.

Contains some material on the Johnson County War.

437   Guinn, J. M.

History of the state of California and biographical record of the Sacramento valley, California. An historical story of the state's marvelous growth from its earliest settlement to the present time, by J. M. Guinn . . . .   Chicago, the Chapman publishing co., 1906. Leather.   Scarce.

12 p.l., [33]1712 p.   ports.   29.7 cm.
Double column; gilt edges.

In a chapter on crime and criminals, the author gives accounts of Murieta and Vásquez.

438   ———

History of the state of California and biographical record

of San Joaquin county, containing biographies of well-known citizens of the past and present. State history by J. M. Guinn .... History of San Joaquin county by George H. Tinkham. Illustrated. Los Angeles, Calif., Historic Record co., 1909. Pub. in two volumes. Three-quarter leather. Scarce.

> Vol. I, 9 p.l., [33]–303 p. 1 port. (with tissue). 29.4 cm.
> Double column; gilt edges.

In a chapter on crime and criminals the author's account of Murieta and Vásquez is virtually the same as that in his other books.

439 ———

Historical and biographical record of southern California, containing a history of southern California from its earliest settlement to the opening year of the twentieth century, by J. M. Guinn .... Chicago, Chapman publishing co., 1902. Leather. Scarce.

> 11 p.l., [33]–1019 p. plates, ports. 28.8 cm.
> Gilt edges.

Some material on the Flores and Vásquez gangs, the Solomon Pico gang, and Jack Powers.

440 ———

A history of California, and an extended history of its southern coast counties; also containing biographies of well-known citizens of the past and present, by J. M. Guinn. Illustrated. Complete in two volumes. Los Angeles, Historic Record co., 1907. Three-quarter leather. Scarce.

> Vol. I, 19 p.l., [33]–1074 p. front. (port. with tissue), ports. (part with tissues). 29.5 cm.
> Index: p. [i]–ix (in front).
> Double column; gilt edges.

In Chapter XXVII, entitled "Crime, Criminals and Vigilance Committees," the author tells of the hanging of Jenkins and the careers of Murieta and Vásquez.

441 Guyer, James S.

Pioneer life in west Texas . . . , by James S. Guyer . . . . Brownwood, Texas . . . , 1938. Pict. cloth. Scarce.

> xi p., 1 l., 3–185 [2] p. illus., plates, ports. 23.4 cm.
> Port. of author on t.p.

The author's chapter on Billy the Kid is full of inaccurate statements. He says Pat Garrett and two deputies "waited in ambush at the Maxwell home waiting for Billy the Kid to meet his sweetheart. About ten o'clock . . . Billy walked slowly into the Maxwell yard, on to the porch, and stepping lightly down the hallway called softly, 'Lucia! Lucia!' Bang! A flash from a small table in the hall, snuffed out the life of William B. Bonney."

442 Hafen, LeRoy R., and Carl Coke Rister

Western America. The exploration, settlement, and development of the region beyond the Mississippi, by LeRoy R. Hafen . . . and Carl Coke Rister . . . .   New York, Prentice-Hall, inc., 1941. Cloth. OP.

xxiv p., 1 l., 698 p. front. (col. map), illus., maps (2 col., incl. front.), facsm. 23.5 cm.
Bibliography after each chapter; index: p. 669–698.
Half title.

Deals with the vigilantes and outlaws over the entire West.

443 Haley, J. Evetts

Charles Goodnight, cowman & plainsman; with illustrations by Harold Bugbee, [by] J. Evetts Haley. Boston, New York, Houghton Mifflin co., 1936. Cloth. OP.

xiii p., 1 l., 485 p. front. (signature in facsm.), illus., double p. map, facsm. 22 cm.
"A note on bibliography": p. [469]–472; index: p. [475]–485.
Half title; vignette; first edition: 1936 under imprint.

Republished by University of Oklahoma Press in 1949 with some changes.

A distinguished biography of an outstanding cattleman, it contains references, scattered but reliable, to certain outlaws of the Southwest.

444 ———

Jim East, trail hand and cowboy, [by] J. Evetts Haley. [Canyon, Texas], 1931. Wrappers. (Cover title.) Scarce.

[23] p. (no pagination). 23.3 cm.

A reprint from the *Panhandle-Plains Historical Review* for 1931, containing some material on Billy the Kid.

445 ———

George W. Littlefield, Texan, by J. Evetts Haley. Drawings by Harold D. Bugbee. Norman, University of Oklahoma press, MCMXLIII. Cloth. In print.

> xiv p., 1 l., 3–287 p. front., illus., ports. 22 cm.
> Index: p. 283–287.
> Half title; vignette; "First edition" on copyright p.

Another good biography of a well-known Texas cattleman with information on various outlaws and on Billy the Kid's visit to the Texas Panhandle.

446 ——

Jeff Milton, a good man with a gun, by J. Evetts Haley, with drawings by Harold D. Bugbee. Norman, University of Oklahoma press, 1948. Cloth. In print.

> xiii p., 1 l., 3–430 p. illus., plates, ports., map. 23.8 cm.
> Index: p. 417–430.
> Illus. t.p.; "First edition" on copyright p.

An excellent biography of one of the famous law-enforcement officers of the Southwest, detailing his activities among its outlaws. As an officer his life was filled with contacts with many outlaws and gunmen, such as John Wesley Hardin, Black Jack Ketchum, John Selman, George Scarborough, Burt Alvord, and Billy Stiles.

447 Hall, Frank

History of the state of Colorado, embracing accounts of the prehistoric races and their remains; the earliest Spanish, French, and American explorations . . . the first American settlements founded; the Rocky Mountains, the development of cities and towns, with the various phases of industrial and political transition from 1858 to 1890 . . . , by Frank Hall, for the Rocky Mountain Historical co. Chicago, the Blakely printing co., 1889–95. Pub. in four volumes. Dec. leather. Scarce.

> Vol. I, xvi p., 1 l., 17–564 p. front. (port.), plates, ports.
> Index: p. 554–564.
> Vol. II (pub. in 1890), xiv p., 1 l., 17–574 p. front. (port.), ports., maps.
> 26.8 cm.

Volume I contains some material on Espinos and Musgrove, Colorado outlaws, and Volume II has more information on Espinos. The author also gives a lengthy account of Billy the Kid, most of it inaccurate. He continues to uphold the legend about the Kid's killing Chisum's cowboys and crediting his account at fifty dollars per head. He says that the Kid went to Maxwell's place to see his sweetheart and that Garrett followed him with a posse. Garrett, according to Hall, entered Maxwell's room through a window, and when the Kid rushed in *with a rifle*, Garret cut him down, ending the Kid's life at the age of *twenty-six*.

448 [Hall, Frank O. and Lindsey H. Whitten]

Jesse James rides again ₁by Frank O. Hall and Lindsey H. Whitten₁. Lawton, Okla., published by LaHoma publishing co. ₁1948₁. Pict. wrappers. OP.

> 3 p.l., 7–48 p. front., plates, ports. 27.8 cm.
> Double column.

A story of J. Frank Dalton, who claimed he was Jesse James, written by two reporters on the *Lawton Constitution* from interviews with this aged character. The authors try to be convincing with the proof of their assertions, but I still do not believe that Dalton was Jesse James.

449 Hamilton, Thomas Marion

The young pioneer. When Captain Tom was a boy. Thrilling tales of a real boy's frontier adventures among Indians, pioneers, scouts, cowboys and bandits, by Thomas Marion Hamilton. Washington, D. C., the Library press ₁1932₁. Cloth. OP.

> 6 p.l., ₁15₁–284 p. 1 plate. 20 cm.
> Half title; vignette.

Unless this was intended to be a collection of tall tales, I feel safe in saying that it is the most ridiculous book ever written. The author says that Billy the Kid was captured by Pat Garrett in *Tombstone, Arizona*, and jailed there. The Kid's sweetheart then came to Tombstone and secured a job as cook in a hotel across the street from the jail, and proceeded to put sleeping drugs in food sent the jail guards, so that Billy could escape.

Albert J. Fountain and his little son were murdered in the White Sands of New Mexico on January 31, 1896, and neither the killers nor the victims were ever found. In spite of the fact that Billy the Kid was killed in 1881, this author states that the Kid warned Fountain of his impending murder as Fountain started his journey. The records show that at this time Billy the Kid had been officially dead for fifteen years; yet Mr. Hamilton says that he followed Fountain and saw him murdered by the Tate gang—whoever they were. According to his account, Billy caught up with this gang, gave them a lecture on their dastardly deed, and, as time passed, killed them one by one. Billy the Kid *told the author all this personally*.

The account of the Kid's killing by Pat Garrett is also preposterous. The Kid's sweetheart had persuaded him to give himself up on the basis of a promise made her by Garrett; but when the Kid arrived at her home, Garrett shot him *with a rifle* while hiding in a peach orchard. The author not only disregards facts, but seems indifferent to getting proper names correct. He spells O'Folliard's name as "O'Foulard," Bowdre's as "Bowder," and says Pat Garrett was killed by Wayne *Bonzell*.

450   Hammond, Isaac B.

Reminiscences of frontier life. Compliments of I. B. Hammond.   Portland, Ore., 1904.   Wrappers.   Rare.

> 4 p.l., [9]–134 [1] p.   illus., port.   21 cm.

Privately printed for friends. While the book was in the press, the author died, and almost the entire edition of the work was then scrapped, only a few copies escaping; hence its rarity. It contains material on some outlaws of the frontier and tells about hangings by the vigilantes and about the last of the Laramie road agents.

451   Hammond, John Hays

The autobiography of John Hays Hammond. Illustrated with photographs.   New York, Farrar & Rinehart, inc. [1935]. Pub. in two volumes (boxed).   Cloth.   OP.

> Vol. I, xiii p., 1 l., 3–383 p.   front. (port.), plates, ports., map.   23.2 cm.
> Half title.
> Vol. II, 4 p.l., 387–813 p.   front., plates, ports.   23.2 cm.
> Bibliography: p. 779–782; index: p. 785–813.
> Half title; paged continuously.

Mr. Hammond was in Tombstone, Arizona, in 1879, and in Volume I he tells of Wyatt Earp, for whom he has nothing but praise. Later the author met Earp again, in Tonopah, where he was consulting engineer, and hired Earp to take care of claim jumpers.

452   Hardin, John Wesley

The life of John Wesley Hardin, from the original manuscript as written by himself.   Seguin, Texas, published by Smith & Moore, 1896.   Wrappers.   OP.

2 p.l., [5]–144 p.   front. (port.), illus., ports.   18.8 cm.

Republished by Frontier Times of Bandera, Texas, in 1926.

The first few copies of the original edition released by the printers have the portrait of Joe Hardin, John's brother, for the frontispiece instead of one of John Wesley Hardin. The book is carefully written; in fact, so well written that it seems to have come from the pen of someone not so illiterate as Hardin. It was probably ghost written, but whoever the writer, he was careful of his names and dates. He tells of his life up to his death, and his death is discussed in an appendix, with a quotation from the *El Paso Herald* of August 20, 1895.

453   Hardy, Allison

Kate Bender, the Kansas murderess. The horrible history of an arch killer, [by] Allison Hardy.   Girard, Kan., Haldeman-Julius publications, 1944.   Wrappers.   OP.

[2]–24 p.   21.4 cm.

A history of the Bender family concluding with various theories and hearsay about their end, but no details of their death have ever been verified.

454   ———

Wild Bill Hickok, king of the gun-fighters, by Allison Hardy. Girard, Kan., Haldeman-Julius publications [1943]. Wrappers.   OP.

1 p.l., [3]–23 p.   21.3 cm.

This is a small book on a large subject, but it is fairly accurate. The author debunks some of the earlier accounts, such as those of Buel and Hough.

455   Harkey, Dee

Mean as hell, by Dee Harkey. Line drawings by Gene Roberts.   [Albuquerque, N. M.], the University of New Mexico press, 1948.   Cloth.   In print.

xvi, 223 [1] p.   illus., plates, ports.   20.2 cm.
Index: p. 219–223.
Half title; illus. t.p.; map on end papers.

A most interesting account of lawlessness in New Mexico. Its frank statements brought threats of lawsuits at its release, causing the publishers to request dealers to use India ink to blot out the word "outlaw" after one of the names in the index. In the second printing this word was omitted. The author had personal experience with many of the outlaws as a peace officer, and he records some facts not found elsewhere.

456 Harlow, Alvin F.

Old waybills, the romance of the express companies, by Alvin F. Harlow. New York, London, D. Appleton-Century co., inc., 1934. Cloth. OP.

> xii p., 1 l., 503 [1] p. front., illus., plates, ports., facsms. 22.5 cm.
> Bibliography: p. 489-[497]; index: p. 499-[504].
> Half title; pub. device; untrimmed; first edition: figure (1) at end of index.
>
> Republished in 1937.

About half of the book deals with train and stagecoach robberies, with information on the Jameses and Youngers, Sam Bass, Black Bart, Evans, Sontag, and others.

457 Harlow, Victor Emmanuel

The most picturesque personality in Oklahoma, Al Jennings, by Victor E. Harlow. Oklahoma City, Harlow publishing co., 1912. Wrappers. Rare.

> 12 p. port. 20.5 cm.

A short sketch of Al Jennings and his activities, which has become very rare.

458 Harman, S. W.

Hell on the border; he hanged eighty-eight men. A history of the great United States criminal court at Fort Smith, Arkansas, and of crime and criminals in the Indian territory, and the trial and punishment thereof before . . . Judge Isaac C. Parker . . . and by the courts of said territory, embracing the leading sentences and charges to grand and petit juries delivered by the world famous jurists—his acknowledged masterpieces, besides much other legal lore . . . . Illustrated with over fifty fine half-tones. By S. W. Harman, compiled by C. P. Sterns. Fort Smith, Ark., the Phoenix publishing co. [1898]. Stiff green wrappers. Exceedingly rare.

> xiii, 720 p. front., illus., plates, ports., map, tables. 21.8 cm.

Later published in an abridged edition:

ix, [1]-9, 10-320 p.   plates, ports.   19.5 cm.

Published again as late as 1953 with some changes:

xiii, 303 p.   plates, ports.   19.7 cm.

The rare original edition has become a collector's item and is the chief source for practically every book and feature story on the old court and Oklahoma outlaws. It is said to have originated from an idea of J. Warren Reed, the criminal lawyer who was such a thorn in the side of Judge Parker.

Although Reed's name does not appear on the imprint, the book was originally his idea, and he financed its publication. He had Samuel W. Harman, a professional juryman, to write it, and it appeared under Harman's name. The book was printed in a first edition of only one thousand copies; and, though statistical and dry, the first edition was soon exhausted on account of the reputation of Judge Parker's court.

A second edition was issued by the print shop of Kendall College, but it was abridged and had four hundred fewer pages, some of the dull part of the first edition being left out. It, too, has become very scarce. Most of the transcripts from court records and biographical sketches in the original edition are said to have been compiled by C. P. Sterns. It contains much material on the outlaws of the Indian Territory who were tried and condemned in this famous court, but some of the material not dealing directly with the court is unreliable.

459   Harrington, Fred Harvey

Hanging judge, by Fred Harvey Harrington. Illustrations from photographs.   Caldwell, Idaho, the Caxton printers, ltd., 1951. Cloth.   In print.

8 p.l., 17-204 p.   front., plates, ports., facsm.   23.6 cm.
Index: p. 200-204.
Half title; map on end papers; headpieces; pub. device; vignette.

Any book about Judge Parker is of necessity full of material about outlaws. This one contains chapters on the Daltons, Belle Starr, and many other Oklahoma outlaws.

460   Harris, Frank

My reminiscences as a cowboy, [by] Frank Harris; illustrations by William Gropper. New York, Charles Boni . . . , 1930. Stiff pict. wrappers.   OP.

7 p.l., 15–217 [2] p. plates. 18.6 cm.
Half title; illus. end papers; vignette.

A London edition was published by John Lane with slight changes in the text and the omission of the last chapter. It was retitled *On the Trail; My Reminiscences as a Cowboy*. Harris's book is full of inaccuracies and is mostly wild imagination. It is included in this work because of his preposterous account of Wild Bill Hickok. He says Hickok was elected marshal of Wichita or Dodge ("he forgot which," and both are wrong) and killed a well-liked railroad man. The deceased's friends ran him out of town. The author claims to have been an intimate friend of Hickok, and says he was brought up in Missouri. He tells of Hickok's first killing over a watch, and I think the author is confused about the story of the Dave Tutt incident. He claims he was with Hickok at Taos, New Mexico, where they were buying cattle and raiding cattle in Mexico, and he tells of their riding the Chisholm Trail together. Hickok never had any interest in cattle, nor is there any record of his ever being in Taos. Altogether, this is a most ridiculous account.

461   Harris, Edward

Outlaws of the Black Hills of Dakota and Wyoming, by Edward Harris. London, 1890. Exceedingly rare.

I have never seen a copy of this book, although I have searched diligently for it over a period of years.

462   Harrison, Benjamin S.

Fortune favors the brave. The life and times of Horace Bell, pioneer Californian, by Benjamin S. Harrison. Los Angeles, the Ward Ritchie press, 1953. Cloth. In print.

xvi p., 1 l., 3–307 p. plates, ports., facsms. 24 cm.
Notes and sources: p. 279–290; bibliography: p. 291–294; index: p. 295–307.
Half title.

A well written story of the life of Major Bell as an early-day Californian, it contains some material on Joaquín Murieta.

463   Hart, William Surrey

My life east and west, by William S. Hart. With illustrations. Boston and New York, Houghton Mifflin co., 1929. Cloth. OP.

vii [1] p., 1 l., 3–[363] p. front. (col.), plates, ports. 22 cm.
Index: p. 355–[363].
Half title; pub. device; first edition: 1929 under imprint.

Contains some information on Wild Bill Hickok, Bat Masterson, and Wyatt Earp.

464 Hawes, Harry B.

Frank and Jesse James in review for the Missouri society. Address by Harry B. Hawes. Washington, D. C., February 25, 1939. Pamphlet. (Cover title.) Scarce.

28 [1] p. 23 cm.

This pamphlet gives some of the high lights of the James brothers' career.

465 Hawkeye, Harry (pseud.)

Tracy, the outlaw, king of bandits. A narrative of the thrilling adventures of the most daring and resourceful bandit ever recorded in the criminal annals of the world, by Harry Hawkeye. Illustrated. Baltimore, I. & M. Ottenheimer, publisher, 1908. Pict. wrappers. OP.

2 p.l., [9]–184 p. front., illus. 18.5 cm.
4 l. adv. at end.

One of the cheap and unreliable paper-backed books on outlaws common forty years ago.

466 Hawley, James H. (ed.)

History of Idaho, the gem of the mountains. James H. Hawley, editor. Illustrated. Chicago, the S. J. Clarke publishing co., 1920. Pub. in three volumes. Cloth. OP.

Vol. I, 8 p.l., 19–895 p. front. (port.), plates, ports. 28.5 cm.
Vols. II and III are biographical.

Has a chapter on lawlessness and the professional "bad man" and contains material on the vigilantes.

467 Haydon, Arthur Lincoln

The riders of the plains. Adventures and romance with the north-west mounted police, 1873-1910, by A. L. Haydon. Illus-

trated with photographs, maps and diagrams.   Chicago, A. C. Mc-
Clurg & co.; London, Andrew Melrose, 1910.   Cloth.   OP.

> xvi, 385 p.   front. (port.), plates, ports., maps (1 fold.), diagrs. (1 fold.).
> 23.3 cm.
> Appendix: p. 355-[380]; index: p. 381-385.
> Half title; pub. device; t.p. in red and black; frontis tissue.

Embodies some material on Soapy Smith, his life and death in the Yukon.

468   Hayes, Augustus Allen, Jr.

New Colorado and the Santa Fe trail, by A. A. Hayes, Jr.
. . . . Illustrated.   New York, Harper and brothers, 1880.   Dec.
cloth.   Scarce.

> 7 p.l., [17]-200 p.   front. (map), illus.   23.2 cm.

This collection of articles reprinted from *Harper's Magazine* and the
International Review contains some material on road agents and stagecoach robberies.

469   Hebard, Grace Raymond

The pathbreakers from river to ocean. The story of the great
west from the time of Coronado to the present, [by] Grace Raymond
Hebard . . . . Four maps and numerous illustrations.   Chicago, the
Lakeside press, 1911.   Cloth.   OP.

> x p., 1 l., 263 p.   front., illus., ports., 4 maps.   19 cm.
> Bibliography: p. 255-257; index: p. 259-263.
> Device.
>
> Republished by Arthur H. Clark, Glendale, Calif., 1932, 1940. Pronounc-
> ing vocabulary added and different illustrations used.

Although she was professor of political economy in the University of
Wyoming until she died and was considered an able historian, the author
continues to give prestige to the Hickok-McCanles legend. "Members
of the McCandlass[*sic*] gang," she writes, "once leagued together to
put him out of the way . . . and at one time a roomful attacked Wild
Bill alone. When the smoke cleared away it was found that ten men
had been killed."

470   Hebert, Frank

40 years prospecting and mining in the Black Hills of South
Dakota, by Frank Hebert . . . .   [Rapid City, S. D., Rapid City Daily
Journal, 1921.]   Cloth.   Scarce.

5 p.l., 199 p. front. (port.), illus., plates, ports. 21 cm.

The author gives information on road agents and on the deaths of Lame Johnny and Fly-Specked Billy.

471 Heermans, Forbes

Thirteen stories of the far west, by Forbes Heermans. Syracuse, N. Y., C. W. Bardeen, publisher, 1887. Cloth. Scarce.

4 p.l., [9]–263 p. 18.4 cm.

In his foreword the author states that these stories "are reports of actual experiences, written up from his note-book, with such changes in names, places and minor incidents as his personal safety seems to require."

But judging from Chapter VII, entitled "The Wedding at Puerta da Luna," his stories are wild fiction. In this chapter he has a preposterous story of Billy the Kid's holding up a wedding dance, killing his own father, and losing his own life in the quicksands of the Pecos River while trying to escape from his holdup victims.

472 Hendricks, George David

The bad man of the west, by George D. Hendricks; drawings by Frank Anthony Stanush. San Antonio, Texas, the Naylor co., publishers, 1941. Cloth. In print.

xv, 310 p. front., plates, ports., facsm. 23.5 cm.
Appendix: p. 271–291; bibliography: p. 295–298; index: p. 301–310.
Half title; illus. end papers; vignette.

The author makes an attempt to analyze the bad man from the psychological point of view, and describes each one's hair, eyes, and characteristics. He tells nothing new, though he does approach his subject from a new angle. His work represents some delving into many books on his subject.

473 Hendron, J. W.

The story of Billy the Kid, New Mexico's number one desperado, by J. W. Hendron. [Santa Fé, printed by the Rydal press, inc., 1948.] Pict. wrappers. In print.

3–31 p. plate, port., plan. 22.7 cm.

This little book was apparently published without being proofread, to judge from the many misspelled words. The author claims that the Kid's mother was born in New Orleans and that she was of French extraction. Other biographers say she was Irish. He also claims that the Kid was

177

born out of wedlock. He is in error when he states that the Kid ran away from his New York home and in 1871 landed in Kansas City, where he loafed around the Kansas City stockyards. He is also in error in the statement that the Kid went to New Mexico with John Chisum's foreman, whom he met at the stockyards. He tells a most fantastic tale about the Kid's escape from the Lincoln County jail and about someone's slipping him a knife and a piece of wood while he was incarcerated. These were hidden in "a *tortita*, a little sweet cake about the size of a biscuit." He states that the Kid kept the knife concealed in his rectum and at every opportunity whittled on the little piece of wood to form a key to fit his handcuffs.

474   Hennessy, W. B.

Tracy the bandit; or, the romantic life and crimes of a twentieth century desperado, by W. B. Hennessy. Twenty-five full page pictures by C. D. Rhodes.   Chicago, M. A. Donohue & co. [1902].   Cloth.   Port. pasted on.   OP.

> 6 p.l., 13–336 p.   front. (port.), plates.   19 cm.
> Also published in wrappers.

Just another book about this outlaw.

475   Henry, Stuart Oliver

Conquering our great American plains. A historical development, by Stuart Henry . . . . Illustrated.   New York, E. P. Dutton & co., inc. [1930].   Cloth.   OP.

> xvi p., 1 l., 3–395 p.   front. (map), plates, ports., plan.   21.5 cm.
> Appendix: p. 353–381; index: p. 383–395.
> Half title.

In the early twenties, the author stirred up quite a controversy throughout the nation by criticizing Emerson Hough's novel, *North of 36*. Most critics excused Hough on the grounds of artistic license. In studying Hough's nonfiction, however, I find him to be just as inaccurate in dates and events. Mr. Stuart devotes the latter part of this book to his side of this controversy, and apparently he is a conscientious historian. Most of the book concerns Abilene, Kansas, when it was wild, and the author gives Wild Bill Hickok considerable attention.

476   Hickman, Dr. Warren Edwin

An echo from the past. A first-hand narration of events of the early history of the Arkansas valley of Colorado, by Dr. Warren Edwin Hickman. Denver, Colo., printed by the Western Newspaper Union, 1914. Stiff wrappers. Scarce.

> 3 p.l., 7–179 p. front. (port.). 19.5 cm.

A story of Colorado during its outlaw days. The author uses fictitious names for his characters, although he states that they "can be readily recognized by people familiar with those times."

477 Hicks, John Edward

Adventures of a tramp printer, 1880–1890, by John Edward Hicks. Kansas City, Midamericana press [1950]. Cloth. Title label pasted on. In print.

> 5 p.l., 11–285 p. 23.6 cm.
> Bibliography: p. 283–285.
> Half title.

In his wanderings over the country as a tramp printer, the author happened to be in St. Joseph, Missouri, when Jesse James was killed there; and he tells something of that tragic event.

478 Hill, J. L.

The end of the cattle trail, by J. L. Hill. Long Beach, Calif., George W. Moyle publishing co. [n. d.]. Wrappers. OP.

> 5–120 p. front., plates. 22 cm.
> Device.

The author has written a splendid little book so far as the cattle trails are concerned; but, like most old-timers, he has written some of it from hearsay. He states that the Lincoln County War originated between sheepmen and cowmen, and that the first man Billy the Kid killed was Black Smith. Evidently he had heard of the Kid's killing a blacksmith early in his career. He says that John Chisum (which he spells "Chisholm") wanted this man out of the way.

Referring to the killing of the Kid, the author says that the kid was to stay at Maxwell's "ranch" on a certain night and sleep with "one of the boys." Garrett and two deputies went to the "ranch" before the Kid arrived. The deputies "lay down flat on the ground a little way from the trail that led into the house" and Garrett went to bed with the "boy the Kid was to sleep with." When the Kid arrived, Garrett raised up and shot him. His information on the James and Younger gang is a little more accurate.

479   Hill, W. A.

Historic Hays . . . , by W. A. Hill.   ₁Hays, Kan., News publishing co., 1938.₁   Pict. wrappers.   Scarce.

> 2 p.l., 7–81 p.   plates, ports.   22.7 cm.

A history of Hays containing information on Wild Bill Hickok and Calamity Jane. The author is more accurate than most of the earlier writers concerning the number of men involved in the Hickok-Mc-Canles fight, but his account of this event is still wrong.

480   Hitchcock, Frank

A true account of the capture of Frank Rande, "the noted outlaw," by the late Frank Hitchcock, sheriff of Peoria county, Ill., for twelve years. Edited by John W. Kimsey . . . .   Peoria, Ill., J. W. Franks and sons, printers and binders, 1897.   Pict. boards.   Scarce.

> 3 p.l., 9–156 ₁2₁ p.   front., plates.   18.5 cm.

One of the few books written about this outlaw.

481   Hitchcock, Mary E.

Two women in the Klondike. The story of a journey to the gold-fields of Alaska, by Mary E. Hitchcock, with 105 illustrations and map. New York, and London, G. P. Putnam's sons, 1899.   Pict. cloth.   Scarce.

> xiv p., 1 l., 485 p.   front. (with tissue), illus., plates, large fold. map in pocket at end.   22.7 cm.
> Index: p. 477–485.
> T.p. in red and black.

Contains some material on Soapy Smith.

482   Hittell, Theodore H.

History of California, by Theodore H. Hittell.   San Francisco, N. J. Stone & co., 1898.   Pub. in four volumes.   Calf.   Scarce.

> Vol. I xxxvi, 27–799 p.   23.5 cm.
> Vol. II, xli, 43–823 p.   23.5 cm.
> Vol. III, xli, 43–981 p.   23.5 cm.
> Vol. IV, xli, 43–858 p.   23.5 cm.
>
> Vols. I–II published by Pacific Press publishing house and Occidental publishing co.
> Vols. III–IV published by N. J. Stone and co.

Book X, Chapter IV deals entirely with Murieta. This account is taken largely from the 1871 edition of John Rollin Ridge's book. Unlike Bancroft, this author credits Ridge as his authority, but admits his source is unreliable. However, the placing of a legend in a history by such a historian strengthened people's belief in the legend.

483   Hobbs, James

Wild life in the far west; personal adventures of a border mountain man. Comprising hunting and trapping adventures with Kit Carson and others; captivity and life among the Comanches; services under Doniphan in the war with Mexico, and in the Mexican war against the French; desperate combats with Apaches, grizzly bears . . . , by Capt. James Hobbs . . . . Illustrated with numerous engravings. Published by subscription only. Hartford, Wiley, Waterman & Eaton, 1872. Cloth. Scarce.

> 8 p.l., [17]–488 p.   front. (col.), illus., plates, ports.   21.6 cm.
> Frontis tissue.

> Republished in 1875.

This scarce book contains a chapter on Joaquín Murieta.

484   Hogg, Thomas E.

Authentic history of Sam Bass and his gang, by a citizen of Denton county, Texas.   Denton, Texas, printed at the Monitor job office, 1876. Wrappers. Exceedingly rare.

> 1 p.l., [5]–143 p.   22.5 cm.
> 1 p. adv. and adv. on both sides of back wrapper.

Republished in Bandera, Texas, by Frontier Times, 1926. Wrappers.   (Cover title.)

> 56 p.   25.9 cm.
> Double column.

Again published by Frontier Times in 1932 in "Museum Edition" with eleven pages added by the publishers.

> 3 p.l., 7–192 p.   18.8 cm.

The original edition of this book is exceedingly rare. It is one of the first books written about Sam Bass. The author was a member of the posse which chased Bass all over Denton County. Both reprints are full of typographical errors.

485 Holbrook, Stewart H.

Little Annie Oakley & other rugged people, by Stewart H. Holbrook. New York, the Macmillan co., 1948. Pict. cloth. OP.

> x p., 1 l., 238 p. 21.5 cm.
> Half title; "First printing" on copyright p.

Contains material on Calamity Jane and the James boys and some unreliable information on Luke Short.

486 ───────

Murder out yonder. An informal study of certain classic crimes in back-country America, by Stewart H. Holbrook. New York, the Macmillan co., 1941. Cloth. OP.

> 5 p.l., 255 p. 24.2 cm.
> Index: p. 249–255.
> Half title; "first printing" on copyright p.

487 ───────

The story of American railroads, by Stewart H. Holbrook. New York, Crown publishers [1947]. Cloth. OP.

> x, 468 p. illus., plates, ports., facsms. 23.5 cm.
> Bibliography: p. 453–457; index: p. 459–468.
> Half title; vignette.

Deals to some extent with train robberies and with such outlaws as the Renos, the Jameses, the Youngers, Sam Bass, and the Evans-Sontag gang.

488 ───────

Wild Bill Hickok tames the west, by Stewart H. Holbrook. Illustrated by Ernest Richardson. New York, Random House. [1952]. Dec. cloth. In print.

> 6 p.l., 3–179 p. illus., plates (col.). 21.8 cm.
> Bibliography: p. 179.
> Half title; illus. end papers (col.); illus. chapter headings (col.); "First edition" on copyright p.

Written for juvenile readers, this book tames down the McCanles fight somewhat, but the author does have McCanles "strapping two revolvers on" as he prepares to go to Rock Creek Station, and even has McCanles's twelve-year-old son arming himself. It seems to me that writers of historical juveniles should be especially careful of their facts, because the impressions that young people receive are more lasting than those of any other age group.

489 Holland, Gustavus Adolphus

"The double log cabin," being a brief symposium of the early history of Parker county, together with short biographical sketches of early settlers and their trials .... Compiled and written by G. A. Holland. ₁Weatherford, Texas₁, 1931. Wrappers. Scarce.

1 p.l., ₁9₁–83 p. illus., plates, ports., facsm. 23 cm.

A privately printed little history of a Texas frontier county, which contains, among other material, information on the Texas Rangers and lawlessness as well as on Sam Bass and Arkansas Johnson.

490 ———

History of Parker county and the double log cabin; being a brief symposium of the early history of Parker county, together with short biographical sketches of early settlers and their trials, by G. A. Holland, assisted by Violet M. Roberts. Weatherford, Texas, the Herald publishing co., 1937. Cloth. OP.

4 p.l., 11–296 p. front., plates, ports., facsm. 23.6 cm.
Index: p. 281–296.

This is an enlarged edition of the 1931 publication with much added material.

491 Holloway, Carroll C.

Texas gun lore, by Carroll C. Holloway. San Antonio, Texas, the Naylor co. ₁1951₁. Cloth. In print.

xii p., 7 l. (1 port., plates), 3–238 p. 21.6 cm.
Index of 800 notorious gun fighters: p. 182–227; bibliography: p. 229–232; index: p. 233–238.
Half title.

A history of guns from flintlocks down to the present, this book contains much material on outlaws and gunmen. The index of eight hundred gun fighters increases its value.

492   Hooker, William Francis

The prairie schooner, by William Francis Hooker.   Chicago, Saul brothers, 1918.   Pict. cloth.   OP.

7 p.l., [17]–156 p.   front. (col.), illus., plates.   18.3 cm.
Half title.

The author devotes only five pages to Wild Hill Hickok. He calls Wild Bill "just a plain gambler and not a very good one," and does not even praise his courage.

493   Hoover, Mildred Brooks

Historic spots in California. Counties of the coast range, [by] Mildred Brooks Hoover. With an introduction by Robert Glass Cleland . . . .   Stanford University, Calif., Stanford University press; London, Humphrey Milford, Oxford University press [1937]. Cloth.   OP.

xxiii, 718 p.   front. (map).   20.7 cm.
Index: p. 687–718 (triple column).
Half title.

Contains some material on Murieta and Vásquez and their hide-outs.

494   Horan, James D.

Desperate men. Revelations from the sealed Pinkerton files, by James D. Horan.   New York, G. P. Putnam's sons [1949].   Pict. cloth.   In print.

xx p., 1 l., 3–296 p.   plates, ports., facsm.   22.2 cm.
Index: p. 293–296.
Half title; map on end papers; untrimmed.

On page 12 the misspelling of Dacus, making it "Bacus," is, I am sure, the fault of the printer. The first half of the book deals with the James-Younger gang, the last half with Butch Cassidy's Wild Bunch.

495   ———

Desperate women, by James D. Horan. New York, G. P. Putnam's sons [1952].   Pict. cloth.   In print.

xi [1] p., 2 l., 3–336 p.   plates, ports., facsms.   22 cm.
Bibliography: p. 323–330; index: p. 331–336.
Half title.

A companion volume to the author's *Desperate Men*, this is an entertaining book. Book I deals with women spies of the Civil War, but Book II is on desperate women of the West, though some of them are not so desperate. Nothing new is added to the stories about Calamity Jane and Belle Starr, although the author does debunk some of the legends about these two characters. He has some new material on Cattle Kate, Pearl Hart, and the Rose of Cimarron, revealing the last woman's identity for the first time.

In his chapter on Belle Starr, he refers to *Frank James, the Only True History of the Life of Frank James, Written by Himself*, stating that he is convinced the book was really written by Frank James. How he determined this is beyond me. See Item 557.

There are at least two typographical errors: on page 216, line 36, there is "hse" for "she," and on page 224, "Soloam Springs" is used for "Siloam Springs."

496 Horan, James D., and Howard Swiggett

The Pinkerton story, by James D. Horan and Howard Swiggett. New York, G. P. Putnam's sons [1951]. Cloth. In print.

> xiii p., 1 l., 3–366 p. front., plates, ports., facsms. 22 cm.
> Appendix: p. 349–358; index: p. 359–366.
> Half title; pub. device.

Written from the confidential files of the Pinkerton Detective Agency, the book contains chapters on many of the train robbers, such as the Renos, Rube Burrows, and the Evans-Sontag gang.

497 Horn, Tom

Life of Tom Horn, government scout and interpreter. Written by himself, together with his letters and statements by his friends. A vindication. Thirteen full page illustrations. Denver, published (for John C. Coble) by the Louthan book co. [1904]. Stiff pict. wrappers. OP.

> 7 p.l., [17]–317 p. front., plates, ports. 18.8 cm.
> Pub. device.

Supposedly written by Tom Horn, this book is considered by many people to have been written by Horn's friend and publisher, John C. Coble. It is an attempt to vindicate the crimes of Tom Horn.

498 Horton, Thomas F.

History of Jack county. Being accounts of pioneer times, excerpts from county court records, Indian stories, biographical sketches and interesting events, written and compiled by Thomas F. Horton. Jacksboro [Texas], Gazette print. [n. d.]. Stiff wrappers. Scarce.

2 p.l., 166 p. 23 cm.

This little book, which contains some material on Sam Bass and his gang, has become quite rare.

499 Hosmer, Hezekiah L.

Montana, an address delivered by Chief-Justice H. L. Hosmer before the Traveler's club, New York city, Jan., 1866. Published by request. New York, printed by the New York printing co., 1866. Wrappers. (Cover title.) Rare.

23 p. 23 cm.

Hosmer was the first chief justice of Montana and brought with him into the territory the first semblance of organized law and order. This work, among the earliest books to give authentic information on the region, includes material on the vigilantes, robbers, road agents, and stage lines.

500 Hough, Emerson

The story of the cowboy, by E. Hough. Illustrated by William L. Wells and C. M. Russell. New York, D. Appleton and co., 1897. Dec. cloth. OP.

xii, 349 [6] p. front., plates. 19.5 cm.
Addenda: p. 345-349; 6 p. adv. at end.
Half title: "The Story of the West Series, edited by R. Hitchcock."

Reprinted many times through the years, but the original edition is quite scarce.

In the chapter "Wars of the Range," the author gives an unreliable history of Billy the Kid. He claims that the Lincoln County War was the bloodiest of all range wars, and makes the exaggerated statement that two or three hundred men were killed in the conflict. In studying all his books on the West, I have found Hough to be careless and unreliable as a historian. He misspells John Chisum's name as "Chisholm" and says that Billy the Kid was killed at the age of twenty-three after he had killed twenty-three men. He says that the Kid killed seven Mexicans "just to see them kick," that he paraded on the platform before the courthouse for half an hour after he had killed his two jailers, and that he took a horse from a "passer-by" when he decided to leave town.

According to Hough, the whole country was an armed camp, and "the wayfarer who saw a body of men approaching was obliged to guess, and guess very quickly, which side he favoured. If he guessed wrong, the coyotes had another meal." Pat Garrett "finally got track of the little ruffian just as he was about to leave the country for Mexico." He learned that Billy was to call at night at a "certain ranch" to tell his Mexican sweetheart good-bye. As the Kid entered the house, he passed two of Garrett's deputies outside. "He apparently was about to repent of having violated his customary rule of shooting first and inquiring afterward, and had pulled his gun from the scabbard [no westerner calls a six-gun holster a scabbard], and was looking out at the men as he came backing into the door, with his boots in one hand." Garrett recognized the Kid and shot him immediately, and the author says that he was "none too quick, for Billy heard him as he rose from behind the bed, *holding* the scared ranchman down with one arm as he fired." He then says that "Billy turned swiftly about and made a quick but ineffectual shot, for he was dead even as he fired." Although the account of the Johnson County War is more accurate, it too can be shot full of holes.

501 ⸺

The story of the outlaw. A study of the western desperado, with historical narratives of famous outlaws; the stories of noted border wars; vigilante movements and armed conflicts on the frontier, by Emerson Hough. New York, the Outing publishing co., 1907. Boards. Scarce.

xiv p., 1 l., 401 p. front., plates, ports., cattle brands. 19 cm.
T.p. in red and black; pub. device; first state has rule at top of p. v.

A writer of Hough's ability, with a following of readers who believed in the authenticity of his accounts, should certainly have made an independent investigation of his subjects and not merely repeated earlier fables, even to incorrect names. In this book he repeats the Buel legend of the Hickok-McCanles fight, and, to make it more sensational, he places the fight in the dark interior of a dugout instead of in the log house from which Wild Bill did his shooting. Although Wild Bill was just a stable hand, Hough calls him a station agent.

Nichols said that his information came from an interview with Wild Bill; and it is possible that Wild Bill, wishing to make himself a hero and having a penchant natural to westerners for "loading" easterners, may have made such statements. Later historians who took the trouble to dig into the records found that Hickok and Wellman had murdered three men in cold blood and had attempted to murder Monroe McCanles, a twelve-year-old boy. David McCanles had never pulled a gun.

Hough also places the date of the fight as December 18, 1861, five months later than the correct date, and errs to the extent of placing Rock Creek Station in Kansas instead of Nebraska. His reputation as a writer at this time gave this misleading account great prestige, even though all the details, such as the number of participants, the use of knives, the time, and the place, are wrong. He states that Wild Bill was alone when attacked by *ten* men, and that he killed eight of them. Such a conglomeration of misinformation and error is unforgivable in a writer of Hough's reputation and ability.

In 1901, Hough had written an article on Billy the Kid for *Everybody's Magazine*, in which he made just as many preposterous statements about the Kid as he does here about Wild Bill. Before writing this book, however, he visited New Mexico again and looked up Pat Garrett. It is said that they traveled over the Billy the Kid country, and Garrett must have enlightened him considerably, because his account of the Kid in this book is entirely different from that in his magazine article and his *Story of the Cowboy*, written nine years earlier. He corrects the spelling of Chisum's name, gives the correct age of the Kid, and tells a more accurate story of the Kid's killing.

502 House, Boyce

Cowtown columnist, by Boyce House. San Antonio, Texas, the Naylor co., publishers [1946]. Cloth. In print.

> xii p., 1 l., [3]–275 p.   20.8 cm.
> Index: p. [273]–275.
> Half title.

There are chapters on Billy the Kid, Sam Bass, Ben Thompson, Belle Starr, and El Paso, the last chapter including such gunmen as John Wesley Hardin, John Selman, and George Scarborough. In his chapter on Billy the Kid, the author repeats the legend of the Kid's playing a game of cards with Bell, dropping a card, having Bell pick it up, and, as Bell did so, jerking Bell's gun from its holster and killing him. House also repeats the false story about Belle Starr's refusing to identify her husband, Jim Reed, after his murder in order to prevent the killer from collecting the reward offered for Reed's capture, dead or alive.

503 House, Edward Mandell

Riding for Texas. The true adventures of Captain Bill Mc-Donald of the Texas rangers, as told by Colonel Edward M. House to Tyler Mason. With a foreword by Colonel House. New York [published by John Day in association with Reynal & Hitchcock, 1936.] Pict. cloth. OP.

xii p., 1 l., 229 p. 19.6 cm.
Half title; untrimmed.

Like most books on the Texas Rangers, this one deals with some of the outlaws of Texas.

504 Howard, James W. ("Doc")

"Doc" Howard's memoirs, written by Sergeant "Doc" Howard, member of Company B, 5th U. S. Cavalry under General Carr, 1867–1872. [N. p., n.d. (ca1931).] Stiff wrappers. (Cover title.) Rare.

24 p. 23.2 cm.
Double column.

This rare little book is said to have been printed in an edition of only fifty copies. It tells of Cheyenne in its wild days and contains some information on Wild Bill Hickok and Calamity Jane. The author calls Deadwood, "Dead Wood's."

505 Howard, H. R.

The history of Virgil A. Stewart, and his adventure in capturing and exposing the great "western land pirate" and his gang, in connexion with the evidence; also of the trials, confessions, and execution of a number of Murrell's associates in the state of Mississippi during the summer of 1835, and the execution of five professional gamblers by the citizens of Vicksburg, on the 6th July, 1835 ..., compiled by H. R. Howard. New York, Harper & brothers ..., 1836. Cloth. Rare.

vi, [7]–273 p. 19.5 cm.
36 p. adv., numbered [1] to 36, of other books by the publisher at end.
Label pasted on spine.

Reprinted in 1839.

The earliest account of a detective's experiences in bringing justice to the Murrell gang.

506 ———

The life and adventures of Joseph T. Hare, the bold robber and highwayman. With 16 engravings. New York, Hillong and brother, 1874. Wrappers. Rare.

> 107 p. illus. 23.4 cm.
> On cover: "By the author of the 'Life of John A. Murrell.' "

Another example of early books on the outlaw.

507 Howard, Joseph Kinsey

Montana, high, wide and handsome, by Joseph Kinsey Howard. New Haven, Yale University press . . . , 1943. Cloth. OP.

> vi, 347 p. 21 cm.
> Acknowledgments and bibliography: p. [330]-339; index, p. [341]-347. Map on end papers.

A well-written book giving some history of Montana, its vigilantes, and some of its more modern outlaws. In his chapter "Nine Holes in Rattlesnake Jake," the author tells of horse thieves, the vigilantes, and the killing of Rattlesnake Jake Fallon and his partner, Long-Haired Owens.

508 ———

Montana margins. A state anthology, edited by Joseph Kinsey Howard . . . . New Haven, Yale University press . . . , 1946. Cloth. OP.

> xviii, 527 p. 24 cm.
> Appendix; p. 517-521; index of authors and acknowledgments; p. 522-527.

Contains a chapter on J. A. Slade from Dimsdale's *Vigilantes of Montana*, and another on cattle rustlers and the later-day vigilantes from Granville Stuart's *Forty Years on the Frontier*.

509 Howe, Charles E.

Dramatic play entitled Joaquín Murieta de Castillo, the celebrated bandit. In five acts. San Francisco, Commercial book and job steam printing establishment, 1858. Wrappers. Rare.

> 42 p. 22.2 cm.

This is an attempt to dramatize the John Rollin Ridge version of Joaquín Murieta's life in a five-act play. There are some changes in names, but this play did much to renew and perpetuate the legend of Murieta. Here Murieta is made a hero instead of the villain he was in actual life. This play also helped to perpetuate the legend of the state's offering a $5,000 reward and of Murieta's scrawling and signing under the poster an offer to give $10,000. The state offered no such reward.

510   Howe, Charles Willis

Timberleg of the Diamond Tail and other frontier anecdota, by Charles Willis Howe. Illustrated by R. L. McCollister. San Antonio, Texas, the Naylor co. [1949].   Pict. cloth.   In print.

ix, 153 p.   21.6 cm.
Half title; illus. chapter headings.

There is a chapter on bad men and the law, dealing with some of the better-known Oklahoma and New Mexico outlaws.

511   Howe, Elvon L. (ed.)

Rocky mountain empire. Revealing glimpses of the west in transition from old to new, from the pages of the Rocky Mountain Empire Magazine of the Denver Post, edited by Elvon L. Howe. With a foreword by Palmer Hoyt.   Garden City, N. Y., Doubleday & co., inc. [1950].   Cloth.   In print.

xiv p., 1 l., 272 p.   21 cm.
Half title; map on end papers; illus. chapter headings; pub. device; untrimmed; "First edition" on copyright p.

Contains a chapter on Bill Carlisle, the lone train robber.

512   Hoyt, Henry Franklin

A frontier doctor, by Henry F. Hoyt; with an introduction by Frank B. Kellogg, and with illustrations. Boston, and New York, Houghton Mifflin co., 1929.   Cloth.   OP.

xv, 260 p.   front. (port.), plates, ports., facsms.   21.3 cm.
Half title; pub. device; untrimmed; first edition: 1929 under imprint.

A well-written book with some new material on Billy the Kid and on life in old Tascosa.

513   Hubbard, Freeman H.

Railroad avenue. Great stories and legends of American railroading, by Freeman H. Hubbard.   New York, London, Whittlesey House, McGraw-Hill book co., inc. ₁1945₁. Cloth. OP.

> x, 374 p. front., illus., plates, ports., map. 23 cm.
> Vocabulary and railroad lingo: p. 331–367; acknowledgments: p. 368; index: p. 369–374.
> Half title; vignette; "First printing" on copyright p.

Contains a chapter on the James gang and its activities in robbing trains.

514 Huckabay, Ida Lasater

Ninety-four years in Jack county, 1854–1948, written and compiled by Ida Lasater Huckabay. ₁Austin, the Steck co., 1949.₁ Cloth. In print.

> xvi p., 1 l., ₁3₁–513 ₁1₁ p. plates, ports., fold. map. tables. 23.5 cm.

In her chapter "Law and Lawlessness on the Frontier," the author deals with outlaws and robberies of West Texas and makes a statement I have never seen elsewhere. According to her, a man named Joe Horner, of Jacksboro, got into trouble and went to the Northwest, where he took the name of Frank Canton and became a well-known peace officer. In his autobiography Canton himself says nothing about having been Joe Horner.

515 Hueston, Ethel (Mrs. Powelson)

Calamity Jane of Deadwood Gulch, by Ethel Hueston. Indianapolis, New York, Bobbs-Merrill co., publishers ₁1937₁. Cloth. OP.

> 3 p.l., 7–306 p. 20.7 cm.
> Half title; untrimmed; "First edition" on copyright p.
>
> Reprinted by Grossett and Dunlap with front. and illus. ₁n. d.₁.

Although written in a factual style, this book is strictly fiction.

516 Hughes, Dan de Lara

South from Tombstone. A life story, by Dan de Lara Hughes. London, Methuen and co., ltd. ₁1938₁. Cloth. Scarce.

> v p., 1 l., 311 ₁1₁ p. 20.3 cm.

A scarce book with some material on the Heath gang of Arizona.

517 Hughes, Marion

Oklahoma Charley, by Marion Hughes . . . . Oklahoma Charley . . . miner, cowboy, corndoctor, Indian scout, invalid, prospector, polygamist, horsetrader . . . snakecharmer, book-agent . . . and booze fighter . . . . St. Louis, John P. Wagner & co. [1910]. Pict. wrappers. Scarce.

2 p. l., [7]–159 p. front., illus. 18.8 cm.

The author writes, among other drivel, a most preposterous tale about Billy the Kid. He relates that the Kid was born in Illinois and named William LeRoy—perhaps the author was a *Police Gazette* fan. Among other things, he has the Kid hold up a stagecoach with a corncob on a stick to prove his bravery to a gang of road agents hanging out in the mountains of Colorado, a gang which he wanted to join. His whole account shows the influence of the *Police Gazette's Billy LeRoy*. The corncob incident was probably suggested by an incident in the *Gazette* novel: when Billy LeRoy's guards wondered at his using a gun as small as a .38, LeRoy answered, "A corn-cob is just as good as a pistol to hold up a coach with."

518 Hultz, Fred S.

Range beef production in the seventeen western states, by Fred S. Hultz. New York, John Wiley and sons, inc.; London, Chapman and Hall, ltd., 1930. Cloth. OP.

xv, 208 p. front., plates, ports., maps, charts, diagrs., tables. 21 cm.
Index: p. 201–208.
Half title.

Although primarily a book on livestock, it has a chapter on the Johnson County War.

519 [Hume, James B., and John N. Thacker]

Report of Jas. B. Hume and Jno. N. Thacker, special officers, Wells, Fargo & co.'s express, covering a period of fourteen years, giving losses by train robbers, stage robbers and burglaries, and a full description and record of all noted criminals convicted of offenses against Wells, Fargo & company since November 5th, 1870. San Francisco, H. S. Crocker & co., stationers and printers . . . , 1885. Wrappers. Rare.

3 p.l., [7]–91 p. 23.5 cm.

This rare report gives the birthplace, age, occupation, physical description, and prison sentences of more than two hundred outlaws who had robbed shipments of Wells, Fargo and Company.

REPORT

OF

JAS. B. HUME and JNO. N. THACKER,

SPECIAL OFFICERS,

WELLS, FARGO & CO'S EXPRESS,

Covering a Period of Fourteen Years,

GIVING LOSSES BY

Train Robbers, Stage Robbers and Burglaries,

AND A FULL DESCRIPTION AND RECORD OF ALL

NOTED CRIMINALS

CONVICTED OF OFFENSES AGAINST WELLS, FARGO & COMPANY
SINCE NOVEMBER 5TH, 1870.

SAN FRANCISCO:
H. S. CROCKER & CO., STATIONERS AND PRINTERS, 215-219 BUSH STREET.
1885.

NUMBER 519

520 Humphrey, Seth King

Following the prairie frontier, [by] Seth K. Humphrey. [Minneapolis], the University of Minnesota press [1931]. Cloth. OP.

5 p.l., 264 [1] p. front. 21.2 cm.
Half title; vignette.

The author gives some information on the Benders, the James-Younger gang, and the Northfield Bank robbery. He is in error, however, when he says, "And when Jesse James was finally shot by one of his own gang, the state of Missouri virtually sent the fellow to prison for life."

521 Hungerford, Edward

Wells Fargo. Advancing the American frontier, by Edward Hungerford. New York, Random House [1949]. Pict. cloth. In print.

xvi p., 1 l., 3–274 p. ports., plates, 2 maps (1 double p.), tables. 23.5 cm.
Bibliography: p. 259–262; index: p. 263–274.
Half title; illus. double t.p.; headpieces; "First printing" on copyright p.

Deals with stage robbers of California, such as Tom Bell, Black Bart, and Rattlesnake Dick.

522 Hunt, Frazier

Cap Mossman, last of the great cowmen, by Frazier Hunt. With sixteen illustrations by Ross Santee. New York, Hastings House, publishers [1951]. Pict. cloth. In print.

5 p.l., 3–277 p. illus. 21 cm.
Half title; illus. end papers (each different); vignette.

During his lifetime the subject of this book was an Arizona Ranger and had many interesting experiences with outlaws in that state.

523 ———

The long trail from Texas; the story of Ad Spaugh, cattleman, by Frazier Hunt. New York, Doubleday, Doran & co., inc., 1940. Cloth. OP.

5 p.l., 300 p. front. (map). 20.6 cm.
Half title; vignette; untrimmed; "First edition" on copyright p.
"This story was published serially under the title 'The Last Frontier.'"

Has some minor information about Wild Bill Hickok and Calamity Jane and material on Doc Middleton and his gang of horse thieves.

524 Hunt, Lenoir

Bluebonnets and blood. The romance of "Tejas," by Lenoir Hunt .... Illustrated with drawings, photographs and maps. Houston, Texas, Texas books, inc. [1938]. Thin boards (imitation cloth). Scarce.

> xv p., 1 l., 3–433 p. front., plates, ports., maps, facsm.   23.3 cm.
> Bibliography: p. 407–409; [notes]: p. 413–427; index: p. 431–433.
> Vignette.
> Colophon (pasted on inside front cover): "Each of five hundred copies of the Founders' De Lux [sic] edition of Bluebonnets and Blood is numbered and autographed by the author."

In a chapter on the Texas Rangers the author mentions such outlaws as John Wesley Hardin and Sam Bass.

525 Hunter, Col. George

Reminiscences of an old timer. A recital of the actual events, incidents, trials, hardships, vicissitudes, adventures, perils, and escapes of a pioneer, hunter, miner, and scout of the Pacific northwest, together with his later experiences in official and business capacities, and a brief description of the resources, beauties and advantages of the new northwest; the several Indian wars, anecdotes etc., by Colonel George Hunter. San Francisco, H. S. Crocker and co., 1887. Pict. cloth. Scarce.

> xxv, 454 p. front. (port.), illus., plates.   20.4 cm.
> Half title; leaf of errata tipped in.
>
> Reprinted the same year with an appendix; again reprinted, Battle Creek, Mich., Review and Herald, 1888.

Contains some information on vigilantes and road agents.

526 Hunt, Rockwell D., and Nellie Van De Grift Sanchez

A short history of California, by Rockwell D. Hunt . . . and Nellie Van de Grift Sanchez . . . . New York, Thomas Y. Crowell co., publishers [1929]. Cloth. OP.

> xiii p., 2 l., 3–671 p. plates, maps (2 fold.).   22.3 cm.
> Appendices: p. 637–647; index; p. 649–671.
> Half title; references for further reading at end of each chapter.

Like most histories of California, this volume devotes some space to California's outlaws—Murieta, Vásquez, and Juan Flores.

527 Hunter, J. Marvin, and Noah H. Rose

The album of gun-fighters, by Marvin Hunter and Noah H. Rose. Decorated and designed by Warren Hunter. ₁Bandera, Texas, 1951.₁ Pict. cloth (in col.). In print.

> xi p., 1 l., 236 p. plates, ports. 31 cm.
> Half title; illus. end papers; illus. double t.p.; leaf of errata laid in.

Published in a limited edition, this volume contains portraits and short sketches of most of the outlaws and gunmen of the Southwest. Rose's pictures have appeared in many western books, but this collection makes a valuable gallery of western gun fighters all under one cover. It is certain to be a collector's item.

528 Hunter, J. Marvin (ed.)

The trail drivers of Texas. Interesting sketches of early cowboys and their experiences on the range and on the trail during the days that tried men's souls. True narratives related by real cowpunchers and men who fathered the cattle industry in Texas. Published under the direction of George W. Saunders, president of the Old Trail Drivers' Association. Compiled and edited by J. Marvin Hunter. ₁San Antonio, Texas, Jackson printing co., 1920–1923.₁ Pub. in two volumes. Pict. cloth. Scarce.

> Vol. I, ₁3₁–498 p. front., ports. 23.3 cm.
> Vol. II, 2 p.l., 3–496 ₁1₁ p. front., plates, ports. 22 cm.
> Vol. I published in 1920; Vol. II, in 1923.
> Crudely bound and printed.

The first volume was exhausted before the second volume appeared; therefore it was reprinted in 1924 with some revisions and additions in an edition of 500 copies with a "second edition" imprint. ₁San Antonio, Globe printing co., 1924.₁ Pict. cloth. OP.

> ₁5₁–494 p. plates, ports. 22.8 cm.

Republished in one volume by the Cokesbury press, Nashville, 1925.

> xvi, 1044 p. front., plates, ports. 23.5 cm.

197

These books are mostly about cattle and, as such, are a valuable contribution, because they record heretofore untold history. They are listed here because they contain an unreliable article entitled "The Killing of Billy the Kid," by Fred Sutton. He has Billy kill a boy companion in New York at the age of twelve, then escape to Kansas, where he worked on a farm for a year and a half before going to New Mexico. The Kid became an outlaw because he killed a rancher for whom he worked. The writer claims to have entered Greathouse's home with Jimmy Carlisle for a parley with the Kid. When they tried to escape, both Carlisle and Sheriff William Bradley [*sic*] were killed. Brady was killed in Lincoln according to all other records, and Sutton has never been mentioned as a member of any posse sent after the Kid. The author also says Garrett killed the Kid in 1882 instead of 1881. Altogether, the account is absurd.

529   Huntington, George

Robber and hero, the story of the raid on the First National Bank of Northfield, Minnesota, by the James-Younger band of robbers in 1876 . . . . Portraits, illustrations and biographical sketches. Compiled from original and authentic sources, by George Huntington. Northfield, Minn., the Christian Way co., 1895. Cloth. Scarce.

v [1] p., 1 l., 119 p. front., plates, ports., plan. 19.7 cm.

This is a carefully written book based upon contemporary newspaper accounts and is considered accurate.

530   Huntington, William (Bill)

Bill Huntington's good men and salty cusses. Illustrated by J. K. Ralston. [Billings, Mont., Western Livestock Reporter press, 1952.] Boards. In print.

3 p.l., 207 p. illus. 21 cm.
Colophon (pasted on inside of back cover): "This is copy number ____ of the limited first edition of 2000 imprints."

Contains some material on Doc Middleton, Tom O'Day, and a few other outlaws of the Northwest.

531   Hutchinson, W. H.

A notebook of the old west, by W. H. Hutchinson. Designed and printed at Chico, Calif., by Bob Hurst for the author [Chico, Calif., 1947]. Stiff wrappers. OP.

> 4 p.l., 11–122 p. illus. 23.3 cm.
> Vignette.

The author tells of Wild Bill Hickok's appeal to women and of his murder by Jack McCall.

532 Hyenne, Robert

El bandido Chileno. Joaquín Murieta en California, por Robert Hyenne. Edición illustrada. Barcelona [and] Mexico [n. d.]. Wrappers. Rare.

> 123 p. plates. 18.6 cm.

This book is supposed to be translated from a French account, which, in turn, was received from Spain. In this Hyenne edition, the author makes Murieta a *Chileño*. The Hyenne edition was retranslated into Spanish, and this translation was issued as *El Caballero Chileño*, by "Professor" Acigar. See Item 534.

533 ———

El bandido Chileno. Joaquín Murieta en California, por Hyenne. Traducido del francés por C. M. Edición illustrada. Santiago, Centro editorial 'La Prensa,' 1906. Wrappers. Rare.

> 2 p.l., [5]–123 [1] p. plates. 18.5 cm.
> Index: p. [124].
> 4 p. adv. at end; Carlos Morla translation.

534 ———

El caballero Chileno. Bandido en California. Unica y verdadero historia de Joaquín Murrieta [*sic*], por el Profesor Acigar. Barcelona (España), Biblioteca Hercules [n. d.]. Wrappers. Rare.

> 206 p. 18.6 cm.

Pirated from the Hyenne edition. Compare with Item 708.

535 Illustrated History

of New Mexico . . . from the earliest period to the present time, together with . . . biographical mention of many of its pioneers and prominent citizens of today . . . . Chicago, the Lewis publishing co., 1895. Cloth. Scarce.

671 [1] p. plates, ports. 30 x 23.5 cm.

Contains an account of the Lincoln County War in the chapter on that county's history, and in it there is much material on Billy the Kid, most of it inaccurate.

536 Informe

de la comisión pesquisdora de la frontera del norte al ejecutivo de la unión en cumplimiento del artículo 3 de la ley de 30 de Setiembre de 1872. Monterey, Mayo 15 de 1873. Méjico, imprenta de Diaz de León y White, calle de Lerdo numero 2, 1874. Wrappers. Rare.

[3]-124 p. 28.7 cm.
Device.

This rare book in Spanish is a report of the commission investigating cattle rustling on the Texas-Mexico border.

537 Ingham, George Thomas

Digging gold among the Rockies; or, exciting adventures of wild camp life in Leadville, Black Hills and the Gunnison country . . . , by G. Thomas Ingham. Philadelphia, Hubbard brothers [1880]. Cloth. Scarce.

xiii p., 1 l., 17-508 p. front., illus. 20 cm.

Republished [n. p.], Edgewood publishing co. [1882].

xiii p., 1 l., 17-452 p. front., plates. 19.5 cm.

Has some material on the road agents of the Black Hills.

538 Inman, Henry

The great Salt Lake trail, by Colonel Henry Inman . . . and Colonel William F. Cody . . . . New York, the Macmillan co.; London, Macmillan and co., ltd., 1898. Pict. cloth. Scarce.

xiii, 529 p. front. (port.), illus., plates, ports., fold. map. 22.5 cm.
Index: p. 525-529.
Half title; vignette; frontis tissue.

Reprinted in 1914.

Contains some material on Joseph A. Slade.

539 Isely, Bliss, and W. M. Richards

Four centuries in Kansas. Unit studies, by Bliss Isely and W. M. Richards. Wichita, Kan., the McCormick-Mathers co. [1936]. Pict. cloth. OP.

> viii p., 1 l., 3–344 p. front., illus., ports., maps. 20.2 cm.
> Bibliography: p. 332–338; index: p. 339–344.
> Illus. end papers; vignette; suggestions for further study and references at end of each unit except Unit XII.

Tells of the Kansas cowtowns and has some material on Wild Bill Hickok.

540 Jackson, Joseph Henry

Anybody's gold, the story of California's mining towns, by Joseph Henry Jackson. Illustrated by E. H. Suydam. New York, London, D. Appleton-Century co., inc. [1941]. Cloth. OP.

> xiv p., 1 l., 3–467 [1] p. front., illus., plates. 23.2 cm.
> "Reading list": p. 447–453; index: p. 455–[466].
> Half title; illus. end papers; illus. chapter headings; untrimmed; first edition: figure (1) at end of index.

Like most of the author's books, this one does much to convince the reader that much of our information on the early California outlaw Murieta is pure fiction. He touches upon practically all of the California outlaws except Vásquez.

541 ———

Bad company. The story of California's legendary and actual stage-robbers, bandits, highwaymen and outlaws from the fifties to the eighties, [by] Joseph Henry Jackson. New York, Harcourt, Brace and co. [1949]. Pict. cloth. In print.

> xx p., 1 l., 3–346 p. plates, ports., relief map, facsms. (all in one section). 22 cm.
> Notes on sources: p. 327–330; appendix: p. 331–335; index: p. 337–346.
> Half title; "First edition" on copyright p.

One of the best books on California outlaws, this volume shows scholarly research. Many accounts of such outlaws as Murieta are revealed as legendary.

542 ———

Tintypes in gold; four studies in robbery, [by] Joseph Henry

Jackson. Decorations by Giacomo Patri.   New York, the Macmillan co., 1939.   Cloth.   OP.

> 5 p.l., 191 p.   20.8 cm.
> Half title; headpieces; illus. end papers; vignette; "First edition" on copyright p.

Thorough studies of four California outlaws—Black Bart, Rattlesnake Dick, Dick Fellows, and Tom Bell—later incorporated into the author's *Bad Company*.

543   Jackson, Mary E.

The life of Nellie C. Bailey; or, a Romance of the west, written by Mary E. Jackson . . . .   Topeka, Kan., R. E. Martin & co., printers and binders, 1885.   Cloth.   Scarce.

> 4 p.l., [7]–399 p.   plates, ports.   19 cm.

Primarily about a strange murder case which created a sensation in the early West, the book gives an account of the hanging of Ben Wheeler and Hendry Brown, the bank robbers.

544   [James Boys]

Bank and train robbers of the West, James boys, Younger boys, etc.   [N. p., n. d.]   Cloth.   (Cover title.)   Scarce.

> 5 p.l., 9–287 p.   front., illus., plates.   20 cm.

545   ———

Frank James and his brother Jesse, the daring border bandits.   Baltimore, I. & M. Ottenheimer, publishers [1915].   Pict. wrappers.   OP.

> 2 p.l., 7–186 p.   front.   18.5 cm.
> 3 l. adv. at end.

One of the many cheap and sensational outlaw books issued by these publishers, none of which are of any historical value.

546   ———

The james boys. A complete and accurate recital of the daredevil criminal career of the famous bandit brothers Frank and Jesse James, and their noted band of bank plunderers, train robbers and murderers. Specially compiled for the publishers.   Chicago, the Henneberry co. [n. d.].   Cloth.   OP.

x, 11–249 p. illus. 19 cm.
6 p. adv. at end.

Also published with the same full title by M. A. Donohue & co., Chicago, without date, in pictorial wrappers and with 8 p. adv. at end.

547 ———

Lives, adventures and exploits of Frank and Jesse James, with an account of the tragic death of Jesse James, April 3rd, 1882. The last daring feats of the James confederacy in the robbery and murder on the Rock Island train, July 14th, 1881; and at Glendale, Mo., September 17th, 1881. [N. p., n. d.] Pict. wrappers. (Cover title.) Scarce.

[3]–96 p. front., illus. 22 cm.

Another book was published under this same title *ca.*1892, with entirely different text and illustrations.

[125] p. (no pagination). front., illus. 18.7 cm.

Both books are worthless historically. The first book has a chapter on the robbery of the Union Pacific by Joel Collins and Sam Bass in order to bring Jesse James into the picture. The author claims that one of the robbers in this holdup was unknown, but declares him to be Jesse James. He also places the value of the loot at $100,000 instead of the $60,000 which the records show was correct. The book contains too much conversation which no one could have reliably recorded. The work is unreliable throughout. Again Liddill is called "Little."

548 ———

The outlaw brothers, Frank and Jesse James. Lives and adventures of the two scourges of the plains . . . . [New York] published by Richard K. Fox, proprietor of Police Gazette [1881]. Pict. wrappers. Rare.

2 p.l., 7–67 p. front., illus., plan. 25 cm.
7 p. adv. at end.

Later published in a revised edition with new illustrations.

Another example of the *Police Gazette's* worthless outlaw series, which have now become scarce collector's items.

549 ———

A thrilling story of the adventures and exploits of Frank and

Jesse James, containing a complete sketch of the romance of guerrilla warfare. Together with a detailed history of the wild bandits
of the border. A graphic account of the tragic end of Jesse James
.... ₍N. p., n. d. (*ca.*1892).₎ Pict. wrappers. Scarce.

₍125₎ p. (no pagination). front. (port.), plate. 18.7 cm.

As in several other such books, Dick Liddill is erroneously called Dick
"Little."

550 ———

Train and bank robbers of the west. A romantic but faithful story of bloodshed and plunder, perpetrated by Missouri's daring outlaws. A thrilling story of adventures and exploits of Frank
and Jesse James, Missouri's twin wraiths of robbery and murder,
containing a complete sketch of the romance of guerrilla warfare.
Together with a graphic and detailed account of the robberies and
murders of twenty years; and the last daring feats of the James' confederacy in the robbery and murder on the Rock Island train, July
14th, 1881, and at Glendale, Mo., Sept. 17th, 1881; to which is added
an account of the tragic end of Jesse James, shot by a confederate,
April 3d, 1882. Together with a record of the wild and reckless
career of the Younger brothers now incarcerated in the penitentiary
at Stillwater, Minn. ... Chicago, Bedford, Clark & co.; St. Louis,
Belford and Clarke publishing co. MDCCCLXXXII. Cloth. Rare.

Part I, 5 p.l., ₍9₎–358 p. front., plates. 19.8 cm.
Part II, viii, ₍9₎–287 p. plates. 19.8 cm.

Part II is the same as Appler's *Guerrillas of the West*, 1876 edition.

551 ———

Wild bandits of the border. A thrilling story of the adventures and exploits of Frank and Jesse James, Missouri's twin wraiths
of robbery and murder .... Chicago, Laird and Lee, 1893. (On
cover: The Pinkerton Detective Series No. 8.) Cloth. Rare.

367 p. front., plates, ports. 19.5 cm.
Pinkerton detective series, No. 8.

Most of these cheap books on the James boys were copied from preceding books. Even the titles are similar.

552 James, Edgar

The Allen outlaws. A complete history of their lives and exploits, concluding with the Hillsville courthouse tragedy, by Edgar James. Profusely illustrated. Baltimore, published by Phoenix publishing co. [1912]. Pict. wrappers. OP.

5 p.l., 13–191 p. front., ports. 19 cm.

There is not much one can say in favor of the cheap books by this author, except that they were perhaps entertaining to readers who cared nothing for facts.

553 ⸻

James boys; deeds and daring. A complete record of their lives and death . . . . Baltimore, I & M. Ottenheimer [1911]. Pict. wrappers. OP.

182 p. front., illus. 19.5 cm.

554 ⸻

The lives and adventures, daring holdups, train and bank robberies of the world's most desperate bandits and highwaymen, the notorious James brothers. The latest and most complete story of the daring crimes of these famous desperadoes ever published. Containing many sensational escapades never before made public, by Edgar James. Baltimore, I. & M. Ottenheimer, publishers [1913]. Pict. wrappers. OP.

3 p.l., 9–192 p. front., illus. 19.6 cm.

555 [James, Frank]

Frank James and his brother Jesse. The daring border bandits. Baltimore, I. & M. Ottenheimer, publishers [1915]. Pict. wrappers. OP.

2 p.l., 7–186 p. front., illus. 18.5 cm.
6 p. adv. at end.

556 ⸻

Life and trial of Frank James. [New York, Frank Tousey, 1883.] Pict. wrappers. Scarce.

205

2–[28], 4 p.   28.4 cm.
Double column.
4 p. adv. at end.

Republished in facsimile in 1952 except for the omission of the second story, "The Clink of Gold," pages 21 to [28] in the original edition, and the change of advertisements.

557 ⸺

The only true history of the life of Frank James, written by himself. [Pine Bluff, Ark., Norton printing co., 1926.] Wrappers. (Cover title.)   Rare.

5 p.l., 7–134 p. plates, ports. 15.2 cm.

This is one of the most brazen bits of writing it has been my experience to read. The author claims to be Frank James, although he says his mother's name was Agnes Collins and his father's name was Nelson. Then, in the latter part of the book, he says that his father was Ed Reed, a brother of Jim Reed, and that he "was a base begotten child."

The real Frank James was pardoned and restored to full citizenship; yet this claimant of the name lived in Newton County, Arkansas, for forty years under the name of Joe Vaughn, trying, he says, to hide his identity. According to his account, most of his life was spent among the Indians of Indian Territory.

Among other unbelievable things, he writes: "Readers, I know it will be hard to make people believe that I am the only Frank James that ever existed, and there never was a real Frank James, that the boy Frank James was none other than Edd Reed." He further states that "the world thinks that Robert Ford killed Jesse James, but I will say right here that the James boys never were captured."

The real Frank James died on the Samuel farm in Missouri, on February 18, 1915. It is a well-known fact that after his pardon he worked as a shoe salesman in Missouri and in Dallas, Texas; that he was employed in St. Louis as a doorkeeper at the Standard Theatre; and that at various times he acted as starter at the fair grounds in St. Louis. He did not have to hide out on a farm in Arkansas afraid to reveal his identity.

The author says his book was finished on December 10, 1925, ten years and ten months after the death of the real Frank James. (The author of this book died on February 14, 1926.) This worthless little tome was published by his daughter, Sarah E. Snow, who upholds her father's claims. It is full of typographical errors, misspelled proper names, and confused geography.

Burton Rascoe, in his *Belle Starr, the Bandit Queen,* says: "It is maudlin, illiterate, vague, confused, pathetic." Yet a few paragraphs later he says, "It is quite probable that, when he was on his uppers, he [Frank James] wrote this story of his life as it was published eleven years after his death. . . . There is something so pathetic about its general style and information that I have a deep suspicion that Frank James may actually have written it and that no 'ghost' or collaborator helped him out in the least."

I fail to see how Rascoe could possibly have arrived at this conclusion if he had actually read the book. Certainly, Frank James, as has been pointed out, did not hide out, nor did he have to hide out, in the hills of Arkansas after his pardon.

Much trash has been written about the James boys, but both Frank and Jesse would turn over in their graves if they knew about this item.

558 [James, Jesse]

Jesse James: the life and daring adventures of this bold highwayman and bank robber and his no less celebrated brother, Frank James. Together with the thrilling exploits of the Younger boys. Written by xxx (one who dare not now disclose his identity). The only book containing the romantic life of Jesse James and his pretty wife who clung to him to the last!   Philadelphia, published by Barclay & co., . . . [1883]. Pict. wrappers. Rare.

> 19–96 p. illus., plates, ports. 23.5 cm.
> Cover title: "The Life and Tragic Death of Jesse James, the Western Desperado."
> Port. of Jesse James on front cover; port of his father on back cover. (Neither authentic.)
>
> Republished in facsimile by William F. Kelleher, Cliffside Park, N. J., in 1951.

559 ———

The St. Joseph Daily Gazette supplement.   St. Joseph, April 9, 1882.   Exceedingly rare.   (Newspaper.)

> 4 p. ports., plan.
> six columns to the page.

This practically unprocurable ephemeron is a separate issue of the newspaper devoted entirely to the life, death, and burial of Jesse James. Printed less than a week after Jesse James' murder, it is the primary source for many of the books on the James boys which followed. This

JESSE JAMES:

THE LIFE AND DARING ADVENTURES OF THIS BOLD

Highwayman and Bank Robber,

AND HIS NO LESS CELEBRATED BROTHER,

FRANK JAMES.

TOGETHER WITH

THE THRILLING EXPLOITS OF THE YOUNGER BOYS

WRITTEN BY ✱✱✱✱✱✱

(ONE WHO DARE NOT NOW DISCLOSE HIS IDENTITY.)

THE ONLY BOOK CONTAINING

The Romantic Life of Jesse James and his Pretty Wife,

WHO CLUNG TO HIM TO THE LAST!

PUBLISHED BY BARCLAY & CO.,
21 NORTH SEVENTH STREET,
PHILADELPHIA, PA.

AGENTS WANTED. MEN EMPLOYED.

NUMBER 558

is the only newspaper item that I have included in this work, but feel that its importance justifies a place here.

560 James, Jesse, Jr.

Jesse James, my father, written by Jesse James, Jr. The first and only true story of his adventures ever written. Published and distributed by Jesse James, Jr. . . . . Independence, Mo., the Sentinel printing co., 1899. Pict. wrappers. Scarce.

> 2 p.l., [5]–194 p. ports. 19.6 cm.

Reprinted, Cleveland, Arthur Westbrook co., ca.1906. Wrappers.

> 2 p.l., [5]–189 p. front., ports. 18.7 cm.
> 3 p. adv. at end.

Jesse James, Jr., says he wrote this book "to correct false impressions that the public have about the character of my father." In the latter part of the book he tells of his own life and the accusation that he was a train robber himself.

561 James, John Towers

The Benders of Kansas, by John T. James, attorney for the defense in the trial of the "Bender woman" at Oswego, Labette county, in 1889–1890. The complete story; facts, not fiction. Wichita, Kan., published by the Kan-Okla publishing co. [1913]. Cloth. Pict. label pasted on. Scarce.

> 4 p.l., [11]–173 p. illus., ports., plan. 20.7 cm.

A full history of these unparalleled killers, related by their defense attorney, who must have known the facts.

562 James, Marquis

The Cherokee Strip; a tale of an Oklahoma boyhood, [by] Marquis James. New York, Viking press, 1945. Pict. cloth. OP.

> 6 p.l., 3–294 p. 21.8 cm.
> Half title; map on end papers; pub. device.
>
> Also published in a de luxe signed edition, and in several trade editions thereafter.

In his youth the author was much impressed with the outlaw Dick Yeager and devotes a chapter to him in this book.

563 ———

They had their hour, by Marquis James . . . . Indianapolis, the Bobbs-Merrill co., publishers [1934]. Cloth. OP.

> 5 p.l., 11–324 p. 23.7 cm.
> Notes: p. 301–302; index: p. 305–324.
> Half title; "First edition" on copyright p.

As in the previous book, Dick Yeager, as well as the Jennings gang, comes in for much attention. The author is mistaken in saying that Charlie Pearce was nicknamed "Tulsa Jack." The real name of the latter was Blake.

564 James, William F., and George H. McMurry

History of San Jose, California. Narrative and biographical, by William F. James and George H. McMurry. Paul Gordon Teal, biographical editor. San Jose, Calif., A. H. Cawston, publisher, 1933. Cloth. OP.

> 2 p.l., [5]–243 [1] p. front., plates, ports. 26.5 cm.
> Biographical sketches: p. [169]–239; index: p. [240]–243.

Contains minor information on Joaquín Murieta and Tiburcio Vásquez.

565 Jelinek, George

Ellsworth, Kansas, 1867–1947, by George Jelinek. Salina, published by Consolidated [1947]. Stiff wrappers. OP.

> 2 p.l., 5–32 p. plates, ports., facsm. 21.5 cm.
> Vignette.

This little book tells of Ellsworth as a cowtown and relates the story of the killing of Sheriff Whitney by Bill Thompson.

566 Jennewein, J. Leonard

Calamity Jane of the western trails, by J. Leonard Jennewein. Huron, S. D., Dakota books [1953]. Stiff pict. wrappers. In print.

> 2 p.l., 5–47 p. plates, ports., facsms. 22.5 cm.
> Bibliography: p. 39–46.

Published in an edition of three thousand copies, this little book gives some new material on Calamity Jane and debunks some of the old.

567   Jennings, Alphonso J.

Beating back, by A. Jennings and Will Erwin. Illustrated by Charles M. Russell.   New York and London, D. Appleton and co., 1914.   Cloth.   OP.

> 6 p.l., 354 [1] p.   front. (port.), plates, plan.   20 cm.
> Half title; pub. device; first edition: figure (1) at end of text.

An autobiography of Al Jennings, edited and with an introduction by Will Erwin. Jennings tells of his start in outlawry, his life in prison, and his come-back after his release. This account was originally published serially in the *Saturday Evening Post* in seven installments, September to November, 1913, which contained eight Charles M. Russell illustrations instead of the three found in the book.

568   ———

Hors le loi! . . . La vie d'un outlaw Américain racontés par lui-même; traduction et adaptation de l'Américain et du slang par Blaise Cendrars.   Paris, B. Grasset [1936].   Wrappers.   Scarce.

> 332 p., 1 l.   front. (port.).   19 cm.
> At head of title: Al Jennings.

569   ———

Through the shadows with O. Henry, by Al Jennings . . . . Illustrated.   New York, the H. K. Fly co., publishers [1921].   Pict. cloth.   OP.

> 6 p.l., [11]-320 p.   front., plates, ports.   21 cm.
> Half title; pub. device.

This book deals mostly with Jennings' prison life and his friendship with O. Henry, who was confined in the same prison. As an Oklahoma outlaw familiar with the officers of that state, the author should have known better than to call E. D. Nix by the name of "Ed Nicks."

570   Jennings, Napoleon Augustus

A Texas ranger, by N. A. Jennings.   New York, Charles Scribner's sons, 1899.   Col. pict. cloth.   Scarce.

> x p., 1 l., 321 p.   19 cm.

Reprinted, Dallas, Southwest press [1930], with a foreword by J. Frank Dobie. Imt. leather.

xv, 287 p. 24 cm.

The first edition is exceedingly scarce and contains much material on Texas gunmen, such as John Wesley Hardin and King Fisher, and on the Taylor-Sutton feud and other border troubles. The reprint has now become quite scarce also.

571 Jensen, Ann (ed.)

Texas ranger's diary and scrapbook, edited by Ann Jensen. Dallas, Texas, the Kaleidograph press [1936]. Cloth. OP.

6 p.l., 13–81 p. front., illus. 19.8 cm.

This small book is composed of short sketches on different subjects, one sketch being on Bass Outlaw and another on the killing of John Selman.

572 Jocknick, Sidney

Early days on the western slope of Colorado, and campfire chats with Otto Mears, the pathfinder, from 1870 to 1883, inclusive, by Sidney Jocknick. Denver, Colo., the Carson-Harper co., MCMXIII. Cloth. Scarce.

4 p.l., [9]–384 p. front. (port., signature in facsm.), plates, ports., map. 20.2 cm.
Appendix: p. [341]–384.

One chapter treats Alfred Packer, his terrible crime of murder and cannibalism; and another, George Howard, the highwayman.

573 Johnson, Francis

Big Goliath; or, the terror of the mines, by the author of steel arm; or, the robbers and regulators of California . . . . New York, Dick and Fitzgerald, publishers [1862]. Pict. wrappers. Rare.

19–107 p. 22 cm.

574 ———

Steel arm; or, the robbers and regulators of California . . . .

212

New York, Dick and Fitzgerald, publishers [1862]. Pict. wrappers. Rare.

19–111 p.   22 cm.

This and the preceding item constitute two more examples of the early dime novel of no historical value, but they are collector's items.

575   Johnson, (Mrs.) Grover C.

Wagon yard, by Mrs. Grover C. Johnson. Illustrated by Jerry Bywaters.   Dallas, William T. Tardy [1938].   Cloth.   OP.

3 p.l., 201 p.   front., illus.   23.5 cm.

This book contains some minor unreliable information on Billy the Kid. The author spells Quantrill's name "Quantrail" and makes the statement that a Kansas jayhawker killed the father of the James boys and shot off one of their mother's arms. History tells us that Pinkerton men were responsible.

Mrs. Johnson says that Kid Lewis and Foster Crawford robbed a bank in Wichita Falls, Texas, but is mistaken in calling them members of the Al Jennings gang. She also gets her information on Jim Murphy mixed, claiming that he was "imported" to trap Sam Bass. She repeats the old fable, too, about Jesse James and the widow whose mortgage was about to be foreclosed by the cruel landlord, whom he paid and then robbed to get his money back. Variations of this legend have been told since the days of Robin Hood.

576   Johnston, Charles Haven Ladd

Famous scouts, including trappers, pioneers, and soldiers of the frontier. Their hazardous and exciting adventures in the mighty drama of the white conquest of the American continent, by Charles H. L. Johnston . . . . Illustrated.   Boston, L. C. Page and co., publishers [1910].   Pict. cloth.   Scarce.

ix, 2 l., 340 p.   front., plates, ports.   20.5 cm.

Republished in May, and again in September, 1911.

xi, 2 l., 348 p.   front., ports.   20.5 cm.
20 p. adv. at end.

The author starts his chapter on Wild Bill Hickok with Wild Bill lying on the floor of a dugout bleeding "from many deep and dangerous wounds." This was after the fight at the Rock Creek Station, which the author erroneously places in Kansas instead of Nebraska.

Johnston misspells McCanles' name and also calls him "Jack" instead of David. He calls Wild Bill's companion " 'Doc' Mills," when his name should be Wellman. He perpetuates the false reputation of the McCanles', having this band "killing more innocent men and running off more horses" than anyone else in the country. He also says that there were ten men in the McCanles party. "Crack! Crack! Crack! went the shots from the pistols of Bill, and at every shot a member of the gang went to the floor—stone dead." With surviving members of the gang crowding him, he slashed right and left with his knife until "the floor was red with blood."

The author claims that this version is true because it is "from Wild Bill's own recital of the fight as reported by James William Buel." The rest of the account is just as unreliable. He states that Jack McCall was a miner and that he killed Wild Bill the day after McCall lost a large sum of money to Wild Bill in a poker game.

577 Johnston, Harry V.

My home on the range. Frontier life in the Bad Lands, by Harry V. Johnston. St. Paul, Minn., printed by the Webb publishing co. [1942]. Pict. cloth. OP.

> 6 p.l., 313 p. front. (port.), illus., plates, ports., cattle brands. 23.5 cm. Vignette.

A book of reminiscences which contains some minor information on Wild Bill and Calamity Jane, as well as unreliable statements about Bill Dalton.

578 Jones, C. N.

Early days in Cooke county, 1848–1873, compiled by C. N. Jones. Gainesville, Texas, [n. d., but *ca.*1936.] Stiff wrappers. Scarce.

> 3 p.l., 5–88 p. front., ports. 23.8 cm.

Though a comparatively recent book, this volume seems to have become exceedingly scarce. It contains some material on outlawry. The author reverses the usual procedure by spelling Jesse Chisholm's name "Chisum."

579 Jones, John P. (Slim)

Borger, the little Oklahoma, by John P. (Slim) Jones . . . . [N. p., n. d.] Pict. wrappers. OP.

> 171 p. 7 plates, 2 ports. in front. 21.5 cm.

A story of much outlawry in Oklahoma during the modern oil-boom days, with some information on Matthew Kimes.

580 [Jones, W. F.]

The experiences of a deputy U. S. marshal of the Indian territory, ₁by W. F. Jones. Tulsa, Okla., 1937.₁ Wrappers. (Cover title.) OP.

> 40 p. front. (port.), 1 plate. 23 cm.

There is much material on Oklahoma outlaws.

581 Juan, Don (pseud.)

Señor Plummer. The life and laughter of an old Californian, by Don Juan. Los Angeles, Times-Mirror, 1942. Cloth. OP.

> 6 p.l., 242 p. ports., plans. 19.5 cm.
> Half title; illus. double t.p.

Interesting reminiscences of an early Californian who lived to a ripe old age. He gives much firsthand information on Vásquez and Murieta and, like many early Spanish Californians, does not believe that the head which was pickled for exhibition was Murieta's.

582 Judson, Katherine Berry

Montana "The land of shining mountains," by Katherine Berry Judson. With twenty-four illustrations and a map. Chicago, A. C. McClurg and co., 1909. Cloth. Scarce.

> vii ₁4₁ p., 1 l., 15–244 p. front. (map), plates, ports., fold. map in front. 19 cm.
> Appendix: p. 179–236; index: p. 239–244.

Contains a chapter on vigilantes and outlaws.

583 Kalbfus, Joseph H.

Dr. Kalbfus' book. A sportsman's experiences and impressions in east and west, by Dr. Joseph H. Kalbfus .... With a preface by his friend and successor, Seth E. Gordon .... ₁Altoona, Pa., the Times Tribune co., 1926.₁ Cloth. Scarce.

> 4 p.l., 342 p. front. (port.), 1 port. 21.4 cm.

The author tells of Slade's killing of Jules Reni and Slade's subsequent hanging by the vigilantes.

584   Keatinge, Charles Wilbur
(Montana Charlie, pseud.)

Gold miners of Hard Luck; or, Three-Fingered Jack, by Charles Wilbur Keatinge (Montana Charlie) .... Cleveland, Ohio, published by the Arthur Westbrook co., 1927.   Pict. wrappers. OP.

> 2 p.l., [7]–203 p.   18 cm.
> [Early western life series, No. 1.]

A fictitious account of Joaquín Murieta and Three-Fingered Jack García.

585   Keithley, Ralph

Bucky O'Neill, he stayed with 'em while he lasted, by Ralph Keithley.   Caldwell, Idaho, the Caxton printers, ltd., 1949.   Cloth. In print.

> 10 p.l., [17]–247 p.   front. (port.), plates, ports., map.   23.5 cm.
> Index: p. [245]–247.
> Half title; pub. device.

A biography of a noted Arizona Ranger, with an account of his chase and capture of the four outlaws who robbed the Atlantic and Pacific train in 1889, the book also gives some information on the Earp-Clanton feud.

586   Keleher, William A.

The fabulous frontier; twelve New Mexico items, by William A. Keleher.   Santa Fé, N. M., the Rydal press [1945].   Cloth. OP.

> ix p., 3 l., 3–317 p.   illus., plates, ports.   23.5 cm.
> Some sources of references: p. 283–286; index: p. 287–317.
> Map on end papers.

> Printed in a limited edition of 500 copies, but has since been reprinted.

This is a scholarly and dependable book which can be safely used as a source for material on Billy the Kid, Pat Garrett, Jim Miller, and other gunmen of New Mexico. Its author is a thorough historian of New Mexico.

587   ――――

Maxwell land grant, a New Mexico item, by William A.

Kelleher. Santa Fé, N. M., the Rydal press [1942]. Pict. cloth. Scarce.

> xiii p., 1 l., 3–168 p. front. (port.), plates, ports. 23.5 cm.
> Sources: p. 155–156; index: p. 157–168.
> Half title.

Although published comparatively recently, this book is becoming quite scarce. It is mostly about Lucien B. Maxwell and the huge land grant which took his name, but does contain some material on Clay Allison, the vigilantes of New Mexico, and Billy the Kid.

588 Kelley, George H. (compiler)

Legislative history, Arizona 1864–1912, compiled by George H. Kelley, state historian.   [Phoenix, Arizona, the Manufacturing stationers, inc.], 1926. Cloth. Scarce.

> xiv p., 1 l., 399 p. front., ports., 11 fold. maps. 21.4 cm.
> Index: p. [381]–399.

Messages of the various governors of the territory and state, some containing reports on outlaws and lawlessness.

589 Kelley, Joseph (Bunco)

Thirteen years in the Oregon penitentiary, by Joseph (Bunco) Kelley. Portland, Oregon, 1908. Stiff wrappers. Scarce.

> 4 p.l., [1] p., 10–142 p. front., illus., plates, ports. 21.2 cm.
> Vignette.

Contains some material on Harry Tracy and Dave Merrill.

590 Kelly, Charles

The outlaw trail. A history of Butch Cassidy and his wild bunch, Hole-in-the-Wall, Brown's Hole, Robber's Roost, by Charles Kelly. With decorations by Bill Fleming. Salt Lake City, published by the author, 1938. Pict. levant. OP.

> 5 p.l., [9]–337 p., 1 l., (acknowledgments). front. (port.), illus., plates, ports. 23.5 cm.
> Bibliography included in acknowledgments.
> Illus. t.p.; map on end papers; headpieces; vignette; 7 blank l. at end: "First edition" on copyright p.

This privately printed book was limited to one thousand copies and is now quite scarce. It is an excellent history of the lives and exploits of the better-known outlaws of the Northwest.

591 Kelsey, D. M.

History of our wild west and stories of pioneer life . . . . A complete story of the settlement and conquest of the western frontier, relating the exciting experiences, daring deeds and marvelous achievements of men made famous by their heroic deeds . . . , by D. M. Kelsey . . . . Chicago, Thompson & Thomas [1901]. Pict. cloth. Scarce.

x [3] p., [15]–542 p. front. (col.), illus., plates, ports. 21.8 cm.

This book contains a long chapter on Wild Bill Hickok in which the author repeats the old legends of the McCanles fight, but says the fight took place on December 16, five months after it actually occurred. He misspells McCanles, calls David by the name of "Jim," and goes into the gory details of the killing of six men and the wounding of two others, although he does let two escape.

592 King, Ernest L.

Main line. Fifty years of railroading with the Southern Pacific, by Ernest L. King as told to Robert E. Mahaffay. Garden City, N. Y., Doubleday & co., inc., 1948. Pict. cloth. OP.

5 p.l., 11–271 p. 22 cm.
Index: p. 265–271.
Half title; illus. double t.p.; "First edition" on copyright p.

Like several other railroad books, this one has a chapter on train robberies. It deals with the De Autremont brothers, Burt Alvord, Grant Wheeler, the Daltons, Sontag, Evans, and others.

593 King, Frank M.

Mavericks. The salty comments of an old-time cowpuncher, by Frank M. King. Illustration by Charles M. Russell. Introduction by Ramon F. Adams. Pasadena, the Trail's End publishing co., inc. [1947]. Cloth. In print.

xii p., 2 l., [5]–271 [1] p. front. (col.). 21.5 cm.
Index: p. [273]–275.
Illus. end papers; illus. chapter divisions; pub. device.

Also published in a de luxe edition of 350 copies, numbered, signed, and bound in morocco.

218

Frank King knew many of the outlaws of the Southwest personally, and his book contains many references to them. These comments are selected from his column "Mavericks," which has run for many years in the *Western Livestock Journal* of Los Angeles. King debunks some of the legends about Billy the Kid. The author, who is a friend of mine, has always deplored the fact that modern writers do not keep the records of the old outlaws straight.

594 ——

Pioneer western empire builders. A true story of the men and women of pioneer days, by Frank M. King. Profusely illustrated, including an original illustration by Charles M. Russell . . . . ₍Pasadena, the Trail's End publishing co., inc., 1946.₎ Cloth. OP.

> 8 p.l., ₍21₎–383 p. front., plates, ports., map, facsm. 22 cm.
>
> Also published in a de luxe edition, signed, numbered, and bound in morocco.

Contains reliable information on Billy the Kid and other outlaws of the Southwest.

595 ——

Wranglin' the past; being the reminiscences of Frank M. King. Illustrated. ₍Los Angeles₎, this first edition privately published for his friends by the author ₍printed by Haynes corp.₎, 1935. Imt. leather. Scarce.

> xi ₍1₎ p., 13–244 p. front. (port.), illus., plates, ports. 23.5 cm.
> Illus. t.p.
> Colophon: "This autograph first edition is limited to 300 copies to be sold at five dollars the copy, of which this is No. ____."

Republished in 1946 by the Trail's End publishing co., Pasadena, with a preface by H. E. Britzman, and an illustration by Charles M. Russell. "First revised edition" appears on t.p., and this edition contains 284 pages.

Both editions contain considerable material on gunmen, such as John Ringo, Billy the Kid, and the Earps, and also tell of the Tonto Basin War.

596 King, Leonard

From cattle rustler to pulpit, by Leonard King. San Antonio, Texas, the Naylor co., 1943. Cloth. In print.

x, 216 p. front. (port.), illus. 21 cm.
Index: p. [215]–216.
Half title.

Taught cattle rustling by his father, this author was a good rustler until he was converted to religion; he later became a minister of the gospel.

597   Kingston, Charles

Remarkable rogues, the careers of some notable criminals of Europe and America, by Charles Kingston, with eight illustrations. London, John Lane, the Bodley Head, ltd.; New York, John Lane co., MCMXXI.   Cloth.   OP.

x p., 1 l., 290 p. front., plates, ports. 22.5 cm.
Index: p. 287–290.

There is a chapter on Belle Starr, in which the author gives a false account of her life and even misspells her name.

598   Klette, Ernest

The crimson trail of Joaquín Murieta, by Ernest Klette. Los Angeles, Wetzel publishing co. [1928].   Cloth.   OP.

4 p.l., 11–215 [1] p. front. 20.2 cm.
Vignette; pub. device.

Though the publishers claim this to be a biography, it is nothing but a piece of romance based on some of the legends preceding it.

599   Kroll, Harry Harrison

Rogues' company. A novel of John Murrell, by Harry Harrison Kroll.   Indianapolis, New York, the Bobbs-Merrill co., publishers [1943].   Cloth.   OP.

5 p.l., 11–412 p. 22.5 cm.
Half title; untrimmed; "First edition" on copyright p.

I have included very few works of fiction in this bibliography, but this novel seems to me to merit inclusion because it is a collector's item with a central character about whom little has been written.

600   Kuykendall, William Littlebury

Frontier days. A true narrative of striking events on the western frontier, by Judge W. L. Kuykendall.   [N.p.], J. W. and H. L. Kuykendall, publishers, 1917.   Cloth.   Scarce.

xi, 251 p. front. (port.). 19 cm.
Appendix: p. 250–251.
Half title.

This book contains some information on the Black Hills outlaws. The author, in a long footnote, gives another false account of the Hickok-McCanles fight. He also has Hickok killing five men and states that McCanles was stabbed through the heart in close fighting. He continues to call Phil Coe, Phil "Cole," a fact which tends to make us believe that he depended for source material on some of the inaccurate books published earlier.

601 La Croix, Arda

Billy the Kid. A romantic story founded upon the play of the same name, by Arda La Croix . . . . New York, J. S. Ogilvie publishing co., 1907. Pict. wrappers. Scarce.

3–128 p. front., plates. 17.9 cm.

This book is based upon the play by Walter Woods and Joseph Santley. The novel version follows the play closely, and, of course, both are fiction. However, this little volume has now become rare and a collector's item.

602 [La Croix, L. F.]

Graphic tale of most daring and successful train robbery in the history of Northwest [by L. F. La Croix]. Capture of the desperadoes and their incarceration in the Helena jail, together with the only truthful narrative ever published giving details of escape on day set for trial . . . . Illustrated . . . . Helena, Mont., State publishing co., publishers, 1909. Wrappers. Scarce.

2 p.l., 7–52 p. front. (port.), plates, ports. 23.4 cm.

603 Lake, Stuart

Wyatt Earp, frontier marshal, by Stuart Lake. With illustrations. Boston and New York, Houghton Mifflin co., 1931. Cloth. First ed. scarce.

xiv p., 1 l., [3]–392 p. front., plates, ports., facsm. 22.2 cm.
Index: p. [377]–392.
Half title; pub. device; first edition: 1931 under imprint.

Often a typographical error will identify a first printing, for the error is usually corrected in the second printing. But the error "senventy-five" (page 25) appears in all editions of this book, even in the "paper short-age" editions of World War II, although the error "ellby" for "belly" on page 54 was corrected. The book purports to be the biography of Wyatt Earp, recorded at the instigation of his third wife, a wealthy woman of San Francisco. Many writers and other men who knew Earp personally in his heyday hold him to be a character entirely different from the one portrayed by Lake. This book leaves out all the shady incidents of Earp's life and does everything possible for his glorification. Frank Waters, in his *The Colorado,* expresses the thought of many old-timers who knew Earp when he writes: "Actually it is not an autobiography at all. It is the most assiduously concocted blood-and-thunder piece of fiction ever written about the West, and a disgraceful indictment of the thousands of true Arizona pioneers whose lives and written protests refute every discolored incident in it." (Page 226.) See Item 1058.

604 Lamb, Arthur H.

Tragedies of the Osage Hills, as told by Arthur H. Lamb . . . . Pawhuska, Okla., published by the Osage printery [1935]. Pict. wrappers. OP.

2 p.l., [5]–203 p. illus., plates. 22.5 cm.
Device.

In dealing with many violent crimes, the author discusses some of the well-known Oklahoma outlaws, such as the Daltons.

605 Lang, William W.

A paper on the resources and capabilities of Texas, read by Colonel William M. Lang before the Farmers' Club of the American Institute, Cooper Union, New York, March 8th, 1881. . . . To which is appended a paper on the social and economic condition of the state. [New York, Wm. H. Thomas, mercantile printer, 1881.] Wrappers. Scarce.

[3]–31 p. large fold. map, tables. 23.2 cm.

Part of this paper deals with lawlessness in Texas. Some issues do not have the map.

606 Langford, Nathaniel Pitt

Vigilante days and ways. The pioneers of the Rockies; the makers and making of Montana, Idaho, Oregon, Washington, and Wyoming, by Nathaniel Pitt Langford. With portraits and illustrations. Boston, J. G. Cupples co., publishers, 1890. Pub. in two volumes. Pict. cloth. Scarce.

> Vol. I, xxvi, 426 p. front., ports. 19.5 cm.
> Vol. II, xiii p., 1 l., 485 p. front., ports. 19.5 cm.
> Index: p. [455]–485.
> Half title; vignette on each t.p.; tissues; 2 l. adv. at end of Vol. II.
>
> Republished in 1895 and 1912 and later issued in one volume.

One of the standard works on the Montana vigilantes and the Plummer gang of road agents.

607 Lardner, W. B., and M. J. Brock

History of Placer and Nevada counties, California, with biographical sketches of the leading men and women of the counties who have been identified with their growth and development from the early days to the present. History by W. B. Lardner and M. J. Brock. Illustrated. Los Angeles, Historic Record co., 1924. Three-quarter leather. OP.

> 11 p.l., [33]–1255 p. plates, ports. 27.3 cm.

Chapter XIII deals with outlawry in Placer County and gives a long account of Richard H. Barter, alias "Rattlesnake Dick," and Tom Bell. Chapter VI of the history of Nevada County has accounts of Murieta and Tom Bell.

608 Last Raid of the Dalton Gang

A lecture. Tackett's production of the last raid of the Dalton gang at Coffeyville, Kansas, October 5, 1892. Folder. Rare.

> 4 p. 19.3 cm.
> Double column.

A folder describing an exhibit of pictures of the Dalton gang.

609 Laughlin, Ruth (Barker)

Caballeros, by Ruth Laughlin Barker; illustrated by Norma van Sweringen. New York, Toronto, D. Appleton and co., inc., 1931. Cloth. First ed. scarce.

> 4 p.l., 379 [1] p. front., illus. 22 cm.
> On cover: "The Romance of Santa Fe and the Southwest."

Republished in 1937. Published again in 1945 by the Caxton Printers, ltd., Caldwell, Idaho, with the addition of a glossary.

4 p.l., 418 p. front., illus. 22 cm.
Map on end papers.

610 Lavender, David

The big divide, [by] David Lavender. Garden City, N. Y., Doubleday & co., inc., 1948. Cloth. OP.

x p., 1 l., 321 p. plates, ports. 22 cm.
Acknowledgments: p. [295]–297; bibliography: p. [301]–307; index: p.
Half title; map on end papers; device; untrimmed; "First edition" on
[311]–321.
copyright p.

The author touches upon many of the western outlaws, such as Billy the Kid, and upon the Johnson County and Lincoln County wars.

611 Lawson, W. B.

The Dalton boys in California; or, a bold hold-up at Ceres, by W. B. Lawson. New York, Street & Smith, publishers [1893]. Pict. wrappers. Rare.

1 l. (adv.), [5]–132 p. 19 cm.
Half title; pub. device; 9 p. adv. at end.

A piece of wild fiction, but a rare collector's item. Its brittle pulp paper has caused it practically to disappear.

612 Layne, J. Gregg

Annals of Los Angeles, from the arrival of the first white man to the Civil War, 1769–1861, by J. Gregg Layne. Special publication number nine. San Francisco, California Historical Society, 1935. Pict. cloth. Illus. label pasted on. OP.

97 p. front., plates (all col., incl. front.). 26.5 cm.
Notes: p. 89–97.
Vignette.

Contains some material on Joaquín Murieta and Jack Powers.

613 Leckenby, Charles H.

The tread of the pioneers . . . . Some highlights in the dramatic and colorful history of northwestern Colorado, compiled by

Charles H. Leckenby. Steamboat Springs, Colo., from the Pilot press [1945]. Cloth. OP.

6–206 [1] p. plates, ports. 23.6 cm.
Table of contents labeled "index"; vignette; copyright notice on verso of flyleaf before t.p.

Privately printed and issued in a small edition, this book contains a chapter on the capture of Harry Tracy and one on Tom Horn.

614 Lee, Charles (ed.)

North, east, south, west; a regional anthology of American writing. General editor: Charles Lee. New England, Sarah Cleghorn; Middle Atlantic, Edroin Seaver; Middle West, A. C. Spectorsky; the West, Joseph Henry Jackson; the South, Struthers Burt. [New York], Howell, Soslin [1945]. Cloth. OP.

xv p., 1 l., 558 p. 23 cm.
Bibliographies: p. [534]–555; index: p. 556–558.
Half title.

Another anthology reprinting Edwin Corle's "The Ghost of Billy the Kid" from his *Mojave*.

615 LeFors, Joe

Wyoming peace officer, by Joe LeFors. An autobiography. Laramie, Wyo., Laramie printing co. [1953]. Cloth. In print.

xiii p., 2 l., 200 p. front., plates, ports. 24.2 cm.
Appendix: p. 187–192; index: p. 195–200.
Tailpieces.

Published by the author's wife after his death, this book reveals some heretofore unwritten history about the Johnson County War and about Tom Horn and other outlaws of the Northwest. LeFors was the man who trapped Horn into a confession.

616 Leuba, Edmond

La Californie et les états du Pacifique. Souvenirs et impressions, par Edmond Leuba. Paris, Librairie Sandoz et Thuillier . . . , 1882. Wrappers. Rare.

2 p.l., [5]–318 p. 19.2 cm.

Chapter XXXII deals with Vásquez and the author's meeting with him as an early French visitor to the American West. He gives some information not published before.

617 Lewis, Alfred Henry

The sunset trail, by Alfred Henry Lewis . . . . Illustrated. New York, A. S. Barnes & co., 1905. Pict. cloth. Scarce.

> x p., 3 l., 393 p. front., illus., plates. 19 cm.
> Half title; device; 3 l. adv. at end.
> Republished by A. L. Burt in 1906.

Mostly a story of Dodge City and its gunmen. O. S. Clark, in his *Clay Allison of the Washita*, quotes part of one chapter from this book.

618 Lewis, John Woodruff
(Don Jernado, pseud.)

The true life of Billy the Kid, [by Don Jernado]. New York, Frank Tousey, publisher, August 29, 1881. Pict. wrappers. (Cover title.) Rare.

> 16 [1] p. 28.7 cm.
> [Wide Awake Library, Vol. I, No. 451.]
> Double column.
> Reprinted in facsimile in 1945 with an introduction by J. C. Dykes.

This is one of the dime novels on the stands almost immediately after the Kid's death. It is utterly false in all details. Very few names are correct; for example, the Kid's name is given as "William McCarthy"; his stepfather is called "Antum" instead of Antrim; McSween is called "McSwain"; and other names are just as incorrect. The author says the Kid was killed on *August* 14, with a *rifle*. It seems that the authors of nearly all the early wild and imaginary tales of western outlaws had little regard for truth; yet they labeled their accounts "true" and used the word "authentic" freely. The author writes that Mrs. McSween played the piano while her home burned. Such tales may be the source of Walter Noble Burns' account. At least they were repeated by other writers until they became legendary.

619 Lewis, Lloyd

It takes all kinds, [by] Lloyd Lewis. New York, Harcourt, Brace and co. [1947]. Cloth. OP.

> ix p., 1 l., [3]-276 p. 20.7 cm.
> Sources: p. [275]-276.
> Half title; "First edition" on copyright p.

226

A collection of Mr. Lewis' newspaper and magazine articles written over a period of years and put under one cover. The book contains a chapter on Billy the Kid, and although the author tells the story through a character whom he calls Tom Blevins, admittedly one with a reputation for tall tales, he does nothing through footnotes or otherwise to correct the preposterous statements made by Blevins. The author himself misnames William Bonney William "Bonner."

The story of Billy the Kid as told by Blevins is one of the most absurd stories about Billy the Kid that I have read. According to the author, the Kid attended college before he came West. A cattleman hired him to kill off the cowboys of a rival ranch at $1,000 per head. During a flood cowboys dragged eleven men from the river, all of whom had been shot between the eyes by Billy the Kid.

Lewis, through Blevins, says that the Kid took care of Pat Garrett during a sick spell and paid his hospital bill, and that once three hundred Negro soldiers surrounded a house in which the Kid had taken refuge. Billy killed five of them before they set the house afire. While the house was burning, the outlaw played "Home Sweet Home" on the piano "as pretty as you please." Perhaps he studied music in college!

During the battle the Kid killed twelve of the soldiers, and, all together, thirty-five men were killed. By actual count the author has the Kid killing forty-five men. He states that Billy was in love with Annie Maxwell, whom he met in Ottaway, Illinois, and that Pete Maxwell did not know Pat Garrett. Although Garrett's first shot in Maxwell's room struck the Kid in the heart, the Kid lived long enough to ask Maxwell, "Who's that in with you, Pete?" and to shoot six times, one shot going through Maxwell's sleeve, the others into the floor. Someone should have told the author that western gunmen carry only five cartridges in their guns.

The author further states that Garrett collected a $12,000 reward from the state and one of $32,000 from the cattle association. Some reward, we might add. All in all this is a most preposterous account, for which we cannot forgive an author writing under the guise of truth.

620 Lillie, Gordon William

Life story of Pawnee Bill. [By Gordon William Lillie . . . . N.p., n.d.] Pamphlet. Scarce.

22 p. 21.3 cm.
Double column.

Contains some material on Jesse James.

621   Linford, Velma

Wyoming, frontier state, by Velma Linford. Drawings by Ramona Bowman. Denver, Colo., the Old West publishing co., 1947. Pict. cloth. OP.

> xii p., 1 l., [3]–428 p. front., plates, ports., maps. 23.2 cm.
> Bibliography at end of each chapter; appendix: p. 407–414; full bibliography: p. 415–418; pronouncing index: p. 419–428.
> Illus. end papers.

Written as a school history, this book contains material on outlaws and the Johnson County War.

622   List of Fugitives from Justice

for 1887. Compiled from reports of sheriffs received at the adjutant-general's office. Austin, State printing office, 1887. Wrappers. (Cover title.) Scarce.

> [1]–101 p. 22.7 cm.
> Index: p. [83]–101.
> Double column; alphabetized by counties.

623   ———

1889, Part V. Compiled from reports of sheriffs received at the adjutant-general's office. Austin, State printing office, 1890. Wrappers. (Cover title.) Scarce.

> 19 p. 23.5 cm.
> Index: p. 17–19.
> Double column.

624   ———

1890. Part VI. Compiled from reports of sheriffs received at the adjutant-general's office. Austin, State printing office, 1890. Wrappers. (Cover title.) Scarce.

> [1]–22 p. 22.7 cm.
> Index: p. [19]–22.
> Double column.

625   ———

for 1900. Compiled from revised reports of sheriffs from fugitive list of 1896, and from subsequent reports of sheriffs received at the adjutant-general's office. Austin, von Boeckmann, Moore & Schutze, state contractors, 1900. Wrappers. (Cover title.) Scarce.

> 203 p. 22.7 cm.
> Index: p. ₁163₁–203.
> Double column.

626 Lockwood, Francis Cummins

Arizona characters, by Frank C. Lockwood . . . . Los Angeles, the Times-Mirror press, 1928. Pict. cloth. OP.

> xiv p., 1 l., 230 p. front., illus., plates, ports. 20.2 cm.
> Half title.

627 ⸻

Pioneer days in Arizona, from the Spanish occupation to statehood, by Frank C. Lockwood . . . . New York, the Macmillan co., 1932. Cloth. OP.

> xiv p., 5 l., 9–387 p. front. (port.), illus., plates, ports., maps. 24 cm.
> Index: p. 379–387.
> Half title; untrimmed.

This book contains considerable material on Arizona outlaws, but the author misnames John Heath "Frank Heith."

628 Logue, Roscoe

Tumbleweeds and barb wire fences, by Roscoe Logue. Amarillo, Texas, printed by Russell stationery co., 1936. Stiff pict. wrappers. OP.

> 5 p.l., 11–110 p. illus., plates, ports. 23.6 cm.
> Vignette; copyright notice on t.p.

In his chapter on Sam Bass, the author errs in saying that the first Texas train holdup by Bass was at Eagle Ford. It was at Allen, Texas. His chapter on Calamity Jane is sympathetic but historically unreliable. He says that she captured Jack McCall by getting the drop on him in a "two-gun play," disarmed him, and locked him up. His chapter on Belle Starr is just as unreliable; it repeats the legend of Belle's refusing to identify Jim Reed so that his assassin could not collect the reward. A short chapter on Cattle Kate is more reliable. There are also chapters on Black Jack Ketchum and the Benders.

629 ———

Under Texas and border skies, by Roscoe Logue. Amarillo, Texas, printed by Russell stationery co., 1935. Stiff pict. wrappers. OP.

> 4 p.l., 5–111 p. illus., plates, facsm. 23.6 cm.
> Vignette; copyright notice on t.p.

In his chapter on Billy the Kid, the author is very sympathetic to the Kid. He repeats the legend of the Kid's card game with Bell while a prisoner at Lincoln, as well as the one about the Kid's going to visit his sweetheart at Maxwell's home the night he was killed.

630 [Long, Green H.]

The arch field; or the life, confession, and execution of Green H. Long. The arch fiend among desperadoes. Who was a member of that celebrated gang, known as the "Banditti of the West," and traveled through the middle, western and southern states, with Hiram Birchead, a notorious English burglar, robbing, counterfeiting, forging, horse-stealing, negro stealing, house burning, gambling, passing counterfeit money, and murdering; carrying devastation, misery, and death, wherever he went, for the space of eleven years, and was finally brought to the gallows, July 27th, 1851, for the treble murder of Col. Darcy, and his two lovely daughters, Beatrice and Juliet, Little Rock, Arkansas. [New York], published by A. R. Orton, 1851. Pict. wrappers. Exceedingly rare.

> 2 p.l., [7]–31 [1] p. front., illus. 20.3 cm.
> Republished in 1852.

This is one of the really rare books dealing with our early outlaws.

631 Long, Haniel

Piñon country, by Haniel Long. Edited by Erskine Caldwell. New York, Duell, Sloan & Pearce [1941]. Dec. cloth. OP.

> xi p., 1 l., 3–327 p. 22.2 cm.
> Index: p. 319–327.
> Half title; map on end papers; "First edition" on copyright p.

There is a chapter on Billy the Kid, but the author tells nothing of the Kid's career, merely holding him as an interest for tourists.

THE ARCH FIEND:

OR

THE LIFE, CONFESSION, AND EXECUTION

OF

GREEN H. LONG.

THE ARCH FIEND AMONG DESPERADOES.

WHO WAS A MEMBER OF THAT CELEBRATED GANG, KNOWN AS

THE "BANDITTI OF THE WEST,"

AND TRAVELED THROUGH THE MIDDLE, WESTERN, AND SOUTHERN STATES, WITH

HIRAM BIRCHEAD, A NOTORIOUS ENGLISH BURGLAR,

ROBBING, COUNTERFEITING, FORGING, HORSE-STEALING, NEGRO STEALING, HOUSE
BURNING, GAMBLING, PASSING COUNTERFEIT MONEY, AND MURDERING;
CARRYING DEVASTATION, MISERY, AND DEATH, WHEREVER
HE WENT, FOR THE SPACE OF ELEVEN YEARS,
AND WAS FINALLY

BROUGHT TO THE GALLOWS, JULY 27TH, 1851,

FOR THE TREBLE MURDER OF

COL. DARCY, AND HIS TWO LOVELY DAUGHTERS,

BEATRICE AND JULIET,

LITTLE ROCK, ARK.

PUBLISHED BY A. R. ORTON

1852.

NUMBER 630

632 Long, Katherine W., and Samuel A. Siciliano

Yuma from hell-hole to haven, by Katherine W. Long and Samuel A. Siciliano. Yuma, Ariz., Yuma County Chamber of Commerce, 1950. Stiff pict. wrappers. In print.

2 p.l., 5–61 p. illus., plates (1 double p.). 19.6 cm.
Double column.

633 [López, Rafael]

Utah's greatest manhunt. The true story of the hunt for López, by an eye witness. ₁Salt Lake, press of the F. W. Gardiner co., n.d.₁ Pict. wrappers. Scarce.

8 p.l., ₁19₁–142 ₁1₁ p. illus. 16.8 cm.
Illus. t.p.; stapled.

The story of a unique manhunt which ended in the underground workings of a mine, but neither the Mexican outlaw nor his bones were ever found.

634 Lord, John

Frontier dust, by John Lord. Edited, with an introduction, by Natalie Shipman. Hartford, Conn., Edwin Valentine Mitchell, 1926. Cloth (title label pasted on). OP.

x p., 1l., 198 ₁1₁ p. 22.2 cm.
Half title.
Colophon: "This book has been designed by Robert S. Josephy and a thousand copies have been printed under his supervision at the shop of Douglas C. McMurtie, N. Y., in December, MCMXXVI."

Although the author of this book says it is an autobiography, he makes some statements we cannot swallow. He claims that Billy the Kid started his outlaw career by killing a cook who had thrown hot grease upon him. He also claims that the Kid and a young Mexican foreman for Maxwell loved the same girl and that this foreman tipped Garrett off that the Kid was in town. Then follows one fantastic tale after another, with the Kid establishing headquarters in the Texas Panhandle and having eighty or ninety men in his gang. The author has him holding up banks, trains, and stagecoaches, something the Kid never did. When the United States government sent a company of cavalry after him for robbing the mails, he and his gang whipped the cavalry in open fight. Lord also says Garrett was a deputy instead of a sheriff.

In telling of the Kid's escape from the Lincoln County jail, he has him merely tapping the jailer on the head, locking him and his *wife* in an empty cell, and then riding off. The author claims that he was sleeping in Maxwell's bed the night Garrett arrived disguised as a Mexican. Garrett got into bed with him, and when the Kid arrived, he slid off the side of the bed and shot him. He states that the Kid was twenty-four years old and says that he had killed twenty-four men.

He also claims that the James boys, under the name of Thompson, were in the cattle business for a year in an entirely unoccupied section of southwestern New Mexico.

The whole book is filled with absurd statements such as those cited above.

635 [Los Angeles County]

An illustrated history of Los Angeles county, California. Containing a history of Los Angeles county from the earliest period of its occupancy to the present time . . . . Chicago, the Lewis publishing co., 1889. Dec. cloth. Scarce.

> 6 p.l., 1 p., 2–835 p. front. (port.), plates, ports. (part with tissues). 30 cm. Double column.

Contains a chapter on Tiburcio Vásquez.

636 Love, Nat

The life and adventures of Nat Love, better known in the cattle country as "Deadwood Dick," by himself. A true history of slavery days, life on the great cattle ranges and on the plains of the "wild and woolly" west, based on facts, and personal experiences of the author. Los Angeles, Calif. [Wayside press], 1907. Pict. cloth. Scarce.

> 3 p.l., [7]–162 p. front. (port.), illus., plates, ports. 23.3 cm.

Although this Negro author is supposed to have been writing of his own experiences, he had either a bad memory or a good imagination. He makes the statement that John Chisum (misspelled "Chisholm") hired Billy the Kid to steal cattle for him. When Chisum failed to settle satisfactorily with the Kid, the outlaw ran him out of the country. He began killing Chisum's employees. According to one of the author's many preposterous statements, "He would ride up to a bunch of cowboys and enquire if they worked for Chisholm [sic]. If they replied in the affirmative, he would shoot them dead on the spot." The author also states that the Kid once pointed out a log cabin as the place where he was born. He misspells many proper names of both people and places.

637 Love, Robertus

The rise and fall of Jesse James, by Robertus Love . . . . New York, London, G. P. Putnam's sons . . . , 1926. Cloth. OP.

ix p., 1 l., 3–446 p.   front. (ports.).   22.2 cm.
Untrimmed.

Probably the most reliable book yet written on Jesse James. Like most biographers, the author is sympathetic to his subject. He places much of the blame for the Jameses' outlawry upon Pinkerton agents and their persecutions. He also repeats the fable about Jesse's helping an impoverished widow hounded by a tyrannical agent. The book contains a chapter on the Union Pacific robbery at Big Springs as an argument against the common belief that Frank and Jesse James were connected with this robbery. His account of this event is fairly accurate except that he calls Joel Collins, "Jim."

638 Lowther, Charles C.

Dodge City, Kansas, by Charles C. Lowther . . . . Illustrated. Philadelphia, Dorrance and co., publishers ₁1940₁.   Cloth.   OP.

4 p.l., 9–213 p.   front., illus.   19.3 cm.
Pub. device.

A book about the gunmen of Dodge City.

639 Ludlum, Stuart D. (ed.)

Great shooting stories, edited by Stuart D. Ludlum. Illustrated by Ted Placek.   Garden City, N. Y., Doubleday & co., inc., 1947.   Cloth.   OP.

xiii p., 2 l., 3–303 p.   illus.   22 cm.
Glossary: p. 301–303.
Half title; illus. end papers; vignette; "First edition" on copyright p.

Contains chapters on Wyatt Earp, the O K Corral fight, and John Wesley Hardin.

640 Lyman, George Dunlap

John Marsh, pioneer. The life story of a trail-blazer on six

frontiers, by George D. Lyman. Illustrated. New York, Charles
Scribner's sons, 1930. Cloth. OP.

> xii p., 2 l., 3–394 p. front., plates, ports., facsm. 22 cm.
> Acknowledgments: p. 339–342; bibliography: p. 343–384; index: p. 387–394.
> Half title; map on end papers; device; untrimmed; first edition: letter "A"
> on copyright p.

641 ⸻

The saga of the Comstock Lode. Boom days in Virginia City,
by George D. Lyman .... Illustrated. New York, London, Charles
Scribner's sons, 1934. Cloth. OP.

> xii p., 1 l., 3–407 p. front., plates, ports. 23 cm.
> Acknowledgments: p. 353–355; notes (in part bibliographical): p. 359–399;
> index: p. 401–407.
> Half title; untrimmed; first edition: letter "A" on copyright p.

This book has several chapters on the bad men of Washoe, such as
"Fighting Sam" Brown and Langford Peel.

642 McCarty, John L.

Maverick town, the story of old Tascosa, by John L. Mc-
Carty, with chapter decorations by Harold D. Bugbee. Norman,
University of Oklahoma press, 1946. Pict. cloth. In print.

> xiii p., 1 l., 3–277 p. illus., plates, ports. 21 cm.
> Bibliography: p. 261–266; index, p. 267–277.
> Half title; map on end papers; illus. double t.p.; illus. chapter headings;
> "First edition" on copyright p.

The first complete history of this wild cowtown, it tells of Tascosa's
gunmen and gun battles and of some of the other outlaws of the Southwest. The chapters on Sostenes l'Archeveque and Billy the Kid are
both reliable.

643 McCauley, James Emmitt

A stove-up cowboy's story, by James Emmitt McCauley.
Introduction by John A. Lomax. Drawings by Tom Lea. ₁Dallas,
Texas₁, published by the Texas Folklore Society, Austin, Texas, and
the University press in Dallas, 1943. Pict. cloth. Scarce.

> xxii p., 1 l., 73 p. front., illus. 22.2 cm.
> ₁Ranch life series.₁
> Illus. end papers.
> Colophon: "700 copies of this book have been printed and the type
> melted."

Contains interesting episodes in a cowboy's life and information on some of the outlaws of Texas and Arizona.

644   McClintock, James H.

Arizona, prehistoric—aborginal—pioneer—modern. The nation's youngest commonwealth within a land of ancient culture, by James H. McClintock.   Chicago, the S. J. Clarke publishing co., 1916.   Pub. in three volumes.   Three-quarter leather.   Scarce.

> Vol. I, x, 312 p.   front., plates, ports., maps.   27 cm.
> Vol. II, vii, 313–633 p.   plates, ports.   27 cm.
> Illus., p. 619–622; index: p. 623–633.
> Vol. III biographical.
> Vols. I and II paged continuously; state seal on t.p.; frontis tissues.

There are chapters with reliable information on all the Arizona outlaws.

645   McClintock, John S.

Pioneer days in the Black Hills. Accurate history and facts related by one of the early day pioneers. Author John S. McClintock, Deadwood, S. D., edited by Edward L. Senn.   Deadwood, S. D., published by John S. McClintock [1939].   Morocco.   Scarce.

> x p., 2 l., 336 p.   front. (port.), plates, ports.   23.5 cm.
> Biographical sketches: p. 280–336.
> Half title.

Contains much material on the road agents and outlaws of the Black Hills and on Wild Bill Hickok and Calamity Jane.

646   McClure, Alexander Kelly

Three thousand miles through the Rocky mountains, by A. K. McClure.   Philadelphia, J. B. Lippincott and co., 1869.   Cloth. OP.

> 8 p.l., 3–456 p.   front., plates.   19.5 cm.
> Appendix: p. 453–456.

Contains some information on the Montana Vigilantes.

647   McConnell, William John

Frontier law. A story of vigilante days, by William J. McConnell, in collaboration with Howard R. Driggs . . . . Illustrated with drawings by Herbert M. Stoops. New York, Yonkers-on-Hudson; Chicago, World book co., 1924. Pict. cloth. OP.

> xii, 233 p. front., illus. 20.2 cm.
> Half title; pub. device; headpieces; tailpieces; 5 l. adv. at end.

648 McGeeney, P. S.

Down at Stein's Pass. A romance of New Mexico, by P. S. McGeeney. Boston, Angel Guardian press, 1909. Pict. cloth. Scarce.

> 3 p.l., 114 p. front. (port.). 18.8 cm.

Although this book is fiction, it is included here because it is a collector's item for material on Billy the Kid. The account of the killing of the Kid by Garrett is based upon fact, but the rest is romance.

649 McGillycuddy, Julia B.

McGillycuddy agent; a biography of Dr. Valentine T. McGillycuddy, by Julia B. McGillycuddy. Stanford University, Calif., Stanford University press; London, Humphrey Milford, Oxford University press [1941]. Pict. cloth. OP.

> xi p., 1 l., 3–291 p. front., ports. 23.5 cm.
> Half title; vignette.

Contains a chapter on Calamity Jane and a good description of the killing of Wild Bill Hickok by Jack McCall.

650 McGinnis, Edith B.

The promised land, by Edith B. McGinnis. A narrative featuring the life history and adventures of Frank J. Brown, pioneer, buffalo hunter, Indian fighter, and founder of the Quaker settlement of Friendswood . . . . [Boerne, Texas, published by Topperwein publishing co., 1947.] Cloth. OP.

> 3 p.l., 7–160 p. illus., ports., map. 23.6 cm.
> "First edition" on verso of dedication p.

Contains some heretofore unrecorded information on Bat Masterson.

651 McGinty, Billy

The old west, as written in the words of Billy McGinty [as

told to Glenn L. Eyler₁. ₁N.p., 1937.₁ Stiff wrappers. (Cover title.) Scarce.

> 108 ₁2₁ p. front., illus. 22 cm.
> Half title.

Some information on Tulsa Jack and other outlaws.

652 McGivern, Edward

Ed McGivern's book on fast and fancy revolver shooting and police training . . . . Springfield, Mass., the King-Richardson co., 1938. Morocco. First ed. scarce.

> 8 p.l., 19–484 p. front. (port.), illus., plates, ports. 23.8 cm.
> Index: p. 479–484.

> Republished several times.

This book about shooting naturally has quite a lot of material on many of the killers of the West.

653 McGowan, Edward

Narrative of Edward McGowan, including a full account of the author's adventures and perils while persecuted by the San Francisco vigilance committee of 1856 . . . . San Francisco, published by the author, 1857. Pict. wrappers. Exceedingly rare.

> viii, ₁9₁–240 p. plates. 17.6 cm.

Contains some material on Tom Powers, with whom the author hid out when the Vigilance Committee was after him.

> Republished in 1917.

> Narrative of Edward McGowan, including a full account of the author's adventures and perils while persecuted by the San Francisco vigilance committee of 1856. Together with a report of his trial, which resulted in his acquittal. Reprinted line for line and page for page from the original edition published by the author in 1857, complete with reproductions, in facsimile of the original illustrations, cover-page title and title page. San Francisco, printed by Thomas C. Russell, at his private press . . . , 1917. Boards and cloth. Scarce.

>> viii, 9–240 p. plates (col.). 20.6 cm.
>> T.p. in red and black.

Colophon: "Limited edition of two hundred copies, printed with hand-set type, and the type distributed. This copy is ____."

Reprinted again in recent years by Biobooks, Oakland, Calif.

654 McGroarty, John Steven

The pioneer. A fascinating chapter from the pages of California's history, by John Steven McGroarty . . . . [Los Angeles, printed by Press publishing co.], 1925. Pict. wrappers. Scarce.

[20] p. (no pagination). front. (port.). 15.3 x 8.5 cm.

Herman W. Hellman, the subject of this little pamphlet and at one time a Wells-Fargo shotgun messenger, tells of some of his experiences with Tiburcio Vásquez, the California bandit.

655 McIntire, James

Early days in Texas. A trip to hell and heaven, by Jim McIntire. Kansas City, Mo., McIntire publishing co. [1902]. Cloth. Rare.

4 p.l., 9–229 p. front., plates, ports. 20.2 cm.
Preface signed "James McIntire."

The author, himself a fugitive from justice, had served as a peace officer in several towns of the West. He tells a great deal about gunmen, such as Billy the Kid and Jim Courtright. The author was city marshall of Las Vegas, New Mexico, when a mob tried to take Dave Rudabaugh from the train while Dave and the Kid were prisoners of Pat Garrett. He refers to the Kid as the "notorious Mexican outlaw."

656 McKee, Irving

"Ben-Hur" Wallace. The life of General Lew Wallace, [by] Irving McKee. Berkeley and Los Angeles, University of California press, 1947. Cloth. OP.

6 p.l., 301 p. illus., plates, ports. 21.6 cm.
Bibliographical appendix: p. 270–282; index: p. 285–301.
Half title.

Unlike Wallace's own autobiography, this book devotes some space to the Lincoln County War and tells of Wallace's contacts with Billy the Kid, and of many of the Kid's actions during that turbulent time.

657 McKeown, Martha Ferguson

The trail led north. Mont Hawthorne's story, by Martha

239

Ferguson McKeown. New York, the Macmillan co., 1948.   Cloth.
In print.

> 5 p.l., 222 p.   front., 2 maps (incl. front.).   21.5 cm.
> Half title.

This is one of a series of books written about Mont Hawthorne's experiences in the West and in Alaska. This one contains some material on Soapy Smith during his stay in Alaska.

658   McLeod, Alexander

Pigtails and gold dust, by Alexander McLeod. Illustrated. Caldwell, Idaho, the Caxton printers, ltd., 1947.   Cloth.   OP.

> 8 p.l., [17]–326 p.   front., plates, facsms.   23.5 cm.
> Bibliography: p. [323]–326.
> Half title; caption title: "A Panorama of Chinese Life in Early California."

Contains a story of Joaquín Murieta and Three-Fingered Jack García and his cruelty to the Chinese. The author is one of many who repeat the legend about the reward notice under which Murieta scribbled his defiance.

659   McNeal, Thomas Allen

When Kansas was young, by T. A. McNeal.   New York, the Macmillan co., 1922.   Cloth.   OP.

> ix p., 1 l., 287 p.   19.5 cm.
> Half title.

This book has become quite scarce. It contains some excellent material on pioneer life in Kansas, including material on outlaws and gunmen.

660   McNeill, Cora

"Mizzoura," by Cora McNeill . . . .   Minneapolis, Mizzoura publishing co., 1898.   Cloth.   Scarce.

> 4 p.l., 391 p.   plates, ports.   20.4 cm.
> Appendix: p. [365]–390; list of errata: p. 391.

A story of the life of the Younger brothers, said to be the only book written about them to which they gave their personal approval. The author uses fictitious names and writes in a fictional style, though the work is said to be fact and she provides affidavits in the appendix as proof that it is.

661 McPherren, Ida (Mrs. Geneva Gibson)

Empire builders, by Ida McPherren. A history of the founding of Sheridan. Dedicated to the memory of John D. Loucks, the founder of the town. ₁Sheridan, printed by Star publishing co., 1942.₁ Stiff pict. wrappers. OP.

72 p. 20.7 cm.

In this story of the founding of Sheridan, Wyoming, the author gives some information on such characters as Calamity Jane, Big Nose George Parrott, and Al Jennings and his gang.

662 ———

Imprints on pioneer trails, by Ida McPherren. Boston, Christopher publishing house ₁1950₁. Cloth. In print.

xi p., 2 l., 17–380 ₁1₁ p. front., plates. 20.3 cm.
Half title; pub. device.

In this book of personal reminiscences the author includes some material on Henry Plummer and Calamity Jane, not any of it too reliable.

663 ———

Trail's end, by Ida McPherren. ₁Casper, Wyo., printed by Prairie publishing co., 1938.₁ Pict. cloth. OP.

4 p.l., ₁9₁–322 p. front. 20.3 cm.
Half title.

This book contains much material on the Johnson County War, but the account has been fictionized.

664 McReynolds, Robert

Thirty years on the frontier, by Robert McReynolds . . . . Colorado Springs, Colo., El Paso publishing co., 1906. Pict. cloth. Scarce.

4 p.l., 256 p. front., plates, ports. 19.5 cm.

Contains a chapter on outlawry in Oklahoma with information about the Daltons and Bill Doolin.

665 Mandat-Grancey, Edmond de, Baron

Dans les montagnes rocheuses, par le Baron E. de Mandat-Grancey, dessins de Crafty et carte spéciale; Courouné par l'Acadé-

mie française, prix Montyon.   Paris, E. Plon, Nourrit et cie., 1884.
Wrappers.   Scarce.

> 2 p.l., 314 p. front., plates, fold. map. 18.5 cm.
> Reprinted: 1889, 1894.

This French nobleman visited the United States and toured the Black
Hills. In writing of his experiences, he must have based his account of
Wild Bill Hickok upon the tall tales fed him by the natives. He
claims that Wild Bill made his living "destroying Sioux—so much for
the scalp of a man, so much for a woman's and so much for a child's."
In dull seasons he hung around Deadwood.

"One day he entered into an inn recently opened by a *Californian*
named Jack McCall," he wrote. "The landlord was standing behind the
bar, against which Wild Bill tottered half drunk."

Wild Bill, according to the author, tried to buy a drink with a hand-
ful of bloody scalps and when refused used a little force. McCall reached
under the bar, secured a gun, and shot Wild Bill *three times* as soon as
he got a chance. Those who know the history of Wild Bill's death will
find this account ridiculous.

666 ———

La brèche aux buffles par le Baron E. de Mandat-Grancey.
Dessins de R. J. De Boisvray.   Paris, E. Plon, Nourrit et cie., im-
primeurs-éditeurs . . . , 1889.   Wrappers.   Rare.

> xvi, 292 p. front. (double p.), illus. (double p.). 18.5 cm.
> Half title; pub. device; tissues; table of contents at end.
> Reprinted in 1894.

This book has become exceedingly rare. It continues this French nobleman's experiences in America. He tells something of Calamity Jane and
attempts to relate the story of Billy the Kid's escape from the Lincoln
County jail when he killed Bell and Ollinger. Much of his information
seems to come from Siringo's writings, but in his translation he seems
to have become confused about some of the facts.

667 Manning, William H.

The gold-dragon; or, the California blood-hound. A story
of Po–8, the lone highwayman.   New York, Beadle and Adams,
1884.   Pict wrappers.   (Cover title.)   Rare.

> 31 p. 31.5 cm.
> Double column.

One of the Beadle dime novels founded upon the activities of Black Bart.

668 [Marlow, Charles and George]

Life of the Marlows, as related by themselves. Illustrated. Ouray, Colo., Plaindealer print, Kelley & Hulaniski publishers [1892]. Pict. wrappers.   Exceedingly rare.

[5]–181 p. front., illus., plates. 19 cm.
Copyright notice on first flyleaf.

Republished with revisions and edited by William Rathmell, Ouray, Colo., Ouray Herald print, W. S. Olexa, publisher [n. d.]. Stiff wrappers.   Scarce.

2 p.l., [7]–100 p. 20.4 cm.

The first edition of this work is exceedingly rare, and the second is quite scarce. The chapters following Chapter XVIII are misnumbered XIV, XV, and XVI. The same mistake is made in the revised edition, but new material is added and changes are made in the latter part of the book. In these books the Marlows tell their side of the trouble they had with the law.

669 Marshall, James

Santa Fe, the railroad that built an empire, by James Marshall.   New York, Random House [1945].   Cloth.   OP.

xvi p., 1 l., 3–465 p. plates, ports., maps, facsms., tables. 22 cm.
Appendices: p. 349–449; index: p. 451–465.
Half title; map on end papers; illus. double t.p.; "First printing" on copyright p.

Another good railroad book containing material on train robbers, such as the James brothers.

670 Marshall, James

Elbridge A. Stuart, founder of Carnation company, [by] James Marshall.   Los Angeles, Carnation co. [1949],   Limp leather. OP.

viii p., 2 l., 3–238 p. front. (port. with tissue), plates, ports. 26 cm.
Appendix: p. 221–238.
Half title; untrimmed; gilt top.
Colophon: "The volume is number ____ of 275 copies issued in memory of Elbridge Amos Stuart founder of Carnation Company on its Fiftieth Anniversary."

Also published in a trade edition.

243

LIFE OF THE MARLOWS

AS RELATED BY THEMSELVES.

ILLUSTRATED.

PLAINDEALER PRINT; KELLEY & HULANISKI PUBLISHERS,
OURAY, COLO.

NUMBER 668

The author tells of some of his subject's experiences in the Wild West around El Paso, Texas, and in New Mexico. He is wrong in saying that Billy the Kid killed twenty-six men and that he was jailed in Las Vegas when he killed his two jailers.

671 [Martin, Charles Lee]

A sketch of Sam Bass, the bandit. A graphic narrative of his various train robberies, his death, and accounts of the deaths of his gang and their history. With illustrations. Dallas, Texas, the Herald steam printing house [Worley and co.], 1880. Pict. wrappers. Exceedingly rare.

[3]-152 [2] p. illus., plates. 20.5 cm.
1 p. adv. in front; 2 p. adv. at end.

This exceedingly rare little book is not to be confused with the Sam Bass volume published in Dallas in 1878. The copy in the Library of Congress is the only copy known to me. The author says that Sam Bass and Joel Collins drove a herd of cattle to Kansas, where they sold them and then used the money to go to Deadwood, *Idaho Territory* (!). Aside from the newspaper quotations and the narrative as told by Jim Murphy, much of the rest of the book parallels Hogg's book published in Denton, Texas. However, in writing of the lives of some of Bass' confederates, such as Underwood, Barnes, and Arkansas Johnson, this author gives much fuller accounts and gives some information not found in the other books on Bass.

672 Martin, Douglas D.

Tombstone's epitaph, [by] Douglas D. Martin. [Albuquerque, the University of New Mexico press, 1951.] Pict. cloth. In print.

xii, 272 p. illus. 23.5 cm.
Half title; illus. end papers; vignette.

This author has done every student of western history a great favor by publishing and putting into circulation these rare items from the files of this noted Tombstone newspaper. Naturally there is much information on the Arizona outlaws, some of it never published in any other book.

673 Martin, George Washington

The first two years in Kansas; or, where, when and how the

Missouri bushwhackers, the Missouri train and bank robber, and those who stole themselves rich in the name of liberty, were sired and reared. An address by George W. Martin . . . . Topeka, State printing office, 1907. Pamphlet. (Cover title.) Scarce.

> 30 p. 22.8 cm.

Revelations, based upon original sources, of vital historical facts not elsewhere available. The author's quotations are from excessively rare files of pioneer newspapers.

674 Martin, Jack

Border boss, Captain John R. Hughes, Texas ranger, by Jack Martin. Drawings by Frank Anthony Stanush. San Antonio, Texas, the Naylor co., publishers, 1942. Pict. cloth. In print.

> xvi, 236 p. front. (port.). 21 cm.
> Bibliography: p. [225]–227; index: p. [231]–236.
> Half title; illus. chapter headings; vignette.

The author tells of the killing of John Wesley Hardin by John Selman. Ranger Hughes, like several others, believes that Pat Garrett was killed by the notorious killer Jim Miller.

675 Masterson, Vincent Victor

The Katy railroad and the last frontier, by V. V. Masterson. Norman, University of Oklahoma press [1952]. Cloth. In print.

> xvi p., 1 l., 3–312 p. illus., plates., ports., maps, facsms., tables. 23.5 cm.
> Bibliography: p. 291–297; index, p. 298–312.
> Half title; "First edition" on copyright p.

Has a chapter which deals with the Daltons and some of their train robberies.

676 Mattison, Ray H.

Roosevelt and the stockmen's association, by Ray H. Mattison. Reprinted from the *North Dakota History*, Vol. 17, No. 2 (April 1950); Vol. 17, No. 3 (July, 1950). Bismark, N. D., the State Historical Society of North Dakota [1950]. Stiff wrappers. In print.

> [3]–59 [3] p. front. (port.), 3 plates at end. 22.8 cm.

Contains much on horse thieves, rustlers, the vigilantes, and bylaws of the Little Missouri Stockmen's Association and the bylaws of the Montana Stock Growers' Association.

677 Maxwell, Hu

Evans and Sontag, the famous bandits of California. San Francisco, San Francisco printing co., 1893. Wrappers. Very rare.

> 248 p. illus., ports. 19 cm.
> On cover: "The California Library No. 1."
>
> Published the same year in New York under the imprint: "Trade supplied by the American News."

An early account of these California train robbers, and another of those brittle pulp publications which have practically disappeared.

678 Menefee, Eugene L., and Fred A. Dodge

History of Tulare and Kings counties California, with biographical sketches of the leading men and women of the counties who have been identified with their growth and development from the early days to the present. History by Eugene L. Menefee and Fred A. Dodge. Illustrated .... Los Angeles, Calif., Historic Record co., 1913. Three-quarter leather. Scarce.

> xiv, [5]–890 p. plates, ports, maps. 27.8 cm.
> Gilt edges.

Chapter XVI, entitled "Great Train Robberies," deals with the Daltons and the Evans-Sontag gang.

679 Mercer, Asa Shinn

The banditti of the plains; or the cattlemen's invasion of Wyoming in 1892. [The crowning infamy of the ages.] By A. S. Mercer. [Cheyenne, Wyo., 1894.] Cloth. Exceedingly rare.

> 5 p.l., [1] p., [12]–139 p. illus., map. 21.3 cm.
> Appendix (confession of George Dunning): p. [107]–139.

This exceedingly rare book has had a tempestuous history. Because the cattlemen of Wyoming objected to being exposed through its publication, the author's print shop was burned to the ground, and with the assistance of a sympathetic judge the cattlemen had most of the books that had already been published seized and burned. The author was ordered to leave Wyoming. Few books have undergone more rigorous

THE

Banditti of the Plains

— OR THE —

Cattlemen's Invasion of Wyoming in 1892

[THE CROWNING INFAMY OF THE AGES.]

By A. S. MERCER.

NUMBER 679

suppression. The state and public libraries of Wyoming have had their original copies stolen or mutilated by descendants of the cattlemen.

Rewritten and republished under the title "Powder River Invasion. War on the rustlers in 1892," by John Mercer Boots. [Los Angeles, 1923.] Cloth. Scarce.

> 7 p.l., [15]–146 p. 19.8 cm.
> Appendix: p. 113–146.

Republished: "The banditti of the plains," I. G. McPherren, Sheridan, Wyo. 1930. Wrappers. Scarce.

> [80] p. 20.5 cm.

Also published in a new edition by the Grabhorn Press, with a foreword by James Mitchell Clarke and illustrations by Arvilla Parker. San Francisco, printed for George Fields by the Grabhorn press, MCMXXXV. Cloth and boards. Scarce.

> xiv p., 1 l., 3–136 p. illus. 24.8 cm.
> Appendix: p. 111–136.
> Illus. chapter headings.

This edition too has become very scarce and quite expensive.

680 Middleton, John W.

History of regulators and moderators and the Shelby county war in 1841 and 1842, in the republic of Texas, with facts and incidents in the early history of the republic and state, from 1837 to the annexation, together with incidents of frontier life and Indian troubles, and the war on the reserve in Young county in 1857. By Jonh [*sic*] W. Middleton .... Fort Worth, Loving publishing co., 1883. Stiff pink wrappers. Exceedingly rare.

> 2 p.l., [5]–40 p. 23.2 cm.

Reprinted by John A. Norris, of Austin, Texas (*ca.*1926), in exact duplication (except for tan wrappers), retaining the misspelled "John" and carrying a statement at the end from Miss Harriet Smither, archivist of the Texas State Library, concerning the exactness of the duplication. Later the book was reprinted by H. N. Gammel, of Austin, with corrected spelling of "John" and with changes on the cover. This edition has the same pagination, but measures 23 cm. Both reprints are now scarce and the original is exceedingly rare.

249

681 Miller, Benjamin S.

Ranch life in southern Kansas and the Indian territory, as told by a novice. How a fortune was made in cattle, by Benjamin S. Miller. New York, Fless & Ridge printing co., 1896. Wrappers. Rare.

3 p.l., [7]–163 [1] p. front. (port.). 20 cm.

The author was the first president of the Cherokee Strip Livestock Association, and his book deals with the cattlemen of that section in the seventies. It contains some firsthand information on Billy the Kid and tells of the attempt by the Las Vegas mob to take the prisoners away from Pat Garrett, an incident which the author witnessed. In reporting the Kid's death the author says Garrett found the Kid *in bed* at Maxwell's and "didn't wait to take him prisoner, but poured a load of *buckshot* into him as he raised up in bed, and that settled it, Billy taking some of the medicine he had been accustomed to administer in such liberal doses to others."

682 [Miller, George, Jr.]

The trial of Frank James for murder. With confessions of Dick Liddil and Clarence Hite, and history of the "James gang." Kansas City, Mo., published by George Miller, Jr. [Columbus, Mo., press of E. W. Stephens, 1898.] Cloth. Scarce.

2 p.l., 5–348 [1] p. front., plates, ports. 19 cm.

Also published in wrappers.

The complete record of the trial, with testimony, addresses to the jury, and pleas of the attorneys.

683 Miller, Joseph (ed.)

The Arizona story, compiled and edited from original newspaper sources, by Joseph Miller, with drawings by Ross Santee. New York, Hastings House, publishers [1952]. Cloth. In print.

xvii p., 1 l., 3–345 p. illus. 20.8 cm.
Half title; map on end papers; illus. double t.p.

This is a collection of excerpts from the early newspapers of Arizona dealing with various subjects, from Indians, lost mines, and outlaws to legends and tall tales. Some of the stories, including an account of Pearl Hart, cover various stage robberies, hangings, and shooting scrapes of the outlaws of that section.

684 Miller, William Alexander

Early days of the wild West, by William Alexander Miller
.... ₁N.p. press of Franc. E. Sheiry₁, 1943. Stiff wrappers. OP.

3–15 p. front. (port.), plates, ports. 23 cm.

This thin book is an address the author delivered before the District of Columbia Society of the Sons of the American Revolution on Washington's Birthday in 1943. The author tells some new stories about Billy the Kid, but they are just as unbelievable as many others which have been told. He also speaks of Lew Wallace's dread of being killed by Billy the Kid while the outlaw was alive.

685 Mills, William (Bill)

Twenty-five years behind prison bars. ₁By Bill Mills, n.p., n.d.₁ Wrappers. (Cover title.) Scarce.

5–60 p. front. 20.2 cm.

686 Mills, William W.

Forty years at El Paso, 1858–1898. Recollections of war, politics, adventure, events, narratives, sketches, etc. . . . , by W. W. Mills . . . . ₁Chicago, press of W. B. Conkey co., 1901.₁ Dec. cloth. Scarce.

4 p.l., 11–166 p. front. (port. with signature in facsm.). 20 cm.

Deals with gun battles and the bloody reign of the city marshals of El Paso, Texas, in its early days.

687 Mitchell, John D.

Lost mines of the great southwest, including stories of hidden treasures, by John D. Mitchell. ₁Phoenix, Ariz., press of the Journal co., inc., 1933.₁ Cloth. Scarce.

4 p.l., 11–174 p. illus., plates. 20.3 cm.

This privately printed little book has a chapter containing the author's personal recollections of the James boys and how the author searched for some of their buried loot when a boy.

688 Moak, Sim

The last of the mill creeks and early life in northern California, by Sim Moak. Chico, Calif., 1923. Stiff pict. wrappers. Scarce.

[3]–47 [1] p. front. (port.). 24 cm.

Contains some material on road agents and Black Bart.

689 Mokler, Alfred James

History of Natrona county, Wyoming, 1888–1922. True portrayal of the yesterdays of a new county and a typical frontier town in the middle west. Fortunes and misfortunes, tragedies and comedies, struggles and triumphs of the pioneers. Map and illustrations, by Alfred James Mokler . . . . Chicago, R. R. Donnelley & sons co., 1923. Cloth. Scarce.

xiv p., 1 l., 477 p. front., plates, ports., map, facsm. 23.5 cm.
Index: p. 475–477.
Half title; frontis tissue.

Privately printed in a small edition and very scarce, this book has some excellent material on train robberies, the Johnson County War, outlaws, and the hanging of Jim Averill and Cattle Kate Watson.

690 Monaghan, Jay

The legend of Tom Horn, last of the bad men, by Jay Monaghan. Indianapolis, New York, the Bobbs-Merrill co., publishers [1946]. Cloth. OP.

10 p.l., 19–293 p. front. (port.), illus., plates, ports. 22 cm.
Acknowledgments, p. 271–274; list of sources, p. 275–284; index: p. 287–293.
Half title; untrimmed; "first edition" on copyright p.

The author gives some new information about Tom Horn, especially about his ancestry and boyhood.

691 Monroe, Arthur Worley

San Juan silver, by Arthur W. Monroe . . . . Historical tales of the silvery San Juan and western Colorado. [Grand Junction, Colo., printed by Grand Junction Sentinel], 1940. Pict. cloth. OP.

ix, 3–250 [1] p. 23.5 cm.

Much about the lawless days in Colorado. The author speaks of the Jinglebob Ranch of New Mexico and erroneously says it is where Billy the Kid and *Sam Bass* got their start. In his chapter on "Creede" there are some stories about Soapy Smith and Bat Masterson.

692 Montague, Joseph

Wild Bill, a western story, by Joseph Montague .... New York, Chelsea House, publishers [1926]. Cloth. OP.

3 p.l., [11]–247 [1] p.   19.3 cm.

This is one of the wildest and most unreliable books on Wild Bill yet published. Even if the author intends it for fiction, I fail to see why he could not get his facts correct. In his first chapter, which he begins with Wild Bill's fight with the McCanles', he misnames the latter "Jim" and "Jack McKandlas" and calls them border outlaws. They are pictured as "drunkards, roisterers and women bullies" whose profession it was to steal horses and plunder the wagon trains and stagecoaches along the trail. The author continues to place Rock Creek Station in Kansas and to have ten men in the gang, all bolstered by liquor.

Of the fight the author says in part: "His [Hickok's] six-gun roared as it shifted from flying target to flying target. Three shots and one from the rifle. Four shots in less than four seconds and there were four men dead on the floor, shot through the brain or heart with appalling accuracy." Although gravely wounded, he continues, Hickok was nursed back to health by his faithful friend Mike Cone. The whole book is the result of a rich imagination and dependence on unreliable secondary sources.

693 [Montana]

History of Montana, 1739–1885. A history of its discovery and settlement, social and commercial progress, mines and miners, agriculture and stock growing .... Indians and Indian wars, vigilantes, courts of justice .... Illustrated.   Chicago, Warner, Beers & co., 1885.   Three-quarter leather.   Rare.

7 p.l., 15–1397 p.   plates, ports., map.   27.8 cm.
Large fold. map in front.

This book has a long history of the vigilantes and their hangings.

694 ———

Montana, an illustrated history of the Yellowstone valley, embracing the counties of Park, Sweet Grass, Carbon, Yellowstone, Rosebud, Custer and Dawson. State of Montana.   Spokane, Wash., Western Historical publishing co. [n.d.].   Full leather.   Scarce.

xxi, 669 p.   front. (port. with tissue), plates, ports. (part with tissues).

253

29.7 cm.
Double column; gilt edges.

A story of the vigilantes and their troubles with the Plummer gang.

695 Moore, Gerald E.

Outlaw's end, by Gerald E. Moore. ₁n.p., n.d.₁ Stiff pict. wrappers. OP.

3 p.l., 101 p. 19 cm.

Information about some outlaws of Oklahoma, including Henry Starr and Bud Wells.

696 Moore, John M. (Tex)

The west, ₁by₁ Tex Moore, the official cowboy artist of Texas, and old time cow-puncher. ₁Wichita Falls, Texas, Wichita printing co., 1933.₁ Pict. cloth. (Cover title.) Scarce.

5 p.l., 147 ₁1₁ p. front., plates, facsm. 24 cm.
Half title; no title page.

A little book of personal reminiscences; but like so many others, it has John Chisum's name misspelled "Chisholm." The book is largely an account of the Lincoln County War and Billy the Kid. The author states that Mrs. McSween played "The Star Spangled Banner" while her home was burning and the bullets flying thick. No one knows how this legend got started, but it seems to be a favorite with many writers.

There are some errors in the account of Billy the Kid, but the author does get his killing by Pat Garrett correct, an item missed by some of the old-timers who attempted to write a book.

697 Mootz, Herman Edwin

The blazing frontier, by Herman Edwin Mootz .... Dallas, Tardy publishing co., 1936. Cloth. OP.

8 p.l., 381 p. plates, ports. 19.5 cm.

A novelized account of some of the Oklahoma outlaws.

698 Morgan, Dale L.

The Humboldt, highroad of the west, by Dale L. Morgan. Illustrated by Arnold Blanch. New York, Toronto, Farrar & Rinehart, inc. ₁1943₁. Cloth. OP.

x p., 1 l., 3–374 p. front. (map), 1 double p. plate. 20.8 cm.
Bibliography: p. 355–365; index: p. 367–374.
Half title; illus. end papers; illus. chapter headings; first edition: "F R" in device on copyright p.

Contains some information about Butch Cassidy and his Wild Bunch.

699 Morgan, Wallace M.

History of Kern county, California, with biographical sketches of the leading men and women of the county who have been identified with its growth and development from the early days to the present. History by Wallace M. Morgan. Illustrated . . . . Los Angeles, Calif., Historic Record co., 1914. Three-quarter leather. Scarce.

xvi p., 1 l., [17]–1556 p. plates, ports. (part with tissues). 28 cm.

Contains some material on the career of Tiburcio Vásquez.

700 Morrel, Ed

The twenty-fifth man. The strange story of Ed. Morrel, the hero of Jack London's *Star Rover*, by Ed. Morrel, lone survivor of the famous band of California feud outlaws . . . . Montclair, N. J., New Era publishing co. [1924]. Cloth. OP.

10 p.l., 390 p. front., illus. 21 cm.
Half title; last 14 p. a bulletin on penology.

A scarce book about the terrible experiences of the last survivor of the Evans-Sontag band of train robbers. The author helped Sontag escape from jail and became a hunted man with him.

701 Morris, Lerona Rosamond (ed.)

Oklahoma yesterday-today-tomorrow, edited by Lerona Rosamond Morris. Guthrie, Oklahoma, published by Co-Operative publishing co., December, 1930. Cloth. OP.

viii p., 9 l., 15–922 [10] p. illus., ports., map. 26 cm.
Index: p. [923–932].
Illus. end papers.

Contains some long chapters on the Oklahoma outlaws.

702   Morrison, Mrs. Anne L., and John H. Haydon

History of San Luis Obispo county and environs, California, with biographical sketches of the leading men and women of the county and environs who have been identified with the growth and development of the section from the early days to the present. History by Mrs. Anne L. Morrison and John H. Haydon.   Illustrated . . . .   Los Angeles, Calif., Historic Record co., 1917.   Three-quarter leather.   Scarce.

7 p.l., [17]–1038 p.   plates, ports.   27.7 cm.

Contains a chapter on such outlaws as Murieta, Jack Powers, and Joaquín Valenzuela.

703   Mumey, Nolie

Calamity Jane, 1852–1903. A history of her life and adventures in the west, by Nolie Mumey.   Denver, Colo., the Range press, 1950.   Boards and leather.   Pict. label pasted on.   Scarce.

xix, 21–146 p. front. (port.), illus. fold. map in front, facsm. of two pamphlets in pocket at end.   26 cm.
Supplement: p. 141–142; index: p. 143–146.
Half title; untrimmed.
Colophon: "This is number ____ of an edition limited to two hundred signed and numbered copies."

The most scholarly research done on this notorious woman. The author seems to have made an honest effort to bring to light every facet of her character. The book is well annotated. Because of the small edition, this book was practically sold out before publication and immediately became a scarce item. The author, a well-known Denver surgeon whose hobby is writing nonfiction, has his books privately printed in small editions; consequently all of them command a premium immediately after release.

The author says Calamity Jane "was supposed to have captured Jack McCall after he shot Wild Bill and held him captive with a cleaver in a meat market until he was taken into custody;" and according to his footnote reference, he got this information from Cunningham's *Triggernometry*. This false story has been repeated until it has become legendary. The author also erroneously states that Jack McCall was re-arrested at Custer City.

704 ———

Creede. History of a Colorado silver mining town. With illustrations and a pictorial map, by Nolie Mumey. Denver, Colo., Artcraft press, 1949. Pict. cloth. Scarce.

> xv p., 2 l., [5]–185 p. plates, ports., 2 maps (1 double p.), large fold. map at end. 24.9 cm.
> Index: p. [179]–185.
> Half title; untrimmed.
> Colophon: "Edition limited to five hundred numbered and signed copies."

A good history of this wild mining town in its early days, it contains an accurate account of the killing of Bob Ford.

705 ———

Poker Alice, Alice Ivers, Duffield, Tubbs, Huckert (1851–1930). History of a woman gambler in the west, by Nolie Mumey .... Denver, Colo., Artcraft press, 1951. Pict. art boards. OP.

> 6 p.l., 47 p. front. (port. tipped in), plates, ports. fold. map at end. 27.4 cm.
> Colophon: "This is No. ____ of a limited edition of 500 numbered and signed copies."

To my knowledge this is the only book written about this unique and famous western character. The first few copies released had the copyright notice on the verso of the second page following the title page, instead of on the verso of the title page. In the folding map, the state of New Mexico was erroneously labeled "Nevada." These errors were quickly corrected, but a few copies escaped the correction and now are considered as the first state of the book.

706 Munsell, M. E.

Flying sparks as told by a Pullman conductor, by M. E. Munsell. Kansas City, Tiernan-Dart printing co., 1914. Pict. wrappers. Scarce.

> xvii, 19–159 p. front. (port. with tissue), illus., port., plates, facsms. 19 cm.

A conductor's experience with some of the Oklahoma outlaws, such as Cherokee Bill, Belle Starr, and Jim Reed.

707 Murdock, John R.

Arizona characters in silhouette, by John R. Murdock. [N.

257

p.₁, Fray Marcos de Niza edition, 1939. Stiff pict. wrappers. Scarce.

> 2 p.l., 7–151 p. illus. (with silhouette drawings). 22.8 cm.
> "First published serially in 1933."

Contains material on the Apache Kid, with a chapter on Bucky O'Neill and some of the train robbers of Arizona.

708 [Murieta, Joaquín]

El caballero Chileno bandido en California. Unica y verdadera historia de Joaquín Murrieta [*sic*] por el Profesor Agigar. Barcelona, Biblioteca Hercules ₍n.d.₎. Col. pict. wrappers. Scarce.

> 6 p.l., ₍13₎–206 p. plates. 18.8 cm.

Compare with Item 534.

709 ———

Joaquín Murrieta [*sic*] el bandido Chileno en California. San Antonio, Texas, "Editorial Martínez," 1926. Col. pict. wrappers. Scarce.

> 4 p.l., ₍9₎–264 p. plates. 19 cm.
> Index: p. 263–264.
> Half title; text in Spanish.

710 ———

The life of Joaquín Murieta, the brigand chief of California; being a complete history of his life, from the age of sixteen to the time of his capture and death at the hands of Capt. Harry Love, in the year of 1853. San Francisco, published at the office of the "California Police Gazette," 1859. Pict. wrappers. Exceedingly rare.

> ₍3₎–71 ₍1₎ p. illus., plates, port. 24.7 cm.
> Double column; 1 p. adv. in front; 2 p. adv. at end.

This book was originally published as a serial in the *California Police Gazette* in ten issues (Vol. I, Nos. 34 to 43, September 3 to November 5, 1859). It is an anonymous rewriting of John Rollin Ridge's biography of Murieta. A name is changed here and there, but the book keeps the general story by Ridge, even to much of the dialogue. The writer changed the name of Rosita to Carmela and created a second mistress named Clarina. Most of the Murieta books which followed, especially the foreign and Latin-American ones, relied on this version.

A comparison of this book with Ridge's substantiates Ridge's charge of plagiarism. But this volume is much better written than Ridge's. The anonymous writer made some of the conversation more reasonable, and the whole thing was re-edited advantageously. Its reissue by the Grabhorn Press in 1932 has made this version more familiar than Ridge's to the modern reader.

The 1859 edition under discussion was illustrated by woodcuts from drawings by Charles Nahl, a well-known artist of his day. It has also become rare, only three or four copies being known to exist. It was republished without three of the plates in 1862.

711 ———

Joaquín Murieta, the brigand chief of California. A complete history of his life from the age of sixteen to the time of his capture and death in 1853. San Francisco, the Grabhorn press, 1932. Pict. boards and cloth. Scarce.

> vii [1] p., 1 l., 116 [4] p. front. (col.), illus. (col.), fold. lithograph at end. 25.6 cm.
> No. 1 Americana reprints.
> Bibliography: last four pages.
> Double column.
> Preface signed in ink by editor, Douglas S. Watson. Introduction and bibliography by Francis P. Farquhar.

This is a modern edition of the *Police Gazette* version and has become quite scarce and high in price.

712 ———

Vida y aventuras de Joaquín Murrieta [*sic*]. San Antonio, Texas, imprenta y Librería de Pablo Cruz [1885]. Pict. wrappers. Exceedingly rare.

> 59 p. 25.5 cm.
> Triple column.

Crudely printed on brittle paper, a fact which perhaps explains its extreme rarity.

713 ———

Vida y aventuras del más célebre bandido sonorense Joaquín Murrietta [*sic*]. Sus grandes proezas en California. Mexico, Tip. y encuadernación de I. Paz, 1908. Wrappers. Rare.

> [3]-281 [1] p. 8 plates. 17 cm.

714 ———

Vida y aventuras del más célebre bandido sonorense "Joaquín Murrietta" [*sic*], y sus grandes proezas en el estado de California. Los Ahleles, [*sic*], Calif., Editores: O. Pazy cía, imprenta "El libro diario," 1919. Wrappers. Rare.

[3]-128 p. 22 cm.
2 p. adv. in front; 6 p. adv. at end (incl. back wrappers).

715 ———

Vida y aventuras del más célebre bandido sonorense Joaquín Murrieta [*sic*] y sus grandes proezas en el estado de California. Los Angeles, Cal., C. G. Vincent & co., editores, 1923. Stiff pict. wrappers. Scarce.

[3]-110 p. 22.2 cm.

716 Murphy, Celeste G.

The people of the pueblo; or, the story of Sonoma, by Celeste G. Murphy. Sonoma, Calif., W. T. and C. G. Murphy, MCMXXXV. Cloth. OP.

xvi p., 2 l., 3-269 p. plates, ports., facsms. 22.7 cm.
Half title.

Contains a chapter on Three-Fingered Jack García.

717 Murphy, J. W.

Outlaws of the Fox river country. Story of the Whiteford and Spencer tragedies, the assassination of Judge Richardson, the execution of John Baird, and the mobbing of J. W. Young . . . , by J. W. Murphy. Hannibal, Mo., Hannibal printing co., 1882. Pict. wrappers. Scarce.

2 p.l., [3]-138 p. front., illus., ports. 20.8 cm.

Another history of the outlaws of the Navoo country depicted so well by Edward Bonney. The author, an editor of Alexandria, Missouri, was personally acquainted with many of the desperate characters in this chronicle.

718 [Murrell, John A.]

Life and adventures of John A. Murrel [*sic*], the great western land pirate, with twenty-one spirited illustrative engravings.

Philadelphia, T. B. Peterson and brothers, 1845. Pict wrappers. Rare.

> 2 p.l., [5]-126 p. illus., port. 23.4 cm.

Republished, New York, H. Long and brother, 1847.

> 2 p.l., [5]-126 p. illus. 22.7 cm.
> Double column.

719 Myers, John Myers

The last chance. Tombstone's early years, by John Myers Myers. New York, E. P. Dutton & co., inc., publisher, 1950. Cloth. In print.

> 4 p.l., 13-260 p. front., plates, ports., maps, plan. 22.2 cm.
> Bibliography: p. 244-246; index: p. 247-260.
> Half title; map on front end papers; vignette; untrimmed; "First edition" on copyright p.
>
> Republished by Grossett and Dunlap under the title *The Tombstone Story* in 1951.

One of the best books about Tombstone yet written, this volume is full of reliable information on all the outlaws and gunmen of Arizona.

720 Ned, Nebraska (pseud.)

Buffalo Bill and his daring adventures in the romantic wild west. Complete biography of the world's greatest scout, buffalo hunter, Indian fighter and scout as narrated for the first time by his old comrade and lifelong friend Nebraska Ned. Baltimore, I. & M. Ottenheimer [1913]. Pict. wrappers. OP.

> 3 p.l., 9-192 p. illus. 19.2 cm.

I can understand why a writer who produces such trash would write under a pseudonym. In this author's account of the Hickok-McCanles fight, he has the *ten* McCandlas' [*sic*] against *Buffalo Bill* instead of Wild Bill. Perhaps the author was attempting to start a legend of his own. He even spells Hickok's name "Hitchcock."

721 Nelson, Bruce

Land of the Dacotahs, by Bruce Nelson. Minneapolis, University of Minnesota press . . . [1946]. Cloth. OP.

> 6 p.l., 3-354 p. plates, ports., double p. map. 23.5 cm.
> Acknowledgments and bibliography: p. 339-343; index: p. 344-354.
> Half title; vignette.

261

The author devotes a chapter to Calamity Jane, mostly in debunking her own autobiography and exposing her true character. He writes: "Calamity's claim of being Wild Bill Hickok's sweetheart was an infamous slander—a fact which Calamity herself admitted in her declining years—for whatever else may be said of Wild Bill, he was at least fastidious."

722 [Nevada]

Pioneer Nevada. Reno, Nevada, lithographed in the United States of America, copyright by Harolds Club, 1951. Stiff pict. wrappers. In print.

> 204 [2] p. illus. 35 cm.
> Map on end papers; vignette; double column.

Each page of this book is a reprint of one of the advertisements published once a week in the newspapers of Nevada during the years 1946 through 1951, and each represents some phase of history or folklore of Nevada. Many of the chapters deal with outlaws and gunmen, such as Nickanoe Rodregues, Farmer Peel, Fighting Sam Brown, Susie Raper, the lady rustler, Jack Harris, and Milton Sharp; other chapters deal with Robbers' Roost, stage robbers, and the vigilantes.

723 Neville, Alexander White

The Red river valley, then and now, by A. W. Neville. Stories of people and events in the Red river valley during the first hundred years of its settlement. Illustrated by Jose Cisneros. Paris, Texas [designed and produced by Carl Hertzog, El Paso, Texas], 1948. Cloth. In print.

> xiii p., 1 l., 3–278 p. plate on leaf before each chapter. 24 cm.
> Half title; map on end papers; t.p. in red and black; vignette.
> Colophon: "Two thousand copies of this book produced at El Paso, Texas. Typography and design by Carl Hertzog; illustrations by Jose Cisneros; silhouettes by Jack Ellis . . . ."

This book contains some new material on Jim Reed, Belle Starr, Frank James, and other outlaws.

724 Newmark, Harris

Sixty years in southern California, 1853–1913, containing the reminiscences of Harris Newmark. Edited by Maurice H. Newmark [and] Marco R. Newmark . . . . With 150 illustrations. New York, the Knickerbocker press, 1916. Leather and boards. Scarce.

xxviii p., 1 l., 688 p.   front. (port. with tissue), plates, ports., facsm.
23.2 cm.
Index: p. 653–688.
T.p. in red and black.
Colophon: "Memorial edition limited to fifty copies. This is No. ____."

Republished by the same publishers in a revised edition and augmented to 732 pages with 172 illustrations in 1926.
Published again in 1930 by Houghton Mifflin co. in an edition of 744 pages with 182 illustrations.

All these books contain much material on Tiburcio Vásquez.

725   Newsom, J. A.

The life and practice of the wild and modern Indian, by J. A. Newsom.   ₁Oklahoma City, Rev. J. A. Newsom, press of Harlow publishing co., 1923.₁   Pict. cloth.   Scarce.

6 p.l., ₁7₁–219 p.   front., illus., ports.   23.6 cm.
Vignette.

Also published in wrappers without place or date.

Contains much material on Oklahoma outlaws and peace officers. See items 428 and 995, especially the comment on the former. This volume apparently provided some of the source material for Sutton's *Hands Up* (Item 974).

726   Nicholl, Edith M. (Mrs. Edith M. Boyer)

Observations of a ranch woman in New Mexico, by Edith M. Nicholl.   London, Macmillan and co., ltd.; New York, the Macmillan co., 1898.   Dec. cloth.   Scarce.

4 p.l., 271 p.   front., plates.   19.4 cm.
Half title; illus. t.p.; frontis tissue.

Republished, Cincinnati, the Editor publishing co., 1901. Cloth.

3 p.l., 260 p.   19 cm.

Although written by a well-educated woman, the book shows a very careless handling of historical facts with which the author should have been acquainted. According to her, Billy the Kid was a dishwasher when he started his outlaw career as the result of being "ill-used by a big burly man-cook." She says that Tunstall (although she calls him "Morton") was killed on the trail at night from behind and his body left to the buzzards. She calls McSween by the name of "Mackintosh" and further states that Billy the Kid's prison guards (Bell and Ollinger) went to dinner and left the Kid alone in jail. While they were gone, he "filed off his fetters." She says that there were fifteen people in Mackintosh's (McSween's) house while it burned and that all except Billy the Kid were brutally murdered. She also relates that the Kid had gone to bed in another room in Maxwell's house the night of his killing, but "finding himself attacked with the pangs of hunger, arose from his couch and, taking a knife, was proceeding to the storeroom to cut himself some meat. Hearing voices in the room of his host, he opened the door and demanded to know who was there." Then Garrett shot him while the Kid was standing in the door *with a lamp in his hands*.

727 Nix, Everitt Dumas

Oklahombres, particularly the wilder ones, by Everitt Dumas Nix, former United States marshal in old Oklahoma territory and the Cherokee Strip, as told to Gordon Hines. ₁St. Louis, 1929.₁ Pict. cloth. OP.

> xix, 280 p. front., plates, ports., facsms. 23.5 cm.
> Chronology of Oklahoma: p. 279–280.
> Half title; illus. end papers; illus. margins and chapter headings; vignette.

Written entirely about the outlaws of Oklahoma and the officers who chased them down.

728 Nolen, Oren Warder

Galloping down the Texas trail, by Oren Warder Nolen. Anecdotes and sketches of the Texas cowboys, rangers, sheriffs, wild cattle, wild horses and gun and game. Written by a native Texan from the experiences of fifty years in the lone star state. ₁Odem, Texas, privately printed, 1947.₁ Cloth. OP.

> 3 p.l., 7–181 p. 23.3 cm.

A little-known book containing some stories of Texas bad men.

729 Nombela, Julio

La fiebre de riquezas; siete años en California. Descubrimiento del oro y explotación de sus inmensos e interesantes relaciones filones. Historia dramática en vista de datos auténticos é enteresantes relaciones de los más célebras viajeros, por Julio Nombela, Tomo I.

Madrid, Administración, Calle de San Bernardo, Núm 11, 1871. Pub. in two volumes. Wrappers. Rare.

> Vol. I, 547 p. front., plates. 20 cm.
> Vol. II, 580 p. plates. 20 cm.

The title page of Volume II is exactly like that of Volume I except for: "Tomo II. Administración, Calle de Serrano, Nún. 14, Barrio de Salamanca, Madrid, 1892."

This two-volume book first appeared serially in Madrid, Spain, in 1871–72. The author writes of early California in a narrative style, but most of the book consists of flights of fancy. In the second part of the first volume the author weaves Murieta into his story and deals with him at length, following the *California Police Gazette* version of Murieta's life very closely, so closely, in fact, that certain parts are merely translations from the English text into Spanish. He calls upon his imagination in relating Murieta's early life and ancestry. Many details of his story appeared in the 1859 version published by the *Police Gazette*. See Item 710.

730 North, Escott

The saga of the cowboy. All about the cattleman, and the part he played in the great drama of the west, by Escott North . . . . London, . . . Jarrolds, publishers, ltd. [1942]. Cloth. OP.

> xii, 13–192 p. front. (port.), plates, ports., cattle brands. 21.8 cm.
> Index: p. 189–192.
> Half title.

Written by an Englishman who came to America and worked as a cowboy, this book gives much material on western outlaws and the cattle wars. The author says that he tried for years to find out something of Wild Bill Hickok's early life, but not until 1930 "did the details of Bill's first killing come to light from the most unexpected source." And of all things, this source was a book written by Frank Harris, one of the most unreliable books I know. Thus he discovers that Wild Bill spent his early life on the *cattle trails!* But then this English author also praises Hough's *The Story of the Outlaw* as being "comprehensive and authentic." He repeats the old legend about the Hickok-McCanles fight with ten men.

He says that Wyatt Earp killed Frank Stillwell in a fair fight, but history tells us that Stillwell was shot from a train without even seeing his assassin. His information on Billy the Kid is also inaccurate; he says, for example, that the Kid was killed on Maxwell's porch.

731   [Northfield Bank Raid]

A story of the heroism of pioneer citizens of Northfield, Minnesota, who frustrated an attempt by the James-Younger gang to rob the First National Bank of Northfield on September 7, 1876. Northfield, Minn., published by the Northfield News, inc., 1933. Wrappers.   OP.

> 3 p.l., 7–32 p.   front. (port.), plates, ports., facsm.   20.3 cm.
> Later reprinted many times.

This, of course, deals with the unsuccessful attempt by the Jameses and Youngers to rob the Northfield Bank.

732   ———

The Northfield Bank raid, fiftieth anniversary finds interest undimmed in the oft-told tale of repulse of the James-Younger gang. Reprinted from the Northfield News of August 27, September 3, 10, and 17, 1926 . . . .   Wrappers.   Scarce.

> 4 p.l., [5]–22 p.   front., plates, ports.   21 cm.
> Double column.

Part of this pamphlet is taken from Huntington's *Robber and Hero;* the latter part was written by old-timers and eyewitnesses to the robbery.

733   Noyes, Alva Josiah

In the land of the Chinook; or, true story of Blaine county, by A. J. Noyes (Ajax).   Helena, Mont., State publishing co. [1917]. Cloth.   Scarce.

> 4 p.l., [7]–152 p.   plates, ports., facsms.   24 cm.
> Device.

Contains some material on Calamity Jane, Kid Curry, and others.

734   ———

The story of Ajax; life in the Big Hole Basin, by Alva J. Noyes.   Helena, Mont., State publishing co., 1914.   Cloth.   Scarce.

> 4 p.l., 158 p.   front., plates, ports.   24 cm.
> Index: p. [153]–158.
> Errata: fourth preliminary leaf.

735 O'Brien, Robert

California called them. A saga of golden days and roaring camps, by Robert O'Brien. Illustrated by Antonio Sotomayor. New York, London, Toronto, McGraw-Hill book co., inc. [1951]. Cloth. In print.

> xv p., 1 l., 3–251 p. illus. 23.5 cm.
> Index: p. 245–251.
> Half title; map on end papers; headpieces; tailpieces; vignette.

This book tells some new stories about Murieta and has some material on other gold-rush bad men.

736 [Oklahoma Authors' Club]

The romance of Oklahoma, Oklahoma's Authors' Club [by various members]. Oklahoma City, 1920. Pict. cloth. Scarce.

> 3 p.l., 86 p. plates, ports. 23 cm.

In Chapter V, "The Triumph of the Law," by Mrs. Zoe Tilghman, there is material on some of the Oklahoma outlaws.

737 [Oklahoma]

Kay county, Oklahoma. Ponca City, Okla., published by Kay County Gas co. [1919]. Cloth. Scarce.

> 75 [1] p. illus., plates (9 fold., 8 double p.), ports. (1 double p.), maps (2 double p.), graphs (1 double p.). 22.2 cm.
> Copyright notice verso of flyleaf.

Contains some material on the Daltons, Henry Starr, and Ben Cravens.

738 Older, Mrs. Fremont

Love stories of old California, with a foreword by Gertrude Atherton. Illustrated. New York, Coward-McCann, inc. [1940]. Cloth. OP.

> xvi p., 1 l., 3–306 p. front., ports. 22 cm.
> Half title; at head of title: "Mrs. Fremont Older."

Among the other love stories, the author tells of Murieta's loves and of the illicit love of Vásquez. In the Murieta chapter she out-Ridges Ridge, using his version of Murieta's life but making it ever so much more romantic.

739 O'Neal, James Bradas

They die but once, the story of a Tejano, by James B. O'Neal.   New York, Knight publications, inc., 1935.   Cloth.   OP.

viii p., 2 l., 228 p.   23.5 cm.
Half title.

The author upholds the legend that Bill Longley was never hanged. He says that the sheriff was a friend of the Longleys, that he planned the execution so no one could see, and that they "hung Bill on a hook for a little while, with a rope under his arms, and pronounced him dead. A doctor bought his body, and they drove the supposed corpse away."

O'Neal makes the statement that the Taylor-Sutton feud was against the Cox outfit, but there is no other record of this. He says that he and his brother Will sold cattle to Cole Younger and Jesse James, who were calling themselves the "Rector brothers."

The subject of this autobiography (so he says) was asked by Ben Thompson to go to Harris's theater some time after he had killed Jack Harris. When O'Neal refused to go with him, Thompson went up the street and met King Fisher. Fisher at first refused also, but finally went, more or less on a dare. History records that Fisher and Thompson were in Austin, and later went to San Antonio together to visit this theater. And, of course, they were killed there. O'Neal makes another broad statement when he says that the James and Younger boys must have killed at least fifteen Pinkerton men.

Like many other old-timers, the author claims that he knew personally nearly all the bad men, such as John Wesley Hardin, Jesse James, Cole Younger, Bill Doolin, and Sam Bass. He says that the law got after Bill Doolin, and that Bill went to New Mexico and was killed there (!), and that Sam Bass came to *Denison*, Texas, and went to work for the sheriff. He means Denton, of course, an example of how many old-timers, having heard a name and then forgotten it, later think that the first name which sounds like it is correct.

The author knew Billy the Kid, too, and says that he wore a "ragged mustache." He hunted buffalo with Pat Garrett before Garrett went to Fort Sumner and opened a grocery store with George Fulton. He says Garrett's reputation was first established when he told some of the Kid's gang who were "raising hell in and around the store" that he'd kill them if they didn't be quiet.

Showing more confusion, O'Neil says that Garrett was deputized by Sheriff Poe, that the Kid owned a ranch on the Pecos where his gang hung out, that the Kid was wounded and jailed, and that when he got well, he killed his jailers Bell and Ollinger.

268

He says that he and Garrett were always friendly and that they were partners in several business deals. Before Garrett was killed, he showed the author a big pile of writing ready for a book. Garrett read him some of it and "some of it I knowed was right, but some of it sounded a little puffed up."

740 O'Reilly, Harrington

Fifty years on the trail. A true story of western life, by Harrington O'Reilly, with over one hundred illustrations by Paul Frenzeny. London, Chatto & Windus, Piccadilly, 1889. Pict. cloth. Scarce.

xvi, 381 p. front., illus. 19.9 cm.
Device; frontis tissue; 32 numbered p. adv. at end.

The subject of this book, John Y. Nelson, who took part in the hanging of Fly-Speck Billy, tells of Doc Middleton's start in outlawry. There is some new information on Joseph Slade.

741 Orton, A. R. (pub.)

"The Derienni"; or, land pirates of the Isthmus. Being a true and graphic history of robberies, assassinations, and other horrid deeds perpetrated by those cold-blooded miscreants, who have infested for years the great highways to California, the El Dorado of the Pacific . . . . Five of whom were shot at Panama by the committee of public safety, July 27th, 1852. Together with the lives of three of the principal desperadoes as narrated by themselves . . . . New Orleans, Charleston, Baltimore, and Philadelphia, published by A. R. Orton, 1853. Pict. wrappers. Exceedingly rare.

2 p.l., [17]-44 p. front., plates. 22 cm.

A lurid tale about the operation of a gang of cutthroats who operated in Panama preying upon the California gold seekers who returned to the States over this route.

742 Osgood, Ernest Staple

The day of the cattleman, by Ernest Staple Osgood. Minneapolis, the University of Minnesota press, 1929. Cloth. OP.

x p., 2 l., 283 p. front., plates, maps (part double), diagrs., facsms. 24.6 cm.

269

Bibliography: p. 259–268; index: p. 269–283.
Half title; illus. end papers.
Thesis (Ph. D.), University of Wisconsin, 1927. (Without thesis note.)

Contains a tabloid account of the Johnson County War.

743   Otero, Miguel Antonio

My life on the frontier, by Miguel Antonio Otero. In two volumes.

Vol. I, My Life on the frontier, 1864–1882; incidents and characters of the period when Kansas, Colorado, and New Mexico were passing through the last of their wild and romantic years, by Miguel Antonio Otero, former governor of New Mexico. Illustrated by Will Shuster.   New York, the Press of the Pioneers, inc., 1935. Cloth.   OP.

> 5 p.l., 293 p.   illus., plates.   23.5 cm.
> Index: p. 289–293 (triple column).
> Half title.

> Published in a limited, signed, and numbered edition. In the trade edition the illustrations were omitted.

Vol. II, My life on the frontier, 1882–1897. Death knell of a territory and the birth of a state . . . , by Miguel Antonio Otero, former governor of New Mexico. Foreword by George P. Hammond . . . .   Albuquerque, the University of New Mexico press, 1939.   Cloth.   OP.

> xi p., 1 l., 306 p.   illus.   23.5 cm.
> Index: p. 301–306 (triple column).
> Half title.

> Published in a de luxe edition limited to 400 copies. Again, in the trade edition the illustrations were omitted.

In Vol. I the author tells the story of Wild Bill Hickok's murder, has quite a few stories about Clay Allison, and tells about the attempt of a mob at Las Vegas to take Dave Rudabaugh away from Pat Garrett. In Vol. II he tells of the lynching of Joel Fowler and has a long chapter on Vicente Silva and his gang.

744   ———

My nine years as governor of the territory of New Mexico, 1897–1906, by Miguel Antonio Otero. Foreword by Marion Dargon, editor. Albuquerque, N. M., the University of New Mexico press, 1940. Cloth. OP.

> viii p., 1 l., 404 p. front. (port.), ports. 23.6 cm.
> Appendix: p. 343–394; index: p. 397–404.
> Device.
> Colophon: "Four hundred de luxe copies printed of which this is No. ____."
>
> Also published in a trade edition.

In a chapter entitled "The Folsom Train Robberies," the author devotes some space to Black Jack Ketchum and his gang, a few members of which were from Butch Cassidy's Wild Bunch. Again the illustrations were omitted in the trade edition.

745 ——————

The real Billy the Kid; with new light on the Lincoln county war, by Miguel Antonio Otero . . . . Illustrated from photographs. New York, Rufus Rockwell Wilson, inc., 1936. Cloth. Scarce.

> xvii p., 1 l., 200 p. front., illus., plates, ports. 23.4 cm.
> Index: p. 197–200.
> Half title.

Although this is a comparatively recent book, it has become quite difficult to find. The author, like many other New Mexicans, is very much in sympathy with Billy the Kid. He holds Pat Garrett to be a cold-blooded killer and cites many opinions of others to prove that Garrett was a horse thief and a coward who shot without giving his victim a chance.

In his foreword Otero states that Charlie Siringo's book on Billy the Kid was "largely copied from Garrett's book." And he declares that the same might be said of Walter Noble Burns' *The Saga of Billy the Kid*. He says, "Each of these authors adds many tales originating solely in their rather vivid imaginations"; and he claims that these tales are "pure fiction, wholly devoid of fact."

Otero toured the Billy the Kid country and interviewed the remaining participants of the war, including Mrs. McSween, Hijinio Salazar, George and Frank Coe, and others. These were all on the Kid's side and had nothing but praise for Billy and condemnation for Pat Garrett. All readily said that Garrett was a cow thief and a coward and that he shot only when he had the advantage.

In this book Martin Chavez tells a different story about the Kid's killing of Bell, and a most plausible one. Most other accounts follow Garrett's. But the world will never know the truth about this episode. There were no witnesses; Bell couldn't talk, and the Kid didn't. All the other accounts of the Kid's killing by Garrett say that the Kid was armed with a butcher knife and a gun, and some even declare that he shot at least once before he died; but Jesus Silva and Deluvina, the Indian slave woman, were the first to enter Pete Maxwell's bedroom after the Kid was killed, and both declare emphatically that the Kid carried only a butcher knife.

746 Ovitt, Mabel

Golden treasure, by Mabel Ovitt. Dillon, Mont., 1952. Pict. cloth. In print.

> 8 p.l., [17]–252 p. front. (port.), plates, ports., facsms. 23.5 cm.
> Appendix: p. [237]–252.
> Half title; plan on end papers.
> Colophon: "The first printing of Golden Treasure is limited to 1000 copies of which this is copy No. ____."

A privately printed and well-written book giving much new material on the vigilantes and road agents of Montana.

747 Paine, Albert Bigelow

Captain Bill McDonald, Texas Ranger. A story of frontier reform, by Albert Bigelow Paine . . . with introductory letter by Theodore Roosevelt . . . . Special subscription edition. New York, made by J. J. Little & Ives co., 1909. Cloth. OP.

> 7 p.l., [13]–448 p. front. (port.), 7 plates (4 col.), facsm. 21.8 cm.
> Appendix: p. [399]–448.
> Frontis tissue.

A biography of one of the better-known Texas Rangers, this volume deals with many Texas and Oklahoma outlaws. Published by subscription, the book was issued in three bindings simultaneously, each to fit the subscriber's pocketbook. The most expensive was bound in full morocco, the next in red cloth with a portrait of McDonald on the cover, and the third and cheapest, the one most commonly seen, in blue cloth.

748 Pannell, Walter

Civil war on the range, by Walter Pannell. Los Angeles, published by Welcome News [1943]. Pict. wrappers. (Cover title: "Civil War on the Range. An Historic Account of the Battle for the Prairies, the Lincoln County War and Subsequent Events.") OP.

> 2 p.l., 5–45 p. 15 cm.
> [Published with "The Empire of the Big Bend," p. 37–45.]
> 3 p. adv. at end.

The author says that Billy the Kid was strictly a hired gunman, "doing murder for wages," and that those wages were paid by John Chisum. He errs in stating that the Kid was in a room next to Maxwell's preparing to go to bed when he decided that he was hungry and went to Maxwell's room to get the key to the smokehouse. He is another writer who states that the Kid pulled the trigger of his gun after he was shot. On page 26, line 20 is repeated.

749   Parker, J. M.

An aged wanderer. A life sketch of J. M. Parker, a cowboy on the western plains in the early days [by J. M. Parker]. San Angelo, Texas, headquarters, Elkhorn wagon yard [n.d.]. Pict. wrappers. (Cover title.)   Rare.

> 32 p.   front. (port. on verso of cover).   21.3 cm.

Also published under the title "The poor orphan boy, a life sketch of a western cowboy." [N.p., n.d.]   Wrappers.

> 2 p.l., [5]-39 [1] p.   front. (port.).   16.6 cm.

Both exceedingly rare little items by an old Texas cowboy, who in his later life became crippled by paralysis and sold these little books for a livelihood as he wandered over the country. Here is another old-timer who claims to have been a close personal friend of Billy the Kid; yet he is certainly confused in his facts. He says that the first man the Kid killed was the Kid's stepfather, whom he killed because he abused his mother; and that the next man the Kid killed was a blacksmith who hit his horse with a hammer while shoeing him.

He further claims that he was with the Kid when he escaped after this killing. Later he and the Kid were joined by five friends and the officers got after them. "We went into a house on the banks of the Pensaque River and some forty armed men surrounded the house trying to capture the Kid," he relates.

The officers set the house on fire, and while it burned, the Kid played the piano, and the author claims he *danced to the music*. He also claims that he was with the Kid when things got so hot for him "we had to scamper away to the far West and remain in the Rocky Mountains until the spring of 1872." (This incident would, according to his date, have occurred when the Kid was twelve years of age.) He further states that the father of the Kid's sweetheart arranged for Pat Garrett (whom he calls the "drunken sheriff") to kill the Kid, and that Garret watched his chance and killed the young outlaw *while he slept*.

750 Parker, Lew

Odd people I have met, by Lew Parker. ₁N.p., n.d.₁ (Cover title, no. t.p.) OP.

3–120 ₁1₁ p. front. (port.), port. 20.8 cm.
Frontis tissue.

Contains some new stories about Wild Bill Hickok and Calamity Jane.

751 Parkhill, Forbes

The wildest of the west, ₁by₁ Forbes Parkhill. New York, Henry Holt and co. ₁1951₁. Cloth. In print.

x p., 1 l., 3–310 p. plates, ports. 21 cm.
Notes: p. 287; bibliography: p. 289–293; index: p. 295–310.
Half title; "First edition" on copyright p.

Contains material on Soapy Smith and many other western outlaws, including some of the underworld characters of Denver.

752 Parks, Charles Caldwell (Carl Gray, pseud.)

A plaything of the gods, by Carl Gray. Boston, Sherman, French & co., 1912. Pict. cloth. OP.

3 p.l., 260 p. 20.8 cm.
Device.

A badly done novel on Joaquín Murieta. Based upon the *Police Gazette* version of his life, it gives a new twist by having Murieta drowned when his boat suddenly capsized.

753 Parrish, Randall

The great plains. The romance of western American exploration, warfare and settlement, 1527–1870, by Randall Parrish .... Chicago, A. C. McClurg & co., 1907. Pict. cloth. OP.

xiv p., 1 l., 17–399 p. front., plates. 21.5 cm.
Index: p. 385–399.
Half title; pub. device; untrimmed.

Contains a chapter on outlaws and desperadoes. Although the author has long been considered an able historian, he repeats the *Harper's Magazine* fable of the Hickok-McCanles fight, stating that Wild Bill was attacked by ten men and that he received eleven buckshot and thirteen knife wounds. He spells the name "M'Kandlas."

754 Parsons, George Whitwell

The private journal of George Whitwell Parsons. Prepared by Arizona statewide archival and records project, division of professional and service projects, Work Projects Administration. Phoenix, Arizona, Arizona statewide archival and records project, November, 1939. Stiff wrappers. Photolithographed. Scarce.

> vi, 335 p. 27.7 cm.
> Printed on one side of paper only.

Written as a diary. The author, very partial to the Earps, tells of the killing of Morgan Earp and Frank Stillwell.

755 Parsons, John E.

The peacemaker and its rivals. An account of the single action Colt, by John E. Parsons. New York, William Morrow and co., 1950. Cloth. In print.

> viii p., 1 l., 3–184 p. front., illus., plates, facsms., tables. 24 cm.
> Notes: p. 159–172; bibliography: p. 173–177; index: p. 178–184.
> Half title; illus. end papers.

Many references to gunmen and their favorite gun.

756 Patterson, C. L.

Sensational Texas manhunt, by C. L. Patterson. [San Antonio, Texas, Sid Murray & son, printers, 1939.] Wrappers. OP.

> 2 p.l., 3–30 p. 19 cm.

A story of the tracking down and capture of the killer Gregorio Cortez.

757 Payne, Doris Palmer

Captain Jack, Modoc renegade, by Doris Palmer Payne. Portland, Ore., Binford & Mort, publishers . . . [1938]. Cloth. OP.

> 6 p.l., [3]–259 p. ports. 20.3 cm.
> Bibliography: p. [257]–259.
> Half title; map on end papers.

A history of a bad Modoc Indian who operated in Oregon and Northern California.

758 Peattie, Roderick (ed.)

The Black Hills, edited by Roderick Peattie. The contributors: Leland O. Case, Badger Clark, Paul Friggens, R. V. Hunkins, Clarence S. Paine, Elmo Scott Watson.　New York, the Vanguard press, inc. [1952].　Pict. cloth.　In print.

> 9 p.l., 17–320 p.　plates, ports., map.　24 cm.
> Index: p. 311–320.
> Illus. double t.p.

Contains a long and fairly accurate chapter by Clarence Paine on Wild Bill Hickok and Calamity Jane. However, Paine writes that Wild Bill was appointed marshal "in the rip-roarin' cow town of Abilene, *Texas*, in April, 1871." I feel sure that this is an oversight (perhaps a typographical error) and that Mr. Paine meant Abilene, Kansas.

759 ⸻

The inverted mountain; canyons of the west, edited by Roderick Peattie. Contributors: Weldon F. Heald, Edwin D. McKee, Harold S. Colton.　New York, the Vanguard press, inc. [1948]. Pict. cloth.　OP.

> x p., 1 l., 3–390 p.　plates, maps.　24 cm.
> Index: p. 379–390.
> Half title; illus. double t.p.

Contains some minor mentions of Butch Cassidy.

760　Peck, Anne Merriman

Southwest roundup, by Anne Merriman Peck. Illustrated by the author.　New York, Dodd, Mead & co., 1950.　Cloth.　In print.

> 4 p.l., 248 p.　illus., map (double p.).　20.8 cm.
> Half title; illus. chapter headings; vignette; untrimmed.

This is a book, seemingly written for young readers, that covers many subjects of the Southwest. The author touches upon the Lincoln County War and Billy the Kid, but spoils her story by saying that the Kid was "trailed to a friend's house in Ft. Sumner where he was cornered by Pat Garrett and shot *after a stiff fight.*"

761　Pelzer, Louis

The shifting cow towns of Kansas, by Louis Pelzer.　Reprinted from the Transactions of the Illinois State Historical Society, 1926.　Wrappers.　OP.

> [3]–13 p.　23 cm.

276

Contains some information on the gunmen of the various wild cow-towns of Kansas.

762 Penrose, Matt R.

Pots o' gold, by Matt R. Penrose. Reno, Nevada, A. Carlisle and co. ₁1935₁. Cloth. Scarce.

xix, 21–233 p., 1 l. front., plates, ports. 20 cm.
Half title.

The author, at one time superintendent of the Nevada state police and later warden of the state penitentiary, tells of some Nevada bad men, including stage and train robbers.

763 Percy, Adrian

Twice outlawed; a personal history of Ed and Lon Maxwell, alias the Williams brothers. A record of highway robbery, horse stealing, romance and murder, to which is added a detailed and graphic account of the arrest and lynching of Edward Maxwell at Durand, Wisconsin, November 19, 1881, by Adrian Percy. Chicago, W. B. Conkey co. ₁n.d.₁. Pict. cloth. OP.

2 p.l., ₁7₁–194 p. 19 cm.

Republished in 1893, Chicago, Morrill, Higgins & co. Pict. wrappers.

2 p.l., ₁7₁–194 p. 18.2 cm.
6 l. adv. at end.

764 Perry, George Sessions

Texas, a world in itself, by George Sessions Perry. Illustrated by Arthur Fuller. New York, London, Whittlesey House, Mc-Graw-Hill book co., inc. ₁1942₁. Cloth. OP.

xi p., 1 l., 3–293 p. 23.4 cm.
Index: p. 287–293.
Half title; illus. map on end papers; illus. chapter headings.

Republished in 1952 by Grossett and Dunlap.

Included in the book is a short sketch of Sam Bass and his death at Round Rock, Texas.

765 Peterson, P. D.

Through the Black Hills and Bad Lands of South Dakota, by P. D. Peterson. Pierre, S. D., J. Fred Olander co. [1929]. Cloth. OP.

4 p.l., 9–189 p. front., illus., plates, ports., maps. 21.8 cm.

Contains a short history of Wild Bill Hickok and some information on Calamity Jane.

766 Peyton, Green (pseud. of Green Peyton Wertenbaker)

San Antonio, city in the sun, by Green Peyton. New York, London, Whittlesey House, McGraw-Hill book co., inc. [1946]. Cloth. OP.

ix, 292 p. plates, ports., maps (1 fold.). 20.8 cm.
Index: p. 277–292.
Half title.

In Chapter 5 the author mentions some of the outlaws who visited San Antonio in the early days, and gives a tabloid, but unreliable, account of the killing of Ben Thompson and King Fisher.

767 Phares, Ross

Reverend Devil, a biography of John A. Murrell, by Ross Phares. New Orleans, Pelican publishing co. [1941]. Pict. cloth. In print.

5 p.l., 263 p. illus., plates. 22 cm.
Bibliography: p. [257]–259; index: p. [261]–263.
Half title; map on end papers; headpieces; vignette.

One of the best books done on this outlaw, based on scholarly research.

768 [Philips, Judge John F., and William H. Wallace]

Speeches of Judge John F. Philips and Wm. H. Wallace . . . in the trial of Frank James at Gallatin, Missouri, for murder committed while engaged in train robbery. [N.p., n.d.] Wrappers. (Cover title.) Scarce.

151–282 p. 2 ports. 17.3 cm.

769 Phillips, Michael James

History of Santa Barbara county, California, from its earliest settlement to the present time, by Michael James Phillips. Illustrated. Chicago, Los Angeles, the S. J. Clarke publishing co., 1927. Pub. in two volumes. Cloth. OP.

> Vol. I, xiv, 15–464 p. front. (port.), plates, ports. 27 cm.
> Historical index: p. 453–461; biographical index: p. 463–464.
> Vol. II is biographical.

Chapter IX, entitled "Bad Men," deals with Jack Powers and Vásquez.

770 Pinkerton, William A.

Train robberies, train robbers and the "hold up" men. Address by William A. Pinkerton. Annual convention International Association Chiefs of Police, Jamestown, Va., 1907. [N. p.] Wrappers. Scarce.

> 3 p.l., 8–84 p. plates, ports. 17 cm.

This book, now scarce, deals with practically all the western train robberies.

771 Pitts, Dr. James Robert Soda

Life and confession of the noted outlaw James Copeland, executed at Augustus, Perry county, Mississippi. Leader of the notorious Copeland and Wages clan which terrorized the entire southern states, as related by himself in prison after he was condemned to death, giving a list of all members of the clan. Mystic alphabet of the clan for their secret correspondence, with an appendix of profound research, by Dr. J. R. S. Pitts. [Hattiesburg, Miss., 1858.] Pict. wrappers. Rare.

> 14 p.l., [31]–237 p. front. (port.), illus. 19.7 cm.
> Appendix: p. [143]–237.
>
> Reprinted in 1909.

Strictly speaking, Copeland was not a western outlaw, but he was on the edge of the early West and was quite a terror in his day.

772 ———

Life and bloody career of the executed criminal James Copeland, the greatest Southern land pirate . . . , by Dr. J. R. S. Pitts. Jackson, Miss., Pilot publishing co., printers, 1874. Pict. wrappers. Rare.

> 220 p. 4 plates. 21 cm.

773 Pleasants, Mrs. J. E.

History of Orange county, California, by Mrs. J. E. Pleasants . . . . Los Angeles, J. R. Finnell & sons publishing co.; Phoenix, Ariz., Record publishing co., 1931. Pub. in three volumes. Leather. OP.

> Vol. I, 3 p.l., 7–567 p. front., plates, ports., map. 26 cm.
> Index: p. 553–567.
> Vols. II and III are biographical.

Chapter IV deals with the killing of Sheriff Barton and the hanging of Juan Flores.

774 Pocock, Roger S.

Following the frontier, by Roger Pocock. New York, McClure, Phillips & co., MCMIII. Pict. cloth. Scarce.

> 4 p.l., 3–338 p. 20 cm.
> Half title; device; untrimmed; 4 l. adv. at end.

In a chapter on outlaws the author touches lightly upon many hunted men of the West from Arizona to Robbers' Roost in Wyoming.

775 Poe, John William

The death of Billy the Kid, by John W. Poe, deputy sheriff under Pat Garrett present at the killing. With an introduction by Maurice Garland Fulton and with illustrations. Boston and New York, Houghton Mifflin co., 1933. Cloth. Scarce.

> xl p., 3 l., 3–59 [1] p. front., illus., plates, ports., facsm., plan. 18.8 cm.
> Pub. device; first edition: 1933 under imprint.

This is one of the best accounts of the killing of the Kid, and the introduction by Mr. Fulton, one of the best living authorities on this aspect of New Mexican history, greatly enhances the value of the book.

776 ———

The true story of the death of "Billy the Kid" (notorious

New Mexico outlaw) as detailed by John W. Poe, a member of Sheriff Pat Garrett's posse, to E. A. Brininstool, 1922. Los Angeles, privately printed by E. A. Brininstool, 1922. Wrappers. OP.

> 5 p.l., [9]–30 p.   19 cm.
> Half title; copyright notice tipped in.

This account first appeared in *Wide World* magazine, London.

777 ———

The true story of the killing of "Billy the Kid" (notorious New Mexico outlaw) as detailed by John W. Poe, a member of Sheriff Pat Garrett's posse, to E. A. Brininstool in 1919. Los Angeles, privately printed by E. A. Brininstool [n.d. (*ca.*1923)]. Wrappers. OP.

> 3 p.l., [7]–15 p.   2 ports. (incl. front.).   22.3 cm.
> Port. on t.p.; double column.
> Colophon (above copyright notice): "Of this booklet, 250 copies were printed for private distribution each copy numbered. This is No. ____."

Three illustrations and a letter from Poe to Brininstool which did not appear in the first printing were added to this edition. Later another printing made its appearance with the price printed on it, but this listing of price seems to be the only difference between this edition and earlier editions.

778 Poe, Sophie (Alberding)
(Mrs. John W. Poe)

Buckboard days, by Sophie A. Poe; edited by Eugene Cunningham. Illustrated with many photographs from the famous Rose collection of San Antonio and from private collections.   Caldwell, Idaho, the Caxton printers, ltd., 1936.   Cloth.   OP.

> 9 p.l., [17]–292 p.   front., plates, ports., facsm.   23.5 cm.
> Notes: p. [269]–287; index: p. [289]–292.
> Half title; map on end papers; pub. device; vignette.
> At head of title: "The Thrilling Experiences On Our Southwestern Frontier of John William Poe, as Buffalo Hunter, U. S. Marshal, Sheriff, Rancher, Banker."

Mrs. Poe relates many incidents in her husband's life, including the story of her meeting him. Her account of the killing of Billy the Kid is very much the same as her husband's, since she got her information from him.

779 Poldervaart, Arie W.

Black-robed justice, by Arie W. Poldervaart. A history of the administration of justice in New Mexico from the American occupation in 1846 until statehood in 1912. [N.p.], Historical Society of New Mexico, 1948. Cloth. In print.

> xi, 222 p. front. (group port.). 23.5 cm.
> Bibliography: p. 213–217; index: p. 219–222.
> Half title.
> At head of title: "Publications in History, Historical Society of New Mexico, Vol. XIII, September, 1948."

The author, law librarian of the Supreme Court of New Mexico for ten years, writes of the various cases on record up to statehood. He tells of the trial and execution of Black Jack Ketchum, of Elza Lay, of train robbery and other outlaw activities.

780 Porter, Henry M.

Pencilings of an early western pioneer, [by] Henry M. Porter. Denver, Colo., the World press, inc., 1929. Cloth. Scarce.

> vi p., 1 l., 198 p. 22.3 cm.
> Device.

The author tells of some of Clay Allison's shooting scrapes. He is inaccurate and even misspells Allison's name.

781 Porter, Millie Jones (Mrs. J. M.)

Memory cups of Panhandle pioneers, by Millie Jones Porter. A belated attempt at Panhandle history with special emphasis on Wheeler county and her relations to the other counties in the long ago as told by the few remaining old times [*sic*] and the records. Clarendon, Texas, Clarendon press, 1945. Cloth. OP.

> xv, 648 p. illus., plates, ports., maps. 23.2 cm.
> Index: p. [617]–648.

This book has some minor material on Jim Courtright and Jim McIntire.

782 Potter, Jack M.

Cattle trails of the old west, by Col. Jack M. Potter . . . . Clayton, N. M., published by the Leader publishing co., 1935. Stiff pict. wrappers. OP.

3–40 p. illus., plates, large fold. map at end. 22.5 cm.
Tailpieces; copyright notice and dedication on t.p.

Republished in 1939 with editing and additions. Edited and compiled by Laura R. Krehbiel. Published by Laura R. Krehbiel at Clayton, N. M. Stiff pict. wrappers. OP.

4 p.l., 9–87 p. illus., large fold. map at end. 20.4 cm.
Tailpieces; vignette.

Although the first edition contains no outlaw material, the second edition has a chapter on Black Jack Ketchum and some material on Mysterious Dave Mathers.

783 ———

Lead steer and other tales, by Jack Potter. Foreword by J. Frank Dobie .... Clayton, N. M., printed ... by the Leader press, 1939. Stiff pict. wrappers. OP.

9 p.l., [13]–116 [1] p. illus., plates, ports. 23 cm.
Copyright and dedication on t.p.

This scarce little book contains a chapter on Black Jack Ketchum.

784 Potter, Theodore Edgar

The autobiography of Theodore Edgar Potter. [Concord, N. H., the Rumford press, 1913.] Cloth. Scarce.

ix p., 1 l., 228 p. front. (port.), ports. 21.5 cm.
Published with half title only.

The manuscript of this book was found after the author's death and published for his children at his written request. The last chapter deals with the capture of the Younger brothers.

785 Powers, Laura Bride

Old Monterey, California's adobe capital, by Laura Bride Powers. Foreword by Dr. Herbert E. Bolton. San Francisco, printed for the San Carlos press, Serra year, 1934. Pict. cloth. OP.

xxii p., 1 l., [3]–299 [1] p. front., plates, ports. 21.2 cm.
Bibliography: p. 289–290; index: p. 293–299.
Half title; map on end papers; vignette.

Contains some information on Vásquez and Murieta.

786 Preece, Harold

Living pioneers. The epic of the west by those who lived it, [by] Harold Preece.   Cleveland, New York, the World publishing co. [1952].   Pict. cloth.   In print.

> 9 p.l., 19–317 p.   21.8 cm.
> Half title; vignette; "First edition" on copyright p.

Tales told by living pioneers themselves and put into a book. There are several chapters containing information on the outlaws, especially those of Indian Territory.

787 Prendergast, Thomas F.

Forgotten pioneers. Irish leaders in early California, by Thomas F. Prendergast.   San Francisco, the Trade Pressroom, 1942.   Cloth.   OP.

> iv p., 4 l., 278 [1] p.   ports.   23.5 cm.
> Bibliography: p. 265–268; index: p. 269–278.
> Half title.
> Colophon: "Of this edition fifteen hundred copies have been printed. . . ."

Has some material on the capture of Murieta and Three-Fingered Jack García.

788 Price, Con

Memories of old Montana, by Con Price (Masachele Opa Barusha).   Hollywood, Calif., the Highland press [1945].   Cloth. OP.

> 4 p.l., 9–154 p.   front.   22.8 cm.
> "First edition" on copyright p.

> Also published in a de luxe edition of 125 copies, numbered and signed by the author and bound in pigskin.

The author has a chapter on Kid Curry in which he tells of the killing of Pike Landusky. There is also a short chapter on the Johnson County War.

789 Price, G. G.

Death comes to Billy the Kid, by G. G. Price.   [Greensburg, Kan., Signal publishing co., 1940.]   Pict. wrappers.   OP.

> 1 l., 16 [1] p.   22.5 cm.

A most ridiculous tale, according to which Billy the Kid was a noble and generous soul persecuted by the cattlemen of New Mexico. The author pictures Pat Garrett (although not mentioning him by name) as "tall and angular with a hawklike face and a beak of a nose. His shaggy brows shading deepset eyes, bony hands hanging almost to his knees."

790   Price, Sir Rose Lambart

A summer in the Rockies, by Major Sir Rose Lambart Price .... With map and illustrations.   London, Sampson Low, Marston & co., ltd., 1898.   Cloth.   Scarce.

> x, 279 p.   front. (port.), plates, fold. map (col.), tables.   19.8 cm.
> Half title; device; frontis tissue; untrimmed.

An Englishman's story of his travels in the American West, telling, among other things, of the Johnson County War.

791   Price, S. Goodale

Black Hills, the land of legend, by S. Goodale Price. Illustrations by Charlotte Gulshall. Drawings made from actual photographs of the period indicated.   Los Angeles, De Vorrs & co., publishers [1935].   Pict. cloth.   OP.

> 8 p.l., [21]-139 [1] p.   illus., plates, ports., map.   19.6 cm.

Like most books on the Black Hills, this one has some information on Wild Bill Hickok, Calamity Jane, and Poker Alice.

792   Prince, L. Bradford

A concise history of New Mexico, by L. Bradford Prince .... Cedar Rapids, Iowa, the Torch press, 1912.   Cloth.   Scarce.

> 4 p.l., [13]-272 p.   front., plates, plans, facsms.   22.2 cm.

Contains some material on the Lincoln County War and Billy the Kid.

793   Pruiett, Moman

Moman Pruiett, criminal lawyer. The life story of a man who defended 343 persons charged with murder. The record shows 303 acquittals and the only client to hear the death sentence pronounced was saved by presidential clemency.   [Oklahoma City, Okla., Harlow publishing co., 1944.]   Cloth.   OP.

> xx p., 1 l., 560 p.   front., plates, ports.   23.7 cm.

285

This prominent lawyer had many associations of a legal character with the outlaws of the Southwest.

794   Quiett, Glenn Chesney

Pay dirt, a panorama of American gold-rushes, by Glenn Chesney Quiett. Illustrated.   New York, London, D. Appleton-Century co., inc., 1936.   Pict. cloth.   OP.

> xxv p., 1 l., 3–506 p.   front., illus., plates, ports., maps.   23 cm.
> Bibliography: p. 483–489; index: p. 491–506.
> Half title; pub. device; untrimmed; first edition: figure (1) at end of index.

This is a thick book containing much material on outlaws of the mining camps, but the author is careless with the spelling of proper names. In his account of the Hickok-McCanles feud he spells McCanles' name "McCaules" and Jack McCall, "McCaul." He admits that the stories told about this fight were tall tales.

795   Quigg, Lemuel Ely

New empires in the northwest . . . ₁by Lemuel E. Quigg₁. New York, the Tribune association ₁1889₁.   Wrappers.   (Cover title.)   Scarce.

> 84 p.   tables.   26 cm.
> Double column.
> Cover title: "Library of Tribune Extras, Vol. I, No. 8, August, 1889."

A collection of thirty-seven letters on the Dakotas, Montana, and Washington signed: L.E.Q. These letters are about travels and observations in the Northwest, dealing with, among other things, the cowboys of Wyoming and the reign of the outlaws in Montana.

796   Quinn, Vernon

War-paint and powder-horn, by Vernon Quinn . . . with frontispiece in color by H. C. Murphy and three illustrations by Louis Schroeder.   New York, Frederick A. Stokes co., MCMXXIX. Cloth.   OP.

> xiv p., 1 l., 298 p.   front. (col.), 4 plates (incl. front.), map.   19.2 cm.
> Half title; illus. map on end papers; pub. device; tailpieces; frontis tissue.

Contains chapters on outlaws and stagecoach holdups.

797   Raht, Carlisle Graham

The romance of Davis mountains and Big Bend country. A

history by Carlisle Graham Raht. Drawings by Waldo Williams. El Paso, the Rahtbooks co. [1919]. Pict. cloth. Scarce.

3 p.l., 381 p. front. (port.), plates, ports., map (double p.). 20 cm.

A good history of the Big Bend country, it is becoming quite scarce. It has much information on lawlessness and on the Texas Rangers of that section.

798 Raine, William MacLeod, and Will C. Barnes

Cattle, by William MacLeod Raine and Will C. Barnes. Garden City, N. Y., Doubleday, Doran & co., MCMXXX. Pict. cloth. OP.

xii p., 1 l., 340 p. front., illus., plates, facsms. 21.2 cm.
Appendix: p. 309–324; index: p. 327–340.
Half title; illus. end papers; vignette; "First edition" on copyright p.

Republished under the title *Cattle, Cowboys and Rangers* by Grossett and Dunlap, 1930.

Although primarily a book on the cattle industry, it gives much information on western outlaws and feuds. The author's story of the Lincoln County War is much the same as appeared in his *Famous Sheriffs and Outlaws*. See Item 799.

799 Raine, William MacLeod

Famous sheriffs & western outlaws, by William MacLeod Raine. Garden City, N. Y., Doubleday, Doran & co., inc., 1929. Cloth. OP.

4 p.l., 294 p. 21.3 cm.
Half title; pub. device; t.p. in red and black.

One of the author's earlier nonfiction books on outlaws, it continues to be a standard work. The author covers the subject of western outlaws thoroughly, but does repeat one or two of the legendary stories about Billy the Kid.

800 ———

Forty-five caliber law; the way of life of the frontier peace officer, by William MacLeod Raine. [Evanston, Ill., Row, Peterson and co., 1941.] Pict. cloth. In print.

2 p.l., [5]–64 p. illus., ports. 23.5 cm.
Half title: "Way of Life Series."
Illus. chapter headings; short biography and port. of author on verso of t.p.

One of a series of short books by different authors. This one deals mostly with law-enforcement officers from marshals and sheriffs to the Texas Rangers and the Northwest Mounted Police.

801 ———

Guns of the frontier. The story of how law came to the west, by William MacLeod Raine. Illustrated. Boston, Houghton Mifflin co., 1940. Cloth. OP.

> x p., 2 l., 282 p. front., plates, ports., facsm. 21 cm.
> Bibliography: p. [271]–274; index: p. [277]–282.
> Half title; First edition: 1940 under imprint.

All of Raine's books on outlaws are reliable. In this one he corrects the fable about Wild Bill Hickok's fight with the McCanles', and he does not seem to hold a very high opinion of Hickok. However, I think he is mistaken in saying that Jack Davis, of the Collins-Bass gang, killed Johnny Slaughter while holding up a stagecoach in the Black Hills. Reddy McKimie claims that honor, and the rest of the gang chased him off for this unwise action.

802 Rainey, George

The Cherokee Strip, its history, by George Rainey. Illustrated. [Enid, Oklahoma., 1925.] Wrappers. Scarce.

> [30] p. (no pagination). illus. 17 cm.

Contains information on the Daltons, the Doolin gang, and other Oklahoma outlaws.

803 ———

The Cherokee Strip, by George Rainey. Guthrie, Okla., Co-Operative publishing co., 1933. Pict. cloth. OP.

> x, 504 p. plates, ports. 22 cm.
> Index: p. 503–504.
> Vignette.

Although it has the same title as the preceding book, this one is entirely different. It also contains information on the Daltons, Dick Yeager, and other Oklahoma outlaws.

804 ———

No man's land. The historic story of a landed orphan, by

George Rainey. ₁Guthrie, Okla., Co-Operative publishing co.₁, 1937. Pict. cloth. Scarce.

> 5 p.l., 245 p. front. (port.), plates, ports., maps, diagr. 21.8 cm.
> Acknowledgments, p. 241–242; index, p. 243–245.
> Half title; copyright notice on t.p.

Some material on the James-Younger gang, the Coe outlaws, and other outlaws.

805   Rak, Mary Kidder

Border patrol, ₁by₁ Mary Kidder Rak. Illustrated. Boston, Houghton Mifflin co., 1938. Cloth. OP.

> ix p., 1 l., 242 ₁1₁ p. front., plates. 21.5 cm.
> Half title; map on end papers; device; first edition: 1938 under imprint.

"The scope of this book has . . . been limited to the border of Arizona, New Mexico and western Texas."—Foreword.

806   Ralph, Julian

Our great west. A study of the present conditions and future possibilities of the new commonwealths and capitals of the United States, by Julian Ralph . . . . New York, Harper & brothers, publishers, 1893. Dec. cloth. OP.

> xi ₁1₁, 477 ₁1₁ p. front., illus., plates, maps. 23 cm.
> Pub. device; 4 p. adv. at end.

A chapter on Montana contains some information on the vigilantes and outlaws of that state.

807   Rankin, L.

No. 6847; or, the horrors of prison life. Including many graphic details in the life of John Wesley Hardin, the noted Texas desperado. Three years in the pen. ₁N.p., printed by No. 6847 himself, *ca.*1897.₁ Wrappers. Exceedingly rare.

> xii, 67 p. 19.5 cm.
> Signed: "L. Rankin."

The author, in his title, claims to give "graphic details in the life of John Wesley Hardin," but barely mentions him. The book is mostly about the author's own life in the Huntsville prison.

808 Rankin, M. Wilson

Reminiscences of frontier days, including an authentic account of the Thornburg and Meeker massacre, by M. Wilson Rankin . . . . Denver, Photolithographed by Smith-Brooks [1938]. Imt. leather. Scarce.

> 5 p.l., 140 p. front., illus., plates, maps. 28 cm.
> Vignette.

This privately printed book is photolithographed and has very crude illustrations. It contains an account of the hanging of Big Nose George Parrott. The author is mistaken in his statement that Joel Collins and Sam Bass fled to the Indian Territory after their robbery of the Union Pacific at Big Springs, and that they were later arrested and sentenced to a prison term.

809 Ransom, Rev. A.

A terrible history of fraud and crime; the twin brothers of Texas. Lives, trial, confession and execution at Savannah, Georgia, for the cruel, but mistaken murder of their beautiful sister, Emily Eganus. With full confession of many other awful murders, incendiaries, highway robberies, and garrotting, while connected with the lawless band of land pirates of Texas and Kansas. Philadelphia, published by M. A. Milliette [1858]. Pict. wrappers. Exceedingly rare.

> [13]–41 [1] p. front., 6 plates (incl. front. and one on back wrapper). 23 cm.

> Published also in German same year under the title of *Die Zwilling-Bruders von Texas.*

This exceedingly rare little book is written in the exaggerated style of the period and is full of imaginary conversation. The subjects were supposedly members of John A. Murrell's gang. Other than in the title there is no reference to the brothers being from Texas. The book is signed "Rev. A. Ransom," and is one of several such stories of crime written by ministers of that period. Perhaps such stories served as an escape for them. In my personal opinion, the book is only a piece of bloody fiction, though its rarity has made it a collector's item.

810 Rascoe, Burton

Belle Starr, "the Bandit Queen." The true story of the romantic and exciting career of the daring and glamorous lady famed in legend and story throughout the West . . . . The true facts about the dastardly deeds and the come-uppence of such Dick Turpins, Robin Hoods and Rini Rinaldos as the Youngers, the Jameses, the Daltons, the Starrs, the Doolins and the Jenningses. The real story with court records and contemporary newspaper accounts and testimony of the old nesters, here and there, in the southwest . . . , by Burton Rascoe . . . . New York, published by Random House . . . , 1941. Cloth. OP.

> viii p., 3 l., 3–340 p. front., plates, ports. 23 cm.
> Chronology and necrology: p. 277–291; glossary: p. 295–298; bibliographical review: p. 301–336; index: p. 337–340.
> Half title: "First printing" on copyright p.

This history of Belle Starr is perhaps the most complete and reliable work done on this female bandit to date.

811   Ray, Clarence E.

The Alabama wolf. Rube Burrows and his desperate gang of highwaymen, by Clarence E. Ray. Illustrated.   Chicago, Regan publishing corp. [n.d.].   Pict. wrappers.   Op.

> 2 p.l., 7–188 p. front., illus. 17.8 cm.

812   ——

The Dalton brothers in their Oklahoma cave. A tale of adventures in the Indian territory, together with the desperate and startling criminal career of the gang, by Clarence E. Ray. Illustrated. Chicago, J. Regan & co., publishers [n.d.].   Pict. wrappers.   OP.

> 2 p.l., 7–189 p. front. 18 cm.
> 3 p. adv. at end.

813   ——

Famous American scouts . . . , by Clarence E. Ray. Illustrated. Chicago, Regan publishing co. [n.d.].   Pict. wrappers.   OP.

> 3 p.l., 7–189 p. illus. 17.8 cm.

This author also follows the Nichols and Hough version of the McCanles fight.

814   ——

The James boys; a complete and accurate account of these

famous bandit brothers, Frank and Jesse James. An authentic account of their noted band of bank plunderers, train robbers and murderers, by Clarence E. Ray. Illustrated. Chicago, Regan publishing corp. [n.d.]. Pict. wrappers. OP.

> 2 p.l., 7–192 p. front., illus. 18 cm.

815 ———

The James boys and Bob Ford. The downfall of Jesse, by Clarence E. Ray. Illustrated. Chicago, Regan publishing corp. [n.d.]. Pict. wrappers. OP.

> 2 p.l., 7–187 p. front., illus. 17.8 cm.

816 ———

The life of Bob and Cole Younger with Quantrell [*sic*]. Daring and startling episodes in the lives of these notorious bandits, by Clarence E. Ray. Illustrated. Chicago, Regan publishing corp. [n.d.]. Pict. wrappers. OP.

> 2 p.l., 7–189 p. front., illus. 17.8 cm.

817 ———

The Oklahoma bandits. The Daltons and their desperate gang, by Clarence E. Ray. Chicago, J. Regan & co., publishers [n.d.]. Pict. wrappers. OP.

> 2 p.l., 7–188 p. front., illus. 18.2 cm.
> 2 p. adv. at end.

818 ———

Rube Burrows, king of outlaws and train robbers. A faithful history of their exploits and adventures, by Clarence E. Ray. Illustrated. Chicago, J. Regan & co., publishers [n.d.]. Pict. wrappers. OP.

> 2 p.l., 7–191 p. front., illus. 18 cm.

819 ———

Tracy, the bandit; or, the romantic life and crimes of a twen-

tieth century desperado, by Clarence E. Ray. Illustrated.   Chicago,
Regan publishing corp. [n.d.].   Pict. wrappers.   OP.

> 2 p.l., 7–185 p.   front., illus.   18 cm.

820 ———

The Younger brothers. An authentic and thrilling history of
the most noted bandits of ancient or modern times, compiled from
reliable sources only, and containing the latest facts in regard to
these celebrated outlaws, by Clarence E. Ray. Illustrated.   Chicago,
J. Regan & co., publishers [n.d.].   Pict. wrappers.   OP.

> 2 p.l., 7–187 p.   front., illus.   18 cm.
> 5 p. adv. at end.

All of these books were written by Ray for sensational reading and sale
on trains, and contain little material of historical value.

821   Ray, Worth S.

Down in the Cross Timbers, by Worth S. Ray (illustrated
by the author).   Austin, Texas, published by Worth S. Ray [1947].
Cloth.   OP.

> 4 p.l., 160 p.   illus.   23.5 cm.
> "First edition 500 copies only."

Photolithographed. Crude illustrations. Contains some information
about Sam Bass taken from other books.

822   Raymar, Robert George

Montana, the land and the people, by Robert George Ray-
mar. Montana biography by special staff of writers. Issued in
three volumes. Illustrated.   Chicago and New York, the Lewis publishing co., 1930.   Pub. in three volumes.   Leather.   Scarce.

> Vol. I, xlvi, 3–634 p.   front. (port.), illus., plates, ports.   26.5 cm.
> Index (in front): p. xv–xlvi.
> Vols. II and III are biographical.

In Chapter IX, "How the Law Came to Montana," the author has written a great deal about road agents and vigilantes.

823   Raymond, Mrs. Dora (Neill)

Captain Lee Hall of Texas, by Dora Neill Raymond; with

illustrations by Louis Lundean and Frederic Remington. Norman, University of Oklahoma press, MCMXL. Pict. cloth. OP.

> xiii p., 1 l., 3–350 p. illus., plates, ports., fold. map, facsm. 22.4 cm.
> Index: p. 345–350.
> Half title; illus. chapter headings; illus. t.p.; "First edition" on copyright p.

A well-done biography which shows scholarly research. There are chapters on Sam Bass and the Taylor-Sutton feud and a good account of the killing of Ben Thompson.

824 Reed, Nathaniel

The life of Texas Jack [by himself] . . . . [Tulsa, Okla., Tulsa printing co., n.d. (ca.1936).] Pict. wrappers. Scarce.

> 3–55 p. front., illus., ports. 22.9 cm.
> Port. of author on t.p.

One of the little books that the author sold for a livelihood in his old age. It has five pages of affidavits on his identity at the end. The author gives much of the same information that he related to Homer Croy, who put it into his book, *He Hanged Them High*. See Item 269.

825 Reno, John

Life and career of John Reno from childhood to the present time, extending over a period of thirty-five years; with illustrations, and including a detailed account of the great safe robbery in Missouri. Written by himself. Indianapolis, Indianapolis Journal co., printers, 1879. Wrappers. Exceedingly rare.

> 2 p.l., [5]–108 p. illus. 18.2 cm.

This well-known outlaw tells the story of his life from childhood to his release from prison. It is claimed by some that this volume was written by L. M. Boland, city editor of the *Seymour Daily Lever* at Reno's dictation. The scarcity of the book is largely due to the fact that relatives of Reno have bought every copy that they could locate, paying all sorts of prices for copies and systematically destroying them. Reverend Robert W. Shields, who has perhaps done more research on the Renos than any other man, told me that Dr. Lucien V. Rule, who has also written an unpublished manuscript on the Renos, owned one of these rare books, but a fire, thought to be the result of arson, gutted his office, destroying the book and all his records.

Republished in 1940 by Robert W. Shields with notes and offset illustrations and with some editorial changes.

5 p.l., 47 [1] p.   front., illus., map.   27.5 cm.   Stiff wrappers.   Scarce.

Printed by a mimeograph dry-stencil process, on only one side of the paper. Since only two hundred copies of this book were printed, it has also become scarce.

826   Rensch, Hero Eugene and Ethel Grace

Historic spots in California. The southern counties, by Hero Eugene Rensch and Ethel Grace Rensch. With an introduction by Robert Glass Cleland . . . .   Stanford University, California, Stanford University press; London, Humphrey Milford, Oxford University press, 1932.   Cloth.   OP.

xxvii, 267 p.   front. (map).   20.7 cm.
Sources: p. 245; index: p. 247–267 (triple column).
Half title; device.

Contains some unimportant information about Murieta and Vásquez, mostly about their hide-outs.

827   Rensch, Hero Eugene and Ethel Grace, and Mildred Brooks Hoover

Historic spots in California. Valley and Sierra counties, by Hero Eugene Rensch, Ethel Grace Rensch, and Mildred Brooks Hoover. With an introduction by Robert Glass Cleland . . . .   Stanford University, California, Stanford University press; London, Humphrey Milford, Oxford University press [1933].   Cloth.   OP.

xxiii, 597 p.   front. (map).   20.7 cm.
Index: p. 569–597 (triple column).
Half title; device.

Here again there is material on Murieta and Vásquez, the authors pointing out and describing the two bandits' hide-outs, which were scattered over the state.

828   Résumé of Facts

connected with the murder of J. H. Tunstall and the plunder of his property in Lincoln county, New Mexico, in 1878.   [N.p., n.d. (ca.1882).]   Folder.   Exceedingly rare.

3 p.   26 cm.

Although this rare little folder has nothing to do with outlaws, I feel that it should be included in this work because the murder of Tunstall is one cause for the many killings done by Billy the Kid, and was oil on the fire of the Lincoln County War. Tunstall's family failed to recover a cent of the fortune that Tunstall had invested in New Mexico.

829 Richards, Rev. A. (ed.)

Zilla Fitz James, the female bandit of the south-west; or, the horrible, mysterious and awful disclosures in the life of the Creole murderess, Zilla Fitz James, paramour and accomplice of Green H. Long, the treble murderer, for the space of six years. An autobiographical narrative, edited by Rev. A. Richards.   Little Rock, Ark., published by A. R. Orton, 1852. Pict. wrappers. Exceedingly rare.

2 p.l., [7]-31 [1] p. front. (port.), plates. 21.9 cm.

An unusual story of crime; yet it is typical of the books issued by this publisher.

830 Richardson, Rupert Norval

Adventuring with a purpose. Life story of Arthur Lee Wasson, by Rupert Norval Richardson.   San Antonio, Texas, the Naylor co., . . . [1951]. Cloth. In print.

xiii p., 4 l. (plates, ports., double p. map), 114 p. 21.6 cm.
Half title.

This book tells something of Black Jack Ketchum but adds nothing new. The author also writes of Sam Bass and his gang, but makes the mistake of saying that Frank Jackson lived out his natural life in New Mexico. After escaping from Round Rock, Texas, Jackson spent the rest of his life in Arizona under the assumed name "Bill Downing."

831 ——, and Carl Coke Rister

The greater southwest. The economic, social and cultural development of Kansas, Oklahoma, Texas, Utah, Colorado, Nevada, New Mexico, Arizona and California from the Spanish conquest to the twentieth century, by Rupert Norval Richardson . . . and Carl Coke Rister . . . .   Glendale, Calif., the Arthur H. Clark co., 1934. Cloth. OP.

6 p.l., [13]-506 p. 6 maps (all double p. except one). 24.8 cm.
Index: p. [489]-506.
Half title; references for additional reading at end of each chapter; pub. device; untrimmed; gilt top.

Contains a chapter on outlaws and vigilantes.

832 Ricketts, William Pendleton

50 years in the saddle, by W. P. Ricketts. Sheridan, Wyo., Star publishing co., publishers, 1942. Cloth. Scarce.

6 p.l., 198 p. front. (port.), plates, map. 23.2 cm.
Half title; device; "First edition" on copyright p.

A privately printed little book of reminiscences now very scarce, it contains some material on the Hole-in-the-Wall country.

833 Ridge, John Rollin (Yellow Bird)

The life and adventures of Joaquín Murieta, the celebrated California bandit, by Yellow Bird. San Francisco, W. B. Cook and co., 1854. Yellow wrappers. Exceedingly rare.

91 p. 2 plates. 22.4 cm.

This was the first work published on Murieta, and nearly all of the books on this outlaw which followed were pirated from this one. No one took into consideration the fiction it contained. Ridge created a legend by cutting his material out of whole cloth. He even resorted to recording conversation and the bandit's inner thoughts. He did more to outline a legend than he did to record any actual event in the outlaw's life. Even the references to Murieta in the standard histories of California have been founded upon the legend created by Ridge.

The author expected to make money from the book, but his publishers pocketed the money for the copies which were sold and skipped out, thus failing to circulate the book properly. Hence the scarcity of the original edition. Before Ridge could finance another edition, the book was copied, reprinted, and translated into several languages with only slight changes.

The book was copyrighted under the names of "Charles Lindley and John R. Bridge" [sic], and the two plates, one of Murieta and one of Harry Love, were done by Anthony and Baker. This edition contained a long publisher's preface and a short one by the editor, in which he assured the reader that the book will be "found to be true."

On page 14 of this edition Ridge inserted one of his poems about Mount Shasta and stated in a footnote that it was written in 1852. This poem was omitted in all later editions, but holds an honored place in his book of collected poems.

This original edition had no chapter divisions, as in the revised edition. Sabin found but one copy of this rare book (listed by him as No. 51,446), and it was located in the New York State Library at Albany, the library which has since burned. The only copy of this edition that I know of is now owned by Mr. Thomas Streeter.

834 ————

Life and adventures of Joaquín Murieta, the brigand chief of California. Killed by Captain Harry Love, in the year 1853. The third edition of this work, comprising a complete history of the desperado and his gang of outlaws, and giving a detailed account of his most prominent acts of murder and violence, and his subsequent capture and death, together with the shooting and dispersal of his band, by the late John R. Ridge. San Francisco, published by Frederick MacCrellish & co., "Alta California" office, 1871. Wrappers. Exceedingly rare.

81 p. 22.8 cm.

This revision, made shortly before the author's death, was in reality only the second edition of his book, but his new publishers were cautious and considered the *Police Gazette* edition of 1859 so patently based on Ridge's first book that it should be considered the second edition of the work. Therefore they labeled this work the third edition.

In his preface to this book, Ridge expressed bitterness toward the persons he accused of plagiarism and wrote in part: "A spurious edition has been foisted upon unsuspecting publishers and by them circulated, to the infringement of the author's copyright and the damage of his literary credit—the spurious work, with its crude interpolations, fictitious additions, and imperfectly designed distortions of the author's phraseology, being by many persons confounded with the original performance."

During the seventeen-year interval between the first edition and this one, the legend of Murieta had grown, and that growth is reflected in this revised edition. Here Ridge dropped his Cherokee name, "Yellow Bird," and used John R. Ridge. He divided this edition into chapters, with summaries at the head of each chapter. He changed some wording, added a number of episodes, and enlarged upon others. All the material in Chapter VI and part of Chapter VII was added. He also used some material from the *Police Gazette* edition which did not appear in his original.

Ridge also made some minor changes in wording and spelling, such as "were" for "have been," "to secure" instead of "to get hold of," and "Hornitas" instead of "Oanetas."

In this revised edition he made some attempt to document his statements by referring to contemporary newspapers, added some minor adventures of the outlaw, and enlarged upon the dialogue and the references to Murieta's early life and persecution.

835 ——

Life and adventures of Joaquín Murieta, the celebrated California bandit. Third edition. Revised and enlarged by the author, the late John R. Ridge.   San Francisco, Fred'k MacCrellish & co., 1874.

> 2 p.l., [5]–81 p.

[Published with]

Career of Tiburcio Vásquez, the bandit of Soledad, Salinas and Tres Pinos. With some accounts of his capture by Sheriff Rowland of Los Angeles. Compiled from newspaper accounts.   San Francisco, F. MacCrellish & co., 1874.   Wrappers.   Rare.

> [85]–98 p.   22.8 cm.
> Cover title: "The Lives of Joaquín Murieta and Tiburcio Vásquez, the California Highwaymen, San Francisco, 1874."
> Double column.

See Item 172.

836   Ridings, Sam P.

The Chisholm trail. A history of the world's greatest cattle trail, together with a description of the persons, a narrative of the events, and reminiscences associated with the same, by Sam P. Ridings. Illustrated.   Guthrie, Okla., Co-Operative publishing co., publishers [1936].   Pict. cloth.   OP.

> 6 p.l., 591 p.   front. (port.), plates, ports., fold. map at end.   23.2 cm.
> Index: p. 587–591.

Although purporting to be a history of the Chisholm Trail, this book also contains much on outlaws, the killing of Ed Short and Charlie Bryant, the Talbot raid, and the Lincoln County War, and a chapter on Hendry Brown.

837   Riegel, Robert E.

America moves west, by Robert E. Riegel . . . .   New York, Henry Holt and co. [1930].   Cloth.   OP.

> x p., 1 l., 3–595 p.   maps.   22 cm.
> Supplementary readings: p. 567–585; index: p. 587–595.
> Half title; pub. device.

The author has some scattered material on many of the western outlaws, such as the James and Younger brothers, Sam Bass, and Billy the Kid.

He makes one statement with which I cannot agree when he says, "Men like Wild Bill Hickok and Sam Bass were all more closely related to the cattle business than to any other phase of life."

838 Ringgold, Jennie Parks

Frontier days in the southwest. Pioneer days in old Arizona, by Jennie Parks Ringgold.   San Antonio, Texas, the Naylor co. [1952].   Cloth.   In print.

> ix, 197 p.   plates, ports., facsms.   21.5 cm.
> Index: p. 189–197.
> Half title; map on end papers (different).

An excellent book of reminiscences of the Southwest when it was wild.

839 Ripley, Thomas

They died with their boots on, by Thomas Ripley.   Garden City, N. Y., Doubleday, Doran & co., inc., MCMXXXV.   Cloth. OP.

> 5 p.l., ix–xx p., 1 l., 285 p.   front., plates, ports.   21.3 cm.
> Bibliography included in "Foreword and Acknowledgments."
> Half title; illus. end papers; 8 ports. before t.p.; 1 p. adv. at end; pub. device; untrimmed; "First edition" on copyright p.

Mostly concerns John Wesley Hardin and his fellow desperadoes of Texas. The author brings in many gunmen of the early days, tells of the killing of Ben Thompson and King Fisher and the hanging of Bill Longley, and gives some information about Wild Bill Hickok. He admits there has been a lot of fiction written about Hickok, but he does refer to Frank Tarbeaux's autobiography and Frank Harris' *My Reminiscences as a Cowboy* as trustworthy books concerning Wild Bill. To me they seem most unreliable.

840 Rister, Carl Coke

No man's land, by Carl Coke Rister.   Norman, University of Oklahoma press, 1948.   Cloth.   In print.

> xi p., 1 l., 3–210 p.   front. (map), plates, ports.   21 cm.
> Bibliography: p. 193–199; index: p. 201–210.
> Half title; "First edition" on copyright p.

This book does not deal with any particular outlaw, but with the general lawlessness of a raw country and the activities of its vigilantes.

841 ———

Outlaws and vigilantes of the southern plains, 1865–1885, by Carl Coke Rister. Reprinted from the *Mississippi Valley Historical Review*, Vol. XIX, No. 4 (March, 1933). Stiff wrappers. OP.

537–554 p.   25.5 cm.

842 ———

Southern plainsmen, ₁by₁ Carl Coke Rister.   Norman, University of Oklahoma press, 1938.   Cloth.   OP.

xviii p., 1 l., 3–289 ₁1₁ p.   plates, fold. map facsms.   23.5 cm.
Bibliography: p. 263–279; index: p. 283–289.
Half title; vignette; "First Edition" on copyright p.

In a chapter entitled "Frontier Justice" the author gives a general picture of lawlessness in the Southwest.

843 ———

Southwestern frontier, 1865–1881. A history of the coming of the settlers, Indian depredations and massacres, ranching activities, operations of white desperadoes and thieves, government protection, building of railways, and the disappearance of the frontier, by Carl Coke Rister . . . .   Cleveland, the Arthur H. Clark co., 1928. Cloth.   OP.

10 p.l., ₁25₁–336 p.   front. (double p. col. map), plates, 2 fold maps.
24.5 cm.
Bibliography: p. ₁311₁–320; index: p. ₁323₁–336.
Half title; pub. device; untrimmed.

This book also has a general picture of lawlessness in the Southwest.

844 Roberts, Daniel Webster

Rangers and sovereignty, by Dan W. Roberts, captain Company "D" of the Texas rangers.   San Antonio, Texas, Wood printing & engraving co., 1914.   Cloth.   OP.

5 p.l., 15–190 p.   front. (port.).   19.8 cm.
Vignette.

A number of Texas Rangers have written their reminiscences. While this is not the most important of these accounts, it does contain chapters on the Mason County War, the Horrel-Higgins feud, and the killing of Sam Bass.

845   Roberts, Lou Conway (Mrs. Dan W.)

A woman's reminiscences of six years in camp with the Texas Rangers, by Mrs. D. W. Roberts, "assistant commander," Company D, Texas frontier battalion.   Austin, Texas, press of von Boeckmann-Jones co., [n.d. (*ca.*1928)].   Wrappers.   OP.

> 2 p.l., 5–64 p.   front., plates, ports.   23 cm.
> Device.

Tells of some of her husband's encounters with outlaws and feudists.

846   Roberts, Gov. O. M.

Message of Gov. O. M. Roberts on appropriations and expenditures under control of the governor, to the Seventeenth Legislature of the state of Texas, convened at the city of Austin, in regular session, January 11, 1881.   Galveston, Texas, printed at the News book and job office, 1881.   Pamphlet.   (Cover title.)   Scarce.

> [3]–23 p.   23 cm.

This rare little pamphlet deals mostly with appropriations and expenditures of rewards for the apprehension of outlaws within the state.

847   Robertson, Ruth T.

Famous bandits; brief accounts of the lives of Jesse James, Cole Younger, Billy the Kid and others . . . . Washington, D. C., the Washington bureau [1928].   Stitched folder.   Rare.

> [4] p.   (Not seen.)

A condensed account of these outlaws' activities, together with the dates and places of their births and deaths.

848   Robinson, William Henry

The story of Arizona, by Will H. Robinson . . . . Illustrated. Phoenix, Ariz., the Berryhill co., publishers [1919].   Cloth.   OP.

> 6 p.l., 13–458 p.   front., plates, map.   20 cm.
> Bibliography: p. 457–458.

In a chapter on saloons and bad men, the author tells of the Earp-Clanton and the Tewksbury-Graham feuds. He refers to Earp as the "criminally inclined officer."

849 Rockfeller, John Alexander

Log of an Arizona trail blazer, by John A. Rockfeller, Tucson, printed by Acme printing co. [1933]. Cloth. Scarce.

xv, 201 p. front., plates, ports. 21.6 cm.

A scarce account of pioneer Arizona containing some material on the outlaws of that state.

850 Rockwell, Wilson

New frontier. Saga of the north fork, by Wilson Rockwell. Illustrations by Josephine McKittrick. Denver, Colo., the World press, inc., 1938. Pict. cloth. OP.

xvi p., 1 l., 3-215 p. illus., plates, ports. 20.5 cm.
Appendix: p. 197-207; bibliography: p. 211-215.
Half title; illus. map on end papers.

Contains some minor information on Billy the Kid.

851 Roenigk, Adolph

Pioneer history of Kansas. [Lincoln, Kan.], published by Adolph Roenigk [1933]. Pict. cloth. Scarce.

6 p.l., 365 [7] p. plates, ports. 24 cm.
Index: 5 unnumbered p. at end.
Vignette.
"The material for the first part was collected and written by John C. Baird."

In a chapter on Abilene, Kansas, the author tells of the killing of Phil Coe by Wild Bill Hickok.

852 Roff, Joe T.

A brief history of early days in north Texas and Indian territory, by Joe T. Roff. [Allen, Okla., Pontotoc County Democrat], MCMXXX. Wrappers. Scarce.

2 p.l., 5-40 p. 17.5 cm.
Device.

Tells about members of the Lee gang and other lesser-known outlaws.

853   Rogers, Cameron

Gallant ladies, by Cameron Rogers; with illustrations by Charles O. Naef.   New York, Harcourt, Brace and co. [1928]. Cloth.   OP.

> 8 p.l., 17–363 p.   front., illus., plates.   22.5 cm.
> Half title; headpieces; pub. device; untrimmed.

Contains chapters on Belle Starr and Calamity Jane. The author repeats the widely circulated legend about Belle Starr's refusing to identify Jim Reed after he was killed in order to keep his assassin from collecting the reward. (Reed was identified by a number of other witnesses.)

854   Rogers, John William

The lusty Texans of Dallas, [by] John William Rogers. New York, E. P. Dutton and co., inc., 1951.   Cloth.   In print.

> 5 p.l., 11–384 p.   front. (port.).   22.3 cm.
> Acknowledgments: p. 366–367; index: p. 368–384.
> Half title; map on end papers (different); vignette; "First edition" on copyright p.

Most of his characters were not so lusty, but Rogers does give some information on Sam Bass, Frank James, Jesse James, and Belle Starr, largely in relation to their lives in Dallas.

855   Rollins, Philip Ashton

The cowboy. His characteristics, his equipment and his part in the development of the West, by Philip Ashton Rollins.   New York, Charles Scribner's sons, 1922.   Cloth.   OP.

> xiv p., 1 l., 353 p.   21.2 cm.
> Half title.

A second edition with illustrations was published in August, 1922.

856   ———

The cowboy. An unconventional history of civilization on the old-time cattle range, by Philip Ashton Rollins. Revised and enlarged edition.   New York, Charles Scribner's sons, 1936.   Cloth. OP.

> xx p., 1 l., 402 p.   front., illus., plates, double p. map, facsms.   22.3 cm.
> Appendix (notes on various statements in text): p. 287–393; index: p. 397–402.
> Half title; illus. end papers.

This is a completely revised edition of Item 855 with a new chapter and illustrations added. All editions contain a chapter on cattle rustling and the Johnson County War.

857   Rollinson, John K.

Hoofprints of a cowboy and U. S. ranger. Pony trails in Wyoming, by John K. Rollinson; edited and arranged by E. A. Brininstool; illustrated with photographs.   Caldwell, Idaho, the Caxton printers, ltd., 1941.   Cloth.   OP.

> 7 p.l., [15]–410 [1] p.   front., plates, ports., map.   23.6 cm.
> Cover title and half title: "Pony Trails in Wyoming"; headpieces; pub. device.

This book contains some material on lawlessness and a mention of Tom Horn. It was later reprinted with a glossary added.

858   ———

History of the migration of Oregon-raised herds to midwestern markets. Wyoming cattle trails, by John K. Rollinson . . . edited and arranged by E. A. Brininstool; illustrated with photographs and maps. Caldwell, Idaho, the Caxton printers, ltd., 1948. Cloth.   In print.

> 9 p.l., [19]–366 p.   front. (col.), plates, ports., maps, facsms.   24.2 cm.
> Appendices: p. [301]–348;   bibliography: p. [349]–351; index: p. [353]–366. Half title: "Wyoming Cattle Trails"; headpieces; pub. device; untrimmed.
>
> Also published in a de luxe edition. Colophon: "The limited edition of Wyoming Cattle Trails is 1000 numbered copies, signed by the author, of which this is No. _____. First edition."

This book has a lengthy chapter on the Johnson County War and the hanging of Cattle Kate and Jim Averill; it also contains material on Tom Horn and Butch Cassidy.

859   Rolt-Wheeler, Francis William

The book of cowboys, by Francis Rolt-Wheeler, with 33 illustrations from photographs, sketches and early prints.   Boston, Lothrop, Lee & Shephard co. [1921].   Pict. cloth.   OP.

> 8 p.l., 13–394 p.   front., plates.   20.5 cm.
> Half title; pub. device.

In the chapter entitled "Barbed Wire," there is considerable material on the Lincoln County War and Billy the Kid, most of it quoted from

Siringo's *Cowboy Detective*. However, the author makes the introductory statement that "one of the worst of all these cattle stealing outfits was Billy the Kid's gang, famous as having held the whole of Lincoln County, *Texas* [!] in a state of guerrilla warfare for years." He later gives the correct location of Lincoln County, in New Mexico.

860 Romer, F.

Makers of history. A story of the development of the history of our country at the muzzle of a Colt. Made into a book by F. Romer. Hartford, Conn., Colt's patent fire arms manufacturing co., 1926. Pict. wrappers. Scarce.

[3]-63 [2] p. front., plates. 17 cm.
Errata tipped in.

Deals with many outlaws, but repeats the legend of the Hickok-McCanles fight.

861 Root, Frank A., and William Elsey Connelley

The overland stage to California. Personal reminiscences and authentic history of the great overland stage line and pony express from the Missouri river to the Pacific ocean, by Frank A. Root . . . and William Elsey Connelley . . . . Topeka, Kan., published by the authors, 1901. Dec. pict. cloth. Rare.

xvii, 630 p. plates, ports., maps (1 fold. at end). 23.5 cm.
Index: p. 615–627; roll of honor: p. 629–630.
Half title; frontis tissue.

Republished in 1950 by Long Book Co.

A very scarce book considered the standard history of the early stage lines. Has some information on stagecoach robberies, Wild Bill Hickok, and Joseph A. Slade.

862 Rose, Dan

Prehistoric and historic Gila county, Arizona, by Dan Rose . . . . Phoenix, Republic and Gazette printery [n.d.]. Wrappers. Rare.

1 p.l., [3]-37 p. 23 cm.

Contains material on the Tonto Basin War and on the Apache Kid and other Arizona outlaws.

863 [Rose, Victor M.]

The Texas vendetta; or, the Sutton-Taylor feud, [by Victor M. Rose]. New York, printed by J. J. Little & co., . . . 1880. Wrappers. Exceedingly rare.

[3]–69 p. 17.8 cm.

Only two copies of this book are known to me, one in the Texas State Library and the other privately owned. The book gives some information not found elsewhere on the Sutton-Taylor feud.

864 Rosen, Rev. Peter

Pa-ha-sa-pah; or, the Black Hills of South Dakota. A complete history of the gold and wonder-land of the Dakotas from the original inhabitants, the whites who came in contact with them; opening up of the country to civilization, and its social and political development, by Rev. Peter Rosen, for seven years a missionary in the Black Hills. St. Louis, Nixon-Jones printing co., 1895. Cloth. Scarce.

xiii, 645 p. front. (port.), illus., plates, ports. 23.5 cm.

A scarce book which includes an account of the death of Wild Bill Hickok.

865 Ross, Edith Connelley

The bloody Benders, by Edith Connelley Ross. Reprinted from *Collections* of the Kansas State Historical Society, 1926–1928, Vol. XVII. Pamphlet. OP.

15 p. 22.8 cm.
Caption title.

A fairly accurate account of the Benders containing some material not found elsewhere.

866 Rothert, Otto A.

The outlaws of Cave-in-Rock. Historical accounts of the famous highwaymen and river pirates who operated in pioneer days upon the Ohio and Mississippi rivers and over the old Natchez Trace, by Otto A. Rothert . . . . Cleveland, Arthur H. Clark co., 1924. Cloth. OP.

8 p.l., [17]–364 p. front. (col.), plates, facsm. 24.5 cm.
Bibliography: p. [335]–345; index: p. [349]–364.
Half title; pub. device; untrimmed; tissues.

A history of the noted Harpes.

867   Rowan, Richard Wilmer

The Pinkertons, a detective dynasty, by Richard Wilmer Rowan.   Boston, Little, Brown and co., 1931.   Cloth.   OP.

6 p.l., 3–350 p. front. (port.), illus., plates, ports. 22.6 cm.
Index: p. 339–350.
Half title; pub. device; t.p. in red and black.

Most of this book deals with the Civil War and eastern outlaws in the Pinkertons' early work, but it does contain a chapter on the Reno brothers, the first train robbers.

868   Russell, Carl Parcher

One hundred years in Yosemite. The romantic story of early human affairs in the central Sierra Nevada, by Carl Parcher Russell. With a foreword by Horace M. Albright.   Stanford, Stanford University press; London, Humphrey Milford, Oxford University press, 1931.   Cloth.   OP.

xvi p., 1 l., 3–242 [2] p. front., plates, ports. 22.9 cm.
Chronology with sources: p. 203–216; bibliography: p. 217–230; index: p. 233–242.
Half title; map on end papers.

Contains some information on Black Bart and his holdups.

869   ———

One hundred years in Yosemite. The story of a great park and its friends, by Carl Parcher Russell. With a foreword by Newton B. Drury.   Berkeley and Los Angeles, University of California press, 1947.   Cloth.   In print.

xviii p., 1 l., 226 p. front., plates, ports. 22.2 cm.
Chronology and sources: p. 179–193; bibliography: p. 197–213; index: p. 217–226.
Half title.

This is a revision of the first edition, with many additions and changes, and different foreword, subtitle, and illustrations.

870 Russell, Jesse Lewis

Behind these Ozark hills. History—reminiscences—traditions featuring the author's family, by Jesse Lewis Russell, veteran newspaper man of the Ozark region. Biographical sketches of outstanding descendants of pioneers.   New York, the Hobson book press, 1947. Cloth.   In print.

> 6 p.l., 205 p.   front. (port.).   21.6 cm.
> Biographical appendix: p. [175]-205 (double column).
> Half title; pub. device.

Contains some interesting sidelights on the James brothers, the Youngers, Henry Starr, and others. The author tells of the James boys' hideout near Harrison, but is mistaken in saying that Jim Cummins lived on the breaks of White River, north of Eureka Springs, spending the remainder of his days there. Cummins spent most of his last days at the Old Soldiers' Home, Higginsville, Missouri, where he died. The author tells of Henry Starr's meeting his doom in Harrison's attempt to hold up a bank in 1921. He also criticizes the book *Only True History of Frank James*.

871 Rutledge, Col. Dick

A few stirring events in the life of Col. Dick Rutledge, only living Indian scout of the early frontier days of the west, and which occurred during the time he was associated with Kit Carson, Phil Sheridan, Buffalo Bill and others. Some of these tales have never before been revealed, all told in brief form . . . . [N.p., n.d.] Wrappers.   Scarce.

> 18 [1] p.   front. (port.).   17.5 cm.
> Cover title: "Brief sketches in the Life of Col. Dick Rutledge, the Last Living Indian Scout."

Contains some material on the James boys, Billy the Kid, and Calamity Jane.

872 Ryan, J. C.

A skeptic dude in Arizona, by J. C. Ryan. Illustrated by Sid Stone.   San Antonio, Texas, the Naylor co. [1952].   Cloth. In print.

> xi, 176 p.   front. (map), illus.   21.6 cm.
> Appendix: p. 175-176.

309

Half title; vignette.

Revives the argument pro and con concerning Wyatt Earp's character, and tells the story of the O K Corral fight.

873 Rye, Edgar

The quirt and the spur; vanishing shadows of the Texas frontier, by Edgar Rye.   Chicago, W. B. Conkey co., publishers ₁1909₁.   Dec. cloth.   Scarce.

> 4 p.l., 9–363 p.   front. (port.), plates.   19.8 cm.

A history of Fort Griffin, Texas, in its wild days, containing material on the early life of John Selman and John Laren. The author misspells Selman's name "Sillman."

874 Rynning, Thomas Harbo

> Gun notches. The life story of a cowboy-soldier, by Captain Thomas H. Rynning, as told to Al Cohn and Joe Chisholm; with a foreword by Rupert Hughes.   New York, Frederick A. Stokes co., MCMXXXI.   Cloth.   OP.

> xvii p., 1 l., 332 p.   21 cm.
> Half title; pub. device; illus. end papers.

This book deals with many of the Arizona outlaws whom Rynning pursued while with the Arizona Rangers.

875 Sabin, Edwin LeGrand

> Wild men of the wild west, by Edwin L. Sabin . . . .   New York, Thomas Y. Crowell co., publishers ₁1929₁.   Pict. cloth.   OP.

> xiv, 363 p.   front., plates, ports.   21.3 cm.
> Half title.

This author covers practically all the gunmen of the West, from the land pirates of the Mississippi to the outlaws of California. In his sketch of Wild Bill he tries to correct the legend of the McCanles fight.

876 Safford, Gov. A. P.

> Message of the governor of Arizona, delivered January 14, 1871, before the Sixth Legislative Assembly.   Tucson, Citizen office print, 1871.   Wrappers.   Rare.

> 13 p.   19.5 cm.

Among other subjects the message treats outlawry in that territory.

877   Sage, Lee

The last rustler, the autobiography of Lee Sage, with illustrations by Paul S. Clowes.   Boston, Little, Brown and co., 1930. Pict. cloth.   OP.

> x p., 1 l., [3]–303 p.   illus.   21.6 cm.
> Half title; headpieces; tailpieces; vignette.

The autobiography of a man born among the outlaws of Robbers' Roost. His mother took her children from this lawless surrounding back to her old home, but the call of the wild was too great to resist, and the author returned West and learned all the tricks of the rustler.

878   Sanders, Helen Fitzgerald

A history of Montana, by Helen Fitzgerald Sanders. Illustrated.   Chicago and New York, the Lewis publishing co., 1913. Pub. in three volumes.   Leather.   Scarce.

> Vol. I, xxxv, 19–847 p.   front., plates, ports., tables, facsm.   27.5 cm.
> Double column; frontis tissue; gilt top.
> Vols. II and III biographical.

This scarce history has chapters on the vigilantes of Montana and on the road agents and other outlaws.

879   Sands, Frank

A pastoral prince. The history and reminiscences of J. W. Cooper, by Frank Sands.   Santa Barbara, Cal., 1893.   Pict. cloth. Scarce.

> xiv p., 1 l., 190 p.   front. (port.), ports.   20 cm.

In his chapter on Murieta the author says: "Today the stories of Murieta look like myths, so enveloped are they with the glamour of enterprise, daring and bravery. Indeed, very many men even doubt the existence of the man, considering him as having been purely a character of fiction, born from the deeds of such men as Jack Powers. Others, admitting that the man actually existed, consider his deeds to have been magnified beyond reason, and affirm that he was only a lieutenant of Powers. But the evidence given by men now living who knew Murieta, both before and during his career of bloodshed and robbery, must count for far more than the doubts of people who know nothing of the matter at all, save from hearsay."

880 Santee, Ross

Apache land, written and illustrated by Ross Santee. New York, Charles Scribner's sons; London, Charles Scribner's sons, ltd., 1947. Pict. cloth. In print.

> vii p., 1 l., 216 p. illus. 23.6 cm.
> Illus. double t.p.; first edition: letter "A" on copyright p.

In a chapter on the Apache Kid the author gives some new material, and since he is thoroughly familiar with the life and history of Arizona, I consider his accounts reliable.

881 Saunders, Charles Francis

The southern Sierras of California, by Charles Francis Saunders . . . . Illustrated from photographs by the author. Boston, and New York, Houghton Mifflin co., 1923. Cloth. OP.

> xii p., 1 l., [3]–367 p. front. (with tissue), plates. 21 cm.
> Index: p. [365]–367.
> Half title; pub. device; untrimmed; first edition: 1923 under imprint.

Contains some material on Murieta and Vásquez.

882 Savage, Richard Henry

The little lady of the lagunitas; a Franco-Californian romance, by Richard Henry Savage . . . . New York, the trade supplied by the American News co. [press of J. J. Little & co.], 1892. Cloth. Rare.

> 3 p.l., [7]–483 p. 20.2 cm.
> 1 l. adv. at end.

A collector's item, but of no historical value. Although purporting to be the life of Murieta, it is done in fictional style.

883 Sawyer, Eugene Taylor

The life and career of Tiburcio Vásquez, the California bandit and murderer; containing a full and correct account of his many offenses against the law, from boyhood up, his confessions, capture, trial, and execution. To which is appended Judge Collins' address to the jury in behalf of the prisoner, by Eugene T. Sawyer. [San Jose, Calif., 1875.] [Printed by Bacon and co., book and job printers, San Francisco, 1875.] Pict. wrappers. Exceedingly rare.

The Life and Career

OF

TIBURCIO VASQUEZ,

THE

California Bandit and Murderer:

CONTAINING A

FULL AND CORRECT ACCOUNT OF HIS
MANY OFFENSES AGAINST THE LAW,
FROM BOYHOOD UP,

His Confessions,

CAPTURE, TRIAL, AND EXECUTION.

TO WHICH IS APPENDED

JUDGE COLLINS' ADDRESS TO THE JURY
IN BEHALF OF THE PRISONER.

By EUGENE T. SAWYER.

Entered according to Act of Congress, in the year 1875, by E. T. SAWYER, in the Office of
the Librarian of Congress, at Washington.

NUMBER 883

2 p.l., [5]–48 p. ports. 22 cm.

Published same year by B. H. Cottle, of San Jose.

One of the rarest of the few books on Vásquez. The author writes with personal knowledge, much of the narrative supposedly coming from Vásquez's lips; in addition the author traveled through Monterey and San Benito counties, interviewing relatives and old acquaintances of Vásquez, from whom he gathered much information.

884 ——————

The life and career of Tiburcio Vásquez, the California stage robber, by Eugene T. Sawyer. Foreword by Joseph A. Sullivan. Oakland, Calif., Biobooks, 1944. Cloth and boards. Scarce.

viii p., 3 l., 3–91 [1] p. front. 24.7 cm.
Specimen of Vásquez's handwriting; vignette.
Edition limited to 500 copies printed by Grabhorn press.

A modern reprint of the original Sawyer edition of 1875, now quite scarce.

885 Scanland, John Milton

The life of Pat F. Garrett and the taming of the border outlaws. A history of the "gun men" and outlaws, and a life story of the greatest sheriff of the southwest, by John Milton Scanland. Published by Carleton F. Hodge, El Paso, Texas.   El Paso, Texas, press of the Southwestern printing co. [1908].   Pict. wrappers.   Exceedingly rare.

42 p. 4 p. plates at end. 23.5 cm.
Port. of Garrett with signature in facsimile on cover.

An exceedingly rare and much sought-after little book. The author starts his narrative by telling of the killing of Pat Garrett by Wayne Brazil, but barely touches upon the killing of Billy the Kid. He makes an error in stating that the Kid went to Pete Maxwell's house the evening he was killed to meet his "lady love." There are some typographical errors such as "rade" for "rode" on page 24, and the author misspells some proper names, such as "O'Fallon" for "O'Folliard." Line 15, page 23, is misplaced, the same line belonging to line 14, page 24. The author makes the statement that the Kid was twenty-two years old and had "killled twenty-seven men—perhaps more." John J. Lipsey, a book dealer of Colorado Springs, Colorado, published a facsimile of this little book in 1952 from a photostat in my library.

886 Schatz, August Herman

Opening a cow country. A history of the pioneer's struggle in conquering the prairies south of the Black Hills, by A. H. Schatz. Ann Arbor, Mich., Edwards brothers, inc., 1939. Stiff wrappers. Scarce.

> x, 107 p., 1 l., 109–141 p. front., illus., plates, ports., maps, plan. 21 cm.
> Appendix: p. 109–141.
> Lithoprinted.

This privately printed and scarce little book devotes a whole chapter to cattle rustling in the Dakotas.

887 Schell, Herbert Samuel

South Dakota, its beginning and growth, by Herbert Samuel Schell. New York, American book co. [1942]. Cloth. OP.

> x p., 1 l., 359 p. front. (double p. map), plates, ports., maps, charts.
> 20.5 cm.
> Appendix: p. 335–344; index: p. 345–359.
> Questions and bibliography at end of each chapter.

888 Schmedding, Joseph

Cowboy and Indian trader, by Joseph Schmedding. Caldwell, Idaho, the Caxton printers, ltd., 1951. Pict. cloth. In print.

> 8 p.l., [17]–364 p. front., plates, facsm. 23.5 cm.
> Half title; map on end papers; headpieces; pub. device; vignette.

Contains some history of Tombstone and the activities of its gunmen. The author tells of the Earps, the Clantons, and their feud.

889 Schmidt, Heinie

Ashes of my campfire. Historical anecdotes of old Dodge City as told and retold, by Heinie Schmidt . . . . Vol. I (only one published). Dodge City, Kan., Journal, inc., publishers [1952]. Stiff pict. wrappers. In print.

> 3 p.l., 9–72 p. plates, ports. 19.5 cm.
> Double column.

Little stories of people and events in Dodge City.

890 Scobee, Barry

The steer branded murder, by Barry Scobee. The true and

authentic account of a frontier tragedy. Documented by eye witnesses, it presents the story of cattlemen, cowboys, and the cattle-country of far western Texas .... ₁Houston, Texas, Frontier press of Texas, 1952.₁ Stiff pict. wrappers. In print.

> 2 p.l., 5–56 ₁2₁ p. front., port. 17 cm.
> Index tipped in.
> Vignette.

A crudely printed and crudely bound little book, but its author seems to have made an honest effort to dig up the facts concerning this well-known Texas incident, which has become legendary. Some of Texas' better-known outlaws are also mentioned.

891 Segale, Sister Blandina

At the end of the Santa Fé Trail, ₁by₁ Sister Blandina Segale. Columbia press, 1932. Cloth. OP.

> 5 p.l., ₁3₁–347 p. front. (port.), plates, ports. 20.5 cm.

Republished by Bruce publishing co., Milwaukee, 1948–1949.

> xi p., 1 l., 298 p. front. (port.), plates, ports. 20.3 cm.
> Footnotes: p. 285–290; bibliography: p. 291–294; index: p. 295–298.
> Half title.

Contains some material on Billy the Kid, but the author is much confused in her dates. She claims to have visited the Kid in jail on May 16, 1882, nearly a year after his death, and she records his death as September 8, 1882.

892 Senn, Edward L.

"Deadwood Dick" and "Calamity Jane." A thorough sifting of facts from fiction, written and published by Edward L. Senn. Deadwood, S. D. ₁1939₁. Pamphlet. (Cover title.) OP.

> 3–15 p. 18.3 cm.

The author here makes an effort to debunk some of the unreliable statements of earlier writers, but gets two dates wrong himself.

893 ——————

"Wild Bill" Hickok, "prince of pistoleers." A tale of facts

and not fiction and romance, written and published by Edward L. Senn. Deadwood, S. D. [1939]. Pamphlet. (Cover title.) OP.

16 p. 18.3 cm.

An abbreviated sketch of Wild Bill, in which the author does much to debunk the fables written about this noted gunman, especially those about the McCanles fight. A newspaperman, the author makes an honest effort to straighten out some garbled history.

894 Sexton, Major Grover F.

The Arizona sheriff, by Maj. Grover F. Sexton, the deputy from Yavapai. Illustrated by Benton H. Clark. [N.p.], published by the Studebaker corp. of America, 1925. Pict. wrappers. (Cover title). Scarce.

2 p.l., 5–46 p. illus., plates, ports., map. 23 cm.

An unimportant little pamphlet which has now become scarce.

895 Shackleford, William Yancey

Belle Starr, the bandit queen. The career of the most colorful outlaw the Indian territory ever knew, by William Yancey Shackleford. Girard, Kan., Haldemann-Julius publications [1943]. Wrappers. OP.

[3]–24 p. 21.3 cm.

The author attempts to compare his information with that of others who have written about Belle Star in an effort to clear up some points.

896 ———

Gun-fighters of the old west, [by] William Yancey Shackleford. Girard, Kan., Haldemann-Julius publications [1943]. Wrappers. OP.

1 l., [3]–24 p. 21.5 cm.

This booklet contains some short sketches of the best-known outlaws of the West. The author attempts to cover the outlaws from the Ohio River pirates of 1800 to the Daltons. He holds to the false story of the Hickok-McCanles fight, and admits "it is quite a thing for one man to whip ten gun fighters and kill eight of them all in the space of four or five minutes." He also calls McCanles "Jim." His whole account of Wild Bill seems to be taken from the *Harper's Magazine* account by Nichols.

Shackleford admits that his account of the Lincoln County War was taken from Emerson Hough's writing, which he says gives the first *authentic* account of this affair. He exposes his ignorance of the West by saying that John Chisum of Lincoln County fame is the same man who gave his name to the famous cattle trail "that the radio cowboys are still caterwauling about." He says that McSween was a preacher. McSween was a religious man, but a lawyer.

The author writes that the first man Billy the Kid killed was a man who slapped the Kid in the face in a barroom when he was twelve years old. He presents a different version of the money owed the Kid, saying that the "murdering preacher" owed him money and "that many people thought that he collected it at the point of a pistol from John Chisum, who had backed McSween."

He names Quantrill, "Charles William Quantrell," and his accounts of the James boys, the Youngers, and the Daltons are just as unreliable as his stories of Wild Bill and Billy the Kid.

897   Shaner, Dolph

The story of Joplin, by Dolph Shaner.   New York, Stratford House, inc. [1948].   Cloth.   In print.

xi, 144 p.   14 full p. plates.   21.6 cm.

Contains some material on the James and Younger brothers, and tells of their visit to Joplin.

898   Shaw, Luella

True history of some of the pioneers of Colorado, [by] Luella Shaw.   Hotchkiss, Colo., published by W. S. Coburn, John Patterson and A. K. Shaw, 1909.   Stiff wrappers.   OP.

vi, [9]-268 [1] p.   front. (port.), plates, ports.   19.8 cm.

There is an account of Jim Reynolds and his gang.

899   Shea and Patten

The "Soapy" Smith tragedy, compiled and copyrighted by Shea and Patten.   Skagway, Alaska [Daily Alaskan print], 1907. Pict. wrappers.   Three-hole tie.   Rare.

[23] p. (no pagination).   13 plates (incl. t.p.).   Oblong 24 x 15.3 cm. Text on verso of plates.

This exceedingly rare little book is said to have been written by H. B. LeFevre, of Skagway. It is a condensed history of the reign of terror and outlawry in White Pass and the Skagway country in 1898, the formation of the vigilance committee, Soapy Smith's counter organization of thugs and cutthroats known as the "Law and Order Committee of 303," and the killing of Soapy and the capture of his gang.

900 Sheldon, Addison Erwin

Nebraska old and new. History, stories, folklore, by Addison Erwin Sheldon . . . . Lincoln . . . , the University publishing co. [1937]. Pict. cloth. OP.

> x, 470 p. front. (map), illus., ports., maps, facsms., plan. 20.8 cm.
> Index: p. 465–470.
> Half title; vignette.

In a chapter entitled "War on the Rustlers," the author tells of the hanging of Kid Wade and the capture of Doc Middleton.

901 Sheridan, Sol N.

History of Ventura county, California, by Sol N. Sheridan. Chicago, the S. J. Clarke publishing co., 1926. Pub. in two volumes. Cloth.

> Vol. I, xviii p., 1 l., 21–472 p. plates. 27.2 cm.
> Index: p. 461–472.
> Vol. II biographical.

In Chapter XXIII, entitled "The Days of the Bandit," the author deals at length on the life of Vásquez.

902 Shields, Robert William

Illustrations for Mule's Crossing, a history of the Reno era; the story of the Reno brothers, the world's first train robbers, America's pioneer wild west gang, and the only criminals ever lynched from the custody of the United States . . . . Franklin, Indiana, R. W. Shields, 1944. Stiff wrappers. Exceedingly rare.

> 1 p.l., 46 plates (incl. ports., facsms.). 27.5 x 21.5 cm.
> "Twelve copies . . . printed . . . ."

There is no text in this book, which contains only the plates used in the back of *The Reno Gang of Seymour* (see Item 1031). These twelve books were made up as souvenirs for Shields' friends. "Mule's Crossing" was the early name of Seymour, Indiana, from which the Renos operated.

903 ———

Seymour, Indiana, and the famous story of the Reno gang who terrorized America with the first train robberies in world history . . . , by Robert W. Shields . . . . Indianapolis, H. Lieber and co., 1939. Stiff wrappers. Scarce.

> 3 p.l., 44 [1] p. illus., fold. map. 26.8 cm.
> Mimeograph dry-stencil process on one side of paper.

One of the few books written about the Renos, it is reliable.

904 Shinn, Charles Howard

Graphic description of Pacific coast outlaws. Thrilling exploits of their arch-enemy, Sheriff Harry N. Morse. Some of his hand-to-hand encounters with bandits, by Charles Howard Shinn (in New York *Sun*). [San Francisco, R. R. Patterson, 1887.] Wrappers. Very rare.

> [3]-32 p. front. (port.). 17 cm.
> Caption title.

A very rare little book dealing with Vásquez, Murieta, and other California outlaws of Spanish descent.

905 ———

Mining camps. A study in American frontier government, by Charles Howard Shinn. New York, Charles Scribner's sons, 1885. Cloth. Scarce.

> xi, 316 p. 21.2 cm.
> Authorities consulted: p. 299-307; index: p. 309-316.
> Half title; 4 l. adv. at end.

Although the author mentions Murieta only briefly, he deals at length with the lawlessness of the early California mines.

906 Shipman, Mrs. O. L.

Letters, past and present . . . , by Mrs. O. L. Shipman. [N. p., n.d.] Stiff wrappers. Scarce.

> 5 p.l., 9-137 p. ports. 22.8 cm.

A series of letters to the author's nephews and nieces containing some material on Billy the Kid, Bill Cook, and Tom O'Folliard.

907 ————

Taming the Big Bend. A history of the extreme western portion of Texas from Fort Clark to El Paso, by Mrs. O. L. Shipman. ₁Marfa, Texas, 1926.₁ Cloth. Scarce.

> viii p., 1 l., ₁3₁–215 p. front., ports., fold. map at end. 23.7 cm.
> Index: p. ₁209₁–215.
> Frontis tissue.

In a chapter entitled "Law West of the Pecos," the author deals with Texas Rangers and lawlessness. In another, there is mention of the Lincoln County War, Billy the Kid, John Wesley Hardin, John Selman, and other gunmen.

908 Shirley, Glenn

Toughest of them all . . . , by Glenn Shirley. ₁Albuquerque, University of New Mexico press, 1953.₁ Cloth. In print.

> ix, 145 p. 21 cm.
> Bibliography: p. ₁137₁–141; index: p. ₁143₁–145.
> Half title.

This book adds nothing new to outlaw literature. The author is mistaken in saying that Billy the Kid "had gotten rid of his handcuffs and leg irons" while Ollinger was running across the street from the restaurant to the courthouse after hearing the shot that killed Bell. It was not that swift and easy. In fact, the Kid had to have it done for him after he killed Ollinger. On page 103, "border" is misspelled "boarder."

909 Siddons, Leonora

The female warrior. An interesting narrative of the sufferings, and singular & surprising adventures of Miss Leonora Siddons . . . . Full and interesting particulars, written by herself. New York, printed for and published by E. E. Barclay, 1844. Wrappers. Exceedingly rare.

> ₁5₁–21 p. front. 22.2 cm.

Miss Siddons could in no sense be classed as an outlaw, but I do believe this little pamphlet should be included, because Miss Siddons is a unique female character. She joined the Texas Army under General Sam

Houston and during the battle at San Antonio was shot and left for dead. Recovering the next morning, she was captured by the Mexicans. After an attempted escape, she was recaptured and taken to Vera Cruz, from which place she was made to walk barefooted over the burning sands to Mexico City, where she was thrown into prison. She escaped from this prison and returned to her friends in 1843.

910   Simmons, Frank E.

History of Coryell county, by Frank E. Simmons.   ₁N.p.₁, published by Coryell County News, 1935.   Stiff wrappers.   OP.

4 p.l., 102 p.   20 cm.

In the chapter entitled "Era of Lawlessness," some of the outlaws of this Texas county are told about.

911   Siringo, Charles A.

A cowboy detective. A true story of twenty-two years with a world-famous detective agency; giving the inside facts of the bloody Coeur d'Alene labor riots, and the many ups and downs of the author throughout the United States, Alaska, British Columbia and Old Mexico. Also exciting scenes among the moonshiners of Kentucky and Virginia, by Chas. A. Siringo . . . .   Chicago, W. B. Conkey co., 1912.   Pict. cloth.   Scarce.

7 p.l., 11–519 p.   front. (port.), plates (2 double p.), ports.   19.7 cm.

Published same year by J. S. Ogilvie.

The author uses the name "Dickenson" for the Pinkerton agency. When he autographed this book for me a few years before his death, he took his pen and, at the chapter heading of Chapter I, scratched out "Dickenson" and wrote "Pinkerton." He also wrote "Tom Horn" beneath the picture of this character which was labeled "Tim Corn." His original title was "Pinkerton's Cowboy Detective," but the agency held up publication of the book through Superior Court action until he changed the title to "Cowboy Detective," and changed the name of Pinkerton to Dickenson, and substituted other fictitious names.

912   ———

Further adventures of a cowboy detective. A true story of twenty-two years with a world-famous detective agency. Giving the inside facts of the bloody Coeur d'Alene labor riots, and the many ups and downs of the author throughout the United States, Alaska, British Columbia and Old Mexico . . . , by Charles A. Siringo. New York, J. S. Ogilvie publishing co. [1912]. Col. pict. wrappers. Scarce.

> 3 p.l., [247]–519 p.   17.4 cm.
> 3 p. adv. at end.

When Ogilvie published *Cowboy Detective*, the company retained the title and issued the work in two volumes, this being the second. The two books were paper bound, being numbered 127 and 128 in the Railroad Series. Both these paper-bound books are exceedingly scarce, though at one time every news-butch carried a plentiful supply.

913 ———

History of "Billy the Kid." The true life of the most daring young outlaw of the age. He was the leading spirit in the bloody Lincoln County, New Mexico, War . . . , by Chas. A. Siringo . . . . [Santa Fé, N. M., the author, 1920.] Stiff pict. wrappers. Scarce.

> 2 p.l., [5]–142 p.   18 cm.
> 1 p. adv. at end.

A very scarce book, written from material the author had scattered through some of his other books plus some new material. Not too reliable.

914 ———

A lone star cowboy, being fifty years' experience in the saddle as cowboy, detective and New Mexico ranger, on every cow trail in the wooly old West. Also the doings of some "bad" cowboys, such as "Billy the Kid," Wess Harding [*sic*] and "Kid Curry," by Chas A. Siringo . . . . Santa Fé, New Mexico, 1919. Pict. cloth. OP.

> 4 p.l., 291 [1] p.   front., plates, ports., facsm.   20.5 cm.

Like many of the author's books, this one contains many repetitions from his previous volumes. In this one the author remembers some incidents he did not tell in his first book. He states in his preface, "This volume is to take the place of *A Texas Cowboy*."

915 ———

Riata and spurs. The story of a lifetime spent in the saddle as cowboy and detective, by Charles A. Siringo, with an introduction by Gifford Pinchot, and with illustrations. Boston, and New York, Houghton Mifflin co., 1927. Pict. cloth. OP.

> xiv p., 1 l., 276 p. front., plates, ports., facsm. 21.2 cm.
> Vignette; first edition: 1927 under imprint.
> "Certain parts of the book are reprinted, in revised form, from the author's privately printed narrative called the Lone Star Cowboy and Cowboy Detective."

The first half of this book was taken from Siringo's *Cowboy Detective*, with real names called. On account of a threatened lawsuit, this edition was recalled after release and pages 120 to 268 were suppressed. All references to the author's experiences with the Pinkerton Agency were cut out and material on bad men substituted. Only a few copies of the original printing got out; hence its scarcity.

916 ———

Riata and spurs. The story of a lifetime spent in the saddle as cowboy and ranger, by Charles A. Siringo, with an introduction by Gifford Pinchot, and with illustrations. Revised edition. Boston, and New York, Houghton Mifflin co. [1927]. Pict. cloth. OP.

> xiv p., 1 l., 261 p. front., plates, ports., facsm. 21.2 cm.
> Half title; vignette.
> "Letters from Gifford Pinchot and Emerson Hough to the author" (1 l. inserted between pages 260 and 261).

In this edition, issued after the recalling of the first printing, the entire last half of the book is changed, but with no explanation. The author used material on bad men he had intended for another book. Reprinted in 1931 under the imprint "Riverside Library."

917 ———

A Texas cowboy; or, fifteen years on the hurricane deck of a Spanish pony. Taken from real life, by Chas. A. Siringo, an old stove up "cowpuncher," who has spent nearly twenty years on the great western cattle ranges. Chicago, M. Umbdenstock and co., publishers, 1885. Pict. cloth. Exceedingly rare.

> 2 p.l., [ix]-xii, [13]-316 p. double front. (col.), illus., ports. 20.cm.
> Added t.p. illus. in col.; dec. end papers.

Republished in 1886 under the imprint of Siringo and Dobson, with the same title page and with an addenda (p. 317-347), an index to the addenda, and a dedication. The second frontispiece of the first edition was used as the only frontis of the second printing. This frontispiece was later used as the cover for the paperbacks of the news-butch editions.

This book was reprinted many times between 1914 and 1926 by various publishers such as the Eagle Publishing Company, Rand, McNally and Company, and finally in a cheap pulp edition by J. S. Ogilvie Publishing Company. It was one of the first books written about the cowboy, and perhaps received wider circulation than any of them; yet it is now hard to find a copy, and next to impossible to locate the first edition.

[Again republished in 1950:]

A Texas cowboy; or, fifteen years on the hurricane deck of a Spanish pony—taken from real life by Charles A. Siringo. With bibliographical study and introduction by J. Frank Dobie and drawings by Tom Lea. Typography by Carl Hertzog.   New York, William Sloane Associates [1950].   Cloth.   In print.

> xl p., 1 l., 3–198 p. illus., facsm. 22 cm.
> Half title; illus. double t.p.; headpieces; first edition: pub. device "WSA" on copyright p.

918 ———

Two evil isms, Pinkertonism and anarchism, by a cowboy detective who knows, as he has spent twenty-two years in the inner circle of Pinkerton's National Detective Agency, by Charles A. Siringo . . . .   Chicago, Charles Siringo, publisher, 1915.   Pict. wrappers.   Exceedingly rare.

> 2 p.l., 109 [1] p. front., illus. 19.7 cm.
> Device; table of contents on verso of t.p.

Out of print since the time it came off the press. From the time Siringo severed connection with the Pinkertons and started writing, the Pinkertons gave him trouble with his books. Most of this edition of two thousand copies, along with the plates, was burned by the Pinkerton Agency on order of a Chicago court, making this book very scarce. A small lot had been shipped west and thus escaped. Siringo seemed determined to reveal what he considered the evils of the Pinkerton methods; and the Pinkertons, in turn, were just as determined that his books would be changed or suppressed.

919 Skelton, Charles L.

Riding west on the pony express, [by] Charles L. Skelton.

Illustrated by Paul Quinn. New York, the Macmillan co., 1937.
Cloth. OP.

> 5 p.l., 196 p. front., illus. 21 cm.
>
> Author's note: "Riding West has some factual matter never before pub-
> lished, including a correct description of J. A. Slade, the most colorful in-
> dividual connected with the pony express."

920 Sloan, Richard E.

Memories of an Arizona judge, by Richard E. Sloan . . . .
Stanford University, California, Stanford University press; London,
Humphrey Milford, Oxford University press, 1932. Cloth. OP.

> xii, 250 p. 20 cm.
> Index: p. 247–250.
> Half title.

Contains accounts of stage robberies, the Earp-Clanton feud, and the
Tonto Basin War.

921 ———

History of Arizona. Hon Richard E. Sloan, supervising editor, Ward R. Adams, author, assisted by an advisory council. Issued
in four volumes, profusely illustrated. Arizona biography by special staff of writers. Phoenix, Record publishing co., publishers,
1930. Pub. in four volumes. Full leather. Scarce.

> Vol. I, 9 p.l., 21–525 p. front. (port.), plates, ports., maps, plan. 27.5 cm.
> Vol. II, 2 p.l., 7–530 p. front., plates, map, plan. 27.5 cm.
> Device; gilt top.
> Vols. III and IV biographical.

Vols. I and II have much good history on the cattle wars and the many
outlaws of Arizona.

922 Small, Floyd B.

Autobiography of a pioneer, by Floyd B. Small; being an
account of the personal experiences of the author from 1867 to
1916 . . . . Seattle, Wash., F. B. Small, 1916. Stiff pict. wrappers. Scarce.

> 2 p.l., 7–106 p. illus. 23.4 cm.
> "Do not read paragraphs marked by red until you come to those marked
> by blue. This was a transposition made by the printer and will be cor-
> rected in the next edition . . . ."—the author.

The author claims to have lived as a close neighbor of Wild Bill Hickok's sister; yet he spells the name "Hecock." He errs in saying that Wild Bill was killed in August of 1877, and makes a bigger mistake when he says that Jack McCall was hanged at Virginia City, Montana. He also gives an account of his meeting with the James boys.

923 Small, Kathleen Edwards, and J. Larry Smith

History of Tulare county, California, by Kathleen Edwards Small, and Kings county, California, by J. Larry Smith. Illustrated. Chicago, the S. J. Clarke publishing co., 1926. Pub. in two volumes. Cloth. Scarce.

> Vol. I, 6 p.l., 15–637 p. front. (port.), plates, map. 27.4 cm.
> Index: p. 627–637.
> Vol. II biographical.

Contains a long chapter on train robbery and the activities of Gratt and Bill Dalton in California and of the Evans-Sontag gang. The Kings County section has some material on Murieta and Vásquez.

924 Smith, Alson Jesse

Brother Van, a biography of the Rev. William Wesley Van Orsdel, by Alson Jesse Smith. New York, Nashville, Abingdon-Cokesbury press [MCMXLVIII]. Cloth. In print.

> 7 p.l., 13–240 p. front. (port.), illus., plates, ports. 20.3 cm.
> Index: p. 237–240.
> Decorative half title; map on end papers: illus. t.p.

This biography has some scattered material on Henry Plummer and his gang, Joseph Slade, and the vigilantes.

925 Smith, Benjamin

A fugitive from hell, by Benjamin Smith . . . . Fifteen years an outlaw. [Joplin, Mo., 1935.] Cloth. Scarce.

> 4 p.l., 9–122 [1] p. front. (port.), plate at end. 19.6 cm.

Another of those little books, often hard to come by, of reminiscences written by former outlaws.

926 Smith, C. Alphonso

O. Henry biography, by C. Alphonso Smith . . . . Illustrated. Garden City, N. Y., Doubleday, Page & co., 1916. Cloth. OP.

v p., 3 l., 3–258 p.   front. (port.), plates, ports. facsm.   24 cm.
Index: p. 253–258.
Half title; pub. device; untrimmed.

Contains some information about Al Jennings, since he was associated with O. Henry during his prison days.

927   Smith, Tevis Clyde

Frontier's generation. The pioneer history of Brown county, with sidelights on the surrounding territory, by Tevis Clyde Smith.   Brownwood, Texas, published by the author [1931].   Stiff wrappers.   OP.

2 p.l., [5]–63 p.   front., plates, ports.   22.2 cm.
Advertisements interspersed throughout.

One section tells of John Wesley Hardin, some of his killings, his capture, trial, and finish.

928   Smith, Wallace

Garden of the sun, by Wallace Smith. A history of the San Joaquin valley, 1772–1939.   Los Angeles, Calif., Lymanhouse [1939].   Cloth.   OP.

v, 558 p., [i]–iii p.   plates, maps, plan.   23.4 cm.
Appendix: p. 541–558; index: p. [i]–iii (at end).
Half title.

Here we have much information on Joaquín Murieta, Tiburcio Vásquez, the Dalton brothers, and Evans and Sontag, the train robbers. The author makes the mistake of stating that the first published account of Murieta appeared in the *California Police Gazette* for September 3, 1859. This did become the best-known edition because of the scarcity of Ridge's original book of 1854.

929   ———

Prodigal sons. The adventures of Christopher Evans and John Sontag, by Wallace Smith.   Boston, the Christopher publishing house [1951].   Cloth.   In print.

7 p.l., 15–434 p.   front. (port.), plates, ports.   22.3 cm.
Appendix: p. 416–434.
Half title; pub. device.

The most extensive book yet written on Evans and Sontag, it is also the most authentic. The author tells more of Evans' childhood and family life than is revealed in any other book I have examined. He has done a scholarly work, and his book can be considered reliable. The word "fact" is used twice consecutively on page 37, an error which might be an identifying point of the first edition.

930 Sonnichsen, Charles Leland

Billy King's Tombstone. The private life of an Arizona boom town, by C. L. Sonnichsen. Illustrated. Caldwell, Idaho, the Caxton printers, ltd., 1942. Pict. cloth. OP.

> 8 p.l., [15]–233 p. front., plates, ports. 23.5 cm.
> Half title; plan on end papers; pub. device.

A different picture of Tombstone than in other books on the subject. A story of a bartender who knew every character in this wild town, it throws some new light upon such characters as Buckskin Frank Leslie, Burt Alvord, and Sheriff John Slaughter.

931 ———

I'll die before I'll run. The story of the great feuds of Texas, by C. L. Sonnichsen. New York, Harper & brothers, publishers [1951]. Cloth. In print.

> xviii p., 1 l., 3–294 p. plates, ports. 21.8 cm.
> Sources and notes: p. 267–294.
> Half title; illus. map on end papers; pub. device; "First edition" on copyright p.

A book on the feuds of Texas which shows serious research, although it does not cover all of the feuds. But feuds are difficult things to write about since descendants are still living. The author, in his "Sources and Notes" (p. 285), makes the error of stating that "the only appearance in print of the Marlow feud is in a story by William McLeod [sic] Raine." The Marlows themselves wrote a book on this feud in 1892, a book that is listed in this work. See Item 668.

932 Sorenson, Al

"Hands up!" or, the history of a crime. The great Union Pacific express robbery, by Al Sorenson. Illustrated. Omaha, Nebr., published by Barkalow brothers, 1877. Wrappers. Exceedingly rare.

> 3 p.l., [11]–139 p. plates. 16.5 cm.
> Half title; 6 p. adv. at end.

Later reprinted by C. B. Dillingham, New York.

This rare book is the first one written about the robbery of the Union Pacific at Big Springs, Nebraska, by Joel Collins, Sam Bass, and company. Giving a detailed account of the robbery, it was published soon after this robbery took place. Since it was published in 1877, it tells nothing of the later events in these outlaws' lives.

933 Sowell, Andrew Jackson

History of Fort Bend county, containing biographical sketches of many noted characters . . . , by A. J. Sowell. Houston, Texas, W. H. Coyle and co., printers, 1904. Cloth. Rare.

xii, 373 p. front. (port.), port. 22.5 cm.

Contains material on the Jaybird-Woodpecker feud.

934 Spalding, William A.

History and reminiscences, Los Angeles city and county, California. Compiled by William A. Spalding. Los Angeles, Calif., published by J. R. Finnell & sons publishing co. [n. d.]. Pub. in three volumes. Leather. OP.

Vol. I, 5 p.l., 13–558 p. front. (port with tissue), plates, ports. 27.4 cm.
Index: p. 523–558.
Vols. II and III biographical.

Contains a chapter on Vásquez and some material on Murieta.

935 Sparks, William

The Apache Kid, a bear fight and other true stories of the old west, by William Sparks. Los Angeles, Skelton publishing co., 1926. Stiff pict. wrappers. OP.

3 p.l., [9]–215 p. 4 plates. 20 cm.

A collection of articles, among which are stories of the Apache Kid and the Diablo Canyon train robbery.

936 Spencer, (Mrs.) George E.

Calamity Jane. A story of the Black Hills, by Mrs. George E. Spencer. New York, Cassell and co., ltd. [1887]. Wrappers. Scarce.

2 p.l., [5]–172 p. 17.8 cm.
12 p. adv. at end.

This book is fiction, but it is a collector's item on Calamity Jane material. It is said to be the first book of fiction published by a South Dakotan.

937 Spindler, Will Henry

Rim of the sandhills. A true picture of the old Holt county horse thief–vigilante days, by Will Henry Spindler .... Mitchell, S. D., published by the Educator supply co. [1941]. Cloth. OP.

7 p.l., [15]–346 p. front., plates, ports. 19.8 cm.

A story of Kid Wade, a horse thief and outlaw hanged by the vigilantes of Nebraska.

938 Splawn, Andrew Jackson

Ka-Mi-Akin, the last hero of the Yakimas, by A. J. Splawn. [Portland, Ore., press of Kilham stationery & printing co., 1917.] Cloth. Scarce.

5 p.l., 436 [6] p. front., plates, ports. 23.5 cm.
Last 6 p. biography and eulogy.

Much information on lawlessness in the Northwest with some heretofore unrecorded material on Boone Helm.

939 Sprague, Marshall

Money mountain. The story of Cripple creek gold, by Marshall Sprague. With illustrations. Boston, Little, Brown and co. [1953]. Cloth. In print.

xx p., 1 l., [3]–342 p. front., plates, ports. 22 cm.
Appendices: p. [297]–302; notes: p. [303]–319; bibliography: p. [321]–327; acknowledgments: p. [328]–330; index: p. [333]–342.
Half title; map on end papers; pub. device; "First edition" on copyright p.

Contains some new material on Soapy Smith and tells much about the lawlessness of this mining town.

940 Spring, Agnes Wright

The Cheyenne and Black Hills stage and express routes, by Agnes Wright Spring .... Glendale, Calif., the Arthur H. Clark co., 1949. Cloth. In print.

8 p.l., [17]–418 p. plates, ports., facsm. (all in one section near end), fold. map at end. 24.5 cm.

Appendices: p. [341]-365; bibliography: p. [367]-371; index: p. [405]-418.
Half title: American Trail Series VI; pub. device.

One of the best books written on the Black Hills and the outlaws of that section, the work reveals much scholarly research by an able historian.

941 ———

William Chapin Deming, of Wyoming, pioneer publisher, and state and federal official. A biography, by Agnes Wright Spring .... Glendale, Calif., privately printed in a limited edition, by the Arthur H. Clark co., 1944. Cloth. OP.

> 9 p.l., [21]-531 p. front. (port.), plates, ports., facsms. 24.5 cm.
> Appendix: p. [495-511]; index: p. [513]-531.
> Half title; device; frontis tissue.

Contains some material on Tom Horn.

942 Stanley, E. J.

Life of Rev. L. B. Stateler; or, sixty-five years on the frontier. Containing incidents, anecdotes, and sketches of Methodist history in the west and northwest, by Rev. E. J. Stanley .... Introduction by Bishop E. R. Hendrix. Illustrations by E. S. Paxson. Nashville, Tenn., Dallas, Texas, publishing house of the M. E. Church South ..., 1907. Pict. cloth. Scarce.

> xvii, 356 [1] p. front., plates, ports. 19.6 cm.

This book contains a chapter on outlaws and the vigilantes of Montana, in which the author tells of the hanging of Henry Plummer and many of his gang and how the vigilantes brought law into that raw land.

943 Stanley, F. (pseud. of Stanley Crocchiola)

Desperadoes of New Mexico, by F. Stanley. [Denver, Colo., printed by the World press, inc., 1953.] Cloth. In print.

> xv, 320 p. plates, ports. 22.3 cm.
> Bibliography: p. 317-320.
> Half title.
> Colophon: "Limited edition of New Mexico Desperadoes. This book number ____ of an edition limited to eight hundred volumes."

A book which covers practically all the well-known outlaws of New Mexico. In it the author tells some things not in other books on this subject. He does, however, repeat several legends about Billy the Kid. Like many writers he has Mrs. McSween playing her piano while her home burns, not once but twice; and this act Mrs. McSween has emphatically denied. Also the author repeats the fable about the Kid playing cards with his jailer, Bell, and dropping a card so that Bell would have to pick it up, thus giving the Kid a chance to slip Bell's gun from its holster. The book shows carelessness in proofreading, as it is full of typographical errors. However, it is most interesting and a valuable addition to the histories of our western outlaws.

944 ———

Fort Union (New Mexico), by F. Stanley. [N.p., 1953.] Cloth.   In print.

> xiii p., 1 l., 305 p.   plates, ports.   22.3 cm.
> Bibliography, p. 301–305.
> Half title.

Contains a chapter on some of the lawlessness in New Mexico, and tells some new stories about Clay Allison.

945 ———

The grant that Maxwell bought, by F. Stanley. [Denver, Colo., printed by the World press, 1952.]   Cloth.   Scarce.

> 4 p.l., 256 p.   15 p. ports. and plates at end, fold. map in pocket at end.
> 28.7 cm.
> Bibliography: p. 254–256.
> Half title; double column.
> Colophon: "Limited edition of the Grant That Maxwell Bought. This book number —— of an edition limited to two hundred and fifty volumes." (Signed.)

This limited edition was immediately sold out and is now scarce. It has a long chapter on Clay Allison, in which the author tries to straighten out some of the legends about this notorious gunman.

946 ———

The Las Vegas story (New Mexico), by F. Stanley . . . . [Denver, Colo., World press, inc., 1951.]   Cloth.   In print.

> xi p., 1 l., 340 p.   plates, ports.   22.3 cm.
> Bibliography: p. 335–340.
> Half title.

A chapter on Vicente Silva and another on outlaws and lawlessness.

333

947 ———

One half mile from Heaven; or, the Cimarron story. Compiled by F. Stanley for the Raton Historical Society .... ₁Denver, Colo., World press publishing co., 1949.₁ Stiff pict. wrappers. OP.

6 p.l., 3–155 p. plates, ports., plan. 21.5 cm.
Bibliography: p. 145–147; notes: p. 148–155.
Half title.

Contains quite a bit of material on Clay Allison and other gunmen of Cimarron.

948 ———

Raton chronicle. Compiled by F. Stanley for Raton Historical Society .... ₁Denver, Colo., World press publishing co., 1948.₁ Pict. wrappers. OP.

7 p.l., 3–146 p. plates, ports. 21.5 cm.
Notes: p. 133–143; bibliography: p. 144–146.
Half title.

Some material on early-day lawlessness in Raton, New Mexico.

949 ———

Socorro: the oasis, by F. Stanley. ₁Denver, Colo., World press, inc., 1950.₁ Cloth. OP.

8 p.l., 221 p. plates, ports. 22.3 cm.
Bibliography: p. 215–221 .
Half title.

Some early-day history of Socorro with a chapter on Joel Fowler and his lynching; also includes information on the vigilantes and on Elfego Baca.

950 Stansbery, Lon R.

The passing of the 3D ranch, by Lon R. Stansbery. ₁Tulsa, Okla., printed for the author by George W. Henry printing co., n.d.₁ Pict. cloth. (Cover title.) Scarce.

92 p. illus., plates, ports. 19.4 cm.

This scarce book gives some heretofore unpublished facts about the Daltons, the Jennings', the Cook gang, and other Oklahoma outlaws.

951 [Starr, Belle]

Bella Starr, the bandit queen, or the Female Jesse James. A full and authentic history of the dashing female highwayman, with copious extracts from her journal. Handsomely and profusely illustrated.... New York, Richard K. Fox, publisher, 1889. Col. pict. wrappers. Exceedingly rare.

> 2 p.l., [5]–64 p. front., illus. 21 cm.
> 8 p. adv. at end.

This book is a rare collector's item, but historically it is worthless. It has been the source, I am sorry to say, of most accounts of Belle Starr by earlier historians, and its information has been repeated so often that even modern historians use material taken from it without knowing its inaccuracies or its source. It is highly imaginative fiction, presented as fact by an anonymous writer of the *Police Gazette* staff. Names, dates, and other essential facts are wrong, even to the spelling of Belle's name. The alleged excerpts of Belle's own letters are pure fabrication. Most writers of the sensational yellow-journalism school of that period used such vehicles to make it appear that their writing was authentic.

952 Starr, Henry

Thrilling events; life of Henry Starr, famous Cherokee Indian outlaw narrates his many adventures from boyhood to date. Written in the Colorado penitentiary by himself .... [N.p.], 1914. Pict. wrappers. (Cover title.) Exceedingly rare.

> 50 [1] p. 19.8 cm.
> Port. of author on cover.

A well-written and most interesting little book about this outlaw's life and his many lawless acts. There are many typographical errors, stretches of misplaced text, and a repetition of two sentences on page 23. The author ends his book with a bitter tirade against society, and has many comments to make on graft in the courts, especially in Judge Parker's court.

953 Stegner, Wallace

Mormon country, by Wallace Stegner. Edited by Erskine Caldwell. New York, Duell, Sloan and Pearce [1942]. Cloth. OP.

> x p., 1 l., 3-362 p. 22.2 cm.

335

BELLA STARR,

THE BANDIT QUEEN,

OR THE

FEMALE JESSE JAMES

A Full and Authentic History of the
Dashing Female Highwayman,
with Copious Extracts from
her Journal.

HANDSOMELY AND PROFUSELY ILLUSTRATED.

PRICE, BY MAIL, - 25 CENTS

New York.
RICHARD K. FOX, Publisher.
1889.

NUMBER 951

Index: p. 351–362.
Half title; map on end papers; "First printing" on copyright p.

Contains a chapter on Butch Cassidy and his Wild Bunch.

954 Stellman, Louis J.

Mother lode. The story of California's gold rush, by Louis J. Stellman. Cover design and decorations by Paul Rockwood. San Francisco, Calif., Harr Wagner publishing co. [1934]. Cloth. OP.

> xv p., 1 l., 304 p. front. (port.), plates, ports. 19.3 cm.
> Index: p. 299–304.

The account of Murieta follows the Ridge version, but the author does state that at one time Murieta's band was composed of almost as many women as men. There is also some material on Black Bart, which tells of his capture.

955 Stephens, Lorenzo Dow

Life sketches of a jayhawker of '49, by Lorenzo Dow Stephens. Actual experiences of a pioneer told by himself in his own way. [N.p., privately printed], 1916. Stiff wrappers. Scarce.

> 2 p.l., [7]–68 p. ports. 23.6 cm.

The author here gives some fresh material on Murieta.

956 Stephenson, Terry E.

Caminos viejos. Tales found in the history of California of especial interest to those who love the valleys, the hills and the canyons of Orange county, its traditions and its landmarks, by Terry E. Stephenson. Published on the Press of the Santa Ana High School and Junior College by its director Thomas E. Williams. Illustrated with photographs, with maps and with woodcuts, the latter by Miss Jean Goodwin and Arthur Ames. Santa Ana, Orange county, Calif., 1930. Dec. cloth. Scarce.

> 9 p.l., 111 p. front., illus., plates, maps (1 large fold. at end). 25.5 cm.
> Half title; illus. end papers; untrimmed.
> Colophon: "This book is one of a de luxe edition of two hundred and fifty copies of which this is No. ____." (Signed by the author and the printer.)
>
> This book was reprinted in another de luxe edition of 500 signed and numbered copies the same year, but this edition was marked "Revised Edition"

on verso of second flyleaf. Both editions are now scarce, and since 1942 this press has been discontinued.

The book has a long chapter on outlawry in Orange County and tells of the killing of Sheriff Barton and the hanging of Juan Flores.

957 [Sterling, Thomas]

Autobiography of Tom Sterling. Seven years of thrilling adventures of a western peace officer . . . . Santa Monica, Calif., Weaver publishing co., 1941. Pict. cloth. Scarce.

2 p.l., 3–118 p. front. (port.), plates, ports. 24.5 cm.
7 blank leaves at end.

Privately printed in a small edition, it is now scarce. It has some material on the gunmen of Dodge City.

958 Stewart, Marcus A.

Rosita; a California tale, by Marcus A. Stewart. San Jose, Mercury steam print, 1882. Cloth. Rare.

3 p.l., [5]–72 p. 20 cm.

In this epic poem the author tries to create another legend about Murieta by having him escape death and go back to Mexico to live a happy life. He makes Rosita the wife of one of Murieta's lieutenants, instead of Murieta himself.

959 Stone, Arthur L.

Following old trails, by Arthur L. Stone, with illustrations. Missoula, Mont., Morton John Elrod, 1913. Cloth. Scarce.

7 p.l., 17–304 p. front., plates, ports. 23.5 cm.
Half title; device.

A chapter on the Montana vigilantes tells of some of their hangings in their effort to bring law and order to the frontier.

960 Stout, Tom (ed.)

Montana, its story and biography. A history of aboriginal and territorial Montana and three decades of statehood. Under the editorial supervision of Tom Stout. Chicago and New York, the American Historical Society, 1921. Pub. in three volumes. Full leather. Scarce.

Vol. I, xlix, 894 p. front., plates, ports. 27 cm.
Vols. II and III are paged continuously, both biographical, and both double column.

Volume I contains a long chapter on the outlaws and vigilantes of Montana based largely on Dimsdale's and Langford's books on this subject.

961 Stout, F. E.

Rube Burrows; or, life, exploits and death of the bold train robber, by F. E. Stout. Aberdeen, Miss., 1890. Pict. wrappers. Exceedingly rare.

2 p.l., [5]–78 p. ports. 15.5 cm.
Port. on t.p. and front wrapper.

Said to be the rarest of all the books about this bold outlaw, it tells of his life from childhood to the day of his death; but the author is wrong in saying that Rube Burrows was on the train at the time of Jackson's capture and that he made his escape dressed as a woman.

962 Stover, Elizabeth Matchett (ed.)

Son-of-a-gun stew; a sampling of the southwest, edited by Elizabeth Matchett Stover; foreword by John William Rogers; illustrations by Harold D. Bugbee. Dallas, University press in Dallas, Southern Methodist University, 1945. Cloth. OP.

x p., 1 l., 216 p. illus. 21.5 cm.
Half title; illus. double t.p.

Also published in wrappers; later republished by Grossett and Dunlap.

This is an anthology of the best articles published in the *Southwest Review* up to 1945, representing a thirty years' file. It was published to commemorate the first Southwest Book Fair held in Dallas in 1945. One article, entitled "Horse Thieves," by J. Evetts Haley, is about outlaws and other persons who later became outlaws; but the author is mistaken when he says Jesse Evans was killed by Billy the Kid at the outbreak of the Lincoln County War.

963 Strahorn, Carrie Adell

Fifteen thousand miles by stage. A woman's unique experience during thirty years of path finding and pioneering from the Missouri to the Pacific and from Alaska to Mexico, by Carrie Adell Strahorn. With 350 illustrations from drawings by Charles M. Russell and others, and from photographs. New York, London, G. P. Putnam's sons, 1911. Cloth. Pict. label pasted on. Scarce.

> xxv p., 1 l., 673 p. front. (port. with tissue), illus., plates (4 col. with tissues), ports. 23.4 cm.
> T.p. in red and black.

Gives accounts of the Montana vigilantes and the Plummer gang.

964 Street, Julian Leonard

Abroad at home; American ramblings, observations, and adventures of Julian Street. With pictorial sidelights, by Wallace Morgan. New York, the Century co., 1914. Cloth. Scarce.

> xiv, 1 l., 3–517 p. front., plates. 22.8 cm.
> Half title; device.
>
> Reprinted in 1918.

Chapter XXVI, entitled "The Tame Lion," is about Frank James.

965 Streeter, Floyd Benjamin

The Kaw; the heart of a nation, by Floyd Benjamin Streeter; illustrated by Isabel Bate and Harold Black. New York, Toronto, Farrar & Rinehart, inc. [1941]. Cloth. OP.

> ix [1] p., 1 l., 3–371 p. front. (map), illus. 21 cm.
> [Rivers of America series.]
> Acknowledgments: p. 351–352; bibliography: p. 353–359; index: p. 361–371.
> Half title; illus. t.p.; illus. end papers; first edition: letter "F R" in device on copyright p.

Contains material on the gunmen of the cowtowns of Kansas. On page 348, line 32, the words "the Congressional school" should read "the Congregational school." If the book is ever reprinted with corrections, this mistake will identify the first state.

966 ⸺

Prairie trails & cow towns, [by] Floyd Benjamin Streeter; with illustrations from old prints. Boston, Chapman & Grimes [1936]. Cloth. OP.

> 5 p.l., 11–236 p. front., plates, ports. 20.8 cm.
> Notes (biographical): p. 219–225; index: p. 227–232; bibliography: p. 233–236
> Vignette; untrimmed.

This able historian gives a good picture of the various famous cowtowns of Kansas, and the activities of the gunmen who lived in them.

340

967 ——

Tragedies of a Kansas cow town, by F. B. Streeter. Reprinted from the *Aerend*, Vol. V, Nos. 2 and 3 (Spring and Summer, 1934). Published quarterly by the faculty of the Ft. Hays Kansas State College ₁n.d. (*ca.*1934)₁. Wrappers. (Cover title.) OP.

 81–162 p. 23 cm.

More material on the gunmen of the cowtowns of Kansas.

968 Stuart, Granville

Forty years on the frontier as seen in the journals and reminiscences of Granville Stuart, gold-miner, trader, merchant, rancher and politician; edited by Paul C. Phillips. Cleveland, the Arthur H. Clark co., 1925. Pub. in two volumes. Cloth. OP.

 Vol. I, 10 p.l., ₁23₁–272 p. front. (port.), plates. 24.4 cm.
 Vol. II, 5 p.l., ₁13₁–265 p. front., plates. 24.4 cm.
 Index: p. ₁243₁–265 (Vol. II).
 Half title: Northwest Historical Series II; pub. device; untrimmed; frontis tissue; gilt top.

Written by a well-educated and influential pioneer of early Montana, this work contains much valuable history. Personally he did much to form a group of later-day vigilantes to break up a band of horse and cattle thieves who became so bold in their operations that drastic measures had to be taken. He gives a good account of the killing of Rattlesnake Jake Fallon and Long-Haired Owens.

969 Sullivan, W. John L.

Twelve years in the saddle for law and order on the frontiers of Texas, by Sergeant W. J. L. Sullivan, Texas Ranger, Co. B, Frontier Battalion. Austin, von Boeckmann-Jones co., printers, 1909. Cloth. Port. pasted on. Rare.

 4 p.l., ₁3₁–284 p. front., plates, ports. 21 cm.
 Errata on verso of third prelim. leaf.

An exceedingly scarce book on the life of a Texas Ranger, it contains chapters on the hanging of Bill Longley, on the Bill Cook gang, feuds, and bank robbers.

970 Supreme Court of the United States

Henry Starr, plaintiff in error *vs.* the United States. Brief of plaintiff in error. In error to the Circuit Court of the United States for the western district of Arkansas. ₁N.p., 1892.₁ Wrappers. (Cover title.) Rare.

> 53 p. 21.7 cm.

The trial of Henry Starr for the killing of Floyd Wilson in the Indian Territory in 1892.

971 Sutherland, William Alexander

Out where the West be-grins, by William Alexander Sutherland. ₁Las Cruces, Southwest publishing co., 1942.₁ Stiff wrappers. OP.

> 2 p.l., 5-94 ₁1₁ p. 23.4 cm.
> Port. on cover.

Gives a short sketch of the killing of Bob Ollinger by Billy the Kid.

972 Sutley, Zachary Taylor

The last frontier, by Zack T. Sutley. New York, the Macmillan co., MCMXXX. Cloth. OP.

> vi p., 2 l., 350 p. fold. map. 22.5 cm.
> Half title; untrimmed.

Contains material on the hanging of Lame Johnny, on Jesse James, Wild Bill Hickok, and Calamity Jane. This author has Calamity Jane born of Mormon parents in Salt Lake City.

973 Sutton, Ernest V.

A life worth living, by Ernest V. Sutton. Introduction by Lee Shippey. End paper painting "When the West Was Young" and chapter headings by Clarence Ellsworth. Pasadena, Calif., Trail's End publishing co., inc. ₁1948₁. Cloth. OP.

> xiv p., 1 l., 350 ₁1₁ p. front. (port.), ports. 22.6 cm.
> Index: p. 347-350.
> Illus. end papers (col.); illus. chapter headings; double t.p.; pub. device; untrimmed; "First edition" on copyright p.
> Edition limited to 2,000 signed copies.

Contains some material on the Benders and Chris Evans.

974 Sutton, Fred Ellsworth

Hands up! Stories of the six-gun fighters of the old wild west, as told by Fred E. Sutton and written down by A. B. McDonald. Illustrated. Indianapolis, the Bobbs-Merrill co., publishers [1927]. Pict. cloth. OP.

> 8 p.l., 13–303 p. front., plates, ports. 21.5 cm.
> Half title; untrimmed.

The author makes some doubtful statements, and according to his narrative it would appear that he had personal contact and friendship with all the outlaws of the Southwest. But, according to his age when he died in 1927, such contacts would have been impossible. He claims to have saved the life of Billy the Kid in Dodge City, but I can find no other reference of the Kid's ever having been in Kansas except as a baby. The author seems to have been "right there" when anything happened to an outlaw, such as his seeing Jesse James immediately after he was killed by Bob Ford. He apparently relies heavily upon such books as Mrs. Tilghman's *Outlaw Days*, Harman's *Hell on the Border*, Wright's *Dodge City*, and Love's *Rise and Fall of Jesse James*. The author also claims that Bat Masterson gave him his gun, calling his attention to the twenty-two notches on the stock. If this really happened, Bat was "jobbing" him, for genuine gunmen did not file notches on their guns. Stuart Lake, in his *Wyatt Earp*, makes mention of this, though he calls no names. He writes that Bat, tired of being pestered by a gun collector, went to a pawnshop, bought a gun, and with a pen-knife cut twenty-two "credits" upon it. Sutton was a gun collector. On the whole, this is a most unreliable book.

975 Swan, Oliver G. (ed.)

Frontier days, edited by Oliver G. Swan. Philadelphia, Macrae-Smith co., publishers [1928]. Pict. cloth. OP.

> 6 p.l., 13–512 p. front. (col.), illus. 12 col. plates (incl. front.). 24.8 cm.
> Illus. end papers (col.); illus. t.p.
>
> Also published in a de luxe edition and boxed.

An anthology with a chapter on "badmen" dealing with road agents, Black Bart, Henry Plummer, Billy the Kid, and others. In a chapter entitled "The Men Who Tamed the Cow-Towns," by Arthur Chapman, the author makes the mistake so many have made before him in calling Phil Coe, Phil "Cole." In another chapter on Billy the Kid, this same author spells John Chisum's name "Chisholm." This story originally appeared in *Outing Magazine* for May, 1905. The author is wrong in most of his assumptions. He says that the Kid "was a New York street waif, from where he *was sent* to Silver City, New Mexico"; that his first job was as a waiter in a Silver City hotel, but that he was soon convicted of "stealing supplies from the hotel, and clothes from a Chinese laundryman." After the Kid made his escape by crawling up a chimney, he got a job as a blacksmith's apprentice and later killed his boss.

Chapman quotes Hough's *Story of the Cowboy* in saying that two or three hundred men lost their lives in the Lincoln County War, a war between cattle owners and cattle thieves.

Chapman's account of the Kid's capture at Stinking Springs is wrong, as is his information on the mob at Las Vegas. He says the mob was after the Kid, although it was really after Dave Rudabaugh for killing a jailer at Las Vegas. He also says that Garrett put his prisoners in a *box car* and that the train could not move for an hour, the mob being bluffed by Garrett and his men all this time. He repeats that old legend about the judge's pronouncing the death sentence on the Kid and this impertinent outlaw's retort "and you go to hell, hell, hell." This, of course, never happened. Chapman also repeats the story about the Kid's killing Chisum's cowboys and sending back a message that he would credit Chisum's account with five dollars for every man he killed. He makes the Kid a thoroughly wanton killer, and follows Hough's account of his killing a bunch of Mexicans "just to see them kick." He does, however, cut the number to three instead of the seven used by Hough. A most unreliable account.

976 Tabor, Silver Dollar

Star of blood, by Silver Dollar Tabor .... ₁Denver, 1909.₁
Stiff wrappers.   Rare.

₁3₁–74 p.   illus., port.   22.3 cm.
Device.

An amateurish story about Allen Dowmen, the outlaw.

977 Tallent, Annie D.

The Black Hills; or, the last hunting ground of the Dakotahs. A complete history of the Black Hills of Dakota from their first invasion in 1874 to the present time, comprising a comprehensive account of how they lost them; of numerous adventures of the early settlers; their heroic struggles for supremacy against the hostile Dakotah tribes, and their final victory; the opening of the country to white settlement, and its subsequent development, by Annie D. Tallent. St. Louis, Nixon-Jones printing co., 1899. Cloth Scarce.

> xxii, 713 p. front. (port.), illus., plates, ports. 23.6 cm.
> Tailpieces; frontis tissue.

The author has Billy the Kid a horse thief and a member of the Exelbee [*sic*] gang in the Black Hills, although she says his name was McCarthy. Perhaps she got his name from some early dime novelist, or perhaps he was another Billy the Kid. Certainly Billy the Kid Bonney was never in the Black Hills. The book contains some information on Wild Bill Hickok, Jack McCall, Dunc Blackburn, stage robbers, and other outlaws.

978 Targ, William (ed.)

The great American west. A treasury of stories, legends, narratives, songs & ballads of western America, edited with an introduction by William Targ. Cleveland and New York, the World publishing co. [1946]. Pict. cloth. OP.

> xii p., 1 l., 3–595 p. 21.8 cm.
> Glossary of western words: p. 587–591; acknowledgments, p. 593–595.
> Vignette.

An anthology of western stories and articles, among which are "Stick 'Em Up," from *Guns of the Frontier*, by William MacLeod Raine, and "Dick Yeager," from *The Cherokee Strip*, by Marquis James.

979 Taylor, Drew Kirksey

Taylor's thrilling tales of Texas, being the experiences of Drew Kirksey Taylor, ex-Texas ranger and peace officer on the border of Texas. Written by himself and narrating true incidents of frontier life. [San Antonio, Guaranty bond printing co.], 1926. Stiff wrappers. OP.

> 2 p.l., 7–93 p. front. (port.), illus. 22 cm.
> Frontis tissue.

The author tells of some gunmen he knew, such as John Selman, John Laren, Clay Allison, and John Wesley Hardin. He claims to have known Billy the Kid personally, but he adds nothing to the information we have on this young outlaw.

980 Taylor, Joseph Henry

Kaleidoscopic lives. A companion book to *Frontier and In-*

345

dian Life, by Joseph Henry Taylor. Illustrated. Washburn, N.D., printed and published by the author, 1896. Cloth. Scarce.

3 p.l., [5]–206 [4] p. front., illus. (part on col. paper), ports. 20 cm.

Some material on lawlessness, including horse stealing, and the vigilantes of the Dakotas.

981 Taylor, T. U.

Bill Longley and his wild career, by T. U. Taylor. Bandera, Texas, Frontier Times [n.d.]. Wrappers. (Cover title.) OP.

31 p. 22 cm.
Reprinted from the *Frontier Times* in 1926.

A fairly accurate account which the author culled from contemporary newspapers, state records, and interviews with personal friends of the outlaw. Contains some typographical errors.

982 ———

The Lee-Peacock feud, by T. U. Taylor . . . . Bandera, Texas, published by Frontier Times [n.d.]. Wrappers. OP.

10 p. 26.4 cm.
Double column.

A separate reprint of an article on this feud which appeared in the *Frontier Times Magazine.*

983 Terrell, Charles Vernon

The Terrells. Eighty-five years Texas from Indians to atomic bomb . . . , [by] C. V. Terrell. Austin, Texas [privately printed, 1948]. Imt. leather. OP.

6 p.l., 13–336 p. plates, ports. 23.3 cm.
Vignette.

This book consists of the personal reminiscences of an old-timer, but the author is mistaken in saying that Sam Bass started his bank and train robbing in Denton County.

984 Thane, Eric (pseud. of Ralph Chester Henry)

High border country, by Eric Thane. Edited by Erskine Caldwell. New York, Duell, Sloan & Pearce [1942]. Cloth. OP.

ix p., 1 l., 3–335 p.   22cm.
Index: p. 333–335.
Half title; map on end papers; "First edition" on copyright p.

Contains quite a bit of material on the Montana vigilantes and the Wild Bunch of later days.

985 ——

The majestic land. Peaks, parks & prevaricators of the Rockies & highlands of the northwest, by Eric Thane. Illustrated. Indianapolis, New York, the Bobbs-Merrill co., inc., publishers [1950].   Cloth.   In print.

5 p.l., 11–347 p.   plates.   22.2 cm.
Index: p. 333–347.
Half title; map on end papers; "First edition" on copyright p.

Contains some material on Montana outlaws.

986   Thomas, D. K.

Wild life in the Rocky mountains; or, the lost million dollar gold mine, by D. K. Thomas. Illustrated by Alice Moseley and M. Reynolds .... [N.p], C. E. Thomas pub. co., 1917.   Cloth.   Pict. label pasted on.   OP.

5 p.l., 13–221 p.   front., illus., plates.   19.5 cm.

Contains chapters on road agents, desperadoes, and the Montana vigilantes.

987   Thomes, William Henry

The whaleman's adventures in the Sandwich islands and California, by Wm. H. Thomes .... Illustrated.   Boston, Lee and Shepard, publishers; New York, Lee, Shepard and Dillingham, 1872.   Cloth.   Scarce.

5 p.l., 9–444 p.   front., plates.   19.7 cm.
"Ocean Life Series."
Frontis tissue.

This seems to have been a popular book in its day, for it was republished in 1876, 1882, 1883, 1885, 1889, and 1890 by various publishers. It tells of the author's encounter with Joaquín Murieta.

988 Thompson, Albert W.

The story of early Clayton, New Mexico, [by] Albert W. Thompson. [Clayton, printed by the Clayton News, 1933.] Wrappers. (Cover title.) Scarce.

> 95 p. plates, ports. (last 5 pages). 21.5 cm.

The last half of this scarce little book deals with the life of Black Jack Ketchum.

989 ———

They were open range days; annals of a western frontier, by Albert W. Thompson. Denver, Colo., the World press, inc., 1946. Cloth. OP.

> viii p., 1 l., 3–193 [1] p. plates, ports., map, plan. 21.5 cm.
> Half title.
> Copyright notice on t.p.

Contains much material on Black Jack Ketchum and the Coe gang, and some on Billy the Kid.

990 Thompson, George G.

Bat Masterson; the Dodge City years, by George G. Thompson. Topeka, printed by Kansas State printing plant . . . , 1943. Wrappers. OP.

> 3–55 p. 22.8 cm.
> Appendix: p. 47–54; bibliography: p. 55.
> (Fort Hays Kansas State College Studies. Language and Literature Series, No. 1. F. B. Streeter, editor. General Series, No. 6.)

A treatise on the life of Bat Masterson during his stay in Dodge City, Kansas.

991 Thompson, Henry C.

Sam Hildebrand rides again, by Henry C. Thompson. Bonne Terre, Mo., printed and published by Steinbeck publishing co., 1950. Stiff wrappers. In print.

> 3 p.l., 113 p. front., 4 plates. 22.2 cm.

One of the few books written about this famous Missouri outlaw.

348

992 Thorndike, Thaddeus

Lives and exploits of the daring Frank and Jesse James, containing a graphic and realistic description of their many deeds of unparalleled daring in the robbing of banks and railroad trains, by Thaddeus Thorndike. Baltimore, I. & M. Ottenheimer, publishers, 1909. Pict. wrappers. OP.

> vi, 7–185 p. front., illus. 19 cm.
> 3 p. adv. at end.

Another cheap, unreliable book on the James boys, it is printed on unusually bad paper.

993 Thorp, Nathan Howard (Jack)

Story of the southwestern cowboy, pardner of the wind, by N. Howard (Jack) Thorp . . . in collaboration with Neill M. Clark. Illustrated . . . . Caldwell, Idaho, the Caxton printers, ltd., 1945. Cloth. In print.

> 10 p.l., [21]–309 p. front., plates, ports., music. 23.6 cm.
> Appendix: p. [285]–301; index: p. [303]–309.
> Half title: "Pardner of the Wind"; pub. device.

This is one of the best western books of recent years. The author gives some frank opinions about Billy the Kid, Sam Bass, and other outlaws, He did not live to see his book in print.

994 Tilghman, Zoe Agnes (Stratton)

Marshal of the last frontier. Life and services of William Matthew (Bill) Tilghman for 50 years one of the greatest peace officers of the west, by his wife Zoe A. Tilghman. Glendale, Calif., the Arthur H. Clark co., 1949. Cloth. In print.

> 9 p.l., [19]–406 p. front. (port.), plates, ports., fold. map at end. 24 cm.
> Index: p. [397]–406.
> Half title: Western Frontiersmen Series III; pub. device.

The only complete biography of this noted peace officer, this book tells of his experiences with the gunmen of Dodge City and the outlaws of Oklahoma.

995 ———

Outlaw days. A true history of early-day Oklahoma characters, revised and enlarged from the records of Wm. Tilghman,

[by] Zoe A. Tilghman (Mrs. Bill Tilghman). [Oklahoma City], Harlow publishing co., 1926. Pict. wrappers. OP.

iii p., 1 l., 138 p. front., ports. 17.3 cm.

See items 428 and 725, especially the comment on the former. Both this volume and Newsom's *The Life and Practice of the Wild and Modern Indian* (Item 725) were printed by the same house. This book has been used extensively as source material by later writers.

996 Tinkham, George H.

History of San Joaquin county, California, with biographical sketches of the leading men and women of the county who have been identified with its growth and development from the early days to the present. History by George H. Tinkham. Illustrated. Los Angeles, Historic Record co., 1923. Three-quarter leather. OP.

ix, [33]–1640 p. plates, ports. (part with tissues). 29.3 cm. Double column.

Chapter XXII, entitled "Courts and Criminals," contains information on Tom Bell and Black Bart.

997 ———

A history of Stockton from its organization up to the present time, including a sketch of the San Joaquin county, comprising a history of the government, politics, state of society, religion . . . and miscellaneous events within the past thirty years, by George H. Tinkham. San Francisco, W. H. Hinton & co., printers, 1880. Cloth. Scarce.

xvi p., 1 l., 397 p. front. (port. pasted in), illus., plates, ports. 22.5 cm. Appendix: p. [387]–397.

This book has some slight information on Murieta.

998 Tittsworth, W. G.

Outskirt episodes . . . . W. G. Tittsworth, the author. [Avoca, Iowa, 1927.] Cloth. Scarce.

3 p.l., [7]–232 [1] p. 20 cm. Port. of author tipped in on t.p.

This extremely scarce book is the personal narrative of the author's life and adventures in the Wyoming country and experiences among the

Rocky Mountain outlaws in the days when the Union Pacific was building westward. The author tells of Tom Horn's killings and his hanging.

999 [Tombstone]

Souvenir of Tombstone, Arizona. [N.p., n.d.] Wrappers.
OP.

[13] p. (no pagination). plates, ports., plan. 22.5 cm.
5 p. adv. at end and adv. on rear cover.

This booklet gives some information on the Earp-Clanton feud.

1000 Tompkins, Stuart Ramsay

Alaska, promyshlennik and sourdough, by Stuart Ramsay
Tompkins. Norman, University of Oklahoma press, 1945. Cloth.
In print.

xiv p., 1 l., 3–350 p. plates, ports., maps. 21 cm.
Bibliography: p. 305–338; index: p. 339–350.
Half title; outline map on t.p.

Contains some minor material on Soapy Smith.

1001 Toponce, Alexander

Reminiscences of Alexander Toponce, pioneer, 1839–1923
[written by himself]. [Ogden, Utah, Mrs. Kate Toponce, 1923.]
Morocco. Scarce.

7 p.l., 15–248 p. front. (port.), plates, ports. 18 cm.
Device.

This privately printed book has several chapters on the road agents and
vigilantes of Montana.

1002 Torchiana, Henry Albert William van Coenen

California gringos, by H. A. van Coenen Torchiana . . . .
San Francisco, Calif., Paul Elder and co. [1930]. Cloth. OP.

5 p.l., 281 p. front. (port.), plates. 19.6 cm.

This scarce book contains some material on Murieta, Black Bart, Chris
Evans, the Sontags, and other California outlaws.

1003 ———

Story of the mission Santa Cruz, by H. A. van Coenen

351

Torchiana. San Francisco, Paul Elder and co., 1933. Cloth. OP.

> xix p., 2 l., 5–460 p. front., plates, maps, facsms. 24 cm.
> Appendix: p. 403–447; index: p. 449–460.

Contains some information on Murieta based on the *Police Gazette* version of Murieta's life.

1004 Townshend, R. B.

The tenderfoot in New Mexico, by R. B. Townshend. London, John Lane, the Bodley Head, ltd. [1923]. Cloth. OP.

> ix p., 1 l., 257 p. front., plates, ports. 22.5 cm.
> Half title; untrimmed
>
> American edition published by Dodd, Mead co., New York, 1924.

One of a series of books by this English author, who spent some time in the American West. In this book he tells of meeting Billy the Kid in New Mexico.

1005 Tracy, Rev. Henry

A confession of the awful and bloody transactions in the life of Charles Wallace, the fiend-like murderer of Miss Mary Rogers, the beautiful cigar-girl of Broadway, New York, whose fate has for several years past been wrapt in the most profound mystery; together with an authentic statement of the many burglaries and murders of Wallace and the notorious and daring thief, Snelling; and an account of the murder, and robbery of Mr. Parks, of Newport, Kentucky, also perpetrated by Wallace; a thrilling narrative of his intercourse with the Brown murderess, Emeline Morere .... From his own memoranda, given at the burning stake, to Rev. Henry Tracy. New Orleans, published by E. E. Barclay & co., 1851. Pict. wrappers. Extremely rare.

> vi, 7–31 [1 p. illus., plates. 23 cm.

A good example of certain earlier publications on criminals; and we note that this one is also edited by a minister.

1006 Train, Arthur

On the trail of the bad men, by Arthur Train .... New York, Charles Scribner's sons, 1925. Cloth. OP.

> xviii p., 3 l., 5–427 p. 21 cm.
> Half title.

The first chapter deals with some outlaws of Arizona and the Earp-Clanton feud.

1007 Travers, James W.

California. Romance of clipper ship and gold rush days, by James W. Travers. Los Angeles, Wetzel publishing co., inc. [1949]. Cloth. In print.

8 p.l., 17–309 p. plates, ports., facsms. 21 cm.

The author gives some information on Murieta, Black Bart, and other stagecoach robbers.

1008 Trenholm, Virginia Cole

Footprints on the frontier. Saga of the La Ramie region of Wyoming, by Virginia Cole Trenholm. [Douglas, Wyo., printed by Douglas Enterprise co., 1945.] Cloth. Scarce.

11 p.l., [21]–384 p. front., plates, ports. 23.5 cm.
Bibliography: p. [362]–365; index: p. [366]–384.
Half title; vignette.
Colophon: "Edition limited to 1000 copies of which this is No. _____."

The author says that Calamity Jane was the first white woman to enter the Black Hills. In making this statement she is very much in error, for Calamity Jane did not go to the Black Hills for several years after the rush there. The book contains some information on Tom Horn and the Johnson County War.

1009 Trenholm, Virginia Cole, and Maurine Carley

Wyoming pageant, by Virginia Cole Trenholm and Maurine Carley. Casper, Wyo., Prairie publishing co. [1946]. Pict. cloth. OP.

4 p.l., [9]–272 p. front., illus. (2 col.), ports., maps, tables. 20.2 cm.
Bibliography: p. 256–262; index: p. 263–272.
Map on end papers.

1010 Triggs, J. H.

History of Cheyenne and northern Wyoming, embracing the gold fields of the Black Hills, Powder River and Big Horn counties..., by J. H. Triggs. Omaha, Nebr., printed at the Herald steam book and job printing house, 1876. Wrappers. Exceedingly rare.

> 3 p.l., 7–144 p. front. (fold. map). 22.5 cm.
> Advertisements: p. 132–144 and back cover.

A very rare early imprint with some material on the vigilantes.

1011 ———

History and directory of Laramie City, Wyoming territory, comprising a brief history of Laramie City from its first settlement to the present time, together with sketches of the characteristics and resources of the surrounding country; including a minute description of a portion of the mining region of the Black Hills. Also a general and business directory of Laramie City, by J. H. Triggs. Laramie City, Daily Sentinel print, 1875. Wrappers. Exceedingly rare.

> [3]–91 p. 22.3 cm.
> Official directory: p. 62–63; general directory: p. 64–91.
> Full page adv. on verso of first 23 pages.

This exceedingly rare imprint gives a frank history of Laramie in its turbulent days and reign of violence.

1012 ———

A reliable and correct guide to the Black Hills, Powder River and Big Horn gold fields. Full description of the country, how to get to it, including a correct map of the gold regions . . . , by J. H. Triggs. Omaha, Nebr., printed at the Herald steam book and job printing house, 1876. Wrappers. Exceedingly rare.

> 1 p.l., [3]–144 p. front. (fold. map). 22.2 cm.
> Adv. on verso of front wrapper and on last 13 p.

With the exception of the first sixteen pages, this is identical with the author's *History of Cheyenne and Northern Wyoming*. Only three or four copies are known to exist. There is a chapter on the vigilantes.

1013 Trimble, William J.

The mining advance into the inland empire. A comparative study of the beginnings of the mining industry in Idaho and Montana, eastern Washington and Oregon, and the southern interior of

British Columbia and of institutions and laws based upon that industry, by William J. Trimble . . . . A thesis submitted for the degree of Doctor of Philosophy, the University of Wisconsin.   Mad-
ison, Wisc., 1914.   Stiff wrappers.   Rare.

> 3 p.l., [7]–254 p.   front. (map).   23.2 cm.
> Bulletin of the University of Wisconsin, No. 638. History Series, Vol. 3,
> No. 2.

A long chapter entitled "The Evolution of Order and Law in the American Territories" deals with the vigilantes and outlaws of Montana and
Idaho.

1014   Trinka, Zena Irma

Out where the west begins, being the early and romantic
history of North Dakota, by Zena Irma Trinka . . . . Illustrated from
photographs by D. F. Barry, the noted Indian photographer. Map
and 74 illustrations.   St. Paul, the Pioneer co., 1920.   Pict. cloth.
Scarce.

> xvi p., 1 l., 432 p.   front. (port.), plates (1 col.), ports., fold. map.   22 cm.
> Index: p. 427–432.
> Frontis tissue.

Contains a chapter on the North Dakota vigilantes.

1015   Triplett, (Colonel) Frank

Conquering the wilderness; or, new pictorial history of the
life and times of the pioneer heroes and heroines of America . . . ,
by Col. Frank Triplett . . . with 200 portraits from life, original and
striking engravings from designs by Nast, Darley and other eminent
artists.   New York, and St. Louis, N. D. Thompson publishing
co., 1883.   Cloth.   Scarce.

> xxxix p., 1 l., 43–742 p.   front., illus., plates, ports.   23.5 cm.
> Republished many times.

This book contains some very uncomplimentary statements about Wild
Bill Hickok. Among other things the author says: "This fellow was a
red-handed murderer without a single redeeming trait, not even pos-
sessing the fearless bravery that usually characterizes the western desperado. It is extremely doubtful if, in his whole career, Wild Bill ever
killed an enemy who had an even chance . . . ."

355

1016 ――――
     History, romance and philosophy of great American crimes and criminals; including the great typical crimes that have marked the various periods of American history from the foundation of the republic to the present day . . . , by Col. Frank Triplett . . . with over 150 fine engravings, representing scenes, incidents and personal portraits. St. Louis, N. D. Thompson and co., 1884. Pict. cloth. Scarce.

    xxxiv p., 3 l., 39–659 p. front., illus., plates, ports. 22.8 cm.

    Republished: Hartford, Conn., Park publishing co., 1885.

The author gives sketches of outlaws from Murrell, the Harpes, and Joseph Hare down through the years to the Benders, Ben Thompson, the Jameses, and the Youngers.

1017 ――――
     The life, times and treacherous death of Jesse James. The only correct and authorized edition. Giving full particulars of each and every dark and desperate deed in the career of this most noted outlaw of any time or nation. The facts and incidents contained in this volume, were dedicated to Frank Triplett, by Mrs. Jesse James, wife of the bandit, and Mrs. Zerelda Samuel, his mother. Consequently every secret act—every hitherto unknown incident—every crime and every motive is herein truthfully disclosed . . . . Chicago, St. Louis, Atlanta, J. H. Chambers & co., 1882. Pict. cloth. Exceedingly rare.

    xvi p., 1 l., [17]–416 p. front., illus., plates, ports. 19 cm.
    Running title: "Life and Times of Jesse and Frank James."

An exceedingly rare book, and the few copies in existence are usually in poor condition. The book was more or less suppressed because it was very bitter toward the Crittendens, influential, citizens of Missouri. It is also said that Frank James objected to the book because it accused him of moral misconduct, and there was some trouble between Mrs. James and the publishers. In a fairly reliable chapter on the Union Pacific robbery by the Joel Collins–Sam Bass gang, the author denies that Jesse James took part in this robbery as stated by many writers. He does, however, make the mistake of calling Joel Collins, "Jim."

1018 Truman, Benjamin Cummings
     Life, adventures and capture of Tiburcio Vásquez, the great

THE LIFE, TIMES

AND TREACHEROUS DEATH

—OF—

JESSE JAMES.

THE ONLY CORRECT AND AUTHORIZED EDITION.

GIVING FULL PARTICULARS OF EACH AND EVERY DARK AND
DESPERATE DEED IN THE CAREER OF THIS
MOST NOTED OUTLAW OF ANY
TIME OR NATION.

The Facts and Incidents contained in this Volume, were Dictated

—TO—

FRANK TRIPLETT,

—BY—

MRS. JESSE JAMES, AND MRS. ZERELDA SAMUEL,

Wife of the Bandit.   *His Mother.*

CONSEQUENTLY EVERY SECRET ACT — EVERY HITHERTO
UNKNOWN INCIDENT — EVERY CRIME AND
EVERY MOTIVE IS HEREIN
TRUTHFULLY
DISCLOSED.

TRUTH IS MORE INTERESTING THAN FICTION.

1882.

J. H. CHAMBERS & CO.,

CHICAGO, ILL.   ST. LOUIS, MO.   ATLANTA, GA.

NUMBER 1017

LIFE, ADVENTURES

AND

CAPTURE

OF

TIBURCIO VASQUEZ.

The Great California Bandit and Murderer.

By Maj. BEN. C. TRUMAN,

Editor of Los Angeles Star.

PRINTED AT
LOS ANGELES STAR OFFICE,
1874.

California bandit and murderer, by Maj. Ben C. Truman, editor of *Los Angeles Star*. [Los Angeles], printed at the Los Angeles Star office, 1874. Pict. wrappers. Exceedingly rare.

> [3]–44 p. front. (map), diagr. 22.8 cm.
> Port. on front wrapper.

Frontispiece on recto of first leaf after cover is a map showing the location of Vásquez's capture. There are advertisements on inside of front wrapper, inside of back wrapper, and outside of back wrapper. Pages 34 to 44 tell in Spanish of Vásquez's capture. This is one of the rarest books on Vásquez.

Reprinted in 1941 by the Clyde Brownes at the Abbey San Encino press, Los Angeles. Cloth and leather. Scarce.

> 3 p.l., [17]–43 [1] p. front. 24.4 cm.
> Half title.
> Colophon: "This edition of Tiburcio Vásquez, designed by the Clyde Brownes, father and son, was set by the latter in linotype's Garmond number 3, and printed on Strathmore Old Laid Book by Frank Masley of the Abbey. The portrait of Vásquez, taken from two dissimilar ones of his day, was drawn by artist Vince Newcomes, the cover fashioned by Earle A. Gray. One hundred copies of this book have been printed, of which this is number ____."

This reprint is not complete, only the first thirty pages of the original being included.

1019 [Tuolumne County]

A history of Tuolumne county, California. Compiled from the most authentic records. San Francisco, published by B. F. Alley, 1882. Calf. Scarce.

> xi, 509 p. ports. 21.5 cm.
> Appendix: p. [3]–48 at end.

Contains a chapter on Murieta.

1020 Turner, Mary Honeyman Ten Eyck (Mrs. Avery Turner)

These high plains, by Mary Honeyman Ten Eyck Turner (Mrs. Avery Turner). Amarillo, Texas [printed by Russell stationery co.], 1941. Cloth. Col. pict. label pasted on. Scarce.

4 p.l., 11–94 p. front. (port.), plates. 24 cm.
Half title.
"Limited to 150 books." (Privately printed.)

Here is another writer who is careless of historical fact. The author states that Billy the Kid was born in July, 1881, the very month and year he was killed. She further states that he was killed when Pat Garrett shot him *in the back.*

1021 Twitchell, Ralph Emerson

The leading facts of New Mexican history, by Ralph Emerson Twitchell . . . . Cedar Rapids, Iowa, the Torch press, 1911–1917. Pub. in four volumes. Cloth. Scarce.

> Vol. I, xx p., 3 l., 3–506 p. front. (col.), plates, ports., facsms., fold. map. 24.8 cm.
> Index: p. [487]–506.
> Half title.
> Vol. II, xxi p., 3 l., 3–631 p. front. (port.), plates, ports., facsms., 3 fold. maps. 24.8 cm.
> Index: p. [611]–631.
> Half title.
> Vols. III and IV biographical.
> Published in a subscriber's edition of 1,500 numbered and signed copies.

The author tells of the Lincoln County War, and he claims Billy the Kid killed only nine men. He misnames Bowdre, "Bowder"; McSween, "McSwain"; and Tunstall, "Tunstel."

1022 Tyler, George W.

The history of Bell county, by George W. Tyler; edited by Charles W. Ramsdell. San Antonio, the Naylor co., 1936. Cloth. In print.

> xxiii p., 1 l., 425 p. front. (port.), plates, ports, 2 fold. maps. 23.4 cm.
> Index: p. 405–425.
> Half title.
> "At [the author's death] the writing was incomplete and some was in the form of rough notes. It was left to the editor . . . to revise and condense the manuscript, and, in a few instances, to fill out the narrative." (P. ix.)

The book contains some material on Sam Bass, Bill Longley, and other Texas outlaws.

1023 Upton, Charles Elmer

Pioneers of El Dorado, by Charles Elmer Upton . . . .

Placerville, Calif., Charles Elmer Upton, publisher, 1906. Cloth. Scarce.

> 3 p.l., [3]–201 [1] p. plates. 20.6 cm.
> Appendix: p. [181]–201.

The appendix gives a complete history of Joaquín Murieta based upon the Ridge account.

1024 Vandor, Paul E.

History of Fresno county, California, with biographical sketches of the leading men and women of the county who have been identified with its growth and development from the early days to the present. History by Paul E. Vandor. Illustrated . . . . Los Angeles, Calif., Historic Record co., 1919. Pub. in two volumes. Three-quarter leather. OP.

> Vol. I, 12 p.l., [31]–1286 [1] p. plates, ports. (part with tissues). 27.8 cm.
> Vol. II biographical.

Several chapters are devoted to California outlaws, one to Vásquez, one to the Evans-Sontag gang, and another to various criminals of the county, including Murieta.

1025 Vestal, Emmett

"Texas Slim" . . . . My ten years in hell, [by] Emmett Vestal . . . . [Montgomery, Ala., printed by Johnson printing co., n.d.] Stiff wrappers. OP.

> 3 p.l., 7–135 p. front., plates, ports. 19.3 cm.

A little-known western outlaw who later became an evangelist tells the story of his life.

1026 Vestal, Stanley (pseud. of Walter S. Campbell)

The Missouri, by Stanley Vestal. Illustrated by Getlar Smith. Maps by George Annand. New York, Toronto, Farrar & Rinehart, inc. [1945]. Cloth. OP.

> x p., 2 l., 5–368 p. front. (double p. map), illus., map. 21 cm.
> [Rivers of America series.]
> Notes: p. 335–343; acknowledgments: p. 345–347; bibliography: p. 349–354; index: p. 355–368.
> Illus. end papers; illus. t.p.; first edition: "F R" in device on copyright p.

Contains some material on Jesse James and other outlaws.

361

1027 ———

Queen of cowtowns, Dodge City. "The wickedest little city in America," 1872–1886, by Stanley Vestal. New York, Harper & brothers [1952]. Cloth. In print.

> viii p., 2 l., 285 p. plates, ports. 21.5 cm.
> Bibliography: p. 271–279; notes: p. 281–282; acknowledgments: p. 283–285.
> Half title; pub. device; untrimmed; "First edition" on copyright p.

This is one of the best books yet done on Dodge City. The author has discovered and presented material not found in other "Dodge City" books. Most of the Dodge City gunmen come in for some attention. Under the bottom illustrations opposite page 21 the caption should read "Civilian Model" instead of "Pavillion Model." The author told me he had asked the publisher to make this correction; so if the book goes into another printing, this error will probably be a mark of identity of the the first printing.

1028 ———

Short grass country, by Stanley Vestal. Edited by Erskine Caldwell. New York, Duell, Sloan & Pearce [1941]. Cloth. OP.

> x p., 1 l., 3–304 p. 22 cm.
> Index: p. 299–304.
> Half title; map on end papers; "First edition" on copyright p.

In two chapters the author deals extensively with lawlessness in the short-grass country.

1029 Vickers, C. L. (ed.)

History of the Arkansas valley, Colorado. Illustrated. Chicago, O. L. Baskin and co., 1881. Morocco. Scarce.

> vii p., 1 l., [11]–889 p. front., plates, ports. 25.3 cm.
> Double column.

Contains chapters on the vigilantes and outlaws of Colorado.

1030 Visscher, William Lightfoot

Buffalo Bill's own story of his life and deeds. This autobiography tells in his own graphic words the wonderful story of his heroic career . . . . His autobiography is brought up to date including a full account of his death and burial, written by his boy-

hood chum and life-long friend, William Lightfoot Visscher . . . .
₁N.p., 1917.₁ Cloth. Port pasted on. Scarce.

xiii, 15–352 p. front., illus., plates, ports. 21.5 cm.

Like most of the books about Buffalo Bill, this one contains some material on Wild Bill Hickok; but unlike most of them, it does not mention the McCanles fight.

1031 Volland, Robert Frederick

The Reno gang of Seymour, by Robert Frederick Volland
. . . . ₁N.p., 1948.₁ Imt. leather. Rare.

ii p., 1 l., 332 p., 1 l. plus 34 p. plates, liii p. plates, ports., facsms. 28 cm.
Plates: p. i–xxxiv; appendix: p. i–xxx; bibliography: p. xxxi–xxxv; index:
p. xxxvi–liii.
Mimeograph dry-stencil process on one side of the paper.

Only twenty-five copies of this book were made and the stencils destroyed. The volume was copyrighted by the Reverend Robert W. Shields, who tells me it served as Mr. Volland's thesis for the degree of Master of Arts at the University of Indiana.

The first few copies of this book were bound in black imitation leather with pages sewn through punched margins. Later copies were bound in red imitation leather and fully sewn. These limited books are scattered through a few libraries, such as the Library of Congress and the Indiana State Library; a number went to various Pinkerton officials, one to the descendants of the Renos, one to the Seymour (Indiana) Public Library, where it will not be released for circulation for twenty-five years, and I was fortunate enough to purchase the last copy which was for sale for my own library.

The book is the best work yet published on the Renos and is well documented. Because of the method of reproduction it is a thick book.

1032 Voorhees, Luke

Personal recollections of pioneer life on the mountains and plains of the great west, by Luke Voorhees. ₁Cheyenne, Wyo., privately printed, 1920.₁ Cloth. Scarce.

3 p.l., ₁7₁–75 p. front. (port.). 22.5 cm.
Device.

Contains some information on stage robbers and Slade's killing of Jules Reni. Published in a very small edition, it is now quite scarce.

363

1033 Waldo, Edna La Moore

Dakota, an informal study of territorial days gleaned from contemporary newspapers, by Edna La Moore Waldo. Bismark, N. D., Capital publishing co. [1932]. Cloth. OP.

> 9 p.l., [3]–297 [3] p. 25.3 cm.
> Bibliography: p. [299–300].
> Half title; vignette; untrimmed.

The book contains some material on Calamity Jane and tells the story of Wild Bill's murder and the hanging of Jack McCall.

1034 Walgamott, Charles Shirley

Reminiscences of early days. A series of historical sketches and happenings in the early days of Snake river valley, by C. S. Walgamott. Pub. in two volumes. Cloth. Scarce.

> Vol. I [n.p., 1926].
> 3 p.l., 127 [1] p. front., ports. 23.3 cm.
> Double column.
> Vol. II [Twin Falls, Idaho, the Idaho Citizen, 1927].
> 4 p.l., 9–127 [1] p. front., illus., plates (1 tipped in). 23.5 cm.

1035 ———

A series of historical sketches of early days in Idaho. Six decades back, [by] Charles Shirley Walgamott. Illustrated by R. H. Hall. Caldwell, Idaho, the Caxton printers, ltd., 1936. Cloth. OP.

> 8 p.l., [17]–358 p. front. (col.), illus., plates. 23.5 cm.
> Half title; illus. end papers; pub. device; frontis tissue.

This book has practically the same text as the two volumes in Item 1034, but now published under one cover. It contains some vigilante, stage robbery, and other outlaw material.

1036 [Walker, Robert C.]

Second annual report of the secretary of the Helena board of trade for the year 1879, territory of Montana. [Helena], Woolfolk, Macquaid and Lacrois, daily and weekly *Independent*, 1880. Wrappers. Rare.

> 40 p. fold. map in front. 22.2 cm.

This rare report contains some outlaw and vigilante material.

1037 Walker, Tacetta B.

Stories of early days in Wyoming; Big Horn basin, by Tacetta B. Walker. Casper, Wyo., Prairie publishing co. [1936]. Cloth. OP.

iv p., 1 l., 271 p. plates, ports., maps. 23.5 cm.
Bibliography: p. 268; index: p. [269]–271.
Map on end papers.

This privately printed book contains chapters on the Johnson County War and the outlaw period, dealing with Butch Cassidy and his gang and the hanging of Tom Horn.

1038 Wallace, Charles (compiler)

The cattle queen of Montana. A story of the personal experiences of Mrs. Nat Collins, familiarly known to western people as "The Cattle Queen of Montana," or "The Cowboy's Mother," in which is included narratives of thrilling adventures . . . and descriptions of the plains, the mines, cattle raising industry and other features of western life, learned during forty years' residence in the far west; compiled by Charles Wallace. Illustrations from special photographs. St. James, Minn., C. W. Foote [Chicago, printed by Donohue and Henneberry], 1894. Stiff wrappers. Rare.

xiii, [15]–249 p. front., illus., plates. 19 cm.

Revised and edited by Alvin E. Dyer and republished in Spokane, Wash., by press of Dyer printing co. [1902]. Stiff wrappers. Scarce.

5–260 p. front. (port.), illus., plates, ports. 20 cm.

Both editions of this book are quite rare. They contain some information on the Montana vigilantes, the hanging of George Ives, Joseph Slade, and others.

1039 Wallace, Lew

Lew Wallace; an autobiography. Illustrated. New York and London, Harper & brothers, publishers, MCMVI. Pub. in two volumes. Cloth. Scarce.

Vol. I, ix p., 2 l., 501 [1] p. front. (port.), illus., plates, ports., map. 21.3 cm.

Vol. II, vii p., 2 l., 503–[1028] p. front. (port.), ports., map, diagrs., facsm. 21.3 cm. Paged continuously with Vol. I.
Index: p. 1005–[1028].
Pub. device; frontis tissues.

Although Wallace was governor of New Mexico and sent there to quell the Lincoln County War, he does not say much about these troubles in his book. He gives some inaccurate information about John Chisum, saying that he imported "about seventy men—murderers, thieves and dangerous men of all classes" from Texas to protect his herds.

1040 Wallace, William H.

The closing speech for the state in the trial of Frank James for murder, held at Gallatin, August and September, 1883. Kansas City, 1883. Wrappers. Scarce.

65 p. 19 cm.

1041 ———

Closing speech for the state made by Wm. H. Wallace, Esq., prosecuting attorney of Jackson county, Missouri, in the trial of Frank James for murder, held at Gallatin, Daviess co., Mo., in Aug. and Sept., 1883. Kansas City, press of Ramsey, Millett & Hudson, 1884. Wrappers. Scarce.

[2]–64 p. 21.7 cm.

Text starts on verso of t.p.

1042 ———

Speeches of Wm. H. Wallace, Democratic nominee for Congress, Fifth Congressional District of Missouri. [By Wm. H. Wallace.] [Kansas City, press of Frank T. Riley publishing co., n.d.] Wrappers. (Cover title.) OP.

1 p.l., [3]–96 p. 22 cm.
Port. on cover.

Contains speeches on "Law and the Bandit" and the "Frank James Trial."

1043 ———

Speeches and writings of William H. Wallace; with autobiography. Kansas City, Mo., the Western Baptist publishing co., 1914. Cloth. Scarce.

> 308 p. front., plates, ports. 24 cm.
> Lettering on back: "Introduction by S. M. Brown."

1044 Walsh, Richard John

The making of Buffalo Bill. A study in heroics, by Richard J. Walsh, in collaboration with Milton S. Salisbury. Illustrated. Indianapolis, the Bobbs-Merrill co., publishers [1928]. Cloth. OP.

> vii p., 3 l., 15–391 p. front. (port.), illus., plates, ports., facsms. 22.6 cm.
> Bibliography: p. 365–370; index, p. 373–391.
> Half title; illus. front end papers; map on rear end papers; device; "First edition" on copyright p.

The author here quotes Wm. E. Connelley in trying to correct the false story of the Hickok-McCanles fight.

1045 Walter, William W.

The great understander. True life story of the last of the Wells, Fargo shotgun messengers. Compiled by William W. Walter. Aurora, Ill., published by William W. Walter [1931]. Pict. cloth. Scarce.

> 5 p.l., 11–315 p. front. (port.). 19.6 cm.

The life of Oliver Roberts de la Fontaine, his experiences in the early West, and his contacts with stage robbers and other lawless persons.

1046 Walters, Lorenzo D.

Tombstone's yesterday, by Lorenzo D. Walters, with illustrations. Tucson, Ariz., Acme printing co., 1928. Cloth. Scarce.

> 7 p.l., [11]–293 p. front., illus., ports. 23.5 cm.
> Pub. device.
> "Tombstone's Yesterday has been appearing as a serial in the 'Progressive Arizona and the Great Southwest,' a Ward Shelby publication, during the past two years and has now been revised and enlarged and offered to the public in book form." (On the second p.l.)

There are chapters in this book on Billy the Kid and Pat Garrett which really do not belong there as Billy the Kid and Garrett had nothing to do with Tombstone. But most authors writing of the West seem to be unable to resist bringing these two popular characters into their efforts.

The author's discussion of Billy the Kid is filled with misstatements from the very beginning, where he intimates that the Kid was a boot-black in New York City. He admits that Billy's father died when he was a mere baby, and says it fell upon him to help support his mother. He says that Billy's mother, after struggling with adverse circumstances for a few years, saved enough money to pay their way to *Texas* (!) where she stayed for some time. And during this stay in Texas she "annexed another husband" by the name of Antrim. All this really happened in Coffeyville, Kansas.

The author continues with the legend that Chisum owed the Kid $5,000 for a split in mavericks, and says Billy threw in with the Murphy-Dolan faction. He says Garrett was imported from Louisiana by Chisum for the express purpose of killing the Kid. And he further states that Baker and Morton "deliberately killed Turnstall [*sic*] just because he was a cattleman." He has the circumstances of Bowdre's killing at Stinking Springs wrong, is careless with the spelling of proper names and with geography, and places the Kid's trial at Las Vegas instead of Mesilla. He uses the Siringo and Burns version of Bell's killing and praises the latter's book as being "the most complete history of Billy the Kid that has ever been published."

The author admits that Garrett had never been to Tombstone, but uses as an excuse for including him in this book the fact that he killed Billy the Kid. He follows Siringo in believing that Garrett was killed by Jim Miller rather than by Wayne Brazil. He covers practically every outlaw who operated in Arizona and some who did not.

1047 Walton, Augustus Q.

History of the detection, conviction, life and designs of John A. Murel [*sic*], the great western land pirate; together with his system of villainy, and plan of exciting Negro rebellion. Also a catalogue of the names of four hundred and fifty-five of his mystic clan fellows and followers, and a statement of their efforts for the destruction of Virgil A. Stewart, the young man who detected him. To which is added a biographical sketch of V. A. Stewart, by Augustus Q. Walton. Cincinnati [U. P. James, n.d.]. Pict. wrappers. Rare.

> 2 p.l., [19]–84, [iii]–xii p. front. (port.), plates. 21.6 cm.
> Pages [iii]–xii at the end give a sampling of a book entitled *A History of the Feud Between the Hill and Evans Parties* . . . , by J. J. Thompson.

Reprinted, Athens, Tenn., G. White, 1835.

> 75 p. 21.6 cm.
> Reprinted, Lexington, Ky., 1835 and again in 185–(?).

1048 Walton, William M.

Life and adventures of Ben Thompson, the famous Texan. Including a detailed and authentic statement of his birth, history and adventures, by one who has known him since a child, by W. M. Walton. Austin, Texas, published by the author [printed by Edwards and Church, newsdealers], 1884. Pict. wrappers. Exceedingly rare.

> 4 p.l., [5]–229 p. front. (port.), plates. 17 cm.
>
> Reprinted, Bandera, Texas, Frontier Times, 1926.

I can remember when a copy of this little paper-bound book could be bought for ten cents, but now it is exceedingly rare and excessively high in price when one is fortunate enough to locate a copy. It was written by a close friend of the subject, who is naturally sympathetic, but his is the only book devoted entirely to this famous Texas gunman.

1049 Walz, Edgar A.

Retrospection, by Edgar A. Walz. [N.p.], October, 1931. Leather. Exceedingly rare.

> 31 [1] p. front. (port.). 18.5 cm.

This privately printed little book, which gives some sidelights on the Lincoln County War, is exceedingly rare. It was written by a man who was in Lincoln County at the time of the conflict.

1050 Ward, William

The Dalton gang, the bandits of the far west. The most desperate train robbers that ever lived. The first true history of the raids and robberies of the gang who terrorized five states . . . as told by a U. S. deputy marshal and set forth by William Ward. Cleveland, published by the Arthur Westbrook co. [n.d.]. Pict. col. wrappers. OP.

> 3 p.l., [7]–179 [12] p. front., illus. 17.3 cm.

This is a sample of the dozens of similar books written on various outlaws by this hack writer. Although he claims the book to be "the first true history" of these outlaws, there is very little truth in the whole account.

1051 Warden, Ernest A.

Infamous Kansas killers, by Ernest A. Warden. [Wichita,

Kan., McGuin publishing co., 1944.] Pict. wrappers. (Cover title.) OP.

> 2 p.l., [5]–48 p. ports. 18.8 cm.
> [Vol. III of "Thrilling Tales of Kansas."]
> "An accurate history of all the legal hangings executed by the State of Kansas up to the present time." (Preliminary page.)

1052 ———

Thrilling tales of Kansas, by Ernest Warden. [Wichita, Kan.], printed by the Wichita Eagle press [1932]. Wrappers. OP.

> 2 p.l., 5–112 p. 19.6 cm.
> Device.

Contains material on the Benders, the Daltons, and the bank robbers Hendry Brown and Ben Wheeler.

1053 ———

Thrilling tales of Kansas, from 1873 to 1938, by Ernie Warden [Wichita, Kan., "second revised edition," 1938.] Pict. wrappers. OP.

> 2 p.l., 3–100 [1] p. 19.3 cm.

Although this book has the same title as the 1932 edition, it is practically a new book, containing much new material and retaining only a few of the chapters from the first printing.

1054 Warman, Cy

Frontier stories, by Cy Warman. New York, Charles Scribner's sons, 1898. Dec. cloth. Scarce.

> 4 p.l., [3]–246 p. 18.2 cm.
> Half title.

Contains a chapter on outlaws.

1055 Warner, Frank W. (compiler)

Montana territory. History and business directory, 1879. Illustrated. Distances, fares, and altitudes. Counties, towns, mining camps. Commercial, mineral and agricultural interests. With a sketch of the vigilantes. Helena, Mont., Fisk brothers, printers and binders [1879]. Boards and cloth. Rare.

> 3 l. adv., 3 p.l., 218 p. illus., plates, fold. map. 21.5 cm.

Prefatory note signed: "F. W. Warner."
Advertising leaves interspersed (in part unpaged) and on inside of front and back covers.

This volume contains a twenty-chapter reprint of Dimsdale's *Vigilantes of Montana.*

1056 Warner, Matt

The last of the bandit riders, by Matt Warner, as told to Murray E. King. Illustrated with photographs. Caldwell, Idaho, the Caxton printers, ltd., 1940. Pict. cloth. OP.

10 p.l., [21]-337 p. front., plates, ports. 23.4 cm.
Appendix: p. [329]-337.
Half title; pub. device; vignette.

An excellent book on the outlaw career of Matt Warner and his association with Butch Cassidy and his Wild Bunch.

1057 Warner, Opie L.

A pardoned lifer. Life of George Sontag, former member notorious Evans-Sontag gang, train robbers. Written by Opie L. Warner. [San Bernardino, Calif., the Index print, 1909.] Cloth OP.

7 p.l., 15-211 p. front. (port.). 19.4 cm.

George Sontag tells his part as a member of the Evans-Sontag gang, his life in prison, and his reason for turning against Evans. Some of his statements do not agree with other published material on this gang of train robbers. There are several typographical errors in the book, such as "wears" for "years," page 49; "leace" for "leave," page 57; "letts" for "letter," page 60; and "persuads" for "persuade," page 60.

1058 Waters, Frank

The Colorado, by Frank Waters. Illustrated by Nicolai Fechin, maps by George Annand. New York, Toronto, Rinehart & co. inc. [1946]. Cloth. OP.

xii p., 3 l., 3-400 p. illus. (1 col.), maps (1 double p.). 20.8 cm.
Rivers of America series.
Reference appendix: p. 289-393; glossary: p. 395-396; index: p. 397-400.
Half title; illus. t.p.

One of the Rivers of America Series, this volume contains some information about Wyatt Earp, but what the author has to say is very uncomplimentary to this Tombstone gunman. (See Item 603.)

1059 Waters, L. L.

Steel tracks to Santa Fé, by L. L. Waters.   Lawrence, Kan., University of Kansas press, 1950.   Cloth.   In print.

> 11 p.l., ₉₋500 p.   plates, port., maps, graphs, tables.   23.6 cm.
> Appendix: p. ₄₈₄₋491; references: p. ₄₉₂₋493; index: p. ₄₉₅₋500.
> Half title; map on end papers.

Contains some material on Newton, Kansas, and its gun battles.

1060 Watrous, Ansel

History of Laramie county, Colorado. Collated and compiled from historical authorities, public reports, official records and other reliable sources..., by Ansel Watrous. Illustrated.   Fort Collins, Colo., the Courier printing & publishing co., 1911.   Leather. Scarce.

> 4 p.l., 7–513 p.   front. (port.), plates, ports.   29 cm.
> Index: p. 505–513.
> Double column; tissues; gilt edges.

Contains material on Joseph Slade and other outlaws.

1061 Watson, Frederick

A century of gunmen; a study in lawlessness, by Frederick Watson.   London, Ivor Nicholson & Watson, ltd., 1931. Cloth. OP.

> vii ₁ p., 295 ₁ p.   22 cm.
> Acknowledgments: p. 291; index: p. 292–₂₉₆.
> Half title; vignette.

Although the author has written an interesting book, most of his quotations have been taken from unreliable sources, such as Sutton's *Hands Up*, Frank Harris' *Reminiscences of a Cowboy*, Emerson Hough's *Story of the Outlaw*, and Lord's *Frontier Dust*. He seems to have had a talent for picking out the most unauthentic books from the many reliable ones which he could have cited.

1062 Weadock, Jack

Dust of the desert. Plain tales of the desert and the border, by Jack Weadock. Illustrations by Jack Van Ryder, with an introduction by George H. Doran.   New York, London, D. Appleton-Century co., inc., 1936.   Pict. cloth.   OP.

xx p., 1 l., 3–306 p.   front., illus.   24.5 cm.
Half title; illus. end papers; pub. device; first edition: figure (1) at end
of text.

In his chapter on Billy the Kid, the author tells about the killing of
Jimmy Carlisle, but he does not tell it the way it actually happened.

1063 Webb, W. E.

Buffalo land: an authentic account of the discoveries, adventures, and mishaps of a scientific and sporting party in the wild
west; with graphic descriptions of the country . . . replete with
information, wit and humor. The appendix comprising a complete
guide for sportsmen and emigrants, by W. E. Webb . . . . Profusely
illustrated from actual photographs and original drawings by Henry
Worrall.   Cincinnati and Chicago, E. Hannaford & co. . . . ,   1872.
Pict. cloth.   Scarce.

xxiii, 25–503 p.   front., plates, ports.   22.6 cm.
Appendix: p. 431–503.

Contains some material on Wild Bill Hickok (whose name is spelled
Hickock). The author admits that Wild Bill gained his reputation
"through *Harper's Magazine*," and says that much that has been written about him is pure fiction. He does not mention the McCanles fight,
and claims Buffalo Bill told him Wild Bill was his cousin.

1064 Webb, Walter Prescott

The Texas rangers, a century of frontier defense. Illustrated
with drawings by Lonnie Rees and with photographs.   Boston,
New York, Houghton Mifflin co., 1935.   Cloth.   OP.

xiv p., 2 l., 3–583 [1] p.   front., illus., ports., facsms.   24.4 cm.
Bibliography: p. 569–[572].
Index: p. 573–[584].
Half title; part tailpieces; pub. device; first edition: 1935 under imprint.
At head of title: "Walter Prescott Webb."

This book was also published in a limited de luxe edition. The trade
edition has gone through several printings. This is the most thorough
work yet published on the Texas Rangers, and it naturally deals with
many Texas outlaws.

1065 Wellman, Paul I.

The trampling herd, [by] Paul I. Wellman; illustrations by
F. Miller.   New York, Carrick & Evans, inc. [1939].   Cloth.   OP.

6 p.l., 13–433 p. illus. 21.8 cm.
"Some books to read": p. 417–419; index: p. 421–433.
Half title; map on end papers; illus. t.p.
At head of title: "The Story of the Cattle Range of America."

Although this is a cattle book, it contains much on outlaws and the Lincoln County and Johnson County wars. However, it brings nothing new, for it is taken from books preceding it.

1066 Wells, Evelyn, and Harry C. Patterson

The '49ers, by Evelyn Wells and Harry C. Patterson. Garden City, N. Y., Doubleday & co., inc., 1949. Cloth. In print.

5 p.l., 273 p. 22 cm.
Half title; vignette.

In Chapter 11, entitled "Bad Men," there is a tabloid life of Joaquín Murieta.

1067 Wells, Polk

Life and adventures of Polk Wells (Charles Knox Polk Wells), the notorious outlaw, whose acts of fearlessness and chivalry kept the frontier trails afire with excitement, and whose robberies and other depredations in the Platte purchase and elsewhere, have been a most frequent discussion to this day, all of which transpired during and just after the Civil War. Written by himself. [N. p.], published by G. A. Warnica, his life long friend and chief financial support [n.d.]. Cloth. OP.

2 p.l., [7]–259 p. front. (2 ports), illus. 22.8 cm.

Although Polk was not as popular with writers as others of his ilk, he was quite an outlaw in his day.

1068 West, Ray B. Jr. (ed.)

Rocky mountain cities, edited by Ray B. West, Jr., with an introduction by Carey McWilliams. New York, W. W. Norton & co., inc. [1949]. Cloth. OP.

14 p.l., 29–320 p. 21.8 cm.
Notes on contributors: p. 318–320.
Half title; pub. device.

One chapter deals with Cheyenne and the Johnson County War.

374

1069 Westerners' Brand Book (Chicago Posse)

The westerners' brand book, 1944. Being a collection of the original papers presented at meetings of the westerners and also of the discussions in which they participated during the first year, March 1944 to March 1945, at Chicago. Chicago, Ill. [1946]. Pict. cloth. OP.

> 5 p.l., 9–151 [8] p. illus., facsm. 23.5 cm.
> Index: p. [157]–[160].
> Half title.

Contains chapters on Calamity Jane and Jesse James.

1070 ———

The westerners' brand book, 1945–46. Being the papers presented during the second year of the westerners (1945–'46), together with some original papers rescued from manuscripts and ephemera. Chicago, Ill. [1947]. Pict. cloth. OP.

> 5 p.l., 9–166 [4] p. illus. 23.5 cm.
> Index: p. [169]–[170].
> Half title; illus. end papers.

Contains papers on Calamity Jane, the James boys, and the Johnson County War. In this volume Clarence Paine offers a theory that Calamity Jane might be a hermaphrodite, but there is no evidence to prove this theory.

1071 Westerners' Brand Book (Denver Posse)

1945 brand book, containing twelve original papers relating to western and Rocky mountain history, edited by Herbert O. Brayer. Denver, Colo., the Westerners [printed by Bradford-Robinson printing co.], 1946. Pict. cloth. OP.

> xiii, 251 p. illus., map. 23.6 cm.
> Appendix: p. [219]–237; index: p. [241]–251.
> Half title.
> Colophon: "Three hundred and fifty copies of which this is No. ____."

This volume contains a chapter on the hanging of Tom Horn.

1072 ———

1946 brand book. Twelve original papers pertaining to the history of the west, edited by Virgil V. Peterson. Denver, Colo. [the Artcraft press], 1947. Pict. cloth. OP.

375

xii p., 1 l., 242 p.   front. (fold. col. panorama), plates (1 col.), ports., maps, facsms.   23.6 cm.
Index: p. 232–242.
Half title.
Colophon: "Five hundred copies of which this is No. _____."

There are chapters on Bill Carlisle, the Wyoming train robber, and Alfred Packer.

1073 ———

1948 brand book. Twelve original papers pertaining to the history of the west, edited by Dabney Otis Collins.   Denver, Colo., the Westerners [printed by the Artcraft press, 1949].   Pict. cloth. OP.

xx p., 2 l., 271 p.   illus., plates, ports., map.   23.6 cm.
Index: p. 265–271.
Half title; facsm. of newspaper advertisements on end papers.
Colophon: "Limited edition of 500 copies of which this is No. _____."

The author of a chapter entitled "Typing the Western Gunman" attempts to compare various types as to build, color of eyes, hair, and their quality of courage. Every notable western gunman comes under his examination, but his hardest words are reserved for Billy the Kid. He says, in part, that "his photograph shows a young man whom any physician would diagnose as an adenoidal moron, both constitutionally and emotionally inadequate to a high degree."

1074 ———

1950 brand book. Vol. VI, edited by Harold H. Dunham. Denver, the University of Denver press [1951].   Pict. cloth.   OP.

10 p.l., 5–312 p.   front., plates, ports., map, facsm.   23.6 cm.
Index: p. [307]–312.
Half title; illus. end papers.

In a chapter on Cattle Kate the author claims the proper spelling of Jim Averill (as commonly spelled) is "Averell." He presents a well-annotated and reliable account of the life of Cattle Kate after her association with Averill.

1075 Westerners' Brand Book (Los Angeles Posse)

The westerners' brand book, Los Angeles corral, 1947.   [Los Angeles, 1948.]   Cloth and leather.   OP.

376

8 p.l., 19–176 p. front., illus., plates, ports. 26 cm.
Bibliography: p. 161–168; errata: p. 169; index: p. 170–173.
Half title; illus. end papers.
Colophon: "The Westerners' Brand Book Los Angeles 1947 is limited to 600 copies."

E. A. Brininstool's chapter on Billy the Kid in this volume is reliable, but Brininstool does make a statement at the end that I have never seen a serious student of the Kid make—that his is "by far the most truthful account of the Kid's activities." The volume also contains a chapter on Jeff Milton and copies of newspaper clippings about Tombstone, Arizona, and its troubles.

1076 ———

The westerners' brand book, Los Angeles corral, 1948. [Los Angeles, 1949.] Pict. cloth. OP.

7 p.l., 17–175 [1] p. front., illus., plates, ports., facsms., 1 double p. col. plate, 2 fold. maps. 26 cm.
Bibliography: p. 163–169; index, p. 170–173.
Half title; vignette.
Colophon: "The Westerners' Brand Book Los Angeles 1948 is limited to 400 copies."

There is material on the Apache Kid, Wyatt Earp, Wild Bill Hickok, Tom Horn, and others.

1077 ———

The westerners' brand book. Los Angeles corral, 1949. [Los Angeles, 1950.] Cloth and leather. OP.

7 p.l., 17–263 [1] p. front., illus., plates, ports., cattle brands, fold. facsm., large fold. map, 84 illus. in col. 26 cm.
Bibliography: p. 251–254; index: p. 257–262.
Half title; illus. end papers; vignette
Colophon: "The Westerners' Brand Book, Los Angeles Corral, 1949 is limited to 400 copies."

Among the historical papers there is a chapter on Black Bart and one on the killing of Ed Masterson.

1078 ———

Westerners' brand book, 1950. Los Angeles corral, 1950. [Los Angeles, 1951.] Leather. OP.

8 p.l., 17–232 p. illus., plates (3 col.), cattle brands, earmarks, facsms. 26 cm.

Contributors: p. 211–214; bibliography: p. 215–226; index: p. 227–230.
Half title; illus. end papers (col.); illus. t.p.

In one article some mention is made of Billy the Kid and Black Jack Ketchum. In an article on the Bell Ranch of New Mexico, the author is careless with his proper names and speaks of the graves of Henry (Charlie) Bowdry [*sic*] and Tom O'Fallord [*sic*].

1079 Wetmore, Helen Cody

Last of the great scouts. The life story of Col. William F. Cody, "Buffalo Bill," as told by his sister Helen Cody Wetmore. Chicago and Duluth, the Duluth press publishing co. [1899]. Cloth. OP.

xiv, 296 p. front., illus., plates. 21 cm.
Half title; device.

Republished, New York, International book and publishing co., 1900.
On cover: "Special Limited Edition."
Republished again by Grossett and Dunlap in 1912, pages 321 to 333 in the reprint being written by Zane Grey.

1080 Wharton, Clarence Ray

L'Archeveque, by Clarence R. Wharton. Houston, Texas, the Anson Jones press [1941]. Wrappers. OP.

21 p. 22.6 cm.

The story of Sostenes L'Archeveque, an outlaw of the Texas Panhandle.

1081 ———

Wharton's history of Fort Bend county, by Clarence R. Wharton. San Antonio, Texas, the Naylor co., 1939. Cloth. OP.

xi, 250 p. front., plates (1 col.), ports., maps (1 fold.), facsms. 23.5 cm.
Appendix: p. 233–235; bibliography: p. 237–238; index: p. 239–250.
Half title; pict. t.p.

Contains an account of the Jaybird-Woodpecker feud and other lawlessness.

1082 Wheeler, Homer Webster

Buffalo days; forty years in the old west. The personal narrative of a cattleman, Indian fighter and army officer, by Colonel Homer W. Wheeler . . . . With an introduction by Major-General

James G. Harbord.   Indianapolis, the Bobbs-Merrill co. [1925].
Cloth. OP.

> 13 p.l., 369 p. front., plates, ports. 22 cm.
> Index: p. 365–369.
> Half title; vignette.

This book was rewritten from the author's *The Frontier Trail*, published in 1923. It was later republished by Grossett and Dunlap.

1083 ———

The frontier trail; or, from cowboy to colonel. An authentic narrative of forty-three years in the old west as cattleman, Indian fighter, and army officer, by Colonel Homer W. Wheeler .... Los Angeles, published by Times-Mirror press, 1923. Pict. cloth. OP.

> 9 p.l., [15]–334 p. front. (port.), plates., ports., facsms. 23.2 cm.

Here we have a new version of the Hickok-McCanles fight, but one just as preposterous as the others. Author Wheeler, however, does not put this account into his own words, but quotes Buffalo Bill Cody in *Hearst's Magazine*.

1084 White, Owen Payne

The autobiography of a durable sinner. [By Owen P. White.] New York, G. P. Putnam's sons [1942]. Cloth. OP.

> vi p., 1 l., 3–344 p. 22 cm.
> Index: p. 339–344.
> Half title.
> At head of title: "Owen P. White."

On account of a threatened lawsuit, the first printing of this book was recalled for some deletions before release date. Only a few copies got into private hands, thus copies of the first printing are scarce. Pages 239–244 were deleted and new material tipped in. The book contains quite a bit of material on the gunmen of the Southwest. Clay Allison is the author's hero, but his remarks about the Earps and Pat Garrett are very disparaging.

1085 ———

Lead and likker, by Owen P. White.   New York, Minton, Balch & co., 1932. Cloth. OP.

> vii p., 1 l., 3–274 p. 21.2 cm.
> Half title; pub. device; untrimmed.

Contains chapters on many of the outlaws from Henry Plummer, John Wesley Hardin, Ben Thompson, and Belle Starr to Chris Evans of California. Most of these chapters are unreliable, especially the one on Belle Starr. Also in this book, as in some of his others, the author says Hendry Brown was hanged by the Medicine Lodge mob, but he was not. Perhaps Brown would have been if he had not been shot down trying to escape.

1086 ———

My Texas 'tis of thee, by Owen P. White. New York, G. P. Putnam's sons, 1936. Cloth. OP.

> 6 p.l., 274 p. 19.6 cm.
> Half title; pub. device.

Contains a not too reliable chapter on Luke Short and his killing of Jim Courtright, and the activities of some other gunmen.

1087 ———

Out of the desert. The historical romance of El Paso, by Owen White. El Paso, Texas, the McMath co., publishers, 1923. Cloth. Scarce.

> 6 p.l., 442 p., 2 l. (1 errata). plates, ports. 23.8 cm.
> Section two, biographical: p. [329]–442.
> Half title; vignette; errata leaf.

A book now scarce and containing much material on the lawlessness of El Paso. Contains a chapter on Dallas Stoudenmire and much information on gunplay in the frontier town of El Paso.

1088 ———

Texas, an informal biography, by Owen P. White. New York, G. P. Putnam's sons [1945]. Cloth. In print.

> ix p., 1 l., 3–268 p. front. (port.), illus., plates, ports., facsm. 20.5 cm.
> Index: p. 265–268.
> Half title; map on end papers.

The last book written by this author before he died, and the poorest one he ever wrote. Like all his books, this one contains much material on gunmen, but he seems to have had the habit of giving unreliable information on this subject. His account of Sam Bass is confused, both as to who planned the Union Pacific robbery and as to the amount secured.

He makes the citizens of Texas appear ridiculous by saying they thought so much of Bass that he could have been elected governor. He paints Ben Thompson with a black brush and an inaccurate one.

1089 ———

Them was the days; from El Paso to prohibition, by Owen P. White, with drawings by Ross Santee. New York, Minton, Balch & co., 1925. Pict. cloth. OP.

6 p.l., 3–235 p. front., illus. 21.4 cm.
Half title; pub. device; untrimmed.

His chapter entitled "The Psychology of Gun-Men" is about John Wesley Hardin and John Selman and the feud between them.

1090 ———

Trigger fingers, by Owen P. White .... New York, London, G. P. Putnam's sons, 1926. Cloth. Scarce.

vii p., 1 l., 3–323 p. 19.2 cm.

This book contains several chapters on various gunmen of the Southwest. The author claims Billy the Kid's first victim was a "black nigger" who tried to cheat him in a card game. He also says that the Kid killed twenty-six men, "not counting Indians," and that he killed Bernstein with no more provocation than that he "didn't like Jews anyhow." He not only has Dave Wall instead of J. W. Bell as the Kid's jail guard, but he has the circumstances of his killing all wrong. Here is another writer who spells O'Folliard's name "O'Phalliard." His account of the Hickok-McCanles fight is also unreliable.

1091 Wickersham, Hon. James

Old Yukon. Tales, trails and trials, by Hon. James Wickersham .... Washington, D. C., Washington law book co., 1938. Cloth. OP.

xi, 514 p. front. (port.), illus., plates, ports., maps. 23.6 cm.
Index: p. 489–514.

Chapter II contains some new and interesting material on Soapy Smith.

1092 Willcox, R. N.

Reminiscences of California life, being an abridged description of scenes which the author has passed through in California and other lands . . . , by R. N. Willcox. ₁Avery, Ohio₁, Willcox print, 1897. Cloth. Rare.

> 3 p.l., 5–290 p. 21.5 cm.

There is some material on Tom Bell, the California outlaw.

1093 Williams, Harry

Texas trails; legends of the great southwest, by Harry Williams . . . pen and ink sketches by Hans Reuter. San Antonio, Texas, the Naylor co. ₁1932₁. Pict. cloth. OP.

> vii p., 2 l., 269 p. 24 cm.
> Index: p. 263–269.
> Half title: illus. end papers; tailpieces; vignette.
> "These stories, some now revised and altered, appeared in the 'Texas Trail' column of the San Antonio Light between the years 1927 and 1931": cf Foreword.

A collection of short stories, among which are tales of Joel Fowler, John Wesley Hardin, and Ben Thompson.

1094 Williams, Henry Llewellyn

"Buffalo Bill" (the Hon. William F. Cody). Rifle and revolver shot; pony express rider; teamster; buffalo hunter; guide and scout. A full account of his adventurous life with the origin of his "Wild West" show, by Henry Llewellyn Williams. London, George Routledge and sons . . . , 1887. Cloth. Rare.

> vi, ₁7₁–192 p. front. 20 cm.
> Half title.

This is said to be the rarest book on Buffalo Bill. It is founded upon the many dime novels of its day and, consequently, is unreliable. In one place the author says, "Lest the authenticity of this early exploit be demurred at let us hasten to say it is recorded by Colonel Prentis Ingraham." Ingraham was one of the prolific and wildly imaginative dime novelists of his day and certainly no authority on anything historical. The whole book is a ludicrous attempt of an Englishman to write of the American Wild West.

1095 ─────

Joaquín (the Claude Duval of California); or, the marauder of the mines. A romance founded on truth. New York, Robert M. DeWitt, publisher ₁1865₁. Pict. wrappers. Scarce.

> 160 p. 23.5 cm.

Republished, New York, Pollard & Moss, 1888.   Dec. cloth. Scarce.

[3]–206 p.   19 cm.
2 p. adv. at end.

Reprinted again in 1889.

This is another fictitious account based on the *California Police Gazette* version of Murieta's life.

1096 Williams, John G.

The adventures of a seventeen-year-old lad and the fortunes he might have won, by John G. Williams.   Boston, printed for the author by the Collins press, 1894.   Cloth.   Scarce.

x, [11]–308 p.   front. (port.), illus.   23.8 cm.
Frontis tissue.

A rare privately printed book in which the author gives an account of his encounter with Joaquín Murieta and Three-Fingered Jack García.

1097 Williams, Llew

The Dalton brothers in their Oklahoma cave. A tale of adventure in the Indian territory, by Llew Williams. . . . Together with the desperate and startling criminal career of the gang. With illustrations from life and the actual scenes of their crimes.   Chicago, M. A. Donohue & co. [n.d.].   Pict. cloth.   OP.

5–234 p.   19.8 cm.

A fantastic tale containing no word of truth, it is one of the cheap "thrillers" typical of its day.

1098 Williams, Judge O. W.

The old New Mexico, 1879–1880.   Reminiscences of Judge O. W. Williams.   [N.p., n.d.]   Wrappers.   Scarce.

48 p.   22.9 cm.

An interesting book of reminiscences with some reference to lawlessness in New Mexico and a mention of Billy the Kid. At the end are the words "To be continued"; but if the second volume was ever published, I have never heard of it.

1099 Williams, R. H.

With the border ruffians. Memories of the far west, 1852–1868, by R. H. Williams, sometime lieutenant in the Kansas rangers, and afterwards captain in the Texas rangers. Edited by E. W. Williams. With portraits. New York, E. P. Dutton and co., 1907. Cloth. Scarce.

> xviii p., 1 l., 3–478 p. front. (port.), plates, ports. 22.3 cm.
> Index: p. 473–478.
> Half title; frontis tissue.

Now quite scarce, this book deals with life during the lawless days of Kansas and Texas.

1100 Williamson, Thames

Far north country, by Thames Williamson. Edited by Erskine Caldwell. New York, Duell, Sloan and Pearce [1944]. Cloth. In print.

> 6 p.l., 3–236 p. 21.8 cm.
> Index: p. 233–236.
> Half title; map on end papers.

Gives a brief story of Soapy Smith.

1101 Willison, George Finlay

Here they dug the gold, by George F. Willison . . . . New York, Brentano's publishers [1931]. Pict. cloth. OP.

> xiii p., 1 l., [3]–299 p. illus. 22.5 cm.
> Half title; map on end papers; pub. device.

Contains much material on the lawlessness in the mining camps of Colorado.

1102 Wilson, Edward

An unwritten history. A record from the exciting days of early Arizona, by Edward Wilson. Cover design by O. D. Brown. [Phoenix, Ariz., the McNail co., 1915.] Pict. cloth. Rare.

> 3 p.l., 7–77 [1] p. 17.3 cm.

Among other stories of early Arizona, the author gives accounts of the Apache Kid, Grant Wheeler, the train robber, and a man called Black Jack. This evidently is Black Jack Christian, for the author says it is not Tom Ketchum. He also says Black Jack Ketchum was light complexioned, but in this he is mistaken.

1103 Wilson, Isaac A.

Four years in a home made hell, by Isaac A. Wilson. Siloam Springs, Ark., the Herald printing co., 1894. Wrappers. Exceedingly rare.

62 p. front. (port.). 19.5 cm.

I know of but one copy of this rare little book. As a member of the Reno gang, the author wrote an account favorable to them, but he gave some accurate information on how the vigilantes worked.

1104 Wilson, Neill Compton

Silver stampede, the career of Death Valley's hell-camp, old Panamint, by Neill C. Wilson. Illustrated. New York, the Macmillan co., 1937. Cloth. OP.

xiv p., 1 l., 319 p. illus., plates, ports., facsm. 22.3 cm.
Index: p. 315–319.
Half title; map on end papers; "First printing" on copyright p.

The history of Panamint in the days of its bad men.

1105 ———

Treasure express. Epic days of the Wells Fargo, by Neill C. Wilson. Illustrated. New York, the Macmillan co., 1936. Cloth. OP.

xii p., 1 l., 322 p. illus., plates, ports., facsm. 22.2 cm.
Acknowledgments: p. 309–311; index: p. 313–322.
Half title; illus. end papers.

A well-written book dealing with stagecoaches and the men who robbed them.

1106 Wilson, Neill Compton, and Frank J. Taylor

Southern Pacific. The roaring story of a fighting railroad. [By] Neill C. Wilson [and] Frank J. Taylor. New York, London, Toronto, McGraw-Hill book co., inc. [1952]. Cloth. In print.

viii p., 1 l., 256 p. plates, ports. 23.5 cm.
Appendix: p. [211]–245; bibliography: p. [247]–248; index: p. [249]–256.
Half title; map on end papers.

Contains a chapter on train robbery, the Daltons, and the Evans-Sontag gang.

1107 Wilson, Rufus Rockwell

A noble company of adventurers, by Rufus Rockwell Wilson . . . . Illustrated from drawings by May Fratz and from photographs.   New York, B. W. Dodge and co., 1908.   Pict. cloth. Scarce.

> 2 p.l., 219 p. front., plates. 19 cm.
> Device.

In a long chapter on the Texas Rangers the author gives accounts of their clashes with outlaws and Texas gunmen.

1108 ———

Out of the west, by Rufus R. Wilson . . . . Illustrations by E. Fletcher.   New York, the press of the Pioneers, 1933.   Cloth.   OP.

> 7 p.l., 425 p. illus. 24.5 cm.

Republished, New York, Wilson-Erickson, inc., 1936.

> xvii, 480 p. front., illus. 24 cm.
> Bibliography: p. 461–468; index: p. 469–480.
> "Only three hundred copies printed."

In the chapter "Turbulent Tombstone," the author makes Wyatt Earp quite a hero and superman, and in another, entitled "Frontier Peace Officers," he repeats some of the legends about Wild Bill Hickok, such as the one about the two men seeking to kill him. One entered from the rear and the other from the front of a saloon; but Wild Bill, "shooting in two directions at one and the same time, killed both of his assailants."

1109 Wilstach, Frank Jenners

Wild Bill Hickok, the prince of pistoleers, by Frank J. Wilstach.   Garden City, N. Y., Doubleday, Page & co., 1926.   Cloth. OP.

> xviii p., 1 l., 304 p. front., plates, ports. 21.4 cm.
> Half title; t.p. in red and black; vignette; untrimmed; "First edition" on copyright p.

This author seems to have made a sincere effort to understand and depict the true character of David McCanles, and tells a more accurate

386

story of the McCanles' fight with Wild Bill than most writers. He labels the Nichols, Buel, and Hough accounts "pure fable," but he is very much in love with the subject of his biography.

1110   Winch, Frank

Thrilling lives of Buffalo Bill, Col. Wm. F. Cody, last of the great scouts, and Pawnee Bill, Maj. Gordon W. Lillie (Pawnee Bill), white chief of the Pawnees . . . .[New York, S. L. Parson and co., inc., 1911.] Wrappers. OP.

224 p.   front., illus., plates, ports., facsm.   19 cm.

1111   Winchell, Lilbourne Alsip

History of Fresno county, and the San Joaquin valley. Narrative and biographical, by Lilbourne Alsip Winchell. Under the editorial supervision of Ben R. Walker . . . .   Fresno, Calif., A. H. Cawston, publisher [1933].   Dec. cloth.   OP.

2 p.l., [5]-323 p.   front. (port.), plates, ports., map.   27.4 cm.

Has a chapter on Murieta and Vásquez.

1112   Winget, Dan

Anecdotes of "Buffalo Bill" that have never appeared in print, by Dan Winget, the last of the old scouts.   Chicago, Historical publishing co., 1927.   Cloth.   Scarce.

5 p.l., 13-230 p.   front. (port.), illus., plate, port., facsm. letter.   20 cm.
Illus. chapter headings; tailpieces; vignette.

Some intimate short stories about Buffalo Bill and the author, among them one about Jesse James. He again tells the old story of the cruel mortgage holder and the widow, but gives it a different setting. Although the author claims to have known all the early notorious gunmen intimately, he misspells many of their names, such as "Quantrall" for "Quantrill," "Hitchcock" for "Hickok," and he calls Joseph Slade, "Simon" Slade.

1113   Winn, Mary Day

The macadam trail. Ten thousand miles by motor coach, by Mary Day Winn. Illustrated by E. H. Suydam.   New York, Alfred A. Knopf, MCMXXXI.   Cloth.   OP.

387

xiv p., 1 l., 3–319 p. front. (col.), full p. illus. 23 cm.
Index: p. i–xii.
Half title; illus. end papers; illus. chapter headings; vignette; "First edition" on copyright p.

Chapter V is about Bill Carlisle, the Wyoming train robber. The book also contains material on the Johnson County War, Jesse James, Billy the Kid, and Calamity Jane, but none of the author's information adds anything of value.

1114 Winslow, Kathryn

Big pan-out, by Kathryn Winslow. New York, W. W. Norton and co., inc. [1951]. Cloth. In print.

x, 3–247 p. plates. 21.8 cm.
Half title; map on end papers.

Contains some material on Soapy Smith while he was in Skagway.

1115 Winther, Oscar Osburn

The old Oregon country. A history of frontier trade, transportation, and travel, [by] Oscar Osburn Winther . . . . Stanford, Calif., Stanford University press; London, Oxford University press [1950]. Cloth. In print.

xvi p., 1 l., 3–348 p. front., plates, ports., maps. 26 cm.
Bibliography: p. 305–323; index: p. 327–348.
Half title.

A special paper-bound edition was published by the Indiana University as No. 7 in its "Social Science Series."

In a chapter on stagecoach travel, the author tells of many of the road agents, such as "Stove Pipe Sam," George Ives, Henry Plummer, and Black Bart.

1116 ———

Via western express and stagecoach, by Oscar Osborn Winther. Stanford University, Calif., Stanford University press [1945]. Pict. cloth. OP.

xi, 158 p. plates, ports., facsms. 26 cm.
Bibliographical notes: p. 149–150; index: 151–158.
Half title; maps on end papers; double pict. t.p. (col.); illus. chapter headings.

Contains information on Murieta, Vásquez, and other California bandits.

1117 Wolle, Muriel Sibell

The bonanza trail, ghost towns and mining camps of the west, by Muriel Sibell Wolle. Illustrated by the author. Bloomington, Indiana University press, 1953. Cloth. In print.

> xvi p., 8 l., 17–510 p. front., illus., maps. 26 cm.
> Glossary: p. 477–482; selected bibliography: p. 483–489; index: p. 491–510.
> Half title; illus. end papers.

The author here has a wealth of material on the vigilantes and the outlaws and gunmen who followed the mining camps of the West.

1118 Wood, M. W. (ed.)

History of Alameda county, California, including its geology, topography, soil and production; together with a full and particular record of the Spanish grants . . . . Separate histories of each of the townships, showing their advancement and progress . . . . Illustrated. Oakland, M. W. Wood, publisher, 1883. Calf. Scarce.

> vii p., 1 l., [9]–1001 p. front. (port.), ports., tables. 26.8 cm.

In a long chapter entitled "Criminal History of the County," the book takes up the story of crime from 1853 through 1881. The better-known outlaws dealt with are Juan Soto, Vásquez, and Rondado.

1119 Wood, Richard Coke

Murphys, queen of the Sierra. A history of Murphys, Calaveras county, California, by Richard Coke Wood. Angel's Camp, Calif., published by Calaveras Californian [n.d.]. Stiff pict. wrappers. OP.

> 3 p.l., 88 p. front. (port.), illus., plates, ports., fold. map. 19.6 cm.
> Notes, p. 83–87; bibliography, p. 87–88.

Has much material on Joaquín Murieta and Three-Fingered Jack García.

1120 ———

Tales of old Calaveras, by Richard Coke Wood . . . . [N.p., n.d.] Cloth. In print.

> 3 p.l., 5–94 [2] p. front. (map), plates, ports. 23.5 cm.
> "Notes" and "references" after each chapter.
> Index: p. [95]–[96].
> Preface on verso of t.p.

Contains chapters on Joaquín Murieta and Black Bart.

1121 Wood, R. E.

Life and confessions of James Gilbert Jenkins; the murderer of eighteen men . . . . Phonographically reorted [*sic*] and arranged for the press by R. E. Wood. Napa City, published by C. H. Allen and R. E. Wood, printed by William P. Harrison & co., 1864. Pict. wrappers. Rare.

> 3 p.l., [7]–56 p. front., illus. 23 cm.

An exceedingly rare little book on one of the early outlaws of California.

1122 Woods, Rev. James

Recollections of pioneer work in California, by Rev. James Woods . . . . San Francisco, Joseph Winterburn & co., book and job printers . . . , 1878. Cloth. Rare.

> 3 p.l., [5]–260 p. 19.4 cm.

Contains some material on Murieta.

1123 Wooldridge, Major J. W.

History of the Sacramento valley, California, by Maj. J. W. Wooldridge . . . . Illustrated. Chicago, the Pioneer Historical publishing co., 1931. Pub. in three volumes. Cloth. OP.

> Vol. I, xxii, 508 p. front., plates, ports. 26.7 cm.
> Vols. II and III biographical.

In a long account of Murieta the author follows the Ridge version.

1124 Wright, Muriel Hazel

The story of Oklahoma, by Muriel H. Wright. Editorially assisted by Joseph B. Thoburn. Oklahoma City, Okla., Webb publishing co. [1930]. Cloth. OP.

> xix, 342 p. front., plates, ports., maps. 19.6 cm.
> Bibliography: p. 320–325; vocabulary: p. 327–330; index: p. 331–342.
> "Points to be remembered" (a summary) after each chapter.

Contains some information on Oklahoma outlaws and Judge Parker's court.

1125 Wright, Robert Marr

Dodge City, the cowboy capital, and the great southwest in the days of the wild Indian, the buffalo, the cowboy, dance halls, gambling hells, and bad men, by Robert M. Wright . . . . [Wichita, Kan., Wichita Eagle press, 1913.] Pict. cloth. Scarce.

> 6 p.l., 9–344 p. front. (col.), plates, ports. 20.3 cm.
> Copyright notice on recto of frontis.

It is said that most of the edition was destroyed by the printer, hence its scarcity. A later edition without date or colored frontispiece is sometimes confused with the first edition. The first edition may be identified by the colored frontispiece with copyright date on recto. The second printing has a portrait of the author in black and white instead of the colored frontispiece. Because the author knew Wyatt Earp well, I think his spelling of his name "Wyat Erb" must be a typographical error. This is one of the first books written about Dodge City, and reveals intimate knowledge of the gunmen of that wild cowtown.

1126 Wyllys, Rufus Kay

Arizona, the history of a frontier state, by Rufus Kay Wyllys. Phoenix, Arizona, Hobson & Herr [1950]. Cloth. In print.

> xiii p., 1 l., 408 p. illus., plates, ports., 9 maps, facsm. 22 cm.
> Guide to references: p. 365–384; index: p. 387–408.
> Half title ("Frontier" misspelled "Frintier"); t.p. in red and black; device; "First edition" on copyright p.
>
> Also published in a de luxe edition limited to 406 copies and signed by the artist, cartographer, designer, and author.

Contains some scattered material on the gunmen of Arizona, the Earps, Clantons, Curly Bill, and others.

1127 Wynn, Marcia Rittenhouse

Desert bonanza. A story of early Randeburg, Mojave desert mining company, by Marcia Rittenhouse Wynn. Illustrated. Culver City, Calif., M. W. Samelson, publisher, 1949. Cloth. OP.

> xv p., 1 l., [3]–263 p. front., plates, map. 22 cm.
> Notes: p. [257]–260; glossary: p. [261]–263.
> Half title; "First edition" on copyright p.

This volume has a chapter on Vásquez's activities in the Mojave.

1128 Young, Charles E.

Dangers of the trail in 1865. A narrative of actual events, by

Charles E. Young. Geneva, N. Y. [press of W. Y. Humphrey], 1912. Cloth. OP.

> 3 p.l., [7]–148 p. illus., plates, map. 19.5 cm.
> There is some mention of outlawry in the early days of Denver.

1129 Young, Harry (Sam)

Hard knocks. A life story of the vanishing west, by Harry (Sam) Young. Portland, Ore. [Wells & co., printers and publishers], 1915. Stiff wrappers. Scarce.

> 4 p.l., [9]–242 p. plates. 19.6 cm.

Although published the same year in Chicago by Laird and Lee, with the same number of pages and bound in cloth, this is said to be the first printing. It is printed upon much better paper than the Chicago edition.

The author claims to have known Wild Bill Hickok personally, but he continues the Nichols' legend about the McCanles fight. He says that Wild Bill was sent to Rock Creek Station especially to wipe out the "McCanles outlaws," that there were nine men in the gang, and that Wild Bill killed them all. He has Hickok receiving three bullet wounds, but does not have him so cut up as some of his contemporaries, letting him receive only two knife wounds.

He calls Tom Smith, the first marshal of Abilene, "Green River" Smith, instead of the correct "Bear River" Smith. He also calls Phil Coe, Phil "Cole," and he has Wild Bill killing twenty-five men while marshal at Abilene.

1130 [Younger Brothers]

Younger brothers of the great west. [Racine, Wis., Whitman publishing co., n.d.] Wrappers. Scarce.

> 3–182 [5] p. 16.2 cm.
> 5 p. adv. at end.

Another of the pulp publications sold by the train butcher boys, this one has become quite scarce. The anonymous author of this tale says the Younger brothers had a cattle ranch in Texas, "which they called home." Neither the Youngers nor the Jameses were ever cattlemen.

1131 Younger, Cole

The story of Cole Younger, by himself. Being an autobiography of the Missouri guerrilla captain and outlaw, his capture and prison life, and the only authentic account of the Northfield raid ever published. Illustrations made expressly for this book. Chicago, press of the Henneberry co., 1903. Stiff pict. wrappers. Rare.

> 5 p.l., [7]–123 [2] p.   front. (3 large ports.), illus., plates, ports., plan. 21.8 cm.

In this rare book Cole Younger tells his own story of the Northfield raid and his life in prison.

1132   Younger, Scout (Bison Bill)

True facts of the lives of America's most notorious outlaws, as told by Scout Younger (Bison Bill).   [N.p., n.d.]   Pamphlet. Wrappers.   (Cover title.)   OP.

> 1 p.l., 3–15 p.   20.4 cm.

Short sketches of the James boys, Younger brothers, Bob Ford, Red Kelley, Belle Starr, Henry Starr, Cherokee Bill, Sam Bass, Bill Doolin, Dick Broadwell, and others.

Index

All index numbers refer to items, not to pages. Authors are arranged alphabetically in the text and are not repeated in the index. Italic figures indicate that, even though the items do not appear in this bibliography, they are mentioned in the work indicated.

Grimes, Curly: *137, 184, 861, 940*
Gringo Doctor: 168
Gringo Gold: 248
Gropper, William: 460
Grounds, Billy: *60, 86, 125, 275, 472, 627, 719, 799, 800, 921, 1046, 1065, 1075, 1105*
Gruelle, Juston C.: 315
Gruver, Homer E.: 59
Guerrillas of the West, The: 31
Guide to Life and Literature of the Southwest: 313; revised ed., 314
Gulshall, Charlotte: 791
Gunfight of the Age, The: 376
Gun-Fighters of the Old West: 896
Guns of the Frontier: 801
Gun Notches: 874
Gun-Smoke: 60

Hall, R. H.: 1035
Hammack, E. S.: 87
Hammond, George P.: 743
Hanging Judge: 459
"Hands Up!" or, the History of a Crime: 932
Hands Up! Stories of the Six-Gun Fighters of the Old Wild West: 974
Hands Up; or, Twenty Years of Detective Life: 241
Harbord, Major-General James G.: 1082
Hardin, Joe: 452
Hardin, John Wesley: *8, 22, 41, 75, 105, 118, 125, 135, 168, 169, 185, 187, 238, 242, 243, 274, 275, 281, 293, 298, 323, 324, 348, 358, 359, 366, 370, 403, 404, 414, 415, 417, 433, 442, 445, 446, 452 454, 455, 472, 475, 491, 502, 524, 527, 570, 593, 603, 639, 642, 652, 674, 686, 719, 730, 739, 751, 756, 778, 797, 798, 799, 801, 807, 810, 823, 839, 860, 875, 890, 907, 914, 915, 927, 931, 943, 966, 974, 979, 993, 1061, 1064, 1065, 1068, 1073, 1075, 1084, 1085, 1086, 1087, 1088, 1089, 1090, 1093, 1109*
Hard Knocks: 1129
Hare, Joseph Thompson: *217, 418,* 506
Hargens, Charles: 103
Harger, Charles Morceau: 238
Harkey, Dee: *446,* 455
Harpe, Wiley ("Little Harpe"): *217, 387, 418, 472, 501, 837, 866, 875, 896,* 1016
Harpe, William Micajah ("Big Harpe"): *217, 387, 418, 472, 501, 837, 866, 875, 896,* 1016

Harper's Magazine: 88, 117, 145, 256, 468, 753, 896
Harris, Jack: 722
Harrison, Nan Hillary: 225
Harry Tracy, the Desperate Outlaw: 182
Harry Tracy, the Desperate Western Outlaw: 183
Hart, Pearl: *6, 196, 252, 380, 406, 495, 527, 644, 683, 848, 921, 993, 1046, 1105*
Heald, Weldon F.: 759
Hear the Train Blow: 87
Hearst's Magazine: 1083
Heath, John: *10, 33, 34, 60, 69, 125, 162, 196, 251, 380, 401, 403, 406, 472, 516, 527, 627, 644, 672, 683, 719, 799, 801, 921, 930, 999, 1046, 1105*
Heffridge, Bill: *79, 169, 185, 186, 275, 318, 404, 417, 484, 491, 498, 544, 558, 603, 637, 801, 915, 916, 932, 940, 978, 1017, 1064, 1088, 1090*
Heffron, Walter J.: 244
He Hanged Them High: 269
Hellcatraz: 405
Helldorado: 125
Helm, Boone: *46, 62, 68, 85, 103, 139, 200, 239, 308, 325, 331, 334, 349, 388, 403, 406, 418, 423, 466, 472, 501, 525, 606, 694, 721, 746, 794, 801, 855, 856, 875, 878, 938, 942, 960, 984, 985, 986, 1055, 1064, 1085, 1108, 1117*
Helms, Jack: *169, 185, 274, 275, 323, 348, 386, 403, 452, 472, 823, 839, 863, 915, 931, 1090*
Hell on the Border: 458
Hendrix, E. R.: 942
Henry, O.: 509, 926
Henry Starr, Plaintiff in Error vs. *the United States:* 970
Here They Dug the Gold: 1101
Heritage of the Valley: 83
Herndon, Albert: *77, 79, 186, 404, 484, 823, 1064*
Herndon, Joe: 770
Heroes of the Plains: 143
Hertzog, Carl: 723
Hickok, James Butler ("Wild Bill"): *2, 6, 8, 13, 14, 16, 21, 25, 50, 62, 86, 88, 98, 105, 106, 108, 117, 118, 119, 125, 127, 128, 135, 137, 143, 145, 146, 147, 149, 150, 156, 157, 169, 181, 184, 185, 194, 197, 204, 219, 220, 221, 222, 223, 234, 235, 237, 238, 241, 249, 250, 256, 257, 262, 271, 274, 275, 286, 288, 291, 292, 312, 316, 320, 324, 329, 336, 342, 345, 346, 348, 351, 359, 366, 370, 381, 385,*

History of Stockton, A.: 997
History of Teton Valley, Idaho: 328
History of Tulare County, California: 923
History of Tulare and Kings Counties, California: 678
History of Tuolumne County: 1019
History of Ventura County, California: 901
History of Virgil A. Stewart, The: 505
History of Our Wild West: 591
History of Yuba and Sutter Counties, California: 297
Hite, Clarence: *264, 418, 513, 637, 682, 1016, 1017, 1069*
Hite, Robert Woodson ("Wood"): *231, 264, 270, 273, 282, 286, 314, 418, 427, 472, 494, 513, 556, 558, 559, 637, 673, 682, 768, 1016, 1017*
Hodges, Stephen: *112*
Hodges, Thomas J.: *see* Bell, Tom
Hodges, William: *112*
Hole-in-the-Wall: 832
Hole-in-the-Wall gang: *165, 166, 590, 615, 674*
Holliday, "Doc": *10, 34, 60, 86, 88, 118, 125, 135, 148, 162, 185, 196, 251, 252, 275, 351, 366, 373, 376, 378, 380, 401, 403, 406, 413, 463, 472, 527, 593, 595, 603, 617, 627, 638, 639, 644, 652, 672, 719, 730, 751, 754, 798, 799, 801, 838, 848, 888, 921, 930, 943, 946, 994, 1028, 1046, 1065, 1073, 1075, 1084, 1086, 1105, 1108, 1117*
Hoofprints of a Cowboy and U. S. Ranger: 857
Hooper, Arthur W.: 333
Horn, Tom: *19, 25, 50, 118, 135, 165, 166, 206, 224, 247, 275, 349, 373, 374, 377, 399, 401, 403, 406, 410, 472, 494, 497, 527, 590, 593, 613, 615, 621, 662, 689, 690, 719, 798, 801, 857, 858, 911, 915, 916, 918, 941, 998, 1008, 1037, 1071, 1073, 1076*
Horrel-Higgins feud: *185, 323, 417, 446, 798, 799, 801, 844, 931, 1046, 1089, 1090*
Horse thieves: *2, 48, 72, 152, 153, 154, 155, 170, 292, 305, 383, 520, 523, 894, 937, 948, 980, 1035, 1083*
Hors le Loi!: 568
Hough, Emerson: *27, 475, 500, 501, 730, 1061, 1109*
Houston, Tex.: 364
Howard, George: 572
Howard, Tex: *33, 34, 60, 125, 162, 380,*

401, 516, 627, 644, 672, 683, 799, 801, 872, 921, 1046
Hudson, Bell: 133
Hughes, Rupert: 874
Humboldt, The: 698
Hunkins, R. V.: 758
Hunt, Zwing: *60, 86, 125, 162, 185, 275, 311, 472, 627, 672, 719, 798, 799, 800, 921, 1046, 1065, 1105*
Hurd, Peter: 362
Hurley, John A.: *see* Lame Johnny
Hurst, Bob: 531

Idaho: *26, 62, 65, 68, 82, 132, 200, 319, 328, 466, 606, 698, 911, 912, 1013, 1034, 1035*
Idaho of Yesterday: 319
I'll Die Before I'll Run: 931
Illustrated History of Los Angeles County, California, An: 635
Illustrated History of New Mexico: 535
Illustrated Lives and Adventures of the Desperadoes of the New World, The: 37
Illustrated Lives of Frank and Jesse James: 278, 279
Illustrations for Mule's Crossing: 902
Imprints on Pioneer Trails: 662
Incidents on Land and Water: 80
Indiana: *487, 496, 770, 825, 867, 902, 903, 1031, 1103*
Indianola Scrap Book: 386
Indians' Last Fight, The: 232
Infamous Kansas Killers: 1051
Informe de la comisión: 536
Ingraham, Col. Prentiss: 143, 146, 1094
Injun Summer: 49
Inland Empire of the Pacific Northwest, The: 393
In the Land of the Chinook: 733
In Old New Mexico: 1098
In the San Juan Colorado: 416
In the Valley of the Cahuengas: 171
"Into the Setting Sun": 414
International Review: 468
Inverted Mountain, The: 759
Iowa: 137, 717, 1067
Irvine Ranch of Orange County, The: 212
It Occurred in Kimble: 368
It Takes All Kinds: 619
It's an Old Wild West Custom: 349
I've Killed Men: 401
Ives, George: *15, 26, 65, 68, 85, 103, 158, 198, 200, 239, 306, 307, 308, 319, 325, 388, 403, 406, 418, 423, 429, 442, 466,*

This book has been set on the Linotype in one size of Granjon, eighteen point, and three sizes, eight point, ten point, and eleven point, of Janson. There are evident differences in design between these two faces, but they are, nevertheless, generations or stages in a continuous line of succession. The first Roman letter forms to be crystallized in type were copies by Nicolas Jenson at Venice, in 1470, of contemporary humanistic Italian manuscript writing. In the sixteenth century, Claude Garamond and other French type-makers modeled their types on that of Jenson, but with inevitable differences, as in penmanship, implicit in individual interpretations of the same basic letter forms. Linotype Granjon is a twentieth-century revival of those French faces. Linotype Janson is a faith-ful reproduction of the type cut in the late seventeenth century at Leipzig by Anton Janson, who was influenced by the French types in general use at that time. Interesting as these technical details are to printers and amateur typophiles, they are significant only as they contribute to the reader's comfort and convenience in using this book.

UNIVERSITY OF OKLAHOMA PRESS

NORMAN